Road Warriors

DANIEL
BYMAN

Road Warriors

*Foreign Fighters in the Armies
of Jihad*

OXFORD
UNIVERSITY PRESS

Library of Congress Cataloging-in-Publication Data
Names: Byman, Daniel, 1967- author.
Title: Road warriors : foreign fighters in the armies of Jihad / Daniel Byman.
Description: New York, NY, United States of America : Oxford University
Press, 2019. | Includes bibliographical references and index.
Identifiers: LCCN 2018036698 (print) | LCCN 2018040087 (ebook) |
ISBN 9780190646523 (Universal PDF) | ISBN 9780190646530 (E-Pub) |
ISBN 9780190646516 (hardback : alk. paper)
Subjects: LCSH: Terrorists—Recruiting. | Terrorism—Prevention. |
Terrorism—Religious aspects—Islam. | Jihad.
Classification: LCC HV6431 (ebook) | LCC HV6431 .B967 2019 (print) |
DDC 363.325—dc23
LC record available at https://lccn.loc.gov/2018036698

9 8 7 6 5 4 3 2 1

Printed by Sheridan Books, Inc., United States of America

CONTENTS

ACKNOWLEDGMENTS

M ANY FRIENDS AND colleagues helped me research and write this book, and a brief note of thanks does not do justice to all they did on my behalf.

This book grew out of a short research project I began with my then Brookings colleague Jeremy Shapiro. He and I traipsed around Europe together, and his many insights, though not his sardonic good cheer, stayed with me as I continued this research. In addition, I had initially planned to coauthor this book with another colleague, Jenn Williams, but she moved on to bigger things. Jenn's ideas remain in the DNA of this book, including the title. My friend Ken Pollack is always there when I need him, and he is a constant source of ideas and inspiration. No matter what I'm working on, Ken spots the toughest problems quickly and then shows me the path out.

Many young researchers assisted me as I did my research. They include Sarah Gilkes, Eliora Katz, Isabelle Mahnke, Ian Merritt, Sam Miller, Israa Saber, Samantha Stern, and Ahmed Zuhairy. Particular thanks go to Zann Isacson for the extensive work she did as a research assistant and editor and to Sahira Akram for her help with Arabic-language sources.

I also benefited from the wisdom of many colleagues and experts who offered insights, read drafts of chapters, shared data, or otherwise kindly offered assistance. Thanks go to Audrey Alexander, Amarnath Amarasingam, Tricia Bacon, Christine Fair, Mohammed Hafez, Stig Jarle Hansen, Thomas Hegghammer, Julie Chernov Hwang, Seamus Hughes, Shiraz Maher, David Malet, Carter Malkasian, William McCants, Chris Meserole, John Mueller, Peter Neumann, Michael O'Hanlon, Jacob Olidort, Truls-Hallberg Tønnessen, Manuel R. Torres Soriano, Lorenzo Vidino, Pope Ward, Benjamin Wittes, and Jeanine Roy van Zuijdewijn.

The book was strengthened by feedback provided at several workshops and conferences. In particular, I'd like to thank Charles Glaser and David Malet for the conferences they organized in Washington and Thomas Hegghammer for arranging time with him and his incredible colleagues at Norway's *Forsvarets forskningsinstitutt* (Defense Research Institute).

Interviews with government experts and policymakers in Europe and the Middle East informed much of my thinking. My promise to most of those involved was anonymity, but this low-profile approach should not detract from highlighting the important contribution that many officials offered my work.

For years now I've had the good fortune to enjoy institutional homes at the School of Foreign Service at Georgetown University and the Center for Middle East Policy at the Brookings Institution. Joel Hellman, Bruce Hoffman, and Keir Lieber have made Georgetown a wonderful home for any scholar and provided support for my work. At Brookings, particular thanks go to Michael O'Hanlon, Natan Sachs, and Tamara Cofman Wittes for their efforts.

David McBride of Oxford University Press has long been a helpful and understanding editor (that's also code for saying that he didn't seem to mind too much when my drafts came in late), and he made several important improvements to my manuscript. Many thanks to my agent Larry Weissman for helping shape and promote my book.

As always, I would like to thank my family: my wife Vikki and my sons Josh and Ben. They enable me to laugh, rather than sigh, during the often lonely and frustrating tasks of research and writing.

CHAPTER 1 | Why Do Foreign Fighters Matter?

HOLDING UP THE severed head of a prisoner, the jihadist smiled into the camera and warned, "Soon on the Champs-Elysées...." The killer featured in the video recording was Samy Amimour, a former French bus driver, just one of over 40,000 foreign fighters whom the Islamic State lured to Syria with promises of glory, gore, and godliness, calling on them to "strike crusaders in their own lands." Eight other jihadists made similar boasts, some in French and some in Arabic, with their leader, Abdelhamid Abaaoud, promising that "we will make rivers out of your blood." Grisly images accompanied these chilling words. The 2015 video displayed jets and military bases with superimposed crosshairs and footage of Western leaders that the Islamic State promised to execute. At the same time, the jihadists exhorted Western Muslims to attack their neighbors and "smash his head with a rock."[1]

The Islamic State would often disseminate bombastic propaganda, but these jihadists' boasts were more than empty threats. On November 13, 2015, the terrorists in the video attacked Paris in an orgy of violence that left 130 people dead: France's bloodiest day since World War II. The Islamic State lauded the killers as "nine lions of the caliphate" who made France "get down on its knees." Amimour, the former bus driver, and two of his comrades threw grenades at concertgoers listening to the Eagles of Death Metal, a rock band playing at the Bataclan Theater, and then started firing machine guns into the crowd. At first, the concertgoers confused the machine-gun fire for the pyrotechnics common to rock concerts, but horror and panic quickly set in. One survivor described the scene as "an abattoir," where he waded through blood and clambered over bodies to escape.[2] When an elite French paramilitary unit arrived at the Bataclan, Amimour blew himself up. Eighty-nine people died at the theater.

The rivers of blood Abaaoud promised also flowed elsewhere in Paris, as his terrorist squad launched six attacks in all, striking restaurants, a café, and a soccer stadium. Abaaoud both directed and participated in the Paris attacks, dropping off the suicide bombers and shooting civilians as well as coordinating operations.[3] Given the ferocity and firepower of the attackers, far more people could have died; the suicide bomber at the Comptoir Voltaire café mercifully took no one with him when he blew himself up. At the Stade de France, where French President François Hollande was attending a soccer match against Germany, a security guard prevented the lead suicide bomber from entering. The bomber then detonated his suicide vest outside the stadium, and shortly afterward his two companions did as well—amazingly, only one innocent person died in these explosions. After firing his own gun into packed restaurants, Abaaoud took the subway to survey the carnage his team had wrought elsewhere in Paris.[4]

Abaaoud and his fellow terrorists came from Belgium and France to fight in the Syrian civil war, which as of 2018 consumed more than 500,000 lives and still grinds on. Abaaoud himself left Belgium with six companions in 2013 as the wave of volunteers began to crest. Among the more than 40,000 Sunni Muslims who traveled to Syria to fight against the "apostates," more than 6,000 originated from Western countries. Europe and the United States have become mass exporters of terrorists to the Middle East. Abaaoud had already launched multiple attacks before the Paris massacre. One of his killers gunned down four people at the Jewish Museum in Brussels in 2014; and the following year, passengers on a train from Amsterdam to Paris, led by three Americans traveling on holiday, disrupted another attack by overwhelming the gunman. In the months before the fateful Paris attack, Abaaoud flitted around Europe, despite being named on several security service watchlists. He traveled back and forth to Syria to elude capture and receive instructions from his Islamic State superiors—proof, he boasted in an Islamic State magazine, that "a Muslim should not fear the bloated image of the crusader intelligence." A Western intelligence official agreed: "Islamic State operatives had little difficulty in piercing Europe's borders."[5] Even after the massacre, a cousin helped Abaaoud hide from authorities.[6]

In addition to the Paris massacre, Syria represented the crucible for Islamic State attacks in Australia, Canada, Indonesia, and other countries—more than twenty in all. The Syrian civil war acted as an operational hive for jihadists as well as a source of inspiration. From his base in Syria, Abaaoud dispensed money and instructions to European jihadists. Police arrested one of his recruits, who warned, "It was a real factory out there and they will really try to hit France and Europe."[7] Abaaoud also sought to expand the Islamic State's ranks. To rile up passions at home, Abaaoud posted videos on Facebook, including one that showed him boasting of his pleasure in seeing "the blood of disbelievers" and another that depicted him driving a truck that dragged mutilated bodies behind it.[8] He recruited women on social media to travel to Syria to "repopulate the caliphate" and convinced his thirteen-year-old brother, Younes (a picture of him with an AK-47 looks like a kid playing soldier), to join the jihad.[9]

The war also transformed many volunteers. Abaaoud himself was a drug-using petty thug who served jail time for theft before going to fight. In Syria he found meaning, as did thousands of jihadists from across Europe and the United States. Moner Abu Salha, the first American suicide bomber in Syria, tweeted before his death that in America he was never happy, despite having "all the fancy amusement parks and restaurants and the food and all this crap and the cars," but in Syria, life is "the best I've ever lived."[10]

The story of Abaaoud and the other Paris attackers demonstrates the danger of foreign fighters. The Syria conflict transformed Abaaoud from an obscure lowlife to Europe's most-wanted man—a highly lethal zealot. He recruited numerous terrorists directly and others through his propaganda, orchestrating plots throughout Europe while enjoying a safe haven from Belgian and other security services. Other important terrorist attacks in the West, including mass transit attacks in Madrid in 2004 and in London in 2005, involved foreign fighters. These were the deadliest terrorist attacks Madrid and London have known, killing 191 and 52, respectively. Foreign fighters also orchestrated the bloodiest terrorist strike in history, the 9/11 attacks.

Yet for every Paris attacker, there are far more volunteers for foreign jihads who have met a less glamorous fate. The U.S. bombing campaign that devastated the Islamic State's short-lived caliphate killed thousands of foreign fighters like Abaaoud. Omar Hammami, a Twitter-happy American jihadist who became an important public face of the Shebaab in Somalia, was hunted down and killed by rivals in the group after he denounced corruption in the leadership. Many, like the jihadist superstar "Barbaros" who led fighters in Bosnia, were arrested after returning to their home countries. And surprisingly common are cases of nonentities like the American Sajmir Alimehmeti, who, when transiting the United Kingdom en route to Syria, got caught with camouflage clothing and nunchucks in his baggage, pictures of him posing in front of an Islamic State flag, and a laptop full of Islamic State propaganda—all of which led to his arrest.[11] Even the Paris attackers would die by the sword. The United States and the French government worked together to systematically eliminate those involved in orchestrating the Paris attacks and other strikes in Europe.[12]

Civil wars often attract foreigners, and figures like Abaaoud, Hammami, and Barbaros are not new to history. The Marquis de Lafayette joined the U.S. fight for liberty; Lord Byron called for "a new Thermopylae" and died in the Greek War of Independence, fighting alongside over a thousand other foreigners; Davy Crockett supported a rebellion against Mexico in the territory of Texas; and Jews from around the world, including Dr. Ruth Westheimer (who served as a sniper), fought for Israel in its 1948 War of Independence, with foreigners constituting the majority of the new state's air force.[13] Decades later, fashion icon Vidal Sassoon recalled being a foreign fighter for Israel's independence as "the best year of my life. When you think of 2,000 years of being put down and suddenly you are a nation rising, it was a wonderful feeling." When asked about his own role in the killing, he responded, "I wouldn't have had any self-respect if I didn't. Somebody had to be one of those somebodies."[14]

Jihadists would share these sentiments of self-worth, sacrifice, and obligation. International Communism proved a particular draw. The Russian Revolution and subsequent civil war drew roughly 50,000 foreign volunteers. George Orwell, André Malraux, and tens of thousands of other idealistic leftists traveled to fight fascism in Spain. Despite the romance that these figures often embodied, in reality, most foreign fighters had little impact on the wars and even less when they returned home. In the drama of war, they were a sideshow, their contributions usually limited to poignant homages to their coming of age or disillusionment.

Like the secular ideologies that preceded it, the jihadist interpretation of Islam inspires adherents around the world, drawing them to battle. The jihadist foreign fighter, in its modern incarnation, appeared in the 1980s, over thirty years ago. Now the movement's duration is starting to approach the five or so decades of international Communism inspiring volunteers to leave their homes and fight for an abstract cause abroad. Yet the latest crop of foreign fighters is far more consequential than its predecessors because these fighters spawn wars in other countries and commit dramatic and bloody acts of international terrorism. In the late 1980s, Arabs who congregated in Afghanistan during the struggle against the Soviet Union founded Al Qaeda, the most consequential terrorist group in modern history, under the leadership of Osama Bin Laden, a young Saudi millionaire who had left home to join the anti-Soviet jihad. Khaled Sheikh Mohammad, who dreamed up the 9/11 plot and organized it under Bin Laden's supervision, also began his life of violence as a fighter against the Soviet Union in the 1980s and later traveled to the war zone in Bosnia. Roughly a decade later, he would recruit Mohammad Atta to lead the 9/11 attacks. Atta became radicalized by the civil war that pitted Russians against Muslims in Chechnya, and he fell into Al Qaeda's hands when he traveled to Afghanistan to train for the fight against the Russians. The foreign fighter problem metastasized further after 9/11 as a steady stream of foreigners joined al-Shabaab in Somalia, and thousands of foreign Muslims flocked to Iraq to fight the United States and the new Shiite-dominated government. While in Iraq, these foreign fighters established Al Qaeda, which made its mark through a massive suicide bombing campaign and an internet propaganda blitz that featured videos of beheadings and attacks on U.S. forces. This branch would later morph into the Islamic State.

These conflicts, however, acted merely as a prelude to what would prove the largest generator of foreign fighters of all modern jihads—the civil war in Syria that began in 2011. At first, this conflict attracted those seeking to oppose the barbarism of Bashar al-Assad's regime. Yet the war became more popular among foreigners as it became more sectarian in 2012 and 2013, pitting the country's Sunni majority against the minority Alawi community that dominated the regime, as well as the regime's Shiite allies from Iran and the Lebanese Hezbollah. Recruitment soared further in 2014, when the Islamic State grabbed world attention with dramatic military successes and the declaration of a caliphate in the territory it controlled in Iraq and Syria. Yet the Islamic State also gained notoriety for its record of brutality, enslaving captured women, throwing homosexuals off towers to their deaths, and burning captives alive. Foreign fighters were at the epicenter of this bloodletting and barbarity.

This brutality would be bad enough, but security officials worry that foreign fighter violence abroad will return back home, mirroring the terrorist attacks that Al Qaeda launched with its network of fighters who had fought in Afghanistan, Bosnia, and other countries. In 2014, British intelligence warned about those going to Syria, "The skills, contacts and status acquired overseas can make these individuals a much greater threat when they return to the UK, even if they have not been tasked directly to carry out an attack on their return."[15] Former FBI director James Comey stated, "All of us with a memory of the '80s and '90s saw the line drawn from Afghanistan in the '80s and '90s to Sept. 11."[16] After officials arrested a man suspected of wanting to bomb the Coney Island amusement park, one of dozens of arrests U.S. officials made in 2015, Comey warned, "This is sort of the new normal."[17] Returnees from Syria fanned the flames in neighboring countries like Lebanon and Turkey and even in conflicts as far away as Libya, Yemen, and the Caucasus.

Fear that the Islamic State's mini-army, like Al Qaeda in the past, would eventually attack the West is one reason why President Barack Obama decided to launch airstrikes in Iraq and Syria, reversing his reluctance to reenter the Middle East quagmire. Obama warned, "If left unchecked, these terrorists could pose a growing threat beyond that region, including to the United States."[18] President Donald Trump continued the campaign against the Islamic State, increasing the U.S. ground presence to fight the group. Although these military campaigns have led to setbacks for the Islamic State, security officials worry that another civil war in the Muslim world could set off a new wave of volunteers drawn from fighters and networks developed in previous jihads.

Road Warriors: Foreign Fighters in the Armies of Jihad provides an analytic history of the contemporary foreign fighter phenomenon. The book begins by dissecting the anti-Soviet Afghan jihad and subsequent growth of Al Qaeda before 9/11. Bin Laden's organization, perhaps uniquely of, by, and for foreign jihadists, sought to spread its tactics and ideas to Muslims around the world. The discussion then turns to how the foreign fighter threat morphed, examining conflicts as disparate as the Balkans, Chechnya, Iraq, and Somalia, all of which saw significant, but quite different, foreign fighter roles. The book then appraises the most important foreign fighter conflict of them all, the conjoined civil wars in Iraq and Syria, and assesses the global jihadist movement's strength in Europe and the United States. As it provides this history, *Road Warriors* offers illustrative stories about a wide range of foreign fighters—Arab and Western, successful leaders and colossal failures, old-school and young punk—and details the histories of the jihadist groups they served like the Islamic State and Al Qaeda. These stories are tied to broader narratives about the key theaters of jihad, making the book also a history of the modern jihadist movement and its impact on the Middle East and the West. The final chapter in the book looks at how governments have tried, often with impressive success, to combat foreign fighters.

Definitions

This book focuses on jihadist foreign fighters, and both the terms "jihadist" and "foreign fighter" demand further explanation. "Jihad" is a contested term. Its linguistic origin is tied to the word "striving," typically in the path of God. Many Muslims embrace this idea as an individual's struggle to act as his or her best self in the face of our baser instincts: to care for loved ones, be kind to strangers, and otherwise be good.[19]

This book, however, employs an alternative, more violent definition that an array of terrorist groups use: a jihadist fights in the name of God. In particular, this book focuses on a subset of Muslims who embrace a puritanical strain of Sunni Islam known as Salafism and believe that following Islam correctly requires fighting "nonbelievers." It is these Muslims who are responsible for 9/11, the 2015 Paris bombings, and other attacks in the West as well as contributing to numerous wars in the Middle East. This subset of Salafists self-identify as jihadist, and they seek to return society to their version of a pure form of Islam as practiced by the earliest Muslims. Their enemies include the United States and European countries, supposed apostate regimes in the Middle East, religious minorities like Shiite Muslims, and fellow Sunnis who do not share their ideas. In their eyes, these supposed unbelievers not only reject God's teachings themselves but also try to prevent the jihadists from living and acting as true Muslims. For them, fighting represents a sacred duty, like prayer or giving to the poor, which one must perform as a good Muslim. The book excludes as principal subjects Shiite Muslims, members of the Muslim Brotherhood, and other non-Salafist Muslims who also may use the term "jihad" to describe their actions.

Defining a foreign fighter can be even trickier. The scholar David Malet, in his excellent overview of a range of (mostly nonjihadist) conflicts involving foreign fighters, defines foreign fighters as "non-citizens of conflict states who join insurgencies during civil conflicts."[20] This definition excludes individuals who travel to areas outside of war zones to prepare to fight, a category important for many jihadist groups profiled in the book. The United Nations takes a different angle, focusing on "individuals who travel to a State other than their own State of residence or nationality for the purpose of the perpetration, planning, or preparation of, or participation in, terrorist acts or the providing or receiving of terrorist training, including in connection with armed conflict."[21] Other experts use the term "travelers" to note that many who go abroad do not fight but participate in other ways, ranging from computer programmers who create social media sites to women who want to raise their children in what they see as a true Islamic society.[22]

I draw on these sources and use a broad definition for the term "foreign fighters": individuals who travel to a state other than their own to join an illicit group and perpetrate or assist in terrorist attacks or armed conflict. This would include not only an individual who went to Syria to blow himself up on behalf of the Islamic State or an Abaaoud-like figure who returned home to wreak havoc but also someone who provided training, designed a website, or otherwise assisted a terrorist or militant group. I seek to exclude those who travel primarily for financial reasons (mercenaries) or do so primarily at the behest of a foreign government.

The definition of "foreign" is also contested. The individuals involved would reject this label, arguing that they are Muslims fighting alongside fellow Muslims. Only Western attempts to divide Muslims by artificial national identities represent the "foreign" aspect in their eyes. Diasporas are another issue. If a Somali who lived in the United Kingdom returned home to fight, is he "foreign"? Making this more complex, what about his son, who is raised in Britain, barely speaks a word of Somali, and yet identifies with his father's homeland? Some groups also recruit heavily from migrant or refugee communities in the immediate neighborhood. Does a Kenyan of Somali ethnicity count as "foreign" if he crosses the border to fight with the Shebaab in Somalia? Although I usually exclude this last category, as it vastly expands the number of foreign fighters while moving away from the core issue that makes the phenomenon most interesting to me, this book adopts a broad definition of "foreign," at times encompassing fighters from neighboring communities and diasporas as well as those from more distant lands.

Finally, data on foreign fighters are often bad or misleading. Many governments ignored the foreign fighter problem and did not gather information about their citizens who traveled abroad to fight. Governments' definitions of "fighting" also vary, as some focus on those who engage in war abroad versus those who simply train or even travel abroad to provide medical services or just live in a land controlled by a jihadist group.[23] Some governments inflate the numbers to gain international support or to justify harsh security measures. Often statistics include both those who tried to go abroad but were arrested and those who successfully made their journeys (a problem that plagues many official U.S. statements on Syria). At times I try to sort this out, but in other cases I try to explain the differences in data to illustrate various arguments I make in the book.

Key Arguments

I argue that the potential threat posed by jihadist foreign fighters is large and growing. In addition to conducting international terrorist attacks, they also radicalize indigenous fighters in civil wars and regionalize conflicts. This form of radicalization intensifies conflicts and makes life worse for people in the affected countries, and the regionalization often provokes neighboring powers to intervene and worsens a war. The foreign fighters, however, often undermine the causes they claim to support. In addition, effective countermeasures can reduce, though not eliminate, many of the potentially dangerous terrorism problems that foreign fighters pose.

My book derives a set of observations on the foreign fighter challenge grouped around three related questions: (1) Why do individuals leave their homes to go fight in faraway lands? (2) What impact do foreign fighters have that makes them of such concern? and (3) How can we better fight foreign fighters?

WHY DO THEY FIGHT?

Foreign fighters are heroes who take up arms in the name of God—or at least that's how they see themselves. Some believe they are defending innocent Muslim women and children from rape and murder at the hands of American, Russian, and other infidel soldiers. Sometimes they see the enemy as even more dangerous, composed of apostate Muslims who themselves have turned away from God and are corrupting Islam from within. For others they are advancing their faith and helping to build an Islamic society, defend it from its enemies, and expand it to new lands. Few have a detailed knowledge of Islam, but all would say that they are fighting for their faith and God smiles on their actions.

Historically, expelling foreign (non-Muslim) occupiers from Muslim lands was the most salient narrative for foreign fighters. Abdallah Azzam, a Palestinian-born preacher and writer who was the prime mover in the foreign fighter universe, articulated the duty of Muslims to remove foreign occupiers during the anti-Soviet struggle in the 1980s. This cry continued in Bosnia, Chechnya, Iraq, and other conflicts. In contrast, fighting against so-called apostate governments (e.g., fights in the 1990s against the government of Egypt or after 2003 in Saudi Arabia) attracted little support from new foreign fighters but led some existing group members to travel abroad, often to train or enjoy the benefits of a safe haven. Syria upended this generalization. Muslim-on-Muslim sectarian fighting proved an important pull for foreign fighters in 2012 and 2013. In 2014, a new narrative began: fighters flocked to Syria once the Islamic State declared a caliphate because they wanted to live in a land ruled according to God's law. This declaration complemented the call to defend the community from unbelievers. For jihadists, Muslims had finally established a true Islamic state, and naturally, Islam's enemies would try to destroy it.

On a more individual level, conflicts initially tend to attract the most idealistic. Over time, the recruits change to include more individuals frustrated with aspects of their lives and who seek the power, legitimacy, community, and opportunity the foreign fighter life affords. And, on a more basic level, some foreign fighters simply want to kill people. Not surprisingly, many recruits for the more popular jihads had criminal records or were otherwise known to law enforcement before taking up arms. In Europe and several other parts of the world, many recruits often interacted with ostensibly peaceful, but politically militant, Salafi groups that promoted radical ideas, extolled war, and helped individuals network with foreign jihadists.

Perceived success bred actual success. Foreign fighters used particular battles or limited achievements to highlight their prowess, and this "winning" narrative attracted additional recruits. When the mujahedin movement scored real successes against the Soviets in Afghanistan, its popularity skyrocketed, but when it became overconfident and simply sent volunteers to be slaughtered, its prestige withered. Similarly, the competence of the Islamic State's government—it collected taxes, imposed its version of law and order, and delivered some social services—demonstrated the group's strength and bolstered its appeal, but when the Caliphate began to collapse in 2016 under the U.S.-led military campaign, foreign fighter flows dried up.

Finally, wars drive foreign fighter flows. The foreign fighters *never* begin the conflicts they participate in and only later play a prominent part. In most cases, they joined civil wars born from nationalist revolts against foreign occupiers or divisions within the country. The foreign fighters usually entered in the middle of the conflict and, even in cases when they participated in the early stages, less radical groups usually dominated at the outset. As the conflict progressed, however, their role would grow. At times groups recruited them, and in other cases they showed up largely on their own. Groups such as Al Qaeda and the Islamic State exploit new wars wherever they can, establishing bases and using the cause to lure new recruits and conduct operations farther afield.

Three factors have changed the scope and scale of foreign fighter flows: a network effect, an expanded technological reach, and ease of travel. The first foreign fighter flow to Afghanistan in the 1980s produced an informal network of "brothers" who encouraged later foreign fighter flows. Subsequent conflicts deepened the network, making the idea of becoming a foreign fighter more exalted in militant circles. War veterans from an earlier conflict act as recruitment nodes for the next, inspiring new volunteers as well as providing practical advice on how to travel and whom to contact.

Groups' ability to harness technology greatly influenced their capacity to reach potential recruits. Many initial recruits had trouble finding Afghanistan on a map, and Arab Afghans fighting the Soviets struggled to produce and disseminate a few magazines. Abu Musab al-Zarqawi, the founder of Al Qaeda in Iraq, in contrast, became a jihadist rock star by uploading gruesome beheading videos to the internet, while the Islamic State churned out more than a thousand video clips each month and used social media to bombard supporters and recruits with propaganda. In most conflicts, the jihadists' virtual triumphs dwarfed their successes on the ground, allowing the prestige of these groups to grow on the internet even while they faced a host of problems .

Finally, ease of travel mattered. Fighting the Russians in Chechnya constituted the most popular jihadist cause in the late 1990s, but Russia's policing of Chechnya's borders (and the attitude of Chechen groups toward most foreign fighters) limited foreign fighter flows. Instead, many of these travelers ended up in Afghanistan to seek the requisite training or simply to do something. Distant battlefields, such as Mali and Somalia, never attracted masses of volunteers in part due to the difficulty in traveling there.[24] Reaching the conflict zone in Syria, on the other hand, proved remarkably easy for the war's first years; once a fighter reached Turkey, usually a cheap plane ride away, established networks would spirit the fighter across the border.

As these factors suggest, foreign fighters are products of an age of globalization. Photos of foreign fighters often resemble a recruitment brochure from an American college, with racially diverse individuals all smiling happily with their arms around one another. Their identities cross borders, they can travel far from their homelands, and they disseminate multimedia propaganda around the world.

WHAT IMPACT DO FOREIGN FIGHTERS HAVE?

Foreign fighters seem to offer many advantages to militant groups fighting in a civil war or otherwise trying to expand their power. Communities and groups in a war zone are often desperate: outmanned, outgunned, and eager for any form of support. Some foreign fighters, but by no means most, brought considerable combat or technical skills to the conflict, having fought in past jihads or spent time at jihadist training camps. They used these skills to fight for locals and often taught them as well. Locals also accepted even unskilled jihadis due to their dedication, which often engendered respect even when it exceeded the fervor of locals. In particular, these relatively unskilled zealots accounted for many of the suicide bombers in some conflicts. The surge in the number of unskilled fighters seeking martyrdom helped some groups, notably the Islamic State, use suicide bombers on an industrial scale. Foreign fighters often acted as logisticians, travel facilitators, passport forgers, propagandists, and recruiters, with their understanding of a foreign culture and how to appeal to that community often serving them in good stead. Such benefits paid off. One study found that the presence of foreign fighters in a conflict makes it harder for the government to achieve victory.[25]

When individuals traveled abroad to fight, they also came under the direction of militant groups in or near a war zone. These groups had their own agendas that were often different and more radical than the fighters' original goals, and they used the foreigners to accomplish them. So individual groups often welcomed fighters even when the community or cause as a whole did not.

Left unchecked or given only modest attention, foreign fighter returnees can prove a major terrorism threat. In many of the biggest attacks in the last thirty years, foreign fighters were instrumental, conducting bombings in Madrid, London, Paris, and of course 9/11, as well as far more attacks in the Middle East and the greater Muslim world. Foreign fighters are often better trained, more highly motivated and networked, and tied to skilled planners back in the war zone. One leading study done before the Syrian civil war found that terrorist plots involving foreign fighter veterans were roughly 50 percent more likely to succeed than those without returning fighters, and when the attack succeeded, on average the fatalities were twice as high.[26]

Even the end of a war does not end the foreign fighter problem. On returning to their home countries with the stature and glory that attends a man who fought for his faith and community, foreign fighters are well-positioned to promote a more extreme version of Islam. As a result, the belief that the West plots to destroy Islam, along with other radical ideas that once found purchase only in narrow segments of the Muslim community, are spreading throughout Muslim lands, in Europe, and in other areas with large Muslim populations. These ideas allow the jihadist movement to endure even without a conflict, as radical groups form in fighters' home countries, ready to seize on the next war when it occurs.

Despite their zealotry and fighting prowess, foreign fighters frequently sow the seeds of their own undoing, leaving both the country in which they operate and the cause they champion worse off in the end. They bring new ideas about who is the enemy and what the goals are to a conflict, creating divisions among the opposition and weakening popular support.[27]

Foreign fighters often make war harsher. They commit atrocities because of their zealotry, their fear of disobeying the harsh discipline of a jihadist group, and their lack of local connections that might otherwise restrain them or give them a protector should they want to disobey the group. In contrast, local groups have personal relations with members of rival communities or at least fear revenge against their own people. In addition, foreign fighters often fiercely oppose any peace deals, using terrorism against all sides to disrupt them.

Groups dominated by foreign fighters often govern poorly. This should not be a surprise. Many foreign fighters are unskilled, and the zealotry they espouse does not easily coexist with a more technocratic approach to government. They traveled to fight, not to pick up the trash. They also usually try to drive out foreign relief organizations, international agencies, and others who might assist local communities, causing basic services to suffer.

Due to their philosophy and background, foreign fighters reject borders. In their eyes they defend the global Muslim community, not artificial lines on a map that define states' boundaries. As such, to them, injustices against Muslims in a neighboring state deserve attention as do injustices in their current base. In addition, foreign fighters leverage travel and logistical networks in other countries to get to a war zone. The same transnational networks that bring fighters into a war zone can just as easily bring fighters and weapons out of a war zone and into new lands. Accordingly, foreign fighters in Chechnya expanded the war to Dagestan; in Iraq, they spread it to Syria; from Afghanistan, they spread it to Pakistan; and so on. Such moves led to new supporters and bases but also brought new enemies and introduced tensions with more nationalistic fighters.

Terrorism that is spearheaded by foreigners against enemies of jihad in distant lands frequently backfires, justifying new or greater foreign intervention against jihadist groups. Al Qaeda, the Chechen jihadists, and the Islamic State all faced increased international intervention when their foreign fighters conducted terrorist attacks outside the conflict zones. In particular, because of the U.S. emphasis on counterterrorism against jihadists post-9/11, the mere presence of groups with links to foreign fighters attracted U.S. attention.

In their zealotry, foreign fighters have difficulty tolerating ambiguity, and in civil wars, many actors change loyalties and play both sides. Some communities may try to cooperate with both the government and insurgents in order to hedge their bets, and many families deliberately plant members in rival groups to ensure that their family will receive protection no matter who wins. States play this game too. Pakistan, Syria, and Turkey have at times supported or tolerated foreign fighter activity, and at other times they cracked down on it. Rather than accepting such vacillations as a hard reality, foreign fighters often retaliate against the state and its citizens. In response, the state comes to see the foreigners and the groups they represent as a direct threat and cracks down. Zarqawi, for example, drew on logistical networks in Iran but later targeted Iranian-backed groups and leaders in Iraq.[28] The 9/11 attacks offer the most egregious example of this tendency, where Al Qaeda's attack on the United States led directly to the overthrow of its host, the Taliban, and the loss of Al Qaeda's training camps.

As foreign fighters consolidate power, they become rivals to local leaders rather than protectors. Foreign fighters who are initially welcomed to balance a hostile government or foreign invaders can later come to represent a direct threat. In Iraq, many Sunnis at first welcomed foreign Arabs to fight against U.S. forces and a government in Baghdad they saw as oppressive. Over time, however, Al Qaeda in Iraq's brutality and hubris provided an opening for the United States to work with Sunni tribes and nationalist forces—the same ones that had shot at and bombed U.S. troops after the 2003 invasion—and decimated Al Qaeda in Iraq. In Chechnya, foreigners initially found the right balance with local fighters, but their ambitions grew, and Moscow mobilized Sufi Muslim leaders against them to devastating effect.

Because of these problems, some local jihadist groups no longer actively seek foreign fighters, particularly Westerners. Al Qaeda in the Arabian Peninsula, for example, claims that the Islamic State's teachings have "contaminated" many foreigners, making them likely to be a divisive force. The foreigners are also hard to control as the Al Qaeda franchise tries to embed itself in local communities, posing as their friend and protector. In addition, Al Qaeda fears attracting more American drones as do the tribes and local leaders who work with the Yemeni Al Qaeda franchise.[29]

HOW CAN WE BETTER FIGHT FOREIGN FIGHTERS?

Many states have tolerated the outflow of fighters only to pay a heavy price later when they returned and conducted terrorist attacks or sought to foster insurgencies. Arab states thought they could dump their radicals, allowing recruits to leave their countries to fight the Soviets in the 1980s, only to see many return and foment radicalism after the Soviet withdrawal. Other states were simply ignorant of the dangers or unable to crack down. After the Syrian civil war broke out, for example, hundreds of fighters left Belgium for Iraq and Syria because Brussels lacked the capacity to monitor and disrupt this flow. A few states even tried to harness the fighters, hoping they could exploit them with no long-term cost, as Yemen did when it used jihadists to fight its civil war in 1994.

Foreign fighters also draw on a broader ideology and private funding mechanisms that a host of states promulgate and enable. Some states, notably Saudi Arabia, fund preachers, educational institutions, nongovernmental organizations, and other bodies that disseminate teachings that reinforce some of the foreign fighters' messages. In the West, some components of the foreign fighters' propaganda machine operated relatively openly, taking advantage of free speech protections, and many fighters emerged from legal organizations that peacefully promoted an extreme interpretation of Islam and, thus, remained unchallenged by government.

The good news is that states are improving laws, security, training, and institutions to deal with foreign fighters even as the numbers of foreign fighters increase. By improving their ability to detect fighters before they leave and when they return, and to disrupt them in transit, states make terrorism less likely. Success in the post-9/11 era of disrupting terrorist havens also hinders groups from organizing and launching attacks from overseas.

Terrorism is a small numbers game. A few sufficiently trained and motivated individuals (nineteen in the final stage of 9/11) can produce a horrific tragedy. But counterterrorism efforts can reduce these numbers and put up barriers in the paths of those who remain, thus dramatically decreasing the odds that foreign fighters will become a security problem. In addition to fighting terrorist groups overseas, counterterrorism should focus on shrinking the network, hindering feeder groups, and trying to prevent one set of foreign fighters from inspiring and directing the next generation. The United States and many allies have learned to do the enforcementside of the equation, but they need new capabilities to persuade potential and actual radicals to turn away from violence.

A successful counterterrorism strategy would aim to disrupt foreign fighters at each stage in a foreign fighter's "life cycle." The life cycle begins with potential volunteers becoming radicalized and then deciding to go abroad to fight. Counterterrorism officials can prevent or dissuade individuals from going to a conflict zone in the first place by undermining the sources of radicalization and disrupting recruitment networks. Many volunteers, however, are not on law enforcement's radar screen or have done nothing illegal until the last minute when they travel abroad to take up arms. Often, ostensibly peaceful domestic groups recruit, radicalize, or otherwise assist potential volunteers by promoting jihadist teachings and creating networks for fighters. For these individuals, it takes ideas, not just arrests, to stop them. Communities and families can act as a source of assistance and work with authorities to prevent their children from traveling to fight, but only if they trust the government.[30] However, in general, governments often fail at developing compelling counternarratives and they also lack community credibility. Increasingly, politicians in the United States and Europe are spouting anti-Muslim rhetoric that further erodes trust in government.

Foreign fighter flows are highly sensitive to the ease of transit. Affecting government policy is vital at this stage, as some governments prove openly or tacitly supportive of fighters, while others take a laissez-faire attitude that indirectly benefits jihadists. Indeed, the international community is far better at disruption of travel than in the pre-9/11 era. Disrupting the transit route via Turkey eventually proved one of the best ways to reduce the flow of foreign fighters to Syria. In addition, bolstering the security services in home countries, enhancing monitoring, and implementing legislation to disrupt travel also hinders the flow of foreign fighters.

For those foreign fighters who make it to a war zone and train and fight there, the United States and its allies can try to shape the course of the war to destroy the groups that use foreign fighters or deter them from doing so. In some cases, as in Iraq and Syria, combating jihadis may involve a mix of bombing terrorist bases and bolstering government and local forces to defeat groups on the ground. It is often necessary to kill jihadists with drones or aid their enemies who will defeat them on the ground. Programs to train and equip local governments and militias can offer modest gains. Off the battlefield, security services should aim to capitalize on the mistrust and cultural distance among foreign fighters and their host groups. To the extent that militias, and especially jihadist groups, see foreign fighters as potential spies or as corrupting cultural influences, they will reduce efforts to recruit foreigners.

Because jihadists thrive in war zones, efforts to resolve wars in the Muslim world can also reduce the production of future fighters. Such diplomacy to end conflicts is difficult, and often it requires funding programs to strengthen governments and local service providers. However, these efforts are far easier and cheaper than intervening in a war.

If the fighters survive the war zone, governments must turn them away from violence and jihad upon return. The most dangerous fighters—those who appear at high risk to conduct terrorism or commit a crime—must be jailed, which requires passing legislation to enable security services to arrest dangerous returnees and providing sufficient resources for these services. However, sending even minor players to jail, particularly if only for a few years, risks exposing them to hardened jihadists in prison and enables them to integrate into broader networks.[31] In addition, an individual may become more likely to commit an act of terrorism and stay with a group if imprisonment seems inevitable because the individual may feel that he has less to lose. Arresting rather than reintegrating returnees is easier politically, however; an individual who conducted a terrorist attack after security services passed on a chance to arrest him would embarrass the service and enrage the public.

Intelligence collection and sharing are vital at every stage of the process. Since 9/11, the United States and its allies have made huge leaps in intelligence sharing and collection. Even so, often there is little collection in the first few years of a new conflict, as security services are not yet focused on a problem. Many European states, for example, did not focus on Syria until the Paris attacks of 2015, and by then thousands of their citizens had left to fight. The United States often acts as the conductor of a global intelligence effort, helping services around the world to share information and to work together against an increasingly global foe. The social media that jihadists use to publicize their cause and direct recruits is often turned against them, helping security services identify real and potential foreign fighters and arrest them before they can do harm.

Alienating Muslim communities and overreacting to even minor terrorist threats and attacks helps the jihadists win. Unfortunately, in the United States and many European countries, rhetoric about terrorism is more alarming than the true threat. Muslims are often criticized, harassed, or worse, creating the risk that cooperative communities will become more supportive of violence or at least less willing to work with governments. In Europe, Muslims are often poorly integrated and live in segregated neighborhoods, which make radicalization more likely in the long term.

Inevitably, security services in the United States and the West in general will miss some dangerous individuals when conflicts attract high numbers of foreign fighters, and some individuals initially deemed nonthreatening might later become a threat. The foreign fighter problem also demands a degree of societal resilience that the United States has lacked thus far, and indeed, resilience has declined since 9/11 even as counterterrorism in general has advanced by leaps and bounds.

Book Structure

The remainder of this book provides a history and assessment of the modern jihadist foreign fighter movement and offers ideas on how to better fight it. Most chapters begin with the story of an individual or small group of foreign fighters who were instrumental in a particular jihad or whose experience illustrates a broader lesson about foreign fighters. The history of the group they joined and the conflict in which they fought usually follows. The initial chapters are a chronological history, while the chapters on Europe, the United States, and policy recommendations cut across various modern jihads.

In chapter 2, I describe the role played by Abdallah Azzam, the founder of the modern foreign fighter movement, who transformed a small and ancillary group of Arab volunteers fighting the Soviets in Afghanistan in the 1980s into the stuff of legend. In addition to incubating future jihads, Afghanistan also gave birth to Al Qaeda, a unique foreign fighter organization. Chapter 3 tells the story of Barbaros, an Afghanistan veteran who seeded the next important jihad for the foreign fighter movement in Bosnia in the early 1990s. Chapter 4 tells the story of Ali Mohamed, an American who joined Al Qaeda and would set up one of the group's most lasting legacies—the archipelago of training camps in Afghanistan that produced some of the most dangerous terrorists the world has ever known, including many of the key perpetrators of the 9/11 attacks. In chapters 5 and 6, I present the story of another Afghan veteran, Khattab, who helped transform the war in Chechnya in the late 1990s into the most important jihadist movement of its time.

The 9/11 attacks, off-the-charts in terms of lethality and impact, marked a turning point for the foreign fighter movement as governments around the world, led and prodded by the United States, began to prioritize arresting or killing foreign fighters. Yet in the post-9/11 era, the foreign fighters enjoyed many successes. Chapter 7 chronicles Abu Musab al-Zarqawi and the foreign fighters in Iraq after the 2003 U.S. invasion. Zarqawi, who fought and trained in Afghanistan, became a jihadist legend through his brutality and use of internet videos, eclipsing even Osama Bin Laden. Yet Iraq was also a disaster for the jihadist cause. In chapter 8, I examine the new leader of the foreigners in Iraq, the Egyptian Abu Ayyub al-Masri, who after 2006 led the jihadists to the edge of defeat, in part because of his messianic insistence on creating an Islamic state. Chapter 9 details how, just as Iraqi jihadists began to flail, another jihadist movement, the Shebaab in Somalia—led by Somalis who fought or trained in Afghanistan—captured the attention of many foreigners. One such foreigner was Omar Hammami, a young American whose humor and use of social media gave him a prominent place in the group's ranks before its leaders brutally turned on him. Chapter 10 examines the most popular jihad of all time in the modern era, the Syrian civil war, which broke out in 2011, and describes how the Islamic State, which grew out of the foreign fighter movement in Iraq, came to dominate the global foreign fighter movement.

The final three chapters cut across this history. Chapter 11 looks at the important role of Europe in the foreign fighter movement as an incubator of jihadist ideas, a generator of volunteers, and, in the end, a victim of terrorism. The story of Amer Azizi, a Moroccan who grew up in Spain and played a key role in

Europe's deadliest jihadist terrorist attack—the 2004 bombings of four trains in Spain that killed 191 people—illustrates these many roles. Chapter 12 looks at a success story: U.S. efforts to hunt down Al Qaeda propagandist Anwar al-Awlaki and the Islamic State cyberteam dubbed "the Legion," a group of mainly British virtual propagandists and operators living in Syria who tried to convince Americans to conduct terrorist attacks in the United States. In the post-9/11 era, U.S. counterterrorism has successfully managed, though hardly solved, the foreign fighter threat to the U.S. homeland. The final chapter of the book offers lessons learned for policymakers seeking to better combat foreign fighters in the future.

CHAPTER 2 | The Prophet: Abdullah Azzam
and the Anti-Soviet Jihad in
Afghanistan

A FGHANISTAN SERVES AS a curious taproot for the global jihadist
movement. The Soviet invasion of Afghanistan in 1979, which aimed
to restore their proxy government to power, initially failed to unify Islamists
worldwide against the foreigners. Islamists had long loathed Communism for
its atheism, yet in the aftermath of the Soviet invasion, they focused instead
on their own, more localized struggles. In Saudi Arabia, fanatics heralding the
return of the messiah seized the Grand Mosque in Mecca in preparation for the
coming apocalypse, while in Egypt, Islamists opposed what they saw as too
secular a regime and sought to Islamize their own society. If Sunni jihadists
obsessed over any foreign event, it was the Islamic revolution in Iran in 1979.
That revolution showed Islam's power; religious leaders could topple a U.S.-
backed dictator whose control seemed insurmountable. Yet Shiite Muslims
led the revolution, who many Sunnis saw as deviant. This mix of inspiration
and loathing electrified many Islamists, while distant events in Afghanistan
seemed like a sideshow at most.

One man, Abdullah Azzam, changed this perception. Azzam was known
as the "teacher and the fighter" by his admirers.[1] Over time, the Afghan
jihad would become a legend for jihadists, a time when heroes gathered to
defy the odds and, with God's grace, defeated a superpower. The reality is
more prosaic. Militarily irrelevant, the foreign fighters represented at best a
curious footnote to the anti-Soviet struggle that the Afghans, not foreigners,

fought and won. In addition, the problems that would plague the foreign fighters in subsequent conflicts—multiple agendas, bitter factionalism, duplicitous state supporters like Pakistan, and brutality toward ordinary Muslims—arose repeatedly. Yet Afghanistan's importance in the history of the modern jihadist movement and the story of the foreign fighters is undeniable. Azzam, through his sermons and writings, would popularize the Afghan cause and promote the idea, which was a curiosity before his time, that Muslims had a personal obligation to travel to distant lands to embrace jihad. Perhaps more important, Azzam also acted as an organizer, creating a bureaucracy and propaganda structure that would continue his great project long after his murder in 1989. Almost every subsequent jihad involving foreign fighters can be traced to individuals who heard Azzam's call and fought in Afghanistan. Perhaps most significantly, the Afghan jihad would bring Azzam together with a young Saudi named Osama Bin Laden, who would go on to found Al Qaeda, which proved perhaps the most consequential terrorist group in modern history.

"Jihad and the Rifle Alone"

Born in the West Bank in 1941, Azzam bitterly remembered Israeli tanks entering his village, without facing opposition, during the 1967 war.[2] Azzam studied in Syria and then traveled to Jordan, where his family moved following Israel's takeover of the West Bank. He then joined a weak Islamist faction of Palestinians fighting Israel, but Marxist and Arab nationalist fighters predominated in the movement as a whole.[3] Palestinian attacks ended in 1970 when the militants clashed with Jordanian security forces, who chased the militants out of the country in a bloody crackdown. Azzam's own group dissolved, and he would become convinced that the Palestinian fighters failed because they did not fight in the name of Islam.[4]

Azzam then completed a Ph.D. at the famous Al Azhar University in Egypt, where many leaders of the Afghan Islamist movement also studied.[5] Egypt in the 1970s acted as a jihadist incubator. President Anwar Sadat unleashed Islamists to oppose leftists and nationalists in Egypt. As with so many countries that played with jihadist fire, Egypt would be burned. In 1981, Egyptian jihadists killed Sadat because he failed to implement Islamic law, and they waged a campaign of terrorism and insurgency against the regime on and off for decades. Azzam left Egypt well before Sadat's killing, but while there he imbibed the ideas of Sayyid Qutb, a radical Egyptian ideologue whose works would inspire future Al Qaeda leader Ayman al-Zawahiri, among others. Azzam first expressed his anti-Communist zeal in his 1978 book *The Red Cancer*.

After completing his degree in Egypt, Azzam returned briefly to Jordan, but his radical views were unwelcome. He made his way to Saudi Arabia, where he taught at King Abd al-Aziz University, where Osama Bin Laden, a young Saudi from a fabulously wealthy family was a student. Azzam's life, and the story of the foreign fighters, would change dramatically in 1979 when the Soviet Union invaded Afghanistan to shore up the Communist regime there. Afghans throughout the country rebelled. Some sought a return of the monarchy, some wanted more autonomy for their region, and a small group wanted to make Afghanistan an Islamic state.[6] The fighting would become fierce, and the war increasingly radicalized many Afghans. It also drew in foreign powers, including the United States, Pakistan, and Saudi Arabia, all of whom wanted to make the Soviet Union bleed.[7]

In 1981, Azzam first went to Pakistan to support the anti-Soviet struggle, joining a handful of other Arabs there. He recalled that he focused on the media and promoting the Afghan cause at student conferences in the United States, Britain, Saudi Arabia, and other countries while, at the same time, trying to get sympathetic Afghan warlords to work together.[8] In 1984, he again crossed paths with Osama Bin Laden, who fell under his spell and whom Azzam declared a "heaven-sent man, like an angel."[9] The two created the Services Bureau, an institution that proved an instrumental step for the international jihadist movement, with Azzam leading it but Bin Laden paying for housing, plane tickets, salaries, and other necessities.[10] The Services Bureau helped organize jihadists, creating structures that facilitated their recruitment, travel, training, fighting, and dispersion. It also offered health care, education, and other assistance to Afghan refugees because, in Azzam's eyes, helping oppressed Muslims meant both humanitarian and military aid.[11] This mix of inspiration and practical assistance would become a trademark of Azzam's jihadist heirs.

Yet while Azzam could be pragmatic, his ideology was uncompromising. "No negotiations, no conferences, and no dialogues," Azzam declared. Instead, the answer was "Jihad and the Rifle Alone." That simple and defiant slogan resonated in an Arab world humiliated by military defeat, political stagnation, and foreign meddling.

But what should the focus of jihad be? Azzam championed the concept that each Muslim had an individual duty to wage violent jihad on behalf of the Muslim community when it is under attack by unbelievers. At a time when jihadists like those in Egypt focused on creating Islamic governments in their home countries, Azzam contended, "When the enemy enters an Islamic land or a land that was once part of the Islamic lands, it is obligatory on the inhabitants of that place to go forth and face the enemy."[12] Azzam believed Christian, atheist, and other unbeliever armies kill and destroy, prevent the practice of Islam, and abuse Muslim women. In such circumstances, jihad, for Azzam, represented an obligatory religious duty for all individual Muslims. Anyone not engaged in jihad "is forsaking a duty, just like the one who eats during the days of Ramadhan without excuse."[13]

Azzam challenged the dominant understanding of the "greater jihad," a supposed saying of the Prophet Muhammad referring to jihad as an attempt to triumph over the darker impulses of one's soul, a benign interpretation many Muslims embrace. Azzam contended that the saying was a fabrication and that true jihad involved "combat with weapons."[14] The peaceful interpretation aimed merely "to distract the Muslims from fighting the infidels and the hypocrites," as one like-minded ideologue explained.[15] Unfortunately, many traditional scholars support Azzam's interpretation.

According to Azzam, God placed an obligation on young Muslims to fight for the oppressed. Azzam also believed violence was cathartic for Muslims as long as it was in the name of God. Fighting would "lift disgrace" off the Muslim community. The Prophet, he noted, constantly fought to defend and expand the faith as did his immediate and most pious successors. More practical reasons included ensuring that leftists and nationalists did not dominate the resistance.[16] Although Azzam bore no love for the West, at this point the jihadist movement was focused on fighting Communism and squabbles in the Muslim world, not in the United States or Europe.

At first, this perceived individual duty of jihad was not popular. In contrast to international Communism or other transnational movements, even the most militant Sunnis of the time did not consider leaving their homes to fight in another country to be a religious obligation. Salafism, the interpretation of Islam that jihadist groups like Al Qaeda and the Islamic State embrace, had only local horizons when the Soviets invaded Afghanistan. Salafist leaders seek to strip Islam of what they regard as innovations and deviations from the Quran and emphasize the authentic sayings and practices of the Prophet Mohammad. They oppose the mysticism of the Sufis and democracy because it elevates man-made law. Shiite Muslims and other religious minorities, such as Syria's ruling Alawi community, are suspect because they venerate figures from Islam's past, giving them near-divine attributes and thus deviating from Salafis' monotheistic purity. Salafism is strong in Saudi Arabia especially (where it is often labeled "Wahhabism" after an important Saudi preacher), and the Saudi state worked with the Salafist religious establishment to consolidate its power. For many Salafists, the Afghans in 1979 did not represent Muslims under attack but rather false Muslims. Although they nominally practiced Islam, the day-to-day teachings and rituals in Afghanistan did not resemble the Islam in Saudi Arabia. Other Muslims thus had no obligation to help them or even care at all. Some religious leaders also argued that young people must ask their parents for permission to go to the battlefield, which often was not forthcoming.

The vast majority of Salafis thought that believers should abstain from politics and other forms of social activism, concentrating instead on their own personal behavior. Even for those who were more political, most leading scholars had argued that those Muslims near the enemy (in this case, the Afghans) must resist directly, but those farther away could rely on their governments to act. This proved a recipe for individual passivity. Azzam argued that when local Muslims are either unable or unwilling to resist, the responsibility to act spreads to those farther away until all Muslims are obligated. In olden times, the difficulty of traveling from one end of the Muslim world to another made such ideas impractical, but with the advent of air travel, that excuse no longer applied.[17]

The small number of Muslims who heeded Azzam's call saw themselves as defenders of their faith. They would say that the Soviet Union and the puppet Afghan government were bent on destroying Islam in Afghanistan. The very real Soviet atrocities there proved Moscow's evil intentions and led to a thirst for revenge and a stain on the honor of those who would not heed the call.

In addition to promulgating the concept of individual responsibility for jihad, Azzam also fostered the idea that Muslims should fight for the entire religious community. Azzam invoked causes ranging from the Philippines to Chad as well as countries in the Arab world and claimed they were part of one struggle that all Muslims share. At the time, the standard rhetoric and mobilization emphasized the Palestinian cause or fighting against supposedly apostate regimes like Egypt. Azzam claimed that fighting the Soviets would help prepare Muslims for the tougher fight against Israel. Afghanistan, he contended, was closer to being a true Islamic state than Palestine and thus should become a base to launch other efforts. More practically, Afghanistan had "3,000 kilometers of open borders" and no functioning security apparatus in much of the state, while in Palestine "the borders are tightly controlled and security is omnipresent."[18]

As the jihadis liberated Muslim lands and Muslims became united, Islam would return to the form of government it had during its centuries of power and greatness: the Caliphate, which had ended when the Turkish government abolished it as antiquated in 1924. Azzam rejected man-made laws, which he believed demonstrated that the community abandoned God. By restoring what Azzam called "God's rule on earth," Muslims would unify under one ruler.[19] For Azzam, however, the Caliphate represented a long-term ambition at best.

By today's jihadist standards, many of Azzam's teachings seem quite moderate. Azzam rejected the ideas that Muslims could declare other Muslims as unbelievers and did not believe the Muslim world was ready for the imminent return of the Caliphate. In general, he was skeptical of calls to revolt against governments in Egypt and Saudi Arabia that were ruled by nominal Muslims, no matter how lax their religious policies. Yet many of his other ideas would form the bedrock of the modern jihadist movement.

The Afghanistan Jihad

In some ways, encouraging Arabs to fight on behalf of Afghans was relatively easy for Azzam compared with his successors. Most traditional Salafis did endorse the idea of jihad as a defensive idea when unbelievers attacked Muslims. This defensive narrative fit Afghanistan and would fit the Russians in Chechnya, the Serbs in Bosnia, and the United States in Iraq. Subsequent jihadists would push the idea of fighting against Muslim rulers for their refusal to apply true Islamic law or, as Al Qaeda would, blaming the United States for the Muslim world's problems and calling for attacks in the West. These ideas had less support among traditional Salafi scholars.[20] The barbarous nature of the Soviet campaign also helped Azzam in his recruitment efforts. One early Arab Afghan (the label often given to Arabs who fought in Afghanistan) recalled, "I used to hang a picture on my room's wall of an Afghani toddler who was completely burned from napalm and crying from pain. Every morning, I would swear in front of this picture that I will fight in Afghanistan."[21]

For Azzam this acceptance of non-Salafis as Muslims was vital. Whereas many Salafis viewed Afghans as de facto unbelievers because they worshipped at graves, embraced forms of mysticism, and seemed primitive in their customs, Azzam argued that most Afghans prayed daily and otherwise embraced the faith. He even turned their supposed ignorance into part of his sales pitch, asking for donations to rebuild demolished schools and to fund volunteer teachers who would guide Afghans along the true path.[22] The Afghans, he stated, sought the counsel and wisdom of pious Arab volunteers, and these volunteers would help them "shake off" the un-Islamic customs and "traditions of defeated generations."[23] The presence of one Arab, Azzam wrote, was worth more than a million dollars.

Indeed, for many Afghans, especially early on, the presence of the Arabs seemed divine. They came speaking the language of the Prophet from legendary places such as Mecca and Medina.[24] Some key figures, notably Sheikh Jalaluddin Haqqani, would embrace the Arab Afghans out of respect for their dedication. Haqqani would emerge as a key anti-Soviet fighter and then an important warlord in the ensuing war of all-against-all, often working with Pakistani intelligence and the military. (His people would also prove a thorn in the side of the United States and its Afghan allies after 9/11.) Many early Al Qaeda leaders cut their teeth working with Haqqani. His support enabled Arabs to gain combat experience, and over time his family proved an important ally.[25]

The reality of the Arabs' presence, of course, was more prosaic, particularly as Arabs became less of a rarity in the struggle. The Afghans often only treated the Arabs well because they saw them as potential donors. Many Afghans wanted little to do with the Arabs. Language differences, the Arabs' poor fighting ability, and other problems hindered ties. The zealous volunteers did not always obey Azzam's call to respect Afghan culture and work with Afghans. In some areas, they raped Afghan women or forced them into marriage, believing that their superior religious status enabled them to take what they wanted. They also would interfere with tribal customs, including honoring the graves of fallen fighters, which the foreigners considered idolatrous. Moreover, for some foreigners jihad was a vacation. They came only for a few days and simply wanted to brag about their bravery back home rather than truly fight; these volunteers were derided as "Gucci jihadis."[26]

Azzam did not have a monopoly on the ideas of Arab Afghans, and many of those who fought embraced visions of jihad that Azzam rejected. Indeed, many of the ideas that would define future jihadist struggles were present in Afghanistan in one form or another, often brought in through contact with foreigners. A key Afghan warlord, Abdul Sayyaf, was a fluent Arabic speaker who had trained in Saudi Arabia and whose language skills and connections made him a favorite of donors there. Sayyaf pushed sectarianism and favored violence against Afghanistan's Shiite Muslim minority, in part to win the support of the anti-Shiite Saudi religious establishment. Indeed, a sermon of his would inspire a young Jordanian named Abu Musab al-Zarqawi, the future leader of the jihadists in Iraq, to first go to Afghanistan.[27] The Saudi money Sayyaf received made him more influential, and in exchange, he helped organize some of the first training courses for Arabs.[28] Another group taught that anyone living in an area the Afghan Communist government controlled was an infidel who deserved to be killed; this policy was a forerunner to similar extreme claims made by groups in Algeria and Iraq. One small Afghan group, foreshadowing the Islamic State, declared their leader the Caliph, enforced Islamic law, and proclaimed that anyone who did not follow him was an infidel.[29] As the war continued, groups like Zawahiri's Egyptian Islamic Jihad established themselves in Pakistan, using the Afghanistan conflict to reorganize after being routed in Egypt. Zawahiri would note that "a Jihadi movement needs an arena that would act like an incubator where its seeds would grow and where it can acquire practical experience in combat, politics, and organizational matters."[30] Syrian fighters, fleeing the regime's crackdown on Islamists in the early 1980s, also traveled to Afghanistan. Some of the Arabs flocking to Afghanistan brought with them the idea that their home regimes were un-Islamic, and those that served them were unbelievers (*kuffar*) who deserved to be killed. Azzam rejected this concept (and so did Bin Laden at the time), but it too spread.[31] These ideas on right and wrong coexisted uneasily. In the best of times for jihadists, they would create animosity and hinder cooperation; in the worst of times, they would lead to outright war.

Azzam recorded and distributed his sermons and authored several influential books, including *Miraculous Signs of God The Compassionate Regarding the Afghans' Jihad, The Defense of Muslim Lands,* and *Join the Caravan.* Starting in 1984, Azzam published *Al Jihad,* an Arabic-language magazine, to publicize the Afghan fight. Long after his death, jihadists would continue to read and find inspiration in his works. Cassette tapes of his sermons appeared throughout the Muslim world, and subsequently the website www.azzam.com disseminated many of his teachings.[32]

One of Azzam's most influential works details the miracles that attended the anti-Soviet fighting. The angels who once fought alongside the Prophet Mohammad now fought alongside the Arab volunteers. Birds would fly down to warn of a Soviet airstrike, while fog would shield fighters from Soviet troops. Afghanistan's fierce scorpions would not sting the jihadists, and Soviet rounds would not explode. Even the dead got into the act. With beatific smiles on their faces, their bodies did not decay and smelled sweet. Their hands clutched their weapons and would only surrender them to other Muslims.[33] Such legends, variations of which were repeated for each subsequent jihad, often led to rude shocks for volunteers when they did not manifest.

Azzam also sought the support of the religious establishment, in contrast to later groups like the Islamic State that explicitly rejected such support. He preached to international Muslim conferences and found prominent religious leaders who would endorse his work. Azzam called on religious leaders to wage "jihad of the tongue" and support the fight in Afghanistan and jihad in general. By wooing and winning these leaders, he greatly expanded the authority of his own calls to jihad.[34]

As these activities make clear, Azzam always recognized the value of propaganda. In his calls for volunteers, he lamented not only the lack of doctors and fighters but also the need for filmmakers to document the struggle. The "Jewish media," he warned, was labeling the fighters as extremists, and the jihadists needed their own media campaign.[35]

Even as Azzam issued stirring calls to fight, he also pleaded for money. With sales pitches that echoed Western charity drives for Africa, he offered price points for different forms of giving to jihad; you could maintain one fighter for $8,000 a year, while $27,000 would open a religious school in Pakistan.[36]

Azzam's ideas spread everywhere, even to the United States. Songwriter Cat Stevens, a convert to Islam, praised jihad and martyrdom in the anti-Soviet struggle in an interview with a jihadist magazine. Azzam repeatedly traveled to America in the 1980s to raise money and established centers in New York; Detroit and Dearborn, Michigan; Los Angeles; Tucson; and San Francisco—fifty-two centers in all. His recruitment center in New York had U.S. government permission to raise money to pay for foreign fighter transit because the United States sought to encourage anti-Soviet sentiment. His magazine *Al Jihad* had many readers in the United States, constituting perhaps half of its total readership.[37]

Azzam the Organizer

Azzam did more than write, proselytize, and preach. He also laid an organizational foundation that would give rise to future generations of jihadists. In particular, his creation of the Services Bureau with Bin Laden's support in 1984 changed jihad from a scattered individual endeavor to an institutionally backed mission, transforming the resources and expertise involved. In the past, jihadists had shown up in ones and twos, and no one kept track of their skillset, their experience, or their fate if they died. Now an organization existed to do just that: recruit volunteers, give them a place to stay when they arrived, train them, and then channel them into the most productive activity or group. If they died, the Services Bureau contacted their families and at times provided some families with monetary support.

The Services Bureau focused on media, fundraising, and religious education in support of the Afghan jihad and charities to help Afghan refugees. It also assisted with travel. The organization gave only limited support to military activities, to Bin Laden's increasing chagrin, a weakness he would correct as time went on. Critically, Azzam focused on propaganda. Much of the Services Bureau's propaganda and educational efforts focused on Arab volunteers and on the Afghans themselves, trying to educate them spiritually as well as militarily.[38]

To appreciate the importance of the Services Bureau, it is useful to recall that simply getting to Afghanistan was difficult and confusing for many recruits as so little was known about the country, how to travel there, and other basic information. In the early 1980s, Afghanistan attracted perhaps a few dozen foreigners in total. The majority of volunteers worked in hospitals or refugee camps, not on the battlefield.[39] The first known Arab fighter death was not until 1985. One early recruit, Wael Julaydan, recalls how he heard about Afghanistan "from the mouths of enemies"—the Western media.[40] Another early arrival, the Algerian Abdullah Anas, recalls, "I had no idea at all where Afghanistan is, how to go there, which language they speak, which airlines go there—a hundred questions."[41] Likewise, one pioneer recalled that he at first didn't know the Afghans were Muslims and assumed the war was like the Contra struggle in Nicaragua.[42]

Most of the arriving Arabs lacked military training, and those who had it from service as draftees learned their craft in the stultifying ranks of Arab armies, not as guerrilla fighters. Militarily, the Arab Afghans' initial efforts were disastrous. After Azzam called on Arabs to join him at one battle, one "brigade" deployed but showed no ability to use terrain, march in the mountains, or otherwise fight effectively. Afghans ushered the group out, and one of the Arab Afghan leaders derided it as the "Brigade of the Humorous."[43]

Slowly but steadily, the first training camps began to emerge. Early efforts involved simply putting foreign volunteers in the same camps training Afghans, and they often trained only on a few basic weapons for a short period of time. Sada was the first camp for Arabs alone, created in 1986 and located in the tribal parts of Pakistan where an Arab Afghan–friendly warlord held sway (some sources claim that Bin Laden tried to keep it secret from Azzam as a way to siphon off the best recruits for his own organization). Isolating the foreign fighters would "save them from the political games of the Afghans."[44] These camps also would help the foreign fighters overcome culture shock as they became acclimated to the rigors and new customs of Afghanistan.[45] In any event, training was only ten days, with an emphasis on basic weapons training. Over the years, Al Qaeda would use other camps more, but Sada did graduate several famous alumni, including Ramzi Yousef, who orchestrated the World Trade Center bombing in 1993; Khalid Sheikh Mohammad, the mastermind of 9/11; and Abu Musab al-Zarqawi, who would lead Iraqi jihadists after the U.S. invasion.[46]

State Support?

Although jihadists' own histories portray the anti-Soviet struggle as a small band of individuals fighting a superpower, the story cannot be told without understanding the policies of several key states, notably Saudi Arabia and Pakistan.

At first, Saudi Arabia was cautious toward the Afghan struggle, with many Saudis considering the non-Salafi Afghans to be false Muslims rather than brothers in need of help. Bin Laden himself recalled that he did not join the fighting initially but confined his aid to financial support because the Kingdom's political and religious leadership was ambivalent in the first years of the war.

Riyadh, however, was strongly anti-Communist. Saudi intelligence, moreover, feared that Iran might gain influence in Afghanistan through Persian-speaking Tajiks and Shiite Muslims who were also taking up arms against the Soviets, and the Saudis sought to strengthen Sunni groups sympathetic to the Kingdom or at least hostile to its enemies.[47] Saudi Arabia funded the militants, but it's important to break down the varieties of Saudi funding, as this issue has caused confusion. The Saudi government, like the U.S. government, gave money to Pakistani intelligence to fund an array of groups, with the Pakistanis controlling the specific allocations. Given Pakistan's myriad connections to mujahedin groups, its importance as a rear base for the fight, and its overall strong position, letting Islamabad take the lead seemed natural. In addition, the Saudi state airline offered a 75 percent discount for those traveling to fight with the Arab resistance. The Saudi government at times tried to block training for Arabs, fearing, with some prescience, that they would become rebels when returning home.[48]

An array of Saudis, however, pursued their own policies. Some Saudi royal family members donated to the cause.[49] Members of the Saudi religious establishment, in direct competition with the Saudi state, gave money to their preferred commanders. Meanwhile, many ordinary Saudis funded medical care, religious education, and other forms of charity for the millions of displaced Afghans. Adding to the complexity, these three categories—state, religious institutions, and wealthy individuals—overlap in Saudi Arabia. A prince who draws a massive stipend from the government might act independently of the government and aid a group or cause, while Saudi intelligence may use religious charities to funnel money and support operations.[50]

Pakistan played a critical role in the anti-Soviet conflict, and the fate of the Arab Afghans and many subsequent foreign fighters would be bound up in the policies of the government in Islamabad. Pakistan told its embassies abroad to give a visa to anyone seeking to join the Afghan jihad. When the CIA backed anti-Soviet groups, it let Pakistan choose which leaders to aid. The CIA focused on killing Soviets but remained unconcerned with who did the shooting and their seemingly petty political squabbles.[51] Pakistan, for its part, feared that the Soviets would attack them, and, indeed, Soviet intelligence launched terrorist attacks in Pakistan itself. Pakistan worked with an array of Afghan groups and at times trying to unite them, but it never wanted any group to gain too much power or too much independence. Money and weapons helped preserve a balance of power. "The water in Afghanistan must boil at the right temperature," Pakistan's dictator, President Zia ul-Haq, told an aide.[52] Murder was part of the game too. One jihadist recalled that "dozens of Afghan field commanders were assassinated."[53]

Even at this relatively early stage, the seeds of what would later prove a disaster for Pakistan were being planted. Foreign fighters recalled going to Pakistan with the support of Pakistani religious groups and noted that the "government has given up" on controlling tribes near Afghanistan. Weapons were everywhere, and the credo of jihad was spreading.[54]

Because Pakistan, and various Saudi funders to a degree, offered their own funding to different Afghan groups, they had less incentive to unite. Azzam himself constantly tried to unify different factions, usually to no avail.[55]

Azzam's End

"History does not write its lines except with blood," Azzam had written, and so it would prove for him.[56] Azzam had few illusions about the Afghan warlords, and their lack of unity in particular disappointed him.[57] Yet he remained committed to their cause. He once declared, "Never shall I leave the land of *jihad,* except under three ways. Either I shall be killed in Afghanistan, killed in Peshawar, or handcuffed and expelled from Pakistan. . . . Blood, carnage, corpses, and souls, they are all fuel for the battle."[58]

By 1989, Azzam had become critical of Pakistan, whose manipulation of the anti-Communist forces led to bloody internecine fighting and numerous losses, as the foreigners and their allies hurled themselves against the better-armed Communists. Different Afghan allies turned on each other and Arab factions followed suit, while Azzam's attempts to mediate failed. Issues ranged from the most naked concerns about power and who received foreign funding to logistical questions about the war and ideology: where the foreign fighters should turn next, how quickly to rush to Islamic governance, the legitimacy of secular rulers in Muslim lands, and other fundamental issues.[59]

On November 24, 1989, a roadside bomb exploded as Azzam and his two sons drove by, killing all the passengers. No one knows who did it; suspects range from the Mossad and the CIA to (more credibly) the Pakistanis or rival militants. Mirroring the entire Arab experience in Afghanistan, Azzam's death entered the realm of legend. Jihadists would later learn that, while other car inhabitants were thrown 100 meters into the air and their remains scattered by the bombing, Azzam's body was discovered "resting against a wall, totally intact, and not at all disfigured."[60]

Azzam never unified the foreign fighters, but his ideas spread in the decades after his death. A jihadist magazine that eulogized Azzam declared that his death led to a "rush of jihad that rose in the souls of the youth all over the Islamic World."[61] Meanwhile, Bin Laden took over many of the networks established by the Services Bureau and expanded them. Over time, these networks would sustain themselves, and their members would create new ones, taking on a lives of their own and feeding various militant causes around the world. Ideas like obligatory jihad, the unity of all Muslims, and the use of constant propaganda became increasingly common. Whereas Azzam inspired hundreds to go fight the Soviets in Afghanistan, twenty-five years after his death, tens of thousands of foreigners would join the fray in Syria.

Enter Al Qaeda

Azzam had wanted to kill Russians, but he opposed terrorism, which he considered a cowardly tactic.[62] Azzam's ideas, however, would give birth to one of the most famous and consequential terrorist groups in history: Al Qaeda. In his writings, Azzam calls for *Al Qaeda al-Sulba*—"a solid foundation."[63] From this base, true Muslims would export jihad throughout the Muslim world and spread the austere Salafi creed. Muslim rebels fighting various regimes would emigrate to this base and find a sanctuary where they could train and form a vanguard, which Azzam described as "a small spark which ignites a large keg of explosives" and one that would "sacrifice their souls and their blood" to defend Muslims around the world.[64]

Osama bin Laden was that spark. Bin Laden quickly achieved local celebrity status because of his family's wealth and position. Who was this young man who would give up millions to live in a cave and risk his life for his fellow Muslims? Bin Laden stood out for his family background and organizational skill, but it was his bravery in battle that catapulted him to the next tier of jihadist stardom. He established the al-Masada ("Lion's Den") Camp in the caves above the village of Jaji just across the Pakistani border. The camp's location near the front was exciting (over time, multiple camps with different training courses would be housed there), and Bin Laden would bring donors to the camp.[65] He formed Al Qaeda as a splinter of the Services Bureau in 1987, but the documented history begins in 1988.[66]

Al Qaeda capitalized on the energy of the Afghan jihad to "form an Islamic army."[67] From the start, the group maintained committees on issues ranging from military and intelligence to money and media, but unlike the Services Bureau, it did not educate Afghans or otherwise do social work.[68] Bin Laden wanted to unify the Arab fighters under a single banner, while Azzam favored dispersing them among the many Afghan mujahedin groups.[69] In addition, Bin Laden and others grew frustrated by what they saw as the Services Bureau's mistakes and, at times, corruption and incompetence. Afghans regularly defrauded it, for example, by taking the same weapons across the border multiple times but charging for each trip separately.[70]

Bin Laden hoped to provoke a battle with nearby Soviet positions. In April 1987, about two hundred Soviet troops, supported by their Afghan allies, tried to overrun the base at Jaji. Along with a few dozen Arabs, including some of his future lieutenants, Bin Laden withstood three weeks of Soviet bombardment and fought to repel attacks. The battle was militarily inconsequential, but holding out against the Soviet onslaught won Bin Laden a resounding propaganda victory. Bin Laden had invited the Arab press to view the fighting, and he gave interviews to journalists portraying his Arab Afghans as a pious band of brothers defiantly confronting the might of the Soviet military, ultimately achieving victory through the grace of God. Accounts of the battle spread across the Arab world, influencing thousands of young men to travel to Afghanistan for jihad. Bin Laden was where the action was. "The youths started coming in waves," according to Al Qaeda propaganda.[71]

After Jaji, young Arabs rushed to join Bin Laden, with some sources claiming that hundreds of Arabs joined in this initial rush of enthusiasm—far higher numbers than Al Qaeda would enjoy later when it was more famous.[72] Saudis, whose numbers were initially small, grew steadily, with jihadist propaganda magazines declaring in 1987 that "most of the Martyrs are Saudis."[73] Thomas Hegghammer, the leading authority on Saudi jihadism, believes the number of Saudi jihadists who joined in this initial period was probably in the low thousands if you exclude those who went for humanitarian work or as a summer holiday just to play jihadist. However, he points out that this is remarkable given that, in contrast to Egypt and other countries, Saudi Arabia had almost no militant jihadist community in the early 1980s.[74] Ironically, more Arabs would go to Afghanistan after the Soviets departed. The "floodgates opened," as one observer noted.[75] Global jihad, while not a mainstream idea, was catching on and becoming the latest transnational identity to inspire young men to go to other lands to fight.

For all their bravado, the Arab Afghans remained woefully unprepared for combat. Their eagerness for martyrdom and lack of training showed, to say nothing of their expectation that angels would fight alongside them. In March 1989, the Afghan mujahedin, with strong Arab Afghan participation, tried to take the city of Jalalabad from the Moscow-backed Afghan Army, which was widely, and wrongly, expected to collapse. Exact numbers are elusive, but hundreds of Arabs and other non-Afghan Muslims (Bengalis, for example) joined the fray, and Bin Laden emptied all his camps to support the fighting.[76] The mujahedin's brutal tactics and refusal of quarter stiffened the Communist forces' resolve, despite fighting for the first time without Soviet support. Bin Laden joined the Arab force and was wounded in combat, bolstering his reputation for battlefield bravery.

The battle raged for three months, but ultimately, the government forces' superior firepower forced the mujahedin to withdraw after losing thousands of fighters. Bin Laden later claimed 170 Arabs died in the battle, which he admitted comprised more than all previous Arab fatalities in Afghanistan.[77] Other sources would put the figure as high as 500. Zeal overcame common sense, which was a consistent pattern. Bin Laden was fiercely criticized; indeed, he owned up to that criticism, for the "waste of the lives of the youth."[78] In addition, the fighting was Muslim on Muslim and was supported by Pakistani intelligence, making it more politically fraught. Mustafa Hamid, a longtime jihadist, argues that this emphasis on "action without attention to consequences" is still strong in the jihadist world.[79]

When the Jihad Ends

Al Qaeda's appeal diminished after Jalalabad and would not fully recover until the late 1990s. Military defeat, along with the withdrawal of Soviet troops, made Afghanistan far less appealing. The Arab Afghans splintered again into different factions, and many Arabs left altogether. As one jihadist put it, Afghanistan was "drinking much blood and offering little hope."[80] The collapse of the Afghan Communist government in 1992 worsened the violence and removed any illusion that this struggle centered on faith. As Hamid recalls, people "lost hope an Islamic state could be established in Afghanistan."[81] For roughly the first half of the 1990s, Al Qaeda focused on training, not on combat or terrorist operations. This too proved negative; young Arabs restless for glory and eager for martyrdom found Al Qaeda useful for learning how to fight but useless for actual fighting. Al Qaeda's ranks diminished to a few dozen trained personnel, though its connections to other fighters and groups continued to grow, expanding its network and maintaining its influence.[82] In this period, it focused primarily on struggles in the Muslim world, not on the United States.

As enthusiasm waned following the Communist collapse, Arab countries ramped up pressure on Islamabad to expel their wayward citizens. Algeria and Egypt in particular struggled with jihadist groups that maintained a presence in Pakistan and trained and fought in Afghanistan. The Communist regime in Kabul finally fell in 1992, so the foreign fighters were less useful. The Pakistani government also feared the United States would label it as a sponsor of terrorism and tried to placate Washington and various Arab countries, ultimately ordering all Arabs to leave by January 31, 1993.[83] Pakistan only intermittently enforced the order at first, with many militants claiming, often accurately, legitimate membership in humanitarian organizations. In 1993, perhaps 2,600 Arab Afghans remained, a sizable number but a stiff decline from previous years.[84] However, in 1994, Pakistan signed an extradition agreement with Egypt to return more than a thousand Egyptians believed to have sought refuge in Pakistan.[85] Pakistan was often willing to ignore its own promises, but some foreigners began setting off bombs in Pakistan as revenge. In addition, Egyptian militants bombed the Egyptian embassy there in what Zawahiri, who was then largely focused on the struggle in Egypt, called a "clear and eloquent message." This resulted in one of "the biggest hunts of Afghan Arabs," according to one jihadist.[86] Bin Laden did not know of the operation. One figure claimed that Al Qaeda would have opposed it "given that Pakistan was still the most important passageway for the Al-Qa'ida Organization from and into Afghanistan" and that Al Qaeda had good relations with Pakistani religious groups that the Pakistani government supported. The number of Arabs in Pakistan plunged further.[87]

Arab Afghans dispersed. Terrorism scholar R. Kim Cragin estimates that 80 percent of Arab Afghans went back to their home countries in the years after the anti-Soviet struggle ended.[88] However, some Arab Afghans had their passports revoked by their home countries or risked arrest on their return and thus had nowhere to go. As one senior Al Qaeda member recalled, Saudis and Yemenis "had no problem with the security services in their homeland," while Egyptian, Syria, Algerian, and Libyan brothers had to stay, choose another place to fight, or find a new haven.[89] Members of several of the more organized groups, such as Zawahiri's Egyptian Islamic Jihad and later Al Qaeda, moved to Sudan, where an Islamist government had taken power in a coup and welcomed terrorist groups of all stripes. Some fled Pakistan for Afghanistan, previously more a combat front than a permanent base, where they worked with local commanders. Others went to fight in Kashmir, often working indirectly for Pakistani intelligence.[90] Still others fled to Yemen, which was one of the biggest sources of recruits for the Afghan jihad, where the government employed them as shock troops in the country's civil war, using them to crush the socialist forces of the south.[91]

Even many of those who at first went home unmolested eventually had a rude awakening. When they had fought the Soviets, these fighters were often lionized. One Saudi jihadist recalled observing the Afghan-style dress of returnees as they walked down the streets of Medina or Jeddah and feeling they looked like "triumphant companions of the prophet."[92] On their return, however, the returnees' governments saw them as possible radicals and threats. Many faced harassment and stayed with jihad because their governments prevented their integration back into society.[93] For others, the government harassment served to justify "proclaiming the government an unbeliever."[94]

The governments' suspicions were warranted, as many returnees proved a disruptive force. Hundreds of Indonesian Muslims had trained in Afghanistan and Pakistan, bringing lessons about guerrilla war home to employ against their government. Indeed, the goal of the Indonesian fighters was to train in Afghanistan, not to fight the Soviets there, because, as one fighter noted, "Studying military tactics is hard to get in Indonesia."[95] Each veteran was told to recruit ten locals, and they would prove the key force behind terrorist attacks that began in Indonesia in the late 1990s.[96] Many of the founders of the Libyan Islamic Fighting Group had fought or trained in Afghanistan.[97] In Algeria, more than a thousand formed much of the leadership and hardcore cadre of the most radical opposition, the Groupe Islamique Armé (GIA), whose armed wing was often called "afghansi." Their motto was "no dialogue, no reconciliation, no truce," and they committed atrocities against civilians that would be seen again in Iraq and Syria in future decades.[98]

The Afghan veterans played multiple roles in these conflicts. With their training and combat experience, they offered a "powerful strike arm" for the most zealous opposition, according to one declassified government assessment.[99] The Afghan veterans also targeted intellectuals and foreigners, while nationalist groups focused on military and government targets, which were generally seen as more legitimate targets. In addition, many attacked rival opposition groups, seeing them as insufficiently zealous. The veterans' actions pushed the civil wars toward the extreme and often discredited the foreign volunteers who ostensibly came to help.

The foreign fighters also touched the United States and other Western countries. In a foreshadowing of 9/11, terrorists placed a bomb in a rental van in the parking garage of the World Trade Center building in 1993. They aimed to topple the building and kill thousands. This grandiose goal failed, but they killed six people and injured nearly a thousand others. A number of those involved in the 1993 World Trade Center attack fought or trained in Afghanistan. The plot's mastermind, Ramzi Yousef, trained in a camp that Bin Laden supported.[100] The infamous "Blind Sheikh," Omar Abdel Rahman (a student of Azzam), was the spiritual leader of an Egyptian jihadist group who helped run a terrorist network out of a Jersey City mosque. He had also found refuge in Afghanistan before eventually making his way to the United States. From the United States, Rahman tried to orchestrate attacks in Egypt, including a plot to assassinate President Hosni Mubarak. In New York, however, Rahman also gathered around him jihadists of varied nationalities, a startling change for the previously Egypt-focused Rahman. He supported attacks on U.S. targets, including a plan to bomb the United Nations building, the Lincoln and Holland Tunnels, the George Washington Bridge, and the New York FBI building.[101] In Paris, Algerian jihadists attacked the Paris subway and the Arc de Triomphe in 1995, bringing together jihadists from France, Italy, Spain, Germany, Switzerland, and the United Kingdom, as well as Algeria who drew on connections formed in Afghanistan or Bosnia.

In contrast to the devastating attack eight years later, Al Qaeda itself did not execute the 1993 bombing. Rather, the networks that Azzam and Bin Laden created brought the perpetrators together. Rahman provided extremist ideas and organizational direction, while Yousef and company provided critical bomb-making skills. Fighting, training, and guest houses in Afghanistan had joined together disparate individual fighters. However, much of the plotting was amateurish. The FBI found a fragment of the van the jihadists exploded that contained the van's vehicle identification number. One of the terrorists, however, hoped to save money and reported the van stolen. He came to the rental agency to get his deposit, where he was quickly arrested.

Warnings Unheeded

Despite these many dangers, the foreign fighters received relatively little attention in the United States and the West in general as they bled out of Afghanistan. The first World Trade Center attack seemed more incompetent than deadly. The countries most at risk—Algeria, Egypt, and so on—seemed like peripheral theaters to a West high on the collapse of Communism and the spread of democracy. United States intelligence services paid little heed. After a string of attacks throughout the early 1990s, the United States began to acknowledge terrorism as a national security threat, but foreign fighters and their jihadist organizations received scant attention. As the 9/11 Commission later found, "Officials continued to think of terrorists as agents of states (Saudi Hezbollah acting for Iran against Khobar Towers) or as domestic criminals (Timothy McVeigh in Oklahoma City)."[102] In the first case, the Saudi group received Iranian support to bomb a U.S. military facility located in the Kingdom; thus, a foreign foe acted with a foreign patron in a foreign land. In the latter, the perpetrator and target were Americans. Al Qaeda and global jihadists, however, were a mix, drawing on their international experience and connections to carry out attacks in the United States.

The foreign fighter problem seemed short-lived. Afghanistan, after all, was unique. Once these remnants died, were arrested, or simply aged and dropped out, the problem would be over. How could such a rag-tag movement ever survive?

CHAPTER 3 | Barbaros: The Red Beard

T HE COLLAPSE OF Yugoslavia into civil war in 1991 dominated
headlines around the world. Serbia, the strongest of the rump republics and the one that inherited the bulk of Yugoslavia's massive military ar-
senal, refused to allow other republics to secede. Meanwhile, Serbia's leader,
Slobodan Milošević, whipped up nationalism, drawing on the country's
Orthodox Christian past to gain popular support. Slovenia seceded first and,
after a few brief skirmishes, established its de facto independence. Serbia
fought a far bloodier conflict with Croatia, but the arena shifted to Bosnia-
Herzegovina in January 1992. Bosnia-Herzegovina was the weakest of the
republics, in part because it had a mixed population of Croats, Muslims, and
Serbs, many of whom shared an identity as Yugoslavs before the conflict.
Serbia wanted to keep Bosnia, using the presence of Bosnian Serbs to justify
its claim. Bosnian Croats at times wanted to join the new neighboring state
of Croatia or to establish their own state within Bosnia, drawing on help
from Zaghreb. Bosnian Muslims eventually sought their own state too. More
than a hundred thousand people would die in fighting across the former
Yugoslavia, which raged through 1995.

For many Europeans and Americans, the strife signified the dark side of the
fall of Communism. The war's many atrocities included widespread expulsions
of civilians from areas where they lived for generations, mass murder, and systematic rape. These abuses garnered near-constant headlines, in contrast to the
Soviet depredations in Afghanistan, and both Europe and the United States
intervened with arms embargoes, no-fly zones, and other limited measures to

protect Bosnian Muslims. None of these halted the killing. Only after the war had raged for three years did the United States and its allies intervene more decisively, using their air forces to help the increasingly powerful Croat and Bosnian ground forces. Serbia sued for peace, and Bosnia became independent.

"I'm proud of what we did in Bosnia and Kosovo," President Bill Clinton would later declare.[1] However, many Muslims saw the conflict as a religious war, with the United States tacitly encouraging Christians to subjugate and slaughter Muslims—"a Christian-Zionist attack on Muslim lands," as one mujahedin charity put it.[2]

This mix of carnage and headlines attracted a range of foreign fighters basking in the afterglow of the Soviet departure from Afghanistan. However, as in Afghanistan, their military impact was limited. Even worse from their perspective, rather than bring true Islam to the Balkans, the Bosnians quickly shunted the foreign fighters aside after winning their independence on the battlefield. In Bosnia, however, the foreign fighters proved that, rather than being a historical curiosity confined to Afghanistan, they were forming a movement that refused to die.

Looking for Jihad

One of the first foreigners to join the fray in Bosnia was the Saudi-born Abd al-Rahman al-Dawsary, who became the first commander of the most famous foreign unit there known as the El Mudzahid forces. Following advice given by the Prophet Muhammad to one of his followers, he had dyed his long beard with henna, prompting his nickname "Barbaros" (the red beard). The name had a considerable pedigree, as it was shared with a famous Ottoman admiral from the sixteenth century.

Originally a family man and an administrator for Saudia Airlines, Barbaros heard the call to jihad from Azzam when the preacher traveled to Saudi Arabia in 1984 to urge young Muslims to join the fight in Afghanistan. Barbaros first made his reputation fighting the Soviets, where his fellow fighters dubbed him "Hown" for his skill with the Russian-made "Hound" rockets. He may have also fought in the Philippines, Kashmir, and Africa. As Barbaros asked himself what to do next after the defeat of Communist forces in Afghanistan, the crisis in Bosnia began. It was a sign from God, and he called on his Arab Afghan brothers to join him.[3]

In 1992, Barbaros led a fact-finding mission from Peshawar to Bosnia, working with a prominent Egyptian imam and jihadist based in Italy named Anwar Shaaban, who sought to assume the role Azzam played in Afghanistan.

The two had met in Afghanistan, and they urged fellow holy warriors to join the latest front.[4] When the war broke out, however, few knew of Bosnia. Indeed, Barbaros later lamented that Muslims only knew of Bosnia via the Western media, which is "far ahead of Islamic media."[5] The ideas Azzam and Al Qaeda promulgated about global obligations did not yet have deep roots, and jihadist organizations still did not have the powerful propaganda apparatuses that would later enable them to spread the word quickly and widely.

The travels of Barbaros and those like him should have scared world intelligence services because they suggested the emergence of a new breed: a professional jihadi not tied to one particular struggle. In the past, jihadists warred against their governments and, in the Afghan case, traveled specifically to fight the Soviets. Barbaros, however, represented a jihadist "looking for jihad" in his words, and the numbers of such men would steadily grow. Jihadism was becoming more like international Communism decades before, with small pools of ideologues here and there willing to travel and fight for a cause that transcended borders.

Inspired to Fight

The horrors Bosnian Muslims suffered appalled Barbaros and his comrades and convinced them that they needed to fight. A PBS *Frontline* documentary describes the atrocities Serbian forces perpetrated:

> Often the paramilitary troops would arrive at a newly conquered town with lists of influential residents who were to be executed; just as often they simply shot, or stabbed, or mutilated, or raped any resident whom they managed to find. These killers, many of whom were criminals who had been released from prison to "reform themselves" at the front, were attracted to the job by their virulent nationalist beliefs, by simple sadism, and by greed. Looting Muslim houses made many of them rich.[6]

A 1992 Human Rights Watch report documenting war crimes in the Bosnian War cites "the 'ethnic cleansing' that is being practiced by Serbian forces," with the victims being "expelled from their homes and villages; rounded up and held in detention camps; deported; killed in indiscriminate attacks; and summarily executed."[7] Rape, torture, and mass murder were common and widely publicized, enraging Muslims and inflaming world opinion in general. International investigators would later determine that some Serb mass murders constituted genocide.

As in Afghanistan, the volunteers saw themselves as defending innocent Muslims against infidels who would oppress and kill them. Barbaros reported, "Many were slaughtered, others were killed, while others were forced to exile. The chastity of their women was infringed upon for the simple reason that they were Muslims."[8] His message, amplified by the world's media, resonated. In this case the perpetrators were Christian Serbs rather than atheistic Russians, but the principle was the same. Similarly, the very real Serbian brutality led the volunteers to see themselves as heroes, in contrast to those who failed to fight. As one British volunteer noted, "You cannot turn a blind eye when Muslims are being massacred, because what will you do when it is happening on your doorstep?" In propaganda videos, British jihadist volunteers mocked their fellow Muslims at home who "like to talk" but then "go back home and they sleep."[9]

Over time, the Muslim world learned of the war in Bosnia from the jihadists' perspective. One of the most famous jihadist videos created near the end of the war in 1995 featured a mix of anti-Western denunciations, bragging about the fighters' military achievements, and emphasizing the gratitude of Bosnia's leaders. Fighters like Barbaros pushed the idea that all Muslims were one people, regardless of state borders. One recruit recalled that his basic motive "was to defend Muslims lands. Otherwise, what would make me leave Saudi Arabia—and I am of Yemeni origin—to go and fight in Bosnia?"[10]

In addition, propaganda also played up the anti-Christian nature of the fighting. One popular video showed jihadists entering an Orthodox Christian church and vandalizing the altar and icons. The propaganda echoed Afghanistan. Some talked about the need to defend fellow Muslims, and fighters claimed that one martyr's body still smelled of musk and did not decompose despite having been in enemy hands for three months before burial.[11]

As with Azzam in Afghanistan, spreading "true" Islam aimed to convince potential funders and recruits skeptical that the Bosnians were worth saving. After decades of Communism, most Bosnians were secular. Pork was a staple of the Bosnian diet, and alcohol flowed freely. In a 1988 poll of Bosnians, only 37 percent of Bosnian Muslims described themselves as religious.[12] One recruiter boasted that the Bosnians who trained with the Arabs eventually embraced Islam because of the foreigners' bravery: "If this is what Islam teaches you, we are fools if we don't practice Islam."[13] One fighter noted that "our educational and intellectual impact on Bosnian society was perhaps greater than our military effect."[14] Barbaros also warned that Iran and the Shiites might fill the void if the Salafist foreign fighters were not supported.[15] But Barbaros and the other volunteers prioritized fighting, not preaching.[16] He lamented that no religious leaders came to help educate Bosnians, noting that he and his fellows "came here seeking martyrdom" rather than "to teach people and educate them."[17]

Propaganda often displayed visceral images, both to outrage Muslims and to show that they were striking back. One recruit working in Italy recalls deciding to join the fight after seeing a video "showing girls who had been raped, old people assassinated, mosques and houses in Bosnia burned."[18] A jihadist video showed photos of Arab volunteers brandishing the bloody heads of Christian Serbs they claimed to have killed.[19] Videos that celebrated the deaths (invariably described as "martyrdom") of fighters often showed parents thanking God for their sons' sacrifices.[20]

Such propaganda from Bosnia now reached well beyond Arabic speakers, with European Muslims and Arab volunteers working together to design materials to inspire Europeans.[21] Collections for charity in Bosnia were a convenient umbrella for funding other ventures as well. Money collected at a gathering in Brooklyn to raise awareness and support for the Bosnian cause enabled jihadists in the United States to set up training camps in America, which would then export fighters to Bosnia and other jihadist theaters.[22]

As Azzam did before him, Barbaros also sought out establishment scholars to bless the jihad. He met with the chief mufti of Saudi Arabia, Sheikh Abdel Aziz Bin Baz, as well as other notable religious leaders, such as Sheikh Al-Albani, a leading Salafist. They duly endorsed the jihad in Bosnia "to make the word of Allah supreme and protect the chastity of Muslims."[23] Barbaros circulated his discussion with some of these leaders as a cassette to raise money and recruits.[24] In addition to blessing Bosnia, however, these religious leaders invoked darker ideas that would form part of the foreign fighter worldview. Some religious leaders declared Bosnia "a war between Islam and Christianity." They noted that the United States, which demonstrated its military prowess in the 1991 Gulf war, refused to defend Muslim lives now that no oil was at stake. With some justification, they portrayed Western measures to limit the fighting, such as an arms embargo, as a pro-Serb measure because the embargo prevented the poorly armed Bosnians from gaining parity on the battlefield.[25]

To publicize the cause and channel fighters into Bosnia, Barbaros and foreign jihadist leaders quickly set up a charity, the International Benevolence Committee, which would fulfill the same role that the Services Bureau did for Afghanistan. Barbaros fundraised in Turkey, Jordan, Pakistan, and especially Saudi Arabia, telling supporters that Bosnia offered a "great opportunity" to "make Islam enter Europe via jihad."[26] The International Benevolence Committee, which also incorporated in America, helped pay for volunteer fighters, met them at Croatia's airport, smuggled them into Bosnia, and sheltered them along the way, while using its humanitarian status to smuggle in weapons and ammunition.[27] The charity also supported Al Qaeda, Chechen rebels, and other causes prominent in the jihadist firmament.

The Saudi Arabian government and people seized on the Bosnian conflict. The royal family was facing criticism from religious dissidents angry at the continued presence of U.S. military forces in the Kingdom after the 1991 Gulf war, and these dissidents criticized the government for being passive as Serbs slaughtered the Bosnians. In addition, two rivals of Riyadh—Iran and the Islamist government of Sudan—tried to exploit the Bosnian conflict by claiming that they, not the Saudis, represented the true champions of Islam.

To win out over these internal and external rivals, the Saudi government followed the playbook it used for Afghanistan. Early on, it allowed its citizens to go without interference. It used symbolic gestures like airlifting wounded Bosnian children out of the war zone for medical care. The royal family established a high-profile "High Committee for Fundraising to the Muslims of Bosnia-Herzegovina," chaired by Prince (and later King) Salman, which raised almost $400 million for the Bosnians. King Fahd bin Abdulaziz Al Saud of Saudi Arabia reportedly gave $8 million of his own money to the Bosnian cause. Diplomatically, the Kingdom pressed the United Nations (UN) and the United States to help the Bosnians, and Saudi Arabia also spent almost $300 million in a covert campaign to arm the Bosnian army. Yet, as all this suggests, the Kingdom was focused on the Bosnian military, not the foreign fighters. By 1995, it had even put restrictions on some of the charities the fighters exploited to raise money and send recruits to the war zone, leading to complaints from Bin Laden, among others.[28]

The Saudi religious establishment went beyond simply blessing those who fought in the Bosnian jihad. Many Saudis would ask their religious leaders how to contribute, and the leaders would gather money or connect them with recruiters.[29] As one former fighter exulted, "All of Saudi Arabia, starting with the government, the religious scholars, and the ordinary people, was on the side of driving youths toward jihad in Bosnia-Herzegovina."[30] Another jihadist recalled "astronomical sums" for equipping fighters. His own journey was sponsored by a schoolteacher who donated her salary that month to pay his way.[31] Kuwait and other Gulf states also proved sources of funds.[32]

Although much of the money came from wealthy donors in the Gulf states, supporters in the West, including the United States, also helped the cause. Barbaros visited the United States to attend the Islamic Assembly of North America in December 1995 in Dearborn, Michigan. Some of the U.S. branches of the Services Bureau set up by Azzam for the Afghan jihad embraced the cause of Bosnia, as did other U.S.-based organizations. One Boston-based group issued a "Call to Jihad in Bosnia" in a pamphlet, noting the death toll and the kidnapping of Muslim girls by the Serbs for "army camps for sex."[33] The U.S. government did little to stop this.

The relief agency and religious network developed for the jihad in Afghanistan continued to blossom. Religious nongovernmental organizations (NGOs) gave money and assistance to military units tied to foreign fighters and provided them with shoes, blankets, and other support. Financiers and recruiters based in London, Milan, and Vienna played important roles in facilitating the flow of fighters. In some countries, former jihadists who had fought in Afghanistan against the Soviets now headed jihadist-linked charities abroad; their past role as fighters gave them connections and credibility. Charities also cared for the wounded back in their home countries, often allowing Al Qaeda members and other jihadists to travel there as humanitarian officials and, in so doing, to serve as recruiters.[34] A U.S. intelligence estimate concluded that nearly one-third of the religious charities acting in Bosnia "facilitated the activities of Islamic groups engaging in terrorism."[35]

Hearing the Call

Heeding the calls of religious leaders and early fighters like Barbaros, Muslims journeyed to Bosnia to join the fray. As in Afghanistan, at first only a handful of Arabs or other foreigners fought, but the number rose to around several hundred by the end of the first year, increasing far more rapidly than in Afghanistan.[36] Records are uneven and fragmentary, and estimates of total volunteers range from three hundred to five thousand from around twenty-five countries, though Barbaros himself was quick to disown higher estimates.[37] Propaganda from the Serbs and others who sought to demonize the Bosnians as foreign terrorists worsen the data problem.

Although Barbaros and most of the foreigners came from the Arab world, perhaps a hundred came from Western countries, with France being the largest contributor.[38] Lower-level fighters often originated from Egypt's Islamic Group or Algeria's Armed Islamic Group, both of which had a significant presence among their countries' diasporas in Europe. Recruits also came from Germany, Great Britain, and other European countries.[39] Often hardened jihadist veterans from Afghanistan fought alongside eager but untrained Europeans.

London, dubbed "Londonistan" by those critical of the foreign presence, became a hotbed for European radicalization in the 1990s. One influential preacher was Omar Mahmoud Othman, commonly known as Abu Qatada, who preached at the Four Feathers Youth Center in central London, primarily on the Algerian jihad. Another radical, Omar Bakri Mohammed, held sway over many British youths, especially through the branch of Hizb ut-Tahrir that he organized in London.[40] The British government described Hizb ut-Tahrir, an organization seeking an Islamic state, as a "radical" organization that holds "anti-Semitic, anti-Western, and homophobic views," but that it is "non-violent."[41] An affiliate of Hizb ut-Tahrir hosted a "Bosnia Week" in 1992 at the London School of Economics that showed films depicting the violence in Bosnia, including *Destruction of a Nation*—a forty-five-minute-long film that showed Serbs castrating captured Bosnian Muslims.[42] Ahmed Omar Saeed Sheikh, charged in Pakistan for the kidnapping and murder of journalist Daniel Pearl, attended the showing of *Destruction of a Nation* and wrote in his diary that the film "shook my heart."[43] In 1994, the *Guardian* reported that Hizb ut-Tahrir controlled most Muslim student organizations on campuses in Muslim-dominant areas.[44] For the Bosnian conflict and for future jihads, organizations like Hizb ut-Tahrir would often prove to be a bridge, introducing individuals to radical ideas and making it easier to get them to take the final step toward violence.

Many Muslim British college students embraced the Bosnian cause. On a Bosnian jihadist video, a twenty-one-year-old Londoner says, "I watch the TV and tears roll down my face when I see the Muslims in Bosnia, Muslims in Palestine, Muslims in Kashmir. And then I come [to Bosnia] and you feel a sense of satisfaction. You feel that you are fulfilling your duty."[45]

As in Afghanistan, some groups sought to exploit Bosnia to fight other enemies. The Algerians saw Bosnia as a base to support their conflict at home, running guns from Bosnia through Europe to Algeria. Al Qaeda sent out a fact-finding mission, meeting with Barbaros and other jihadists there.[46] In addition to seeking to support the Bosnian cause, Al Qaeda sought to use Bosnia as "a base for operations in Europe against al-Qaeda's true enemy, the United States," according to a U.S. Department of Justice indictment.[47] Some Arabs who fought in Bosnia, however, claim that Bin Laden provided, at best, lukewarm support.[48]

Some volunteers traveled to Bosnia because it was the best of a set of bad options. The allure of Afghanistan was declining while Pakistan was pressing Arab fighters to leave the country. As a Saudi spokesman for the foreign fighters at the time noted, "The Algerians cannot go to Algeria, the Syrians cannot go to Syria, or the Iraqis to Iraq. Some will opt to go to Bosnia."[49]

Foreigners regularly invoked Afghanistan as they trumpeted the Bosnian cause. The Serbs mirrored the Russians—both were Slavs, and both were Communists (or, in the Serb case, former Communists). Yet the jihad in Bosnia never had the appeal of Afghanistan or the allure of Iraq and Syria in the future. Before the anti-Soviet rebellion, some Afghan commanders spent time in the Arab world and had ties to religious figures in Saudi Arabia, while religious figures in Bosnia had few such links. In addition, the question of whether Bosnians were truly Muslims also arose. Afghans in general were practicing Muslims (if still deviant from a strict Salafi point of view), while most Bosnians were openly secular, leading many to question whether the Bosnians were worth saving. One future Al Qaeda figure who considered going to Bosnia was told by other jihadists that in Bosnia he would "find moral corruption" and that "the blonde European girls might influence you."[50]

Another key difference from Afghanistan was the lack of a rear base. In contrast to Pakistan, where trucks of weapons could be sent into Afghanistan, Barbaros lamented that smuggling often occurred a weapon or two at a time.[51] In addition, Bosnia was far from the home of most Arab fighters and never part of their cultural world. Barbaros noted that, at first, "we were unable to understand where Bosnia was, was it in America or the southern hemisphere or in Asia?"[52] Whereas many countries encouraged or quietly tolerated the participation of their nationals in the Afghan conflict, this attitude changed by the time violence reached its height in Bosnia. The end of the Cold War, the 1993 attack on the World Trade Center, and jihadist violence in Algeria and Egypt made most states skeptical at best of foreign fighters.

A Mixed Reaction in Bosnia

Bosnia's president, Alija Izetbegović, welcomed the foreigners as a symbol of the Muslim world's backing of Bosnia. Izetbegović was an Islamist, though not a jihadist, and had served time in prison for his views. Now leading Bosnia, he promoted an agenda that mixed nationalism and Islamism, conveniently allowing backers of both views to see him as sympathetic (and opponents to paint him as secular or fanatical, depending on their agendas).

The Bosnian army desperately needed help, especially military aid, at the beginning of the war in 1992. It lacked a formal army and had far fewer weapons, particularly heavy weapons, as well as equipment, qualified officers, and other basics than Croatia and Serbia. At the outset of the conflict, Bosnian Serbs were better organized and armed than their Muslim counterparts and enjoyed strong support from Serbia itself. One witness observed that "this was not an army that was established, equipped." Rather, "It looked like a peasant uprising of some sort."[53] As one Bosnian refugee put it, "I am not a fundamentalist, but I will take a gun from the fundamentalists and thank them for it."[54] The U.S. intelligence community reported the Bosnian army had few tanks or artillery pieces and that its forces had no real training. It judged that it "can neither hold its territory against determined offensives nor permanently retake lost ground." Without outside help, "It will slowly deteriorate."[55]

Some foreigners like Barbaros had significant training and fighting experience from their Afghan days. Now, unlike in Afghanistan, the foreigners brought skilled fighters to the fray. The foreigners were particularly useful for offensive operations, especially dangerous ones. As one UN military official in Bosnia noted, "Their presence indicates imminent conflict."[56] The foreign presence proved vital in the early days of the war when the Bosnians were the most vulnerable. "I think the Muslims wouldn't have survived without this," argued Richard Holbrooke, the American diplomat who eventually negotiated an end to the war.[57]

In August 1993, the foreign fighters founded the "El Mudzahid" unit under Barbaros's leadership. El Mudzahid was created after Bosnian army and public complaints about the foreigners' brutality and lack of discipline as well as the foreigners' view that they could not rely on local Bosnians to stand and fight when the time came.[58] The unit was technically integrated into, supplied by, and under the command of the Bosnian military. Although the training did not match what Al Qaeda would later achieve in Afghanistan, El Mudzahid required volunteers to take a six-week religious course and then a six-week military course.[59]

The unit followed the Al Qaeda model of a single leader (emir) with military and religious councils underneath him. After Barbaros, who left to fundraise and recruit, a Libyan led El Mudzahid, followed by an Algerian, and then, finally, Egyptian commanders gained control—casualties among the leadership were heavy. The fighters lacked ranks and uniforms. They did, however, carry a black flag with Arabic writing similar to that which the Islamic State would later use.[60] Most members had not fought in Afghanistan, but veterans of the Afghanistan war often served as key trainers and leaders.[61]

Headquartered in an abandoned factory in Zenica, El Mudzahid had its own hospital and prayer hall. At first, only foreigners comprised El Mudzahid, but by 1995, the unit contained more local Muslims than foreign ones; one estimate put the number of foreigners at only 20 percent of the total, though this ratio is disputed. By 1995, the unit grew to as many as five hundred fighters. Local Bosnians joined because it was better organized, had higher morale, and had religious ardor.[62]

Even by the standards of a brutal war, the foreign fighters stood out. Foreign soldiers looted, destroyed Christian religious sites, and killed civilians in "senseless massacres," as one Bosnian commander put it.[63] After one of their military victories, they starved and tortured the Serb prisoners to death, forcing them to fight each other and cutting off the heads of those who died. They made videos of many of their executions, disseminating them to supporters (though, in a pre–social media age, they lacked the vast reach the Islamic State would later attain).[64] A UN investigation alleged that detainees held by the foreign fighters "were beaten, electrically shocked with wires attached to a car battery, stomped on and hit with shovels, pieces of iron and police batons." Female prisoners were raped as well as beaten.[65] One foreign veteran recalled his unit killing Croat prisoners of war, with his commander asking him, "Have we come to Bosnia to help the Croats, to save their lives, or to kill each and every one of them?" He related how he saw trucks filled with bodies with blood dripping out of the back, "And I saw that these killed men had no heads."[66] One researcher claims the El Mudzahid unit sent President Izetbegović twenty-eight Christian heads as a gift.[67]

The internal divisions that plagued the foreign fighters in Afghanistan continued in Bosnia. Some fighters were part of existing groups, like Egypt's Islamic Group, some of whose members had found refuge in Europe or otherwise could not return home.[68] In addition to the El Mudzahid unit, foreigners joined other Bosnian units or operated on their own. For example, although Barbaros originated from Saudi Arabia, he mainly commanded Egyptians and North Africans, while Saudis and other Gulf state fighters joined another faction. Nor did they integrate seamlessly into the Bosnian military structure. As one veteran recalled, even if the Bosnian army requested they attack, "we wouldn't take part in that attack" if El Mudzahid leaders said not to do it.[69]

Barbaros, however, claimed that the foreign fighters were relatively unified, at least compared with Afghanistan.[70] The volunteers in Bosnia, though often extreme in their own politics, proved less disruptive than later generations of jihadists. Their leaders declared allegiance to Bosnian President Izetbegović and made him their honorary commander, even though some fighters back in Afghanistan saw him as an apostate because he deviated from pure Salafi beliefs.[71] Barbaros aimed to help the Bosnians rather than impos his will on them, in contrast to fighters in future jihads. Barbaros declared that in the end "it is up to the Bosnian people to decide" and that he and his comrades would leave whenever the government told them to go.[72]

The foreigners had a limited but real military impact. They excelled as guerrillas, harassing civilians and ambushing enemies in parts of Bosnia under Serbian or Croat control.[73] All other sides fought with tanks and artillery, but the foreigners lacked such heavy weapons. This hindered the foreign fighters' ability to sustain operations or defend themselves when the Serbs counterattacked with artillery support. The lack of firepower, combined with their bravery, led to heavy casualties.

The foreigners in Bosnia had their own equivalents of Jaji, the victorious battle in Afghanistan where the Arab volunteers like Bin Laden proved, to themselves at least, that they could fight. These notable wins occurred near the war's end in 1995, when the Croats and Muslims began to work together, putting the Serbs on the defensive. The foreigners participated in three successful operations against the Serbs—"Black Lion," "Miracle," and "Badr," the latter name coming from a key victory of the Prophet Muhammad during Islam's early years.[74] In Black Lion, the foreigners seized control of Serb positions in a vital mountainous area, preventing further Serb shelling of civilians in this region and exposing Serb supply lines to disruption.[75]

Their next major operation, Miracle, occurred just after Serbian troops massacred almost 10,000 Muslim civilians in Srebrenica, a town supposedly under UN protection. The unwillingness of the peacekeepers to act as Serb forces slaughtered civilians before their eyes outraged world opinion. In the Muslim world, many saw the massacre as proof of Western complicity in the Serb killings. Saudi Arabia's leading cleric called for "weapons, financial assistance, and prayers" and for "Muslims throughout the world to assist their brothers."[76] The foreigners charged into well-defended Serb positions and took heavy casualties, but they captured several objectives, and even a Serb tank. They dubbed their victory "Miracle" because they felt God was behind them.

Badr was the last major operation and the most successful. It aimed to capture another set of positions in the mountains—two peaks with a transmitting tower, overlooking roads and the town of Vozuca. The Serbs fled as the foreigners attacked, and the foreigners continued to advance, again taking heavy casualties.

None of these operations individually turned the tide, and even in these select operations, regular Bosnian military units often played the critical roles. Nevertheless, they demonstrated the commitment of the foreigners, who proved willing to take on the most dangerous operations. And, as with Jaji, propaganda helped spread a sense of victory. Foreign fighters documented some of their operations, highlighting the Serb tank they captured in the Miracle operation and showing brave jihadists charging forward in the face of heavy Serbian fire. They also videotaped the aftermath of their victory in Badr, including their butchery of many of the Serb prisoners.[77] A Saudi-backed NGO distributed the video of the operation to raise money and general awareness.[78]

The money foreign governments provided and the fighting skills of the foreigners offset any embarrassment they caused and made the Bosnian government reluctant to crack down on the foreigners, despite pressure from Croatia. One foreign fighter recalled that the foreigners would destroy a café where alcohol was served without punishment. "We enjoyed police immunity. We had somebody's support," he said.[79]

The foreign fighters also tried to indoctrinate locals.[80] As in Afghanistan, the training camp curriculum included calisthenics, weapons training, and a lot of slogan shouting.[81] Indeed, the camps emphasized proselytizing far more than in Afghanistan during the anti-Soviet period, where Azzam and others feared that attempts to indoctrinate Afghans would anger them and lead to divisions. In Bosnia, Barbaros and others believed indoctrination promoted unity and spread the true faith.[82]

Many Bosnians appreciated the foreigners' bravery even when they did not share their ideology. One foreign veteran recalls that locals would often conduct reconnaissance before the operation began, as they knew the terrain better than the foreigners, but that "we were going first" when it came to any difficult attack.[83] "These men don't know what a bullet is," said one Bosnian soldier. "Where other men will crawl into battle, they walk upright."[84] Another Bosnian fighter noted, "They came here to be killed. For them there is no going back."[85]

The locals' admiration, however, often mixed with private contempt, and the foreign fighters and Bosnians soured on each other as the war dragged on. As one Bosnian Muslim put it, the foreigners "come here full of ideals about dying in battle and going to paradise. Bosnians are not so stupid. We want to live for Islam, not die for Islam."[86] Off the battlefield, the foreign fighters often alienated locals. Some foreigners wanted to kill Bosnian fighters who drank alcohol or otherwise strayed from the true path.[87] As one foreign volunteer later admitted, "It must be said that some of the brothers looked down upon the local population."[88] One private memo from jihadists at the time lamented that when the foreigners arrive and "find no knowledge of Islamic behavior," they try to step in and impose it, becoming "tyrants even worse than those we despise."[89] One longtime holy warrior in Afghanistan recalls volunteers "talked all the time about how the Bosnians were not real Muslims. They said the women didn't wear headscarves and the men didn't go to mosque. That they drank alcohol and ate pigs."[90] Another noted that some Muslims would even wear a cross around their neck, ignorant of its meaning.[91] Bosnian religious leaders often rejected the proselytizing of the foreign fighters and the religious aid agencies backing them, considering the Salafis strident and backward.[92]

In addition to alienating many ordinary Bosnians, the foreigners also had trouble navigating the conflict's foreign relations. Two countries bordered Bosnia—Croatia and Serbia. Traveling through Serbia, the ultimate enemy, was out of the question, but Croatia was hardly a friend to the Bosnians and especially to the foreign fighters. When the war broke out in 1992, Croatian leaders viewed Serbia as their primary enemy and allowed foreign fighters to pass through. The Croatian government even gave foreign fighters identification cards as humanitarian workers.[93] One former fighter recalls that agency workers in Croatia "were excellent at forging IDs, documents, and passports." Some of the foreigners even gained UN identity cards.[94] Croatia, however, became more restrictive over time, with tensions running particularly high when Muslim and Croat unity collapsed, and the two communities fought in central Bosnia in 1993.[95] The bribes required to pass through grew, and at times the Croats arrested or even fought with foreigners trying to transit. The Croatian government would skim money and weapons off the top of military aid. "For each bullet reaching the mujahedin, one bullet had to be given to the Croatian border guards," recalled one fighter.[96]

Some of the foreign fighters refused to accept Croatia's on-again, off-again support and acted against Croatia after one of their own was killed and others taken prisoner. Working with sympathetic Bosnian Muslims, they kidnapped Croatian intelligence officers, soldiers, and even one of the senior Croat military commanders to force a prisoner exchange. This succeeded, and the Croats released their foreign fighter prisoners in a UN-brokered exchange. However, the incident bolstered the Croatian government's hostility, which further impeded efforts for the foreigners to reinforce and sustain their forces.[97] The Croats would remain hostile to the foreign fighters in the last years of the conflict.

Serbia used the foreigners' presence as proof that it fought Muslim fanatics. Further, the foreigners kidnapped, tortured, and murdered several British advisers and occasionally targeted Western aid workers, leading some relief agencies to suspend operations to the desperate Bosnians.[98] These attacks on Western peacekeepers and aid workers damaged the Bosnians' claim to be victims in the conflict.

An Abrupt End

When Bosnia won its freedom in 1995, it rejected the foreign fighters who helped it survive in its darkest days. The Dayton Accords, the U.S.-brokered settlement that ended the war in 1995, required that all forces "which are not local origin," including foreign fighters, leave Bosnia. The United States pushed hard for the expulsion of foreign fighters, and given that Bosnia depended on U.S. support for the deployment of international peacekeepers (including tens of thousands of American and allied NATO troops), choosing between America's wishes and gratitude to the foreigners proved easy.[99]

The Bosnian military disbanded the El Mudzahid unit and ordered its members to leave the country. In contrast to Afghanistan, Bosnia had a government—a weak and corrupt one, but nevertheless, one that could impose its will on a small number of jihadists. Even before the fighting ended in 1995, many foreigners had left Bosnia, disillusioned by their failure to convert Bosnian Muslims to "true" Islam. Some Arabs like Barbaros returned to their home countries, but increasingly they faced arrest and harassment upon return, and it didn't help that many brought beheading videos or other propaganda with them.[100] Others, like the Egyptians and Algerians, whose governments actively hunted jihadists, sought political asylum in other European states. A few of the most zealous or most desperate sought to go to Chechnya, which was emerging as a new conflict zone, or to havens as far away as Somalia and the Philippines, where governments had collapsed or were weak.[101]

Many foreign fighters saw their expulsion as a betrayal. A leading Bosnian jihadist ideologue denounced Dayton as "a humiliation" and a "conspiracy to destroy Islam."[102] The world, in their eyes, only intervened once the Muslims began to fight back effectively. "As soon as the Muslims began to fight back and win, they ended the war," complained one British volunteer.[103] Indeed, many foreign fighters saw their victories in 1995 as the key to defeating the Serbs and hoped that the Bosnian Muslims would continue the war.

Some foreign fighters retaliated. In October 1995, fighters linked to an Egyptian jihadist group with a strong presence in Bosnia used a suicide bomber, the first in Europe, to attack police headquarters in the Croatian town of Rijeka as revenge for the deportation of one of their leaders to Egypt. Michael Scheuer, who headed the CIA's Bin Laden unit, claimed the United States worked with the Egyptian and Croatian governments to covertly arrest and deport the senior terrorist back to Egypt.[104]

Not all the foreigners left. Dozens received Bosnian citizenship (often because they married local women) and stayed in the country, while several hundred may have stayed illegally or acquired forged documents, exploiting the weakness and corruption of the Bosnian government.[105] Passports were for sale and not for a high price. Often with the tacit approval of Bosnian authorities, some of the foreigners terrorized Serbs and Croats who remained and vandalized or destroyed their churches. The Bosnian government also resisted extradition requests by Egypt, Italy, and other governments.[106]

Some of the foreigners, however, nestled in Bosnian villages, almost in self-contained communities, where they pushed an austere Salafi way of life and lived under religious law.[107] In general, the weak Bosnian government reluctantly allowed these villages to self-govern, and the foreigners enjoyed some sympathy among members of Bosnia's military and intelligence services.[108]

In addition, foreign-backed relief agencies continued to proselytize, funding mosques and local religious leaders, and spread their austere and anti-Western form of Islam.

Saudi Arabia also changed course. After terrorist bombings in Saudi Arabia in 1995 and 1996, the Kingdom became far more hostile to former foreign fighters, leading to outrage from Bin Laden, among others.[109] Saudi security officials arrested hundreds of suspected jihadists during investigations, although only a small number were involved in terrorism, with many tortured while in custody. Barbaros, once a hero, spent time in prison in Saudi Arabia.[110]

Saudi and other security officials had good reason for their suspicions. Alumni of Bosnia included 9/11 plot mastermind Khaled Sheikh Mohammad, two of the 9/11 plot leaders,[111] the highest-ranking jihadist in Germany,[112] two of the senior figures involved in the 1998 Dar es Salaam and Nairobi embassy bombings and the 2000 USS *Cole* bombing, and a man who helped inspire the 2005 bombings in London.[113] Abu Walid, a French convert to Islam originally named Christophe Caze, led an Algerian jihadist network in France known as the "Roubaix Group," which committed numerous attacks in France before he was killed in 1996. Many members of the Roubaix Group had trained and fought in Bosnia, and they smuggled weapons to France from the Balkans to conduct armed robberies to raise money for the Algerian struggle.[114]

After 9/11, fears grew that the remaining foreign fighters and their supporters in Bosnia would pose a new terrorism threat. One U.S. official described Bosnia as "an R&R destination" where terrorists "chill out" to escape from pursuit elsewhere, though UN officials later estimated that only a few dozen of the remaining several hundred foreign fighters had links to terrorism.[115] The U.S. government worked with the Bosnian government to disrupt several terrorist attacks against U.S. and Western facilities, and the Bosnian government passed new laws that deprived these several hundred former foreign fighters of their Bosnian citizenship.[116]

In some ways, Barbaros and his fellow fighters did win despite their ignominious fate after the war ended in 1995. The Balkans cause kept the foreign fighters' flame alive after the anti-Soviet struggle, which came at a crucial transition point between the end of the jihad in Afghanistan and the emergence of conflict in Chechnya coupled with Al Qaeda's growth in Afghanistan in the late 1990s. Indeed, Bosnia and the Balkans would eventually prove fertile recruiting grounds for the Islamic State. A generation after the Bosnian war for independence, the Balkans would have the largest number of volunteers for the war in Syria per capita of any area in Europe.

CHAPTER 4 | The Trainer: Ali Mohamed and
Afghanistan in the 1990s

U NITED STATES SPECIAL operations forces are known for killing
terrorists, not training them. Yet one of the most important figures in
the history of jihadism is Ali Abdul Saoud Mohamed, a U.S. Army sergeant
who taught his fellow soldiers at the John F. Kennedy Special Warfare Center
and School at Fort Bragg, North Carolina. Although subsequent investigations
linked Mohamed to several of Al Qaeda's most audacious attacks, including
the 1998 bombing of two U.S. embassies in Africa, his true contribution fit one
of the classic missions of special forces: unconventional warfare, featuring the
covert training of local fighters in "a variety of tactics, including subversion,
sabotage, [and] intelligence collection."[1] Mohamed, known as Abu Mohamed
al-Amriki ("the American"), helped establish a network of training camps and
otherwise organized jihadists in Afghanistan. There he built the foundation
for Al Qaeda and many other terrorist organizations and tranformed foreign
fighters from zealous incompetents into deadly instruments of terrorism and
insurgency. A senior counterterrorism prosecutor declared him "the most dangerous man I have ever met."[2]

Mohamed's life story, a jihadist mix of James Bond and Severus Snape,
is the stuff novels are made of. He began his career in the Egyptian army,
serving for seventeen years and attaining the rank of major. A proficient mar-
tial artist, he spoke four languages, including Hebrew. However, while in the
army, he fell in with the Egyptian Islamic Jihad and its young leader, Ayman
Zawahiri—the future head of Al Qaeda—who then led a jihadist faction that

wanted to overthrow the Egyptian government and was responsible for killing President Anwar Sadat.

These associations led to Mohamed's discharge in 1984, and from there his storied career took off. First, probably at Zawahiri's behest, he traveled to Germany to serve the CIA. He was tasked to infiltrate a mosque associated with the Lebanese terrorist group Hezbollah, but he then openly told its members there that he was an American agent.[3] The CIA knew about his double-cross through another asset in the mosque, though this didn't stop Mohamed from taking advantage of his service to the U.S. government to secure expedited travel to America. He married an American woman he met on the flight over, became a citizen, and enlisted in the U.S. Army. He rose to the rank of sergeant and was stationed at Fort Bragg, North Carolina from 1986 through 1989. His supervisors rated him "beyond reproach," and his 1989 discharge documents commended his "patriotism, valor, fidelity, and professional excellence."[4] He appears to have served as an FBI informant despite the CIA warning, using this status to shield himself from any investigation.[5]

While stationed at Fort Bragg, Mohamed took leave in 1988 to train Afghans and fight the Soviets himself, later returning and giving away the uniform belts of two Soviet soldiers he claimed he killed there. He continued operating in Afghanistan after the Soviets departed and as Al Qaeda was getting on its feet, fighting in the Afghan civil war. When Mohamed returned to the United States, he trained jihadists like El Sayyid Nosair, who assassinated extremist rabbi Meir Kahane in 1990 when the rabbi was giving a speech in Brooklyn, and Mahmud Abouhalima, a taxi driver who was supposed to drive the getaway car, though a nervous Nosair jumped into the wrong taxi by mistake. Abouhalima was also involved in acquiring and transporting explosives for the first World Trade Center bombing in 1993. Mohamed often worked through a Brooklyn center set up by Azzam and others to help Afghans displaced by the Soviet invasion but also to recruit foreign support and train those bound for Afghanistan. When Ayman Zawahiri came to the United States in 1993 to fundraise, it was Mohamed who provided him with forged papers and introduced him to American supporters. His terrorist accomplishments grew and grew. Mohamed organized Bin Laden's personal security, served as a liaison to other terrorist groups like the Lebanese Hezbollah, and reconnoitered targets in Africa, which would culminate in the bombing of U.S. embassies in Kenya and Tanzania in 1998, killing 224 people.[6] One of his fellow jihadists claimed that, for all his prowess, Mohamed was "not a good practitioner of Islam," but another noted that he was "very, very strict" as a taskmaster—a classic drill sergeant, in other words.[7]

Establishing and improving training camps proved Mohamed's most lasting achievement. In contrast to young Communists or nationalists looking to fight in another country, jihadists did not have a state sponsor with a military and intelligence service eager to train volunteers. Not surprisingly, most jihadists were long on zeal but short on skill. Mohamed would help change that. As early as 1991, he was training jihadists in Afghanistan and Pakistan to smuggle small knives and other weapons onto planes. Some of his prize students included Osama bin Laden and Ayman al-Zawahiri.[8] Often using translated documents, Mohamed transferred his knowledge of U.S. special operations forces doctrine, which had been used to promote guerrilla war to fight Communists, making the Arabs experts at ambushes, raids, and bomb creation. When U.S. forces seized the jihadist training camps after 9/11, they found some facilities used U.S. Marine Corps material on how to move in small fire-teams. Others employed Army Ranger material on how to conduct reconnaissance.[9] Indeed, Mohamed often trained the trainers. His pupils would themselves have a legacy of developing new terrorists, and among those who trained in the facilities he established were several of the 9/11 hijackers.[10]

Mohamed put his knowledge on paper (real and virtual), contributing to what would become known as the "Encyclopedia of Afghan Jihad," the project initiated by Azzam to preserve and pass on the knowledge the jihadists were amassing in their struggles. This multivolume tome became a bible for jihadists worldwide, with topics including explosives, intelligence, topography, and hand-to-hand fighting.

Mohamed's most violent success proved his undoing. Mohamed had helped case the embassies Al Qaeda blew up in 1998. One of the bombers in the Nairobi embassy attack did not martyr himself as planned, but instead survived. After being treated at a local hospital and contacting Al Qaeda leaders over a monitored phone line, Kenyan officials picked him up and transferred him to U.S. custody. He talked, and his confession—along with subsequent interrogations of his colleagues and the trove of information discovered in once-secret safe houses in Kenya—enabled the CIA and FBI to unravel the web of conspiracy and link Mohamed to the attacks.[11] He pled guilty, but that is not the end of the story. The ever-adaptable Mohamed has so far avoided sentencing, probably by cooperating with U.S. officials against his former comrades.[12] The camps he established, however, lived on, with devastating implications.

Mohamed's story is fascinating in itself, but it is interwoven with a key element of the foreign fighter movements: the transformation callow youths undergo when they travel to fight. In the 1990s, volunteers would often travel to Afghanistan with simple goals such as expelling a foreign invader like Russia from Chechnya, but while in Afghanistan, they would see their struggle in a new context. Seemingly disparate conflicts in Libya, Yemen, Pakistan, and the Philippines would all be linked together as the struggle of Muslims against their oppressors, be it apostate regimes or foreign invaders and occupiers. As their worldviews expanded, their skill sets sharpened. In training camps like the ones run by Mohamed, they would learn to fight, becoming deadly warriors and skilled terrorists. They also helped train and bring together jihadists from Egypt, Indonesia, and other countries that already were indoctrinated against a local enemy but now found wider horizons. The camps, in other words, played an integral role in Al Qaeda's history and would help make it one of the world's most formidable terrorist groups. As one jihadist noted about Mohamed, "It is not an exaggeration to say that Ali Muhammad is the actual founder of the 'terrorist' organisation al-Qaeda."[13]

Jihad at a Crossroads

When Mohamed began his work, the story of the foreign fighters seemed to be ending with a whimper. After the Soviet troops withdrew from Afghanistan, the Afghan mujahedin turned their guns on one another, with some foreign fighters joining the fray and others turning away in disgust. Military defeats like Jalalabad took the bloom off the Al Qaeda rose. In 1991 and 1992, these problems, along with Pakistani pressure on suddenly unwanted foreign organizations, led Al Qaeda and other foreign jihadists to decamp to Sudan, which was then under the control of an Islamist government that opened its doors to terrorists from around the world. Bin Laden offered to help the Islamist government fight African Christians in the south of the country as well as build roads and otherwise spread his wealth. While in Sudan, he forged ties to even more groups and individuals, creating a network that would become stronger and stronger. Mohamed helped organize the move, handling logistics and security and then, when in Khartoum, establishing training camps and teaching fighters there. He did all this while commuting back and forth to the United States to recruit in American mosques.[14]

While in Sudan, Bin Laden and his organization flitted from cause to cause, at times trying to work with Afghan groups, considering a jihad in Yemen, and even weighing resignation from the fight altogether. His efforts to unify various jihadists failed, and rival jihadists from small and even more extreme groups tried to kill him, believing he was not pure enough in his interpretation of Islam. Bin Laden turned more against Arab regimes, including his own government in Saudi Arabia, supporting critics of the royal family based in London. Riyadh in turn froze his assets, a devastating blow.[15]

Bin Laden and other foreign jihadists eventually wore out their welcome in Sudan. Egyptian jihadists' use of Sudan as a base in their attempt to assassinate the Egyptian president when he was visiting neighboring Ethiopia led the United Nations (UN) to sanction Sudan. This cost, and the continuing pressure from Saudi Arabia, Egypt, and the United States, led the Sudanese government to expel various jihadist groups. The Libyans went first, with Bin Laden unable to shield them from the government's wrath. Al Qaeda itself got the boot in 1996, with the Sudanese government also seizing Bin Laden's assets in its country.[16]

During Bin Laden's time in Sudan, Al Qaeda turned decisively against the United States and the West in general. Bin Laden never harbored any positive feelings toward America, but in Al Qaeda's early days, it focused primarily on fighting Communism and promoting change in the Muslim world. It carried out its first anti-American operation, a botched attempt to kill U.S. troops transiting Yemen to deploy in a peacekeeping mission in Somalia, because it thought the American deployment was part of a plan to occupy the Horn of Africa. In subsequent years, however, jihad seemed to be failing in Algeria, Bosnia, Egypt, and elsewhere while the United States propped up local allies and its military role in the Middle East continued, with large deployments of troops in Saudi Arabia in particular. Bin Laden and Al Qaeda came to see the United States as the head of the snake, evil in its own right but also a foe that, if it could be defeated, would lead to the collapse of America's Arab world allies and Israel.

Bin Laden was not eager to return to Afghanistan. His group was broke and desperate, and the constant warring there made the country unappealing. Many jihadists thought Bin Laden was done with jihad, as Al Qaeda had done little to support fighters in Bosnia or Chechnya, the two most popular anti-foreign jihads among the fighters.[17]

Pakistan seemed a fickle friend. A limited Pakistani crackdown in the early 1990s had led Bin Laden and other Arab fighters to leave in the first place, and in 1995, fearing the return of foreign fighters from the Balkans, the Pakistani government initiated another major crackdown.[18] Yet Pakistan wanted to keep the jihadist flame alive to further its fight against India and advance its interests in Afghanistan. In addition, the Pakistani government outsourced much of its fighting in Afghanistan and Kashmir to a range of Islamist non-state groups, helping organize, train, and direct them. These groups often trained in camps in Afghanistan, and many saw eye to eye with the foreign jihadists on the need for an Islamic government. Pakistani security officials apparently hoped to use Al Qaeda camps to train fighters for Kashmir in their war against India, but their expectations were probably low; indeed, Bin Laden came with only around fifty followers.[19]

Bin Laden returned to Afghanistan when a new movement, the Taliban, was making its mark. Led by Mullah Omar, a one-eyed veteran of the anti-Soviet struggle, the Taliban emerged in 1994 from the refugee camps of Pakistan. Pakistan was one of only three countries in the world to recognize the Taliban government, and Pakistani intelligence provided it with money and weapons. United States government officials also reported that Pakistani military forces covertly fought with the Taliban as it extended its reach in Afghanistan.[20] The Taliban's power base was among Afghanistan's fractious Pashtun majority, whom it was eventually able to unify as it consolidated control of southern Afghanistan. In 1996, the Taliban captured the capital, Kabul, and would steadily extend its reach into non-Pashtun areas until, on the eve of 9/11, it controlled perhaps 90 percent of the country. Ahmad Shah Massud, the anti-Soviet hero whom Azzam had admired, led beleaguered fighters concentrated in the Tajik north in their increasingly desperate fight against the Taliban.

As the Taliban spread its control, Afghanistan became a base, indeed *the* base, for Al Qaeda and other foreign fighter groups. At first, it was questionable whether the Taliban, with its local focus, would mesh well with the foreign fighters. When Al Qaeda relocated from Sudan in 1996, it went to the territory of Afghan warlords it had fought alongside in the past. One report even claims that Bin Laden had no idea who or what the Taliban was when he returned to Afghanistan.[21] They allowed Bin Laden to stay, however, due to their common identity as Muslims and a sense of obligation to a man who had fought with and financially supported the anti-Soviet resistance. Bin Laden also promised to help them build roads, improve irrigation, and defend Kabul with his fighters; buying Mullah Omar and some of his lieutenants expensive automobiles didn't hurt either.[22] Many Arab foreign fighters also married Afghan women, giving them personal connections to important Afghan leaders.[23] Of the $30 million a year or so Bin Laden's organization raised in the pre-9/11 era, the bulk, roughly $10–20 million, went to supporting the Taliban.[24]

Military cooperation between Al Qaeda and the Taliban became increasingly important, though it was not the core of the relationship. Foreign jihadists formed what became known as the "055 Brigade." These fighters learned to use artillery, tanks, and land mines, as well as more traditional guerrilla tactics, and they had a reputation for ferocity.[25] Some of the Arab fighters would even charge through landmine-strewn fields to open up a path for their Taliban allies to follow.[26] That being said, the foreigners were only a small part of the

Taliban's overall force, and their military contributions were limited. Many were Pakistanis, working more with militant religious organizations and associated violent groups in Pakistan, and that country's intelligence service, than Al Qaeda. Similarly, Uzbeks and other Central Asians outside Al Qaeda's control were often more important for the Taliban than Arabs linked to Al Qaeda. Most Arabs sought to gain combat experience to help advance causes in other countries, not the Taliban in Afghanistan, and Al Qaeda often used fighting for the Taliban as a way of testing the mettle of potential members. Many often ended up fighting alongside the Taliban because they had few other places to fight; one Arab commander noted in 2000 that "if we open the doors of Chechnya now—in the fighting season—70 percent of the youth" would go there.[27]

Perhaps even more important, Al Qaeda also used its terrorist capability on behalf of the Taliban. Just before 9/11, two men pretending to be Arab journalists went to interview Massud. They hid explosives in their camera equipment and blew themselves up, killing the famed commander, who had been the biggest threat to the Taliban.[28]

Zawahiri argued that the "jihadist movement needs an arena that would act like an incubator where its seeds would grow and where it can acquire practical experience in combat, politics, and organizational matters"—a perfect description of what he and other Al Qaeda leaders achieved in Afghanistan in the late 1990s.[29] From its haven in Afghanistan, Al Qaeda became bolder and bolder, launching sophisticated attacks around the world. Al Qaeda embraced a "Far Enemy" strategy, arguing that the United States was the world's puppet master conducting a war on Islam, propping up dictators in Egypt and Saudi Arabia, providing military support to Russia in Chechnya and India in Kashmir, and otherwise undergirding every threat. "If America falls, the other regimes, including Israel, will fall," Bin Laden told his followers.[30] In addition to the 1998 embassy bombings, in 2000 Al Qaeda attacked the USS *Cole* in a harbor in Yemen, killing seventeen American sailors. It also plotted attacks in Europe, the Middle East, and the United States. As Michael Sheehan, a senior U.S. counterterrorism official in the 1990s, remarked: "Afghanistan was the swamp these mosquitos kept coming out of."[31] In February 1998, Bin Laden, Zawahiri, and leaders of several other organizations with a presence in Afghanistan formed what they called the "World Islamic Front." They argued that America was engaged in mass murder of Muslims, the humiliation of Islam, and other grave crimes. Thus, as Azzam had argued, it was the individual's duty "to kill the Americans and their allies—civilians and military."[32]

Al Qaeda's reputation would grow as it launched a series of attacks on U.S. targets. Bin Laden hoped to bring the war home to the United States and convince American leaders to withdraw from the Middle East, believing that a few big hits would eventually lead America to withdraw its forces.[33] The situations in Beirut in 1983, when Hezbollah's bombings of the U.S. embassy and Marine barracks led America to beat a hasty retreat from Lebanon, and in Mogadishu in 1993, when the downing of a U.S. helicopter and deaths of eighteen Army Rangers led to a similar withdrawal from Somalia, convinced Bin Laden the United States was a paper tiger, reliant on technology but vulnerable to hardened guerrillas who would fight with "faith and conviction."[34] Even if the United States intervened more instead of withdrawing, this too would be a win; the U.S. intervention would inspire Muslims to rise up, swelling the ranks of the jihadists and eventually leading the United States to leave, as the Soviets had done in Afghanistan. Attacks on the two U.S embassies in 1998, the USS *Cole* in 2000, and 9/11 followed this general strategy.[35]

But these strategic reasons were only part of the story of Al Qaeda's operations. Al Qaeda also attacked the United States as a form of advertising, hoping that it would raise the group's prestige, inspire young Muslims, and bring them to train in Afghanistan. Indeed, part of why Al Qaeda launched the 1998 embassy attacks was simply to make sure their existing members did not defect to other groups.[36]

Spectacular attacks also made for spectacular images. Building on Azzam, Khattab (discussed in chapter 5), and others, Al Qaeda also put the media and propaganda effort front and center, with a magazine published by a fighter with the amusing nom de guerre of Abu Musab al-Reuters. Al Qaeda also videotaped important operations, using the subsequent images to inspire new recruits and draw them to Afghanistan. In a propaganda video, Bin Laden recited a poem about fighters who "charged and destroyed a destroyer that fearsome people fear, one that evokes horror when it docks and when it sails," followed by images of a blast blowing a hole in the USS *Cole*.[37] Invariably, they referred to Afghanistan as Khorasan, using the ancient name that the Prophet had used when he said that black standards—the flags that serve as the inspiration for those used by the Taliban, Al Qaeda, and most notably the Islamic State—"will come from Khorasan, nothing shall turn them back until they are planted in Jerusalem."

Al Qaeda's anti-U.S. campaign would culminate on September 11, 2001, when its operatives killed almost three thousand people in attacks in New York and Washington, D.C., as well as in a plane crash when United Airlines Flight 93 was downed over Pennsylvania as its passengers and crew tried to overpower the hijackers and prevented an attack on the U.S. Capitol. These attacks would prove a high-water mark for Al Qaeda violence but also a turning point for the foreign fighter movement as a whole.

Why Did Fighters Go to Afghanistan?

Looking back, we tend to conflate the foreign presence in Afghanistan with the Al Qaeda story and the road to 9/11 because of the latter's devastation and shocking impact. But a wide range of fighters and organizations found their way to Afghanistan in the days before 9/11. Exact numbers are elusive, but the 9/11 Commission estimated that between 10,000 and 20,000 foreigners trained in Afghanistan's camps, not all of which Al Qaeda controlled. Jihadists' estimates are higher, with one reputable jihadist putting the number at over 30,000, with Saudi Arabia sending by far the largest number, followed by Yemen and Egypt.[38] Other recruits came from all around the world, including North Africa, China, and Canada.[39]

No single, or simple, profile exists of the recruits who went to Afghanistan. In contrast to most theaters that attracted foreign fighters discussed in this book, Afghanistan in the 1990s was less about joining a particular fight and more about joining the jihad in general. Some individuals went because they wanted to fight in Chechnya, then the most popular cause.[40] It may seem odd to go to Afghanistan because you want to fight in Chechnya, but Russia had effectively sealed the borders to Chechnya. Moreover, the Chechen fighters only wanted a few foreign volunteers, and only trained ones at that. So would-be jihadists often made their way to Afghanistan, hoping it would be a way station. Mohammad Atta, who led the 9/11 attackers, was one such would-be foreign fighter in Chechnya. For others, Afghanistan was simply a refuge. Khalid Sheikh Mohammed, who masterminded the 9/11 plot, fled to Afghanistan in 1996 after the United States tried and failed to capture him in Qatar.[41] Less dramatically, many veteran foreign fighters from the anti-Soviet struggle or the fight in Bosnia also could not return home for fear of imprisonment or death, leading them to Afghanistan.

Yet other factors brought foreigners to Afghanistan too. In 1996, the Taliban's leader, Mullah Omar, took what Afghans believed to be the cloak of the Prophet Mohammed from its shrine in the city of Qandahar—the first time it had been removed in decades. He donned it before a large crowd containing many religious leaders who shouted, "Commander of the Faithful."[42] Finally, it seemed, Muslims would unite in the name of God under one commander. Enthusiasm for the Taliban grew outside Afghanistan as word spread. In 2000, an important Saudi cleric declared the Taliban to be a true Islamic government, leading to a surge in Saudi recruits.

The Taliban's massacres of Shiite Muslims, which some allege were begun by Arabs in their ranks, also appealed to some individuals from the Gulf states with a sectarian agenda.[43] The Shiite community of Afghanistan fought the

Taliban, at times with limited support from Iran, and suffered grievously when the Taliban conquered their lands (the Taliban massacred thousands in 1998).[44] For the Taliban, and especially for their foreign supporters, the Shiites veneration of Ali, the prophet's son-in-law and cousin whom Shiites consider his true heir, and other "deviations" from a strict Salafi interpretation of Islam made them apostates.

Just as they did during the anti-Soviet period, militant groups around the Muslim world saw Afghanistan and Pakistan as a refuge from persecution at home. The Islamic Group and the Islamic Jihad organizations from Egypt established a presence after devastating setbacks in Egypt itself in the mid-1990s, and Libyans and Algerians also showed up after reverses in their home countries. In the early 1990s, all these groups believed they would triumph against the "near enemy" in their home countries, but now they needed a sanctuary to hide and rebuild. Perhaps fourteen groups in all showed up.[45] The Taliban also hosted a large Uzbek foreign fighter presence.[46] Of these groups, only five had joined Al Qaeda in "declaring war" on the United States in 1998.

Getting There

Getting to Afghanistan was not without its challenges. The trip itself involved airfare to Pakistan and subsequent travel to the training camps, a cost not all would-be fighters could pay. In contrast to today's media-saturated environment, a would-be fighter often had to have a personal contact to explain to him where to find a local facilitator in Pakistan to help find the camps. Many individuals who did make it had access in their home countries to existing militant groups with links to Afghanistan, but if the facilitator was arrested or left, travel from that country or region might no longer be feasible. As the scholar Timothy Holman notes, "Without access to a social network with links to facilitators, travel to Afghanistan at this time was not possible."[47] Once they arrived, the Arabs and Westerners, even those of Pakistani origin, stood out in Pakistan and in Afghanistan. This made them easy prey for Pakistani security officials, who alternated between crackdowns and toleration. Sometimes they had to pay smugglers to get them into Afghanistan.[48]

Al Qaeda and other groups were rightly terrified of spies; many were in Afghanistan because intelligence services in their home countries had penetrated and then decimated their ranks. You couldn't just show up and expect to be trusted. New fighters often brought letters of introduction with them from a respected member of an existing jihadist group, vouching for their sincerity and trustworthiness.[49] Again, this required some access to existing group members or supporters. For security reasons, each recruit took a nickname,[50] often incorporating a prominent figure from Islamic history, the recruit's country of origin, or another important aspect of his life. For example, Al Qaeda's first military chief was "Abu Ubaidah," after a companion of the Prophet, and then "al-Banshiri" in remembrance of the Panshir Valley in Afghanistan where he fought.

Nor was the trip out of Afghanistan easy. Because the returnees were linked to violence and extremism in the Middle East and Europe, if a fighter had a Pakistani stamp on his passport, he might receive extra scrutiny or even face arrest on returning home or to the West.[51] Al Qaeda created another path of entry to Afghanistan via Iran, probably with the toleration of Iranian officials, as Iran would allow jihadists to transit the country without having their passports stamped.[52] Tehran's exact motivations are not clear, but it appeared Tehran wanted to maintain relations with this fractious but violent set of groups, as well as help instigate problems among rivals like Saudi Arabia and Egypt.

To overcome these many transit problems, Al Qaeda created a vast apparatus to identify travel routes, forge passports, create false identities, store the passports of dead fighters for use by others, and pay for travel.[53] On the internet, it put out guidance ranging from what types of deodorant to wear to the need to avoid clothing made in countries like Pakistan, which would draw attention from border officials.[54] Another innovation was the use of charities as fronts to support operations. Although charities played an important role in Bosnia and the anti-Soviet fight, they had state support and many openly backed the fighting; now they operated more independently and below-the-radar (though often this was due to states ignoring their activity rather than clandestine skill). Al Qaeda members often operated in war zones, with hospitals damaged or nonexistent, food lacking, and other basic services missing. Al Qaeda both penetrated existing charities and created its own. Taking advantage of Islam's call for believers to donate to those in need, Al Qaeda relied heavily on a network of donors in the Gulf states, particularly Saudi Arabia, which was often referred to as the "Golden Chain."[55] Often with winks and nods on all sides, it was easier to raise money for the poor and suffering of Afghanistan, Bosnia, Chechnya, or another country than it was for the fighters themselves; using charitable fronts allowed their financial backers to escape scrutiny at home or at least claim ignorance of support for violence. By posing as charitable workers, the foreign fighters had an excuse to raise money, which was often untraceable in the form of cash, and a legitimate reason for traveling to and from war zones.[56] Many also genuinely did good. In addition to being a master terrorist, Zawahiri is a doctor who worked in a hospital in Pakistan, treating wounded Afghans. For many jihadists, serving the cause as an aid worker and serving as a fighter were complementary ways of pursuing their faith.

Actual operations were cheap, but that cost excludes the far more expensive components of the terrorist network. These ranged from paying fighters to maintaining camps to procuring documents. So while the 1998 embassy attacks directly cost only $10,000, and 9/11, probably the most expensive terrorist attack in history, cost $400,000, Al Qaeda would spend millions of dollars a year maintaining its training and camp infrastructure.[57]

What Did Fighters Learn in the Camps?

For Al Qaeda and other groups, spending this money on fighters, camps, and other infrastructure was vital, for Afghanistan would transform foreign fighters from a historic curiosity to a major force. In his memoir of the camps, former jihadist Omar Nasiri recounts the prominent role played by anti-Soviet fighters. He and other recruits looked up to them, and they had firsthand experience to impart on guerrilla war and military operations in general.[58]

The Afghan camps comprised an archipelago featuring dozens of facilities big and small. The Khalden camp, for example, focused on training recruits for operations outside Afghanistan. Not all the camps were run by Al Qaeda, but they all were linked to one another. The Sada camp established by Azzam in the 1980s remained independent of Al Qaeda but still coordinated with the group, with Al Qaeda training recruits there to fight in Afghanistan—"limited duration" fighters—as well as identifying "open duration" recruits who would receive more advanced training.[59] Derunta was really a complex of distinct camps, where different mujahedin groups would train. Different Afghan warlords controlled some camps in the complex, while others were for Arabs or for those fighting India in Kashmir.[60] The Farouq facility was Al Qaeda's primary camp. One recruit described it as "a military college where cadets passed through a number of stages and levels until they finally graduated at the command level," enabling them to lead fighters anywhere around the world.[61] Recruits often trained at multiple camps, receiving specialized or advanced training depending on the camp's focus.[62]

Although the camps have been described as terrorist factories that churned out killers who attacked in London, New York, and other Western cities, their primary purpose was to train soldiers to fight on behalf of the Taliban and guerrilla armies in the Muslim world.[63] The training at Al Qaeda's primary camp, Farouq, is instructive; it focused on weapons familiarization, laying land minds, small team tactics, and other basics of conventional and guerrilla warfare.[64] Much of the course involved conditioning familiar to soldiers around the world. Recruits did calisthenics, daily runs, and other physical exercise and followed an early to bed, early to rise rhythm. Part of the purpose was physical, but part of it was to break down recruits, bond them together, and ensure their commitment.[65] One recruit recalled that trainees were deliberately exposed to severe conditions—not being allowed to eat or drink, for example—in order for trainers to observe "their obedience, discipline, and patience."[66] To build the toughness of recruits going off to Chechnya, Kashmir, and other jihads, they ran through rivers and up and down mountains, carrying weapons, in Afghanistan's brutal heat and piercing cold.[67] Trainers tried to use a uniform curriculum across camps, helping foreign fighters overcome some of their language differences and other sources of disunity. During the anti-Soviet struggle, the U.S.-backed fighters had fought differently from one valley to the next. One U.S. official noted, "We couldn't get them on the same page." Now, they could fight more effectively as one team even when they hadn't trained together.[68] Indeed, recruits recalled that the camps supplemented the battlefield experience many had, with one describing it as "dotting the i's and crossing the t's" after combat.[69]

The skills taught to recruits in the 1990s were staggering, a far cry from the few weeks of basic weapons training given during the early years of the Afghan war. Nasiri writes: "I learned how to drive a tank, and how to blow one up. I learned how to lay a minefield, and how to throw a grenade to inflict maximum damage. I learned how to fight in cities, how to stage assassinations and kidnappings, how to resist torture. I learned how to make deadly bombs out of even the simplest ingredients—coffee, Vaseline. I learned how to kill a man with my own hands."[70] And then there were the guns. Nasiri recalls training on guns as varied as the Walther PPK (James Bond's preferred gun), the Israeli-made Uzi, the AK-47 (the universal guerrilla weapon), sniper rifles like the Dragunov, antitank weapons, and even large artillery. Ammunition was plentiful. "We never had to conserve ammunition, and there was always something new to try," Nasiri exulted.[71] He even remembers going "fishing" with the plastic explosive Semtex; the explosion in the lake led hundreds of dead fish to rise to the surface for dinner. His experience duck hunting with a sniper rifle did not go off so well. He recalled that the armor-piercing bullets blew the prey into tiny shreds.[72]

More advanced recruits, who represented only a fraction of the total trained, learned bomb-making, surveillance, and other techniques for terrorism, usually at different and smaller camps. One espionage class taught "observing foreign embassies and facilities." There, recruits learned how to use codes, communicate secretly, and recruit spies.[73] Nasiri recalls learning how to work with many different types of explosives, from Semtex to a mix improvised from paint and fertilizer.[74] Surveillance, of buildings and of people, was also an important part of the curriculum.[75]

Part of the reason for Al Qaeda's success was that it recognized the power of bureaucracy. It had committees for media, military operations, security, and fundraising, enabling it to specialize. Al Qaeda required its recruits to train and otherwise closely monitored personnel. Members were paid—not well, but enough to get by, and more if they had a family.[76] The group even had generous vacation leave, with one week off for every three weeks on for married recruits.[77]

Using its bureaucratic skills, Al Qaeda used the camps to separate the wheat from the chaff, with the wheat going to Al Qaeda itself. From its inception, Al Qaeda decided that many would enter a "testing camp and the best brothers of them are chosen in preparation to enter" the group. Recruits must not only prove dedicated fighters, but they needed to be "referred from a trusted side" (i.e., vetted for security) and be "obedient" with "good manners." The others would simply be fodder for various jihads around the world.[78] One trainee recalls that only three of fifty fellow volunteers were asked to join Al Qaeda.[79] Perhaps surprisingly, many recruits had tremendous freedom on where to go next. Al Qaeda's primary camp, for example, allowed graduates to go on to the fight of their choice (though a nudge or two from an instructor often made a huge difference).[80]

That Al Qaeda helped train many foreign fighters who did not join the group subsequently led to a lot of confusion as to whether someone trained by Al Qaeda should be considered part of the terrorist group. Adding to the confusion, Al Qaeda also allowed members to have ties or even membership in other groups. Many of the group's senior leaders had ties to the Islamic Jihad group of Egypt. Al Qaeda's military commander, in fact, was the military leader of both groups.[81]

Al Qaeda camps also taught recruits how to resist interrogation. This ranged from exposing them to brutal techniques to prepare them for capture to explaining how they might release false information to frighten or mislead their interrogators. Nasiri claims that Ibn al-Sheikh al-Libi, one of the most important camp instructors, used this technique after 9/11 when he was captured and interrogated in Egypt. He provided deliberately false information that claimed Iraq was giving Al Qaeda information about weapons of mass destruction. This "confession" supposedly contributed to the Bush administration's disastrous decision to go to war in Iraq. Libi, like many jihadists, wanted Saddam toppled and America trapped in a war in the Muslim world, and with his false claim, he got both.[82]

The camps were also highly bureaucratic in both the good and bad sense of that word. Upon arrival, recruits gave groups their names, contacts at home, past military training, and other information. During their time training or in the field, they often submitted tedious paperwork and accounting, ranging from the location of a grave to the need to write down the cost of various vegetables for reimbursement.[83] Despite the annoyance and labor such detailed organization required (and later, as we shall see, despite the counterintelligence risks it entailed), such thoroughness enabled Al Qaeda and other groups to organize and train large numbers of recruits, identify specialized assets, and otherwise form the basis of an army.

The camps also tried to instill a similar mindset among recruits. Nasiri recalls learning that there are many ways to wage jihad, ranging from proselytizing to charitable giving, but the noblest way of all is holy war. When possible, military instruction drew on religious legitimacy for authority. One class taught that fighters should not retreat without orders from their leader— a standard instruction—but couched it with the Quranic verse, "Do not retreat, but stay steady."[84] At the same time, recruits learned about the abuses under British and French colonialism, the U.S. bombing of civilians in World War II, and, of course, Israeli brutality against the Palestinians.[85] One recalled seeing a picture "of a Jewish soldier breaking the limbs of a Palestinian child" with no one moving to help.[86] Azzam's teachings featured heavily in their indoctrination, but so too did the teachings of Egyptian jihadists who stressed the apostasy of their own regimes and of other Islamists who did not embrace the jihadist cause.[87] Each class of recruits learned from past successes. Al Qaeda recruits watched the film *The Destruction of the American Destroyer Cole* (the luckier ones also watched *The Great Escape*).[88] Training reinforced these points; targets for shooting practices were in U.S. uniforms with American names.[89] The particulars of the indoctrination also served narrower agendas. By socializing recruits with a similar worldview, they would be more likely to stay loyal to Al Qaeda or whoever was training them rather than the myriad competitor groups that were also fighting.

Seeds nurtured in the camps would blossom in later fights. Recruits learned that the Caliphate "is the best and only solution" to the Muslim world's many problems.[90] The Palestinian cause was constantly stressed, as was Kashmir (Hindus, apparently, "were the descendants of a Jewish tribe that had wandered to India many centuries earlier," greatly simplifying things). In places like Bosnia and Chechnya, where Muslim land was considered occupied, Muslims also needed to fight. Infidels pretending to be Muslims ruled places like Egypt, Libya, and Algeria. America was the great Satan, but "American wasn't really America; it was controlled by Israel." The Shiites were also on the list. They were trying to "destroy Islam from within," and were thus more dangerous than America or even Israel.[91] The indoctrination, however, was varied and often so broad as to give the movement an incoherent set of priorities. One publication in the camp warned about how "the Beatles and the hippies" were undermining Europe.[92]

In the 1990s, as with Azzam, jihad also meant restraint. This would often be absent in practice but at least was preached. Nasiri learned that holy war demanded no indiscriminate killing. Corpses should not be mutilated, schools and churches should be preserved, and women and children were protected. Yet even at this early stage, we see the seeds for more indiscriminate killing. Nasiri recalls that while the enemy might simply be seen as those with guns, the definition "can be expanded to include the entire supply chain," ranging from those who give money or food to fighters or even to journalists who might aid an enemy's cause.[93]

Individuals also formed networks. Recruits from over twenty countries trained in the camps.[94] Fighters from different antiforeign jihads like Chechnya and Bosnia would mingle with groups fighting "infidel" governments like Algeria and Egypt, as well as with locals fighting in Kashmir and Afghanistan. These networks reinforced the idea that they were all part of one struggle and helped fighters form connections for wars in the future. In later years, it would prove common for individuals originally from different causes to work together after meeting in the camps. Indeed, for Al Qaeda, the networks would soon prove vital for its survival. After 9/11, various Pakistani jihadist groups, which had trained fighters in Afghanistan for war against India, helped host foreign fighters fleeing Afghanistan.[95]

Many recruits suffered under these conditions, however. At times the training was dangerous. One jihadist recounted that recruits threw grenades at one another in training, and one of them would have to hurl it far away to make sure it exploded and did not kill them all. Some died learning how to build bombs, while others perished in the cold and heat. Even for those who endured, life was austere. Nasiri recalls that he missed life in the West, ranging from cigarettes to soft sheets. "More than anything, I missed sex," he said.[96]

These gripes aside, the camps were often life-changing, giving recruits a sense of belonging and brotherhood that went beyond the specifics of the indoctrination. Nasiri loved that at the camps "everyone was equal." He recounted, "It was wonderful to know that every one of the brothers would lay down his life for me, just as I would for them. I had never felt so loved in my life, so taken care of." There was an emir who gave orders, but he could be challenged. Nasiri explained in his memoir that "it was the most democratic place I had ever been." Another jihadist recalled that "colors and races dissolve. There are no foreigners among us."[97] Egalitarianism also had its limits, as some volunteers were more equal than other. Nasiri recalled that Saudis would go to the camps for short periods only, but "they were there for a holiday." They didn't have to run or train, and only joined the group in the afternoon "to play with the guns."[98]

As Al Qaeda's reputation grew, it also increased its control over various training camps. Khalden, for example, was run independently of Al Qaeda, sent fighters to zones like Chechnya and Algeria where Al Qaeda had little presence, and did not respect the Taliban's leadership. It even distributed materials that "proved" Bin Laden's "deviation" from Islam because of his ties to the Taliban.[99] Bin Laden worked to close it down, and when the Taliban shut its gates in 2000, many of its volunteers ended up in Al Qaeda's clutches.

Tensions in the Ranks

It is tempting to tell the Afghanistan foreign fighter story as a steady arc, growing in both power and hatred of the West, beginning with Azzam and culminating in the 9/11 attacks. But the foreign fighters remained deeply, grievously divided, and these splits continue to this day. Indeed, decades later, jihadists would lament the "plethora of groups and organizations" that divided the jihadist cause.[100] Despite attempts at indoctrination and uniformity, Afghanistan was a hothouse for jihadist groups, with new splinters emerging while old groups morphed or joined forces.

Foreign fighters would still depict themselves as heroes fighting Islam's enemies, but they disagreed as to who was the top enemy, with candidates ranging from the numerous regimes in the Muslim world the jihadists deemed apostates to Israel, Russia, and India for their wars against local Muslim communities. Increasingly for the Al Qaeda leadership, the United States enjoyed pride of place, but even they spent heavily to support the Taliban in its quest to control Afghanistan and aided an array of groups fighting local regimes.

A basic divide was over a fundamental question: Who is a true Muslim? Traditional Islamic leaders, including the vast majority of Salafis, were reluctant to denounce any Muslim as an apostate. They argued that it was hard to know what was truly in a person's heart and warned that such charges would divide believers, a grave crime. A number of groups, however, justified their rebellions against ostensibly Muslim leaders like Egypt's Mubarak or Libya's Qaddafi by claiming that the governments they were fighting consisted of false Muslims. The regimes were not implementing Islamic law, which was a sure sign that they were unbelievers, and thus, rebellion was necessary. Once the door was open to declaring even a few nominal Muslims to be untrue, the question became when to close it. In Algeria in the 1990s, groups denounced not only the government but also anyone fighting for it. When this was not enough, they declared that anyone who was not fully on the side of the jihadists was really an apostate and proceeded to slit the throats, disembowel, mutilate, and otherwise slaughter ordinary citizens, including women and children.[101] This tendency toward brutality remained strong. Indeed, one leading jihadist claimed Bin Laden denounced the Saudi government in the mid-1990s in order to preempt this trend toward a war against all from emanating from Algeria and spreading in the Kingdom. Bin Laden hoped his declaration would instead focus jihadists there against the West.[102]

During the 1990s, this question of who is a true Muslim centered around the legitimacy of secular regimes and societies, but even then, sectarianism raised its head, with some volunteers seeing the Shiites as Islam's biggest enemies. For Al Qaeda, sectarianism was and would continue to prove a dilemma. Al Qaeda considered sectarianism a diversion from its anti-U.S. agenda, and in any event, it cooperated with Iran, the dominant Shiite power, using the country as a limited haven and secondary transit route after Pakistan for entry into the camps. Sectarian sentiment, however, was politically popular among the jihadist rank-and-file. Al Qaeda tried to walk a fine line; it downplayed sectarianism but also quieted any talk of its cooperation with Iran despite exploring transit routes there.[103]

Foreign fighters also quarreled over the legitimacy of the Taliban. Some prominent foreigners called for supporting the Taliban, for all its imperfections, because it was trying to implement Islamic law. Others, like the Libyans, considered the Taliban infidels because they tolerated the decoration of graves, an Afghan tradition. In addition, in their eyes, the Taliban did not crack down hard enough on Sufism and other "deviant" forms of Islam. Other charges included the Taliban's willingness to work with the United Nations to gain international recognition, fighting other Muslims in the Afghan civil war, and ties to Pakistan and Saudi Arabia (which some jihadists considered to be apostate regimes).[104] Prejudice also showed up, as some Arabs considered Afghans and the Taliban to be "primitive, backward, dirty, and chaotic."[105] The Taliban, for its part, feared that the Arabs' penchant for discord and denouncing enemies as infidels would create splits in their own ranks.[106] The foreigners often called on the Taliban to close down the camps and offices of their rivals.[107]

One Afghan jihadist even took over part of Afghanistan's Kunar Province and declared an Islamic state there, establishing Islamic law courts and trying to end crime and drug use. Supported by donors in Saudi Arabia and Saudi intelligence, he demanded that Bin Laden swear loyalty to him. Many Afghans opposed the supposed emirate, with one leader declaring, "When we finish with the Communists, we will start with the Wahhabis." An Egyptian jihadist assassinated the would-be state's leader, and rival Afghan forces overran Kunar. Several years later, an Arab Afghan tried to establish another Islamic state, but local tribes turned against him. When the Taliban took over Kunar in 1996, the would-be state's leadership prudently removed themselves to London.[108]

Despite the haven foreign fighters enjoyed in Afghanistan and Pakistan, Al Qaeda often showed little respect to their hosts. The Taliban did not seek to strike the United States and other "Far Enemy" targets. The Afghan group even negotiated directly with U.S. officials, though usually with no results. The Taliban often urged restraint on Al Qaeda. In 1996, after Bin Laden called for attacks on U.S. military forces, the Taliban asked him to stop making provocative media statements and relocated him to Kandahar, the heart of their territory and an area from which they thought they could control him directly.[109] Bin Laden's May 1998 declaration of war against the United States, three months before he attacked two U.S. embassies without telling the Taliban, infuriated Mullah Omar. "There is only one ruler. Is it me or Osama?" he reportedly exclaimed.[110] The Taliban closed down several training camps, creating a "crisis" and "discontent," according to other Arab foreign fighters.[111] Two leading jihadists wrote in 1999 that Bin Laden "has caught the disease of screens, flashes, fans and applause" and urged him to apologize to the Taliban.[112] After the embassy attacks, the Taliban confiscated his phone, leading Bin Laden to say that "two entities are against our jihad. One is the U.S., and the other is the Taliban's own foreign affairs ministry."[113] The Taliban issued identity cards to Arabs in order to control foreign fighters, and in 2001, Mullah Omar appointed an Uzbek fighter, Juma Namanjani, as their overall commander, with Bin Laden being the leader of the Arab contingent.[114]

The Weak Response

For some U.S. government officials, the 1998 embassy attacks were a wake-up call about the dangers of Al Qaeda and the growth of the jihadist infrastructure in Afghanistan, but eradicating this presence did not become a priority until after the 9/11 attacks.[115] As the 9/11 Commission found, key parts of the government such as the FBI, the U.S. military, and the State Department did not prioritize counterterrorism or Al Qaeda.[116] Thus, while the United States was often able to disrupt Al Qaeda plots, the foreign fighter camps kept churning out new ones with little interruption. Similarly, although the CIA did try to target Al Qaeda's money, the 9/11 Commission judged these efforts to be weak and uneven in the pre-9/11 era. Heavy hitters like the Treasury Department did not get involved until after the attacks. Intelligence was often lacking on who the financiers were and how the money was transmitted, and the United States lacked an effective legal and regulatory framework to stop terrorist financing. Other countries, such as Saudi Arabia and the United Arab Emirates (UAE), had less capacity and far less desire to stop the flow of money.[117] As a result, the foreign fighters enjoyed a haven to train, organize, plan, and indoctrinate in Afghanistan, as well as a significant presence in Pakistan. Outside Afghanistan and Pakistan, they also enjoyed a permissive environment in many countries to recruit and fundraise for groups in the camps and then, when the training was done, for individuals to return home and inspire more recruits or wreak havoc.

Travel restrictions did help, but these were episodic at best (though their considerable impact, even when they were weak, shows how the freedom to travel is a foreign fighter Achilles heel). In Jordan and Egypt, those who went to Afghanistan were often presumed to be terrorists, and the capable security services of these countries would monitor and arrest them on return. Arab governments kept an eye out for travel to Pakistan, seeing it as a red flag for training experience in Afghanistan. Al Qaeda often encouraged operatives to transit via Iran, despite often tense relations with Tehran, because Iran did not stamp their passports to avoid tipping off security officials in home countries. Some European officials also saw the flow of fighters to and from Afghanistan as dangerous, but they put up no barriers to transit and often did not monitor those who returned.[118]

When the United States did use military force, it often backfired. Indeed, the Al Qaeda–Taliban relationship was saved by U.S. efforts to fight it. After Al Qaeda attacked the two U.S. embassies in 1998, the United States retaliated by launching cruise missiles at foreign fighter camps in Afghanistan. The strikes killed a few fighters (most of them Pakistanis training to fight in Kashmir) and missed Bin Laden. It made the United States seem weak while at the same time elevating Al Qaeda's stature further. Now, if the Taliban expelled Al Qaeda, it would be publicly caving to the United States and surrendering a guest they claimed to honor—an impossible concession from its perspective. "What is there left to talk about now?" Mullah Omar asked after the strikes.[119] A year later, Afghan religious leaders affirmed this decision, telling Mullah Omar that if they surrendered Bin Laden, "America would also demand that we remove the veil of women" and otherwise put an end to the Islamic nature of the state.[120] On the eve of 9/11, the Taliban's former interior minister claimed Mullah Omar had moved so close to Bin Laden "that he was ready to sacrifice his people, his country, everything for him."[121]

The 9/11 Disaster

Led by Bin Laden, the foreign fighters proved the Taliban's undoing and, indirectly, destroyed their own position in Afghanistan. Because of their lethality, the 9/11 attacks are often portrayed as Al Qaeda's greatest accomplishment, and the strikes did prove a lasting propaganda accomplishment. Bin Laden, more than any terrorist in history, was a household name. The Lafayettes, Byrons, and Guevaras of transnational jihadism were emerging. However, in terms of advancing the goals of the foreign fighters as a whole, the 9/11 attack was a disaster that almost destroyed the entire jihadist movement. One prominent jihadist had warned Bin Laden to avoid international terrorism, which jeopardized the Taliban's rule, noting, "We are in a ship that you are burning."[122] On 9/11, his prophecy came true. The attacks "cast jihadists into a fiery furnace," he lamented, "a hellfire which consumed most of their leaders, fighters, and bases."[123] Prominent religious leaders in Egypt, Saudi Arabia, and elsewhere, often under pressure from their government, condemned the attacks.[124]

Bin Laden apparently hoped the United States would invade Afghanistan and become bogged down in a bloody quagmire, as had happened with the Soviets. And he was willing to sacrifice the Taliban to achieve this end. Bin Laden's scorn for the United States proved disastrous. At most, two thousand Arabs, and probably fewer, stayed behind to fight the United States. Some did so out of zeal, but others because they had nowhere else to go.[125] Although the U.S. campaign did not completely destroy Al Qaeda, it did devastate its ranks. Al Qaeda lost almost 80 percent of its members in fighting the United States and its allies.[126]

Beyond these huge losses to Al Qaeda and other foreign jihadists, support from U.S. special operations forces and air power, as well as money to warlords provided by U.S. intelligence, enabled the anti-Taliban opposition to rapidly turn the tables on Al Qaeda's protector. The United States began its military campaign in October 2001, and by December the Taliban had been routed almost everywhere.[127] Years later Zawahiri himself recalled the death of his family and lamented, "And to this day I do not know the location of the graves of my wife, my son, my daughter, and the rest of the three other families who were pulverized."[128]

The jihadists took their last stand in the Shah-i-Kot valley in 2002. The valley is only a few miles at its widest point and around five miles long, but it is surrounded by imposing mountains that dominate the few entrances. During the Soviet-Afghan War, Afghan mujahedin and foreign jihadists built extensive fortifications including bunkers, trench lines, and firing positions on the ridgelines, producing some of the heaviest mountain fighting of the war. Two decades later, the reeling Al Qaeda fighters reoccupied these same positions.[129] Although the foreign fighters suffered many losses, the battle also demonstrated how far they had come since their sorry showing during the anti-Soviet period.[130] As one U.S. military analyst wrote, Taliban fighters fought poorly while the foreigners were "resolute and capable fighters" and a "well-trained, disciplined force."[131] Despite extensive surveillance of the area before the battle, Al Qaeda fighters successfully hid many of their firing positions from the United States and its allies.[132] Their gunners surprised U.S. special operations forces, destroying helicopters and ambushing U.S. troops. "The Al Qaeda soldiers moved quickly from position to position in black tunics and head wraps like Ninjas," wrote one U.S. officer describing the battle. They also surprised U.S. forces by their eagerness to fight. Before the battle, the U.S. concern had been trapping the fighters in the valley before they had a chance to flee. The problem soon became the opposite; Al Qaeda fighters streamed into the valley from Pakistan, seeking combat with the Americans.[133] At least dozens, and probably hundreds of Al Qaeda and Taliban fighters also died, but their ferocity and skill made a mark on the United States as well, with eight soldiers lost and eighty-two wounded.

These casualties, however, were little consolation for jihadists in 2002. The foreign fighters had lost their haven in Afghanistan and, with it, the archipelago of training camps that had made them more formidable and a magnet for new recruits. Less dramatically, but perhaps most important, the United States orchestrated a global manhunt that netted not only Al Qaeda members but also foreign fighters of any stripe who might be affiliated with them. The factional differences that consumed jihadists mattered little to a wounded and angry America, and any link to Al Qaeda made a foreign fighter an enemy. In the face of U.S. pressure and attacks, the many disparate factions came together, and the Taliban rallied around Al Qaeda. Some did so out of conviction, but many found themselves unable to escape the taint of their connections to Al Qaeda.

Afghanistan after 9/11

The legacy of those who trained in Afghanistan in the 1990s is one of the most fruitful in the history of terrorism. Terrorism linked to those who trained in the camps in Afghanistan continued well after the United States or its Afghan allies conquered and disbanded the camps themselves. Mohammad Sidique

Khan, for example, who masterminded the July 2005 transportation bombings in London, had trained in the Afghan camps.[134]

Yet Afghanistan itself steadily declined in importance to the foreign fighter movement. Despite the reemergence of a threat that rallied foreign fighters in the past—foreign occupation of Afghanistan, in this case, with the United States replacing the Soviet Union—many foreign fighters kept their distance.[135] Some blamed Al Qaeda for its rash attack on the United States, which jeopardized the jihadist project worldwide as well as toppled the one "true" Islamic government, the Taliban. Over time, the attraction of other theaters like Iraq and later Syria, which better captured the Muslim public's imagination, made Afghanistan a sideshow in the overall jihadist struggle.

Some existing fighters stayed on in Pakistan after 9/11 to continue the fight or simply because they had no other options. Pakistani militant groups often provided safe houses or other logistical support, and they worked with Al Qaeda and other foreign fighters to conduct attacks. Some had married local women, gaining close ties to the community and, by tribal custom, an obligation of their new kinsmen to protect them. In general, the foreigners stayed in the background, working with various local groups as well as a welter of less prominent but deadly organizations like the Haqqani network or Hizb-e Islami, often building on relationships forged in the 1980s and 1990s, as well as with various tribal groups fighting the Americans. Over time, Pakistan would become more important than Afghanistan for Al Qaeda's remnants.[136]

Pakistan's role evolved in response. In the pre-9/11 era, Pakistan was vital to Al Qaeda and other foreign fighters, serving as a place for safe houses, logistics routes, and other forms of support. It also sent thousands of "volunteers" to fight with the Taliban. In the post-9/11 era, Pakistan often targeted anti-U.S. foreign jihadists even as it continued to work with the Taliban and various Pakistan-based groups fighting India in Kashmir. Pakistani tribes and religious groups, many of which had worked with the foreigners for years before 9/11, regularly gave them sanctuary, lighting bonfires to guide their way when they fled Afghanistan into Pakistan. Many foreigners found shelter in tribal parts of Pakistan that were traditionally no-go zones for the Pakistani state.[137]

Pakistan's balancing act of suppressing some jihadists while supporting others gradually spiraled out of control. Its failure to crack down fully on jihadists angered the United States and other allies. However, its pressure on Al Qaeda and other groups led some organizations to criticize the Pakistani government for killing and imprisoning holy warriors and justified targeting of the Pakistani state itself. Most of these groups were Pakistani, not foreign, but Arab foreign fighters ran training camps in tribal parts of Pakistan. The camps helped train Afghans and Pakistanis in opposing their governments, and Uzbeks were pioneers of grizzly beheadings in the country.[138] In the years following 9/11, jihadists killed thousands of people in Pakistan with suicide bombings, roadside bombs, and guerrilla attacks. They often targeted Shiite Muslims, Christians, and other religious minorities as well as police and soldiers. In 2007, they assassinated former Prime Minister Benazir Bhutto, using a suicide bomber to kill her while she was campaigning.

The U.S. invasion of Afghanistan and its enduring presence initially brought the Taliban closer to Al Qaeda and other foreign fighters. No longer did Al Qaeda have to justify the Taliban's war against other Afghan Muslim factions, for it was now a classic defensive war against a foreign "aggressor." In addition, the near enemy and the far enemy merged into one, as U.S. forces were on Afghan soil. The Taliban and Al Qaeda now shared a common enemy.[139] The Taliban, however, kept the foreigners at arm's length. When they withdrew from Kabul in 2001, they did not tell the foreign fighters, leaving them to their fates. Even when foreigners eventually returned, Al Qaeda fighters played at best a small military role in the larger struggle in Afghanistan that the Taliban was waging.[140] According to some reports, Taliban officials oppose Arab military and political groups because they cause disturbances.[141] "We have never felt the need for a permanent relationship [with Al Qaeda]," noted the Taliban's leader in 2007. In addition, the Taliban never integrated foreign fighters into their leadership, in contrast to groups in Somalia, Iraq, Syria, and elsewhere.[142]

Nevertheless, Al Qaeda itself persisted in the region. Its ties to the Haqqanis, forged in the 1980s and sustained ever since, paid dividends as the Haqqanis gave them shelter in Pakistan and otherwise protected them. Al Qaeda decentralized its structure, seeking to support the Taliban and foment guerrilla war against the United States and the new Afghan government.[143] It continued to churn out jihadist tutorial videos, inspirational speeches, and images of combat against U.S. and allied troops. Brian Glyn Williams, an analyst of the region, notes that "the Arab fighters seemed much more concerned about photographing and filming themselves than their simple Afghan hosts."[144] Afghanistan itself gained more attention as Iraq turned sour at the end of the 2000s. Nevertheless, by 2010, the U.S. government estimated that the number of Al Qaeda members in Afghanistan was only in the "double digits," though there were probably many additional foreign fighters from Central Asia as well as others who were not members of Al Qaeda.[145]

Because of the direct line between Al Qaeda's presence there and the 9/11 attacks, Afghanistan in the 1990s has fundamentally shaped our understanding of foreign fighters. But supposed lessons from the Afghanistan experience can be misleading. Al Qaeda often prioritized attacks on the United

States and Europe. Most foreign fighters, however, joined struggles like the anti-Soviet fight in Afghanistan, the anti-Russian cause in Chechnya, or, later, the fights in Iraq and Syria, which were more local and regional than focused on the West. Yet in the aftermath of 9/11, it seemed that all foreign fighters not only opposed the United States and the West but also saw them as the main enemy.

Similarly, 9/11 showed the lethality of groups like Al Qaeda, and that image has remained in our consciousness even though nothing near the scale of the 9/11 attacks has occurred in the post-9/11 era. For all the continued attacks in Pakistan and the Taliban's successes in Afghanistan, the loss of the haven in Afghanistan and massive training camp infrastructure was a devastating blow to foreign fighters. For without the camps, the jihadist cause became far less formidable. As one U.S. military officer noted, camp materials on bomb making were "for somebody who is smart."[146] But without teachers and trainers, even smart people would fail. Added to this loss was the continuing manhunt for jihadists, which made it far harder for them to operate in countries with strong and competent governments.

Finally, the Afghan experience in the 1990s revealed many of the limits and problems created by foreign fighters. The groups bickered constantly, and their zealotry alienated the locals. In addition, they often expanded the war in self-defeating ways, hurting their hosts and their cause in general. So while the era should be remembered as one where Al Qaeda was able to inflict a devastating blow on the United States, it is also a time when Al Qaeda brought the cause as a whole to the edge of the abyss.

CHAPTER 5 | The Sword of Islam: Khattab and
the Struggle in Chechnya

K HATTAB IS THE most important jihadist you've never heard of. In one
2011 survey, aspiring jihadists ranked this "Sword of Islam" as more inspirational than giants like Bin Laden, Zawahiri, and Zarqawi.[1] Khattab was
a jihadist Che Guevara, inspiring young Muslims with his style and image as
well as his words and deeds. Important figures like Zarqawi and Mohammad
Atta, the leader of the 9/11 attackers, initially sought to fight with Khattab
rather than join Al Qaeda.

Khattab went to Chechnya to fight in 1995, and he would die there fighting
seven years later, the victim of a Russian assassination. Under Khattab's leadership, the Chechen conflict marked the first time foreign fighters transformed
a local struggle into a regional one—a truly strategic impact. However, as
would happen again and again, the foreign fighters brought about their
own underdoing: their zealotry and regional ambitions proved a disaster
for Chechnya and eventually for the jihadist cause in the region as a whole.
Chechnya would become the jihadists' graveyard.

As for many important jihadists, there was no single moment or clear origin story for Khattab's decision to embrace jihad. Born Samir ibn Salih ibn
'Abdallah al-Suwaylim, Khattab grew up in the town of 'Ar'ar in northern
Saudi Arabia in a religious family (the norm in Saudi Arabia), and he was a
promising student. He turned his back on school, however, and, according to
the narration in a hagiographic video, left a good job, a big house, a beautiful
wife, "and immense wealth." Angered by violence against the Palestinians and

Afghans, "a kind of Islamic rage" grew in him and, like thousands of other Saudis, he made his way to Afghanistan for "caves to dwell in, gravel to sleep on, and the sky to cover with."[2] He arrived in May 1988, with letters vouching for him from Saudi aid organizations that backed the anti-Soviet struggle. He took his nom de guerre from the second caliph, Umar ibn al-Khattab, who was known for his piety and for his military prowess. The Caliph Umar had devastated the Persians and the Byzantines and conquered modern-day Iraq, Iran, Israel, Syria, Jordan, and parts of Central and South Asia in the name of Islam.

Khattab's time in Afghanistan would shape his subsequent outlook on jihad and the role of foreign fighters. Khattab fought along with Bin Laden in the battle of Jaji, the first time Arab volunteers played a significant independent military role against the Soviets.[3] He also was part of the subsequent conquest of Jalalabad and Kabul in 1993.[4] Later, when asked whether he had received formal military training, he replied, "No, for me school was Afghanistan."[5] Indeed, he still couldn't believe he and his fellow volunteers had won. "If you had told me back when we were in Afghanistan that one day we would be fighting jihad in Russia itself," he exclaimed, "I would never have believed you!"[6]

Although Al Qaeda would lionize the Arabs' role in fighting the Soviets in Afghanistan, Khattab was dismissive and more accurate. "We didn't really do jihad in Afghanistan. The Afghans did almost everything," he would later recall. He blamed inadequate training for the Arabs' poor military performance.[7]

As for Barbaros and other jihadists, the collapse of the Soviet Union was miraculous, and yet it posed a question: What to do next? As another jihadist would write, this time "was the darkest period," as various jihadist groups turned their guns on each other and Pakistan began intermittent crackdowns. Khattab, like many others, would leave Afghanistan. In his case, it was for the moral clarity of continuing the fight against the Russians.

With the collapse of the Soviet Union, chaos enveloped the Caucasus and Central Asia, and numerous small wars broke out among successor states. Although the West largely ignored these seemingly petty conflicts in distant lands, Russia often intervened to play kingmaker in what Moscow saw as its own backyard. Small numbers of Afghan Arabs traveled to fight in places like Abkhazia, Nagorno-Karabakh, and Tajikistan. Although this was new territory for jihadists, they had friends on the ground. Some sympathetic Central Asian Muslims may have trained in camps run by Al Qaeda and other groups in Afghanistan and Pakistan in the years after the Soviet withdrawal from Afghanistan.[8]

Khattab would work with the Islamic Renaissance Party in Tajikistan in the early 1990s. He claims his own band was at most 120 men. They based themselves on the Afghan side of the Amu Darya River and conducted raids into Tajikistan, where they worked with several hundred more locals. Khattab recalls in his memoirs traversing the wild river, whose crossing itself "was a jihad," and then going over "mountains and mountains the likes of which my eyes had never seen."[9] The Tajikistan struggle was failing, however, and some of his Tajik companions were more criminals than holy warriors.[10] Military operations seemed fruitless, money was short, and terrain and the weather prevented his group from making significant inroads. Many fighters would flee to Afghanistan or Uzbekistan to join jihadist groups in these countries.[11] Khattab later lamented that "Tajikistan was neglected" by the world's Muslims.[12] Khattab himself, however, established a reputation as a serious fighter, losing two of his fingers throwing a hand grenade.[13]

All this is a prelude to Khattab's story. Like Bin Laden, he would become a jihadist hero fighting the Russians, but he would do so in Chechnya, not Afghanistan.

Russian Dogs

No part of the former Soviet Union was more poised to rebel against Russian rule than Chechnya, where hatred of the Russians ran deep. The Russian conquest of the Caucasus spanned most of the nineteenth century, with Russia proving victorious through sheer numbers, total war (including the widespread deforestation of Chechnya), and extensive ethnic cleansing.[14] Leo Tolstoy, who witnessed the resistance of the Chechens and respected their independent spirit, famously wrote in his novel *Hadji Murat*:

> The feeling, which all Chechens, young and old experienced, was stronger than hatred. It was not hatred, but a refusal to recognize these Russian dogs as people, and such a disgust, horror and incomprehension of the monstrous cruelty of these creatures that the urge to kill them, like the urge to kill rats, poisonous spiders, and wolves, was as natural a feeling as the instinct of self-preservation.[15]

Caucasian rebels waged a series of holy wars on the Russian invaders, giving their revolts a religious hue. Imam Shamil led the Caucasian Imamate, which had a brief existence from 1840 to 1859. As the title "Imam" suggests, Shamil was a Sufi holy man from Dagestan. (Sufism is a mystical form of Islam embracing saint worship, visits to the saints' tombs, and ritualistic dance that was and remains prevalent in Chechnya.) Shamil led a guerrilla war for more than two decades against the Christian Slavic invader. His call for defensive jihad united the otherwise fractious peoples under a Sufi Muslim banner until his ultimate defeat and capture in 1859.[16] These uprisings involved not only Chechens but also neighboring Dagestanis and Ingush tribes, and regional connections endured. These Caucasian peoples shared religious and cultural ties, and they often fought together against the Russians at different historical periods. A common identity—fragile, often fractious, but with a religious and anti-Russian orientation—was born.

The Russian suppression of the Caucasus in 1860 led to a mass exodus. Over 100,000 residents fled to Ottoman Turkey, with some eventually settling in Jordan, Iraq, Syria, and other countries. This resettlement created an emotional bridge that would endure even as these parts of the world moved in different directions.[17] In Jordan, for example, almost 10,000 Jordanian-Chechens retain a distinct cultural tradition, including the Chechen language.[18]

When Moscow's boot was off Chechnya's throat, as it was during the Russian civil war that followed the 1917 Russian revolution, rebellion inevitably followed. Again, Chechens allied with neighbors from Ingushetia and Dagestan to oppose Russia. Because of these rebellions, Moscow constantly feared revolt and treated the Chechens with a level of suspicion, which extended to paranoia. In 1944, well after Russia had turned the tide against German forces, Stalin feared that the Chechens, among other groups, would ally with the invaders (who never entered Chechnya), and he deported the entire community to Kazakhstan. Over half of those deported died before they were allowed to return home in 1956 following Stalin's death.

Under Soviet rule, Russian migrants controlled political life in the Chechen area, and Russian was the dominant language. Over time, Russia seemed to have won, and while local customs endured, Islam in Chechnya seemed to be in decline. Yet memories of Russian abuses remained strong, and Chechens never forgot the deportation and mass death. And even after Soviet dominance was secure, Chechnya remained poor, its language and customs disdained, and its people excluded from top jobs and higher education.[19]

As the Soviet Union declined and the country opened up, some among the Chechen diaspora began to return, largely to visit but also, in a few cases, to stay. At the same time, religious sentiment in the Caucasus grew, with mosques and Islamic societies rapidly spreading, filling the ideological void left by the collapse of Communism. Preachers from the Gulf states began to push their austere interpretation of Islam, believing that they could convert these fallen Muslims, most of whom were Sufis. Salafis saw Sufi practices as smacking of polytheism and thus as anathema, and many jihadists would see these practitioners as apostates. In neighboring Dagestan, religious sentiment also grew, and intellectuals and religious figures there began voicing support for bringing the various peoples in the Caucasus together in a single Islamic state.[20]

Indigenous Salafists in the region began reaching out to foreign preachers and charities, seeking help and, of course, money. One journalist account describes a Jordanian missionary entering a destitute village in the early 1990s, handing out money to converts, and offering a free feast to the village every week.[21] Early Salafi missionaries in Chechnya and Dagestan would offer local religious leaders $1,000 as a signing bonus and up to $150 a month if they embraced the more austere Saudi-style form of Islam. More humble converts also got a bonus of $30.[22]

The First Chechen War

Chechnya, unlike many other parts of the Soviet Union, did not gain independence when the Soviet Union was abolished in 1991. Russian leaders made a legalistic argument, contending that countries like Kazakhstan were "independent" entities within the "Union" of various Soviet Socialist Republics, while Chechnya was part of the Russian republic and thus had no right to secede. Russian leaders feared that Russia itself might break up if secession were allowed to go unchecked, with disastrous political and economic consequences. Many Chechens, for their part, had bitter memories of Russian rule, resented Russian settlers, and wanted their own language to be the official tongue.[23]

Chechen leaders declared independence anyway in 1991 under the leadership of former Soviet Major General Dzhokhar Dudaev. At first, Russia tried to control events by giving pro-Russian forces in Chechnya money and clandestine military aid, but this failed to dislodge the separatists. In 1994, over the objection of many of Yeltsin's advisers and senior military officers, Russia decided to go to war to reassert its control over Chechnya. Khattab and his fellow jihadist volunteers would use this nationalistic struggle to enter the fray.

These volunteers seemed a mere curiosity in 1994, when fighting in Chechnya began. Dudaev was a thoroughgoing nationalist; he did not even know how many times a day a Muslim should pray,[24] and as a Soviet air force general, he had bombed Arab fighters in Afghanistan in the 1980s.[25] Dudaev appealed to the West for recognition and support, but, fearing it would anger Russia, the West ignored his pleas.

Dudaev initially downplayed Islam, but after Russia invaded, he found "holy war" a valuable slogan to convince young Chechen men to fight. He also began to visit Middle Eastern countries and cultivated local religious leaders. Chechnya's leading religious figure, Akhmad Kadyrov, declared a jihad against Russian forces. As under Imam Shamil, Islam was a way to unify a country where clan divisions were strong and also a way to contrast Chechnya's distinct identity with Christian Russia.[26] Kadyrov was a Sufi, and Sufi Brotherhoods were particularly important forces mobilizing Chechens to defend Islam. But nationalism and Sufism were both a far cry from mujahedin-style jihadism, which rejected both these identities as worshipping false gods.

Russia bombarded Grozny with a ferocity not seen in Europe since World War II. Of roughly one million Chechens, tens of thousands died, and hundreds of thousands became displaced. As these death tolls suggest, Russian forces often obliterated civilian areas. Nor was bombing the only Russian crime. In April 1996, Amnesty International bluntly informed the United Nations Commission on Human Rights that "men, women, and children have been victims of extrajudicial executions, hostage-taking, torture and ill-treatment in detention."[27] In the village of Samashki, for example, Russian forces killed over a hundred civilians, "torching houses and cellars with grenades and flame-throwing rockets, burning residents alive or shooting them at point-blank range in the streets and courtyards."[28]

Yet the Chechens endured. They lacked Russia's firepower, but they too abused Russian prisoners and killed Chechens suspected of collaborating. Russia routinely lies about its casualty figures, but nongovernmental sources like the Committee of Soldiers' Mothers of Russia put its total losses at 14,000.[29] Ethnic Russians living in Chechnya also died, often the victims of Russian bombardments, but most fled. The Russian population of the republic shrank from almost 300,000 to less than 20,000.

Enter the Jihadists: Khattab and Basaev

To many jihadists, Chechnya seemed like the new Afghanistan—same aggressor and same part of the world—and a few slipped in to join the fray. One of the earliest arrivals was a Jordanian-Chechen, a veteran of the anti-Soviet conflict, who convinced Khattab that Chechnya was a worthy struggle. However, at first Khattab had to search for Chechnya on the map because it was so obscure to him and to other foreigners. Yet Khattab, along with a dozen other veteran fighters, would enter Chechnya in February 1995.[30]

Khattab modeled his forces on the International Islamic Brigade, the force led by Barbaros in Bosnia. Other jihadists were also entering Chechnya at this time, in part because the Dayton Accords in Bosnia led them to be expelled from that country. The Chechen jihadists also drew on the same network of charities founded to support jihad in Afghanistan, Bosnia, and other parts of the world. Once established, these institutions endured beyond the conflicts that spawned them. Often, personal connections among fighters from past conflicts helped ensure continued cooperation.[31]

Khattab formed a deep bond with Shamil Basaev, one of the leading Chechen commanders who, like Khattab, had fought throughout the region as well as in Chechnya. Basaev would declare Khattab to be his "brother," a vital endorsement in a society where kin ties shaped so many relationships and where outsiders were suspect. It was this tie to a top local commander that enabled Khattab to have such a decisive impact.

Basaev was a computer salesman in Moscow when the USSR dissolved in 1991. He quickly returned home to take part in the fledging independence movement, but his first fighting was not in Chechnya. Violence had broken out throughout the region and, with Russian support, Basaev created his own special forces unit. As a foreign fighter himself, Basaev fought on the side of Abkhaz separatists, who were trying to break away from the newly independent Georgia.[32] He led the "Confederation of Mountain Peoples of the Caucasus"[33] during the Georgian-Abkhaz conflict in 1992–1993, showing an early interest in the independence of other Muslim Caucasian republics, not just Chechnya, a prelude of things to come. Basaev also traveled to Pakistan and Afghanistan in 1994 before the Chechen war broke out, bringing with him Chechens who would be trained there. He went on to retain this broader outlook, with devastating consequences.

In 1995, Basaev masterminded one of the most dramatic raids of the Chechen war. He led around 120 men disguised as Russians to the quiet city of Budyonnovsk, 70 miles north of Chechnya. They attacked the police station before ransacking the town, and in the process they collected hundreds of hostages who were shepherded into the main hospital. They then fortified the hospital, and Basaev issued an ultimatum for the Russians to end the war. Russian forces repeatedly launched brutal Soviet-style assaults that resulted in untold numbers of dead hostages, but they were unable to dislodge the Chechen fighters. Humiliated, the Russian government negotiated with Basaev and agreed to temporarily halt military operations in Chechnya.[34]

Basaev emerged a national hero, and he proceeded to conduct even bolder attacks.[35] Along with future President Aslan Maskhadov, Basaev led the storming of Grozny, Gudermes, and Argun in August 1996. The offensive trapped the numerically superior Russian forces inside their bases and checkpoints. Chechen forces then repeatedly ambushed hastily supplied Russian relief columns, compelling Russian President Boris Yeltsin to end the war.[36] Such military accomplishments and derring-do made Basaev particularly popular among young militants.[37]

Just as they had before the first Chechen war began, Basaev's horizons went beyond Chechnya after it ended, and his perspective became increasingly religious. At the start of the conflict, he was an ambitious nationalist and saw neighboring Dagestan in particular as part of his struggle. But he was not a jihadist. During the war, however, Russia attacked his village, killing his wife and six children.[38] These and other attacks made Basaev more radical, and over time he took on Khattab's worldview. As one former friend declared, "He changed from a Chechen patriot to an Islamic globalist."[39]

Khattab shared Basaev's love for daring acts, particularly raids and ambushes. Khattab himself made his reputation on April 16, 1996, when he and his fellow fighters ambushed a Russian motorized rifle regiment outside the village of Yarysh Mardy. Roughly a hundred well-hidden ambushers destroyed the regiment's communications vehicles in their first attack, preventing calls for reinforcements. They then destroyed the armored personnel carriers in the front and back of the column, trapping the Russian soldiers. To finish up, they fired armor-piercing grenades into the trapped vehicles one by one while mowing down anyone who tried to escape.[40]

The propaganda was even better than the operation. Khattab filmed the ambush, and the video shows dark smoke emerging from burned Russian vehicles. Amid the carnage, a swarthy Arab with a long beard and black beret brandishes an AK-47 and proclaims, "Allahu Akhbar." Copies of the video were soon everywhere, winning over Chechens to the foreign fighters and making Khattab a hero in radical mosques around the world.[41]

Part of Khattab's success came in part from his policy of "*jihad* through the media."[42] He declared that "the media has become more important than rifles and guns," and a video team always traveled with his band. He would document and film his victories, contributing to his renown.[43] At first he distributed videos and CDs, new tools for jihadists,[44] with images of fighters shooting down helicopters, blowing up armored personnel carriers, and accepting the surrender of Russian soldiers with peaceful assurances.[45] Off the battlefield, videos showed fighters chanting, playing with children, and praying together, contrasting their peaceful brotherhood with the fierce fighting. Some featured fighting in neighboring Dagestan as well. Chechen jihadists also developed jihadi snuff films, showing the torture and beheading of Russian prisoners,[46] a genre that subsequent groups would come to perfect. Voiceovers would commend the brothers for leaving "affluent, beautiful lives" to fight for God, who would surely accept them as his favorites.[47] "Russian Hell" was a particularly popular video, and it had several sequels of the same name.[48] Khattab would also pioneer the use of the internet, developing websites to disseminate propaganda (though, at the time, low bandwidth meant that hosting large video files was impractical). One snippet of propaganda sums up a common jihadist theme: "Today thousands of your fellow Muslims are being killed, yet where is your support for us?"[49] As a result of media outreach, the Chechen conflict became far better known than the struggle in Bosnia, and Khattab achieved celebrity status around the jihadist world.[50]

Khattab and his followers also benefited from the increasingly influential role of radical preachers congregating in London and other European cities starting in the early 1990s. Following the Soviet-Afghan War, several Arab religious leaders relocated to Europe, often to avoid the security services awaiting them in their home countries. Radical preachers influenced sympathizers throughout the United Kingdom and the rest of Europe, further developing and expanding the informal network of Afghan Arabs and bolstering the ideological underpinnings of the movement.

During much of the 1990s, these preachers, while sympathetic to globally oriented groups like Al Qaeda, often embraced more traditional antiforeign jihad in the Muslim world or rebellions against Middle Eastern regimes. From their mosques in London, they encouraged Muslims to fight in Bosnia, Algeria, and Chechnya, rather than attacking the West. Toward the end of the decade, Chechnya became the primary focus, especially after the Dayton Accords resulted in the expulsion of foreign fighters from Bosnia, and infighting among jihadists in Algeria became increasingly bitter.[51] They used images of Russian atrocities against innocent Muslims, and there were many, to raise money and encourage volunteers to fight.

For all of Khattab's successes, however, the Chechen cause's popularity was not matched by the flow of volunteers. During the 1994–1996 war, the number of foreigners from outside the Caucasus region was tiny: perhaps eighty Arabs, along with a few dozen Turkish and Central Asian fighters. Given the thousands of Chechens who took up arms, the foreigners were a drop in the bucket. The Chechen resistance did not lack manpower, and many foreign fighters were poorly trained despite their enthusiasm. Language differences, rough terrain, and a harsh climate also made it difficult for foreign fighters to contribute, so Khattab often limited the number of foreign volunteers. Biographies of many jihadists reveal they sought to fight in Chechnya but did not do so.[52] Fatefully, Khattab's websites and those of other jihadist networks encouraged volunteers to first train in Afghanistan, where his representative vetted potential fighters.[53] Locals seemed to exploit foreigners more than value them, and they worked with them primarily to solicit donations from wealthy Arabs.[54]

Transit routes proved a constant problem, and Khattab himself noted that many Arab brothers could not reach Chechnya. Russia controlled most of Chechnya's border. To get to Chechnya, one had to try to either bribe his way through or hike over the Caucasus mountains via Georgia, and these mountains were patrolled, making the trip harder over time. Khaled Sheikh Mohammad, the 9/11 plot mastermind, tried to enter Chechnya via Azerbaijan in 1997 but was turned back, fatefully putting him in Afghanistan.[55] Ayman Zawahiri, who went on to head Al Qaeda, also tried to reestablish his Egyptian group in Chechnya, but he too was briefly arrested while trying to enter, convincing him that he had no choice but to throw in his lot with Bin Laden.

Yet even with all these limits, the Afghan veterans began to make their mark. Perhaps because the overall number of foreign fighters was small, they were disciplined and coherent, in contrast to their role in many other conflicts. The Chechens soon learned that a pitched battle with better-armed and more highly trained Russian forces was a recipe for disaster. Foreign volunteers helped them learn Afghan-style guerrilla methods such as ambushes and improved explosive devices. As the former Chechen foreign minister told scholar Brian Glyn Williams, "I did not personally like Khattab and his foreign fighters, but they did make a great contribution to our struggle by teaching us the tactics of the Afghan guerillas."[56]

The Interim: Exploiting the Vacuum

In 1996, under the Khasavyurt Accord, Russia withdrew its troops and rejected war "forever." Both sides recognized each other and were to build relations "on the generally recognized principles and norms of international law."[57] The war in Chechnya had embittered and exhausted Russia, and Moscow seemed to have little appetite for resuming the war. However, there was no Dayton Accord equivalent that forced the foreigners to leave. If the Chechnya conflict had ended in 1996, the foreign fighter role would have been similar to that in Bosnia—more a historical curiosity than a landmark event.

However, a Russian counterterrorism success would eventually make the terrorism problem in Chechnya much worse. Shortly before the first war ended, the Kremlin began seeking a diplomatic resolution and agreed to meet with Chechen President Dudaev. However, when Dudaev came out of hiding to speak on the phone with a Duma member to coordinate the meeting, Russian aircraft intercepted his signal and killed him with laser-guided missiles.[58] Both Russia and Chechnya would pay a heavy price for this tactical success. Dudaev was a secular figure respected throughout Chechnya, and his death led to a power scramble. Zelimkhan Yandarbiyev briefly became acting president and then, after elections, Aslan Maskhadov took over. Maskhadov had little authority and even less legitimacy.

When Maskhadov came into power in 1997, he faced an almost impossible task. Most Chechens wanted independence, and while Moscow was willing to grant considerable autonomy, the Yeltsin government balked at formal secession, fearing that other parts of Russia might follow suit, resulting in Russia's political humiliation. The Russian military sought revenge for its defeat, and with every violent incident in Chechnya (and there were many), voices proclaimed the Chechens couldn't be trusted. Russia established a de facto blockade of Chechnya with rings of troops and checkpoints, claiming, with some justification, this was an attempt to prevent chaos from spreading back into the rest of Russia. Chechens saw it as an attempt to starve them into submission.[59] In tactics that would become familiar decades later in Ukraine and other countries, Moscow also supplied the opposition with money, assassinated key leaders, and otherwise tried to sow chaos and undermine confidence in the new government.[60]

Perhaps more important to ordinary Chechens, education, health care, and other services had collapsed and unemployment reached a staggering 80 percent.[61] Moscow had promised aid, but little was delivered, and both Russian and Chechen officials stole a large amount of the allocated funds. Much of the middle and educated classes left during the war and resulting chaos and never returned. Drug trafficking, robbery, and kidnappings became commonplace, with local warlords exploiting the Chechens for money and power.[62] Almost two thousand people were kidnapped for ransom, including many Russians in Chechnya, despite the wishes of Maskhadov.[63] All this made Chechens desperate for any solution that promised law and order.

Although the foreigners' military impact had been minimal in the first war, they had gained goodwill and admiration. Maskhadov declared that "the Chechens will always remember them" for their sacrifices.[64] The Chechen government at the time lauded Khattab, giving him medals, the rank of general, and other rewards. "Khattab" was a popular name for newborn Chechen babies.[65]

Foreign fighters exploited their popularity, eventually going from the sidelines to center stage. Their divine mission, it seemed, continued. They had won in Afghanistan and Bosnia, and now they were beating Russia again in Chechnya. Khattab embraced the idea of building a base within a state. Fighters were required to define and advance the borders of this base, and true Muslims were needed to be its subjects. Salafists in Chechnya drew on foreign funding to spread their teachings and reward recruits. They recruited more

Arabs and Turks from Central Asian areas along with hundreds of Dagestani and Chechen volunteers. As in Afghanistan, training and proselytizing mixed, with religious instruction and weapons instruction incorporated into the curriculum. Foreign ideologues, along with some like-minded Chechen and Dagestani preachers, pushed the idea that the war was not over because the North Caucasus was not truly free of foreign rule given Moscow's control of neighboring Dagestan.[66]

Khattab, working with Basaev, established at least four training camps in the mountainous east of Chechnya. Arabs, Chechens, Dagestanis, and other Muslims from the region all trained together in the camps. More foreign fighters began to enter Chechnya, with the number of Arabs growing to five hundred or more by 2001. Indeed, more Arabs came to Chechnya between the first and second Chechen wars than during the wars themselves. Of these new arrivals, more than half were from Saudi Arabia, with Yemenis, Egyptians, and Kuwaitis also playing a significant role. Perhaps two thousand Dagestanis also trained in the camps.

At these camps, trainees imbibed jihadist teachings along with instructions in weapons, explosives, and ambush tactics. As in Afghanistan and later in Syria, these camps would be incubators. They were "like a beehive," Khattab would later claim, though many foreign fighters did not actually fight. They had an even bigger impact by training others, providing weapons, fundraising, preaching, and otherwise supporting the conflict.[67]

In contrast to many future jihadist leaders, Khattab did not demand purity from his followers. Khattab claimed most of them were actually Sufis. He stressed the need to work with the locals and to not force a foreign interpretation of Islam on them. Flexibility was vital. Khattab also sought to integrate his fighters to avoid having them be seen as outsiders. He and many others married local women, delivered food to villages, and otherwise tried to show solidarity with the locals. What Khattab did demand, however, was discipline; he expelled almost half of his volunteers for not meeting his high military standards.[68]

Jihad, with its promise of endless fighting, had natural allies in the local warlords. Most had been nobodies before the conflict; war is what made them prominent. If a local warlord worked with foreign fighters, he had access to foreign money, making him better armed and more formidable, which proved another draw. Many warlords simply mouthed Islamist slogans to gain foreign cash and maintain their independence from the central government. Yet their lip service had lasting consequences. Many local recruits were dead-enders, "poor, drug-addicts, and alcoholics" according to one commander, but the training and fighting changed them. Many emulated their foreign comrades, growing bushy beards and embracing an austere Islam. They renounced alcohol, cigarettes, music, and other supposedly decadent activities, wearing green headbands with the words "God Is Great" on them.[69] As one observer commented, people didn't join because they were Islamists, but they became Islamists in order to fit in with their new comrades.[70] Khattab would claim that the foreigners were "giving an Islamic flavor" to what had been a nationalistic struggle.[71] Other Chechen leaders may have been more pragmatic. They feared the war would resume, and Khattab himself claimed that he and his fellow fighters were asked to continue the training mission "because nobody was convinced the Russians would completely withdraw."[72]

Chechen President Maskhadov, for his part, initially pushed a secular agenda and allied with local Sufis, trying to portray local warlords who opposed his rule as being in bed with foreign zealots. He also tried to work with Russia, drawing the ire of Basaev and other radicals who went so far as to claim Maskhadov did not believe in God.[73]

Fighting among the government, the warlords, and the foreigners made the chaos even worse. Maskhadov supporters battled with Salafists, trying to arrest Khattab and expel those who "came to spread the ideology so foreign to the Chechen nation," particularly those coming from Arab countries and Pakistan.[74] No one listened. Maskhadov's own vice president worked with Basaev to save the foreign fighters, with Basaev singling out his brother Khattab for praise.[75] With the blessing of many warlords, the radicals established Islamic courts in defiance of the government.[76] As one Chechen observer said at the time, "People are fed up with disorder all around them. They think that introducing Shariah will bring an immediate halt to crime."[77]

As the state neared collapse, Maskhadov did an about-face. He tried to co-opt the radicals by declaring Islamic law, separating girls and boys in school, and allowing Islamic courts. Maskhadov also brought leading militants, including Basaev, into government. Supposedly, Basaev and Khattab threatened Maskhadov at gunpoint to bring about such changes.[78] Maskhadov also framed the conflict more as a regional struggle than one confined to just Chechnya. The radicals, however, opposed any hint of compromise, and they used their newfound influence to block security cooperation or other concessions to Russia.

Although many Chechens hoped that the war was over, for Khattab the ceasefire was just a chance to reload. In 1997, in a prelude to similar raids that sparked the Second Chechen War a few years later, Khattab led roughly a hundred men—a mix of Arabs, Chechens, Dagestanis, Ingush, and other Central Asians—on a raid into neighboring Dagestan, striking a tank battalion of Russia's 136th Mechanized Infantry Brigade. Khattab's force destroyed many of the battalion's tanks (Khattab would claim a total of three hundred vehicles) and then scattered, fleeing in trucks and using hostages to ensure safe passage back to Chechnya.[79] Khattab's raiders took heavy casualties, but the raid electrified supporters. This was no "terrorist attack" but rather a full-on strike against the core of a hated enemy's military forces.

Khattab reached the peak of his influence around this time. Indeed, from the end of the first Chechen war in 1996 to the beginning of the second in 1999, Khattab's position seemed stronger than that of Bin Laden's. Khattab was more admired in the key fundraising hub of Saudi Arabia. Most Saudi clerics backed him over Bin Laden, in part because the Saudi government did not want youths to fight with Bin Laden, who was openly hostile to the Saudi regime.[80] Khattab even filmed himself with the Saudi flag, which helped him retain the support of prominent Saudi religious leaders who supported the Chechen fighters but were also loyal to the Saudi government.[81] The Saudi government did not crack down on fundraising for Chechnya as most Saudis saw it as charity and freedom fighting, not terrorism.[82]

While Khattab and Bin Laden were on friendly terms, Khattab's focus on Chechnya rather than the broader anti-U.S. fight frustrated Bin Laden.[83] One former jihadist noted that, for Al Qaeda, "Khattab was a big threat," and he repeatedly refused Al Qaeda's attempts to co-opt him.[84] Khattab was living the legacy of Azzam, embracing Islam as a way of repelling foreign invaders.[85] Captured correspondence would reveal that Khattab and Bin Laden disagreed strongly over where to focus the energy of jihadists. Khattab emphasized liberating Muslim lands from foreign occupiers like Russia and guerrilla war, not international terrorism. Al Qaeda's frustration grew even greater when the organization was driven from Afghanistan after 9/11 and Khattab refused its members sanctuary in Chechnya itself.[86] Yet while Khattab kept his distance from Bin Laden, Al Qaeda's efforts to help the broader jihadist movement still had an impact. In Afghanistan, Al Qaeda financed and trained Arabs and other volunteers, perhaps including some Chechens, who would later fight in Chechnya.[87]

Khattab seemed like a winner on the battlefield, but his attacks and other violence in Chechnya played into the hands of hardliners in Moscow. Russia demanded the Chechen government hand over the perpetrators of cross-border attacks, but Maskhadov did not, and could not, comply with this demand. Moscow dragged its feet on negotiations and rejected outright independence, while Russian military and intelligence officials began preparing for another war. Khattab and the foreign fighters would help Moscow justify this war, and in the end, they would destroy the very independence of the Chechen state they came to save.

CHAPTER 6 | Hubris and Nemesis: The Chechen Foreign Fighters' Overreach

K HATTAB AND BASAEV wanted to do more than save Chechnya: they wanted to liberate the entire Caucasus region. For both, this goal was nothing new. Basaev had already fought for the nearby Abkhaz against Christian Georgia, while Khattab had fought in Tajikistan and Afghanistan. It was Dagestan, however, that was next on the list. Dagestan and Chechnya share historical and cultural ties. Like Chechnya, Dagestan is majority-Muslim but primarily Sufi. Also, like Chechnya, many of Dagestan's people historically resented the Russians, though not as much as their Chechen neighbors did.

Khattab had gained followers in neighboring Dagestan as well as Chechnya, and he even married a seventeen-year-old Dagestani girl.[1] In addition to the raid he led in 1997, in 1998 he and Basaev convened the Congress of the Chechen and Dagestani People (the Congress) to unite the two regions under the flag of Islam. Hundreds of Dagestanis were training in Khattab's camps in Chechnya, and Khattab and Basaev established an Islamic International Peacekeeping Brigade composed of foreign fighters, Chechens, and especially Dagestanis.

Basaev, for his part, wanted to become the Imam of Chechnya and Dagestan, as Imam Shamil had been in the past.[2] He sought "the removal of all Russian presence from the Caucasus." The Dagestan issue also played into internal politics. For Basaev, the Dagestan issue was a way of separating himself from Maskhadov's negotiations with Russia. Maskhadov even warned Russia about the risk of attacks into Dagestan by Basaev and other radicals.[3]

Several villages in Dagestan, including the one from which Khattab's wife hailed, declared they were creating an embryonic Islamic state where Islamic law would be enforced and women would wear a full veil (alien to the region's traditional Sufi teachings). Makeshift border posts separated these villages from the rest of Dagestan. One Sufi leader recounted that, at first, the Salafis tried to sway locals through money and preaching, "but by 1999, they were saying, 'Join us or we'll cut your head off.'"[4] Presaging this trend, in August 1998, Salafis murdered the Sufi mufti of Dagestan.

The so-called Congress cheered on radicals in Dagestan who defied Moscow, and Khattab at first sent them weapons and then fighters. Russia, in turn, surrounded the villages with troops, clearly indicating its intentions to subdue them. Basaev and Khattab, who had received religious rulings from clerics in Pakistan and Saudi Arabia in support of military action (as well as a hefty $25 million in donations), led hundreds of fighters across the border to the enclave, supposedly to protect it from world Zionism (which, of course, was linked to Russia and apparently took a deep interest in Dagestan). They conquered over thirty more villages, proclaimed the Islamic State of Dagestan, and declared war on Russia. "The mujahedin will force Russia to leave Dagestan," Basaev declared. He also claimed that locals welcomed him and that in early fighting with Russian forces his forces shot down helicopters, destroyed armored vehicles, and in other ways proved to be victorious.[5]

Almost immediately, Russia struck back—again brutally. Even worse for Khattab, many Dagestani peasants rallied to Russia, rejecting the Salafis' alien teachings and predilection for war. Russian forces expelled Khattab and his followers in a matter of days, with the nationalities of the dead consisting of fourteen Chechens, eight Dagestanis, five Arabs, three Turks, two Uzbeks, and two Ingush, reflecting the multinational nature of Khattab's forces.[6] A former jihadist would later describe the Dagestan effort as "a complete failure."[7]

Because this move would prove so disastrous to Chechnya, Khattab later went to great lengths to justify his actions in Dagestan. Russian generals, he pointed out, openly told Chechens that "we'll be back," and constant assassinations, flyovers, and support for the anti-Islamist forces made Russia's intentions clear. "Are we supposed to wait for Russia to come and annihilate us?" he asked.[8] Indeed, he argued that his fighters' presence in Dagestan was a reaction to Russia's aggression. Many in Russia certainly were eager for renewed war, but Khattab's own responsibility is considerable.

Far worse than being pushed out of Dagestan, Khattab gave Russia a pretext to again invade and occupy Chechnya itself. The Yeltsin government initially intervened reluctantly, but by early 2000, a new leader, Vladimir Putin, had taken power. The once-obscure Putin seized on the war to rally Russians under his banner, promising a return to law and order and a restoration of respect for Russia's might. Russia's renewed military campaign reversed the losses of the first war and, over time, succeeded to the point where it was able to install a brutal and corrupt Russian proxy government to rule Chechnya. Both to justify the war at home and to gain victory in Chechnya, Russia exploited the presence of foreign fighters, using their zeal to gain support for crushing Chechen separatism in general.

At first, however, the renewal of violence led most Chechens to embrace the rebels and reject negotiations. Even Maskhadov, who had tried to control the radicals and placate Moscow, called for holy war. This turn of events gave Moscow the war it wanted—against "terrorists" and jihadists rather than oppressed nationalists—but made peace impossible.

Again, Chechnya suffered. Tens of thousands, and perhaps even more, Chechen civilians died directly from shelling, bombing, and other forms of war or indirectly from starvation and disease. Russia used artillery, cluster bombs, and fuel air explosives to attack rebel positions, happily pulverizing the city if it meant the rebels died in its ruins. Virtually every building suffered damage, and one reporter conjured up an image of Berlin in 1945.[9] The United Nations in 2003 would declare Grozny the most destroyed city in the world.

As Khattab had hoped, money from abroad poured in, particularly from donors in Saudi Arabia and other Gulf states. Estimates vary widely, but most agree the foreign money was considerable. From 1997 through 2002 the United States estimated that foreigners contributed around $100 million to Chechnya (Russia claims much more).[10] The foreign money came from militant groups in Pakistan and sympathetic donors and charities in the Gulf, not from governments.[11]

As the war reignited, fresh recruits joined either in small groups or as individuals. Volunteers came from Algeria, Palestine, Lebanon, and other lands.[12] Again, senior Saudi religious leaders issued decrees declaring the war to be a legitimate jihad. In addition, a relatively new technology, satellite television, meant that the destruction and bloodshed were beamed into the Kingdom, horrifying Saudis and raising awareness there.[13] Over half the Arab volunteers were from Saudi Arabia. Almost all these recruits sought to fight under Khattab, attracted by his star power.

The new war fit the foreign fighters' modus operandi, which stressed guerrilla war over conventional conflict. They used a mix of car bombs, kidnappings, suicide attacks, ambushes, raids, and other indirect methods to hit the Russians. Their tactics included fading into the mountains or trying to blend among the people to hide. The Chechens did the bulk of the fighting, but foreigners played vital roles. As a Russian military spokesman argued, "The Arabs are the specialists, they are the experts in mines and communications."[14]

What began as a secular struggle for an independent Chechnya morphed into a regional jihad. The foreigners sought to create a state under Islamic law and use Chechnya as a launching pad for further expansion. At the struggle became fiercer and the rebels lost ground, more Chechen leaders embraced Basaev's calls for independence of the entire Caucasus (not just Chechnya) in an attempt to unify and inspire the overall resistance.[15] Over time, Dagestan and other neighboring areas would become the center of conflict.

Suicide bombers took the war to Russia, and other attacks targeted civilians, often justifying these actions as a response to Russian brutality against Chechen civilians. In 2002, around forty Chechen militants acting on Basaev's orders seized the Dubrovka Theater in Moscow, taking almost a thousand hostages. Over a hundred died when Russian forces used an incapacitating gas in an attempt to render everyone unconscious. In 2004, two female Chechen terrorists blew themselves up on two passenger airplanes going to Volgograd and Sochi, killing eighty people.[16] That same year, Chechen and Ingush terrorists working under Basaev's leadership seized a school and took over a thousand hostages (including almost eight hundred children) in the town of Beslan.[17] Russian security forces stormed the school, using tanks and other heavy weapons. Over three hundred people, including almost two hundred children, died. Although more moderate leaders like Maskhadov denounced the attacks, Putin dismissed such denunciations as rhetoric, lumping together Maskhadov and radicals like Basaev. In all these cases, Russia used the outrages to justify its war and to strengthen the government's authority in Russia itself.

Russia Exploits the Foreign Fighters' Presence

From the start of the second Chechen war, Russian leaders exploited terrorism to justify intervention to Russians embittered by misadventures in Afghanistan in the 1980s and the first Chechen war. In September 1999, a series of explosions devastated four apartment blocks in Buynaksk, Moscow, and Volgodonsk, killing almost three hundred and wounding more than a thousand more. The sudden and unexpected violence in metropolitan Russia panicked and terrified the public. Before any investigations could even get underway, much less conclude, Putin immediately blamed Chechen terrorists.[18] The Russian public eagerly welcomed Putin's firm leadership and promises of harsh retaliation after such a traumatic experience. The bombings transformed the politics of war: instead of an obscure conflict in a peripheral, backward region, the conflict was now an assault on the Russian people in their homes. Khattab himself was singled out for blame without much evidence. In response, he and Basaev denied responsibility, claiming (rather dubiously) their fighters opposed killing innocent civilians.[19]

Although conspiracy theories are common regarding terrorism and the justification for war, this one may be true: the Russian government (or some part of the state apparatus, probably linked to Putin) may have deliberately bombed the apartment buildings to blame it on Chechens and create a pretext for another war. The most damning evidence took place in the town of Ryazan. A resident of a city apartment building noticed suspicious men carrying sacks into the building's basement and notified the local police. When the police arrived, the men had already left, but they discovered the sacks left behind, labeled as sugar, contained large quantities of the military-grade explosive RX/hexogen (the same used in the other bombings) set to detonate early the following morning (the same time as the other bombings). Later that evening, a local telephone employee overheard a suspicious conversation related to the bombing that the police traced to the local Russian intelligence office. The intelligence office began furiously denying everything before claiming it was merely involved in a training mission, which only contributed to the general mistrust and appearance of a cover-up. Almost immediately, many people, including serious media institutions, began to question the official story.[20] After the successful bombings, authorities demolished the crime scene quickly, and there was no thorough, transparent inquiry following the event. Later revelations found that a nearby special service military base had stored kilograms of the explosives used in bags labeled as "sugar."[21]

As the decision to blame Khattab for the bombings suggests, Russia also exploited foreign fighters in its propaganda. In the first war, when less than a hundred Arabs fought on behalf of the Chechens, Russia claimed there were six thousand.[22] As the second war went on, Russia painted all Chechen separatists with a jihadist brush. Although Chechen jihadists thought terrorism would shock Russians into withdrawing, Russia instead doubled down, with terrorism justifying the intervention and bolstering Putin's popularity rather than fostering support for a withdrawal.[23]

Russia's attempt to depict all Chechens as terrorists became far more successful after 9/11, when Moscow was able to link its fight to the U.S. "war on terror." Just as third world countries cloaked themselves in anticommunism to fight local rebels during the Cold War, now countries used counterterrorism to gain U.S. support. Those whom Russia used to label "Chechen bandits" now became "international terrorists," directed and funded by Bin Laden and Al Qaeda. (They also tried to link the Chechen rebels to Boris Berezovskiy, a Russian oligarch whom Putin deemed an enemy.[24]) Talking to moderate leaders, Russian officials argued, was like having "talks with Mullah Omar," the Taliban leader.[25] Worldwide efforts to crack down on terrorist financing also deprived Chechen foreign fighters of important sources of revenue.[26]

The confusing nature of Al Qaeda made it easier to conflate the Chechen cause and Bin Laden's organization. Khattab and Bin Laden had long been respectful rivals, and Khattab never embraced Bin Laden's focus on the United States and the West. However, the overlapping networks of training camps, funding, and effective Russian counterintelligence—Russian spies planted reports of a Chechen presence within Al Qaeda—led the United States to lump them together. As the scholars Cerwyn Moore and Paul Tumelty point out, "The legend of the Chechen foreign fighter was born."[27]

In addition to using foreign fighters to discredit the Chechens internationally, Moscow also exploited their presence within Chechnya itself. Although Khattab himself called for working with locals, many of the foreign fighters he attracted were far more brutal and alienated many of the locals they came to save. In addition to their hostility toward the Sufi beliefs that predominated in Chechnya, the foreigners called for banning music, replacing local traditional dress with more modest clothing, and applying extreme corporal punishment (such as cutting off the fingers of those who drank alcohol). Not surprisingly, this angered many Chechens. As one Chechen scholar pointed out, "If we did not become Russian after 70 years of Soviet rule, we are not about to become Arab today."[28]

Even when the locals may have sympathized with the more extremist rebels, fear of Russia made them reluctant to embrace the foreigners who were magnets for Russian counterattacks. They often asked them to leave the village, but the foreign fighters would refuse.[29] One Russian intelligence official claimed that "Chechen villagers refuse to bury the foreigners in their cemetery."[30]

In 2000, taking advantage of the hostility the foreigners displayed toward Sufis, Moscow chose Akhmad Kadyrov to administer Chechnya. Kadyrov, once the Sufi mufti of Chechnya, was hardly an obvious choice for Moscow: he had declared jihad against the Russians during the first war. Now, however, he argued it was "they, or we" when it came to the Salafis.[31] Many ordinary Sufis, no friends of Russia but repelled by the jihadists' brutality, began to side with the pro-Russian government.[32] The hostility was mutual. A local Islamic court "tried" Kadyrov in absentia and sentenced him to death; the sentence would be carried out in May 2004, when a bomb exploded during a military parade he attended.[33] Basaev claimed credit for the killing. Kadyrov's son Ramzan took his place and remains in power to this day, drawing on Russian government support and using a mix of assassination, terror, and corruption to stay in power.

The Kadyrov regime also raised local militias. These militias, backed by several thousand Russian troops and paramilitary forces, bore the brunt of the day-to-day fighting, limiting the direct burden on Russia.[34] Because these militias often had better knowledge of local communities and could identify the fighters, and because the risk of opposition forces defecting to the militias was high, Chechen rebels often prioritized targeting them, thus reducing Russian casualties and taking further pressure off the Putin government.[35]

Jihad took its toll on Khattab, as his family, particularly his mother, pleaded for him to return home. He would later warn fellow jihadis that "the biggest obstacle that stands between us and jihad is family," noting that "every time I talk to my mother on the phone, she asks me: 'when will you return home my son?'" But if he and others listened to these pleas, he warned, "Who would carry on this burden?"[36]

Russian intelligence would exploit this filial loyalty when they eventually caught up with Khattab in 2002 after several failed operations. While there has never been (and likely never will be) a verified description of Khattab's assassination, Russian authorities and the Russian media have implicitly confirmed the account released by Khattab's fellow foreign fighters. Russian intelligence allegedly turned or planted a double agent as a courier within Khattab's inner circle, a man who may have felt betrayed by Khattab's refusal to give sanctuary to fleeing Al Qaeda members.[37] The courier arrived from Baku to deliver a letter supposedly from Khattab's mother that was laden with poison (perhaps sarin)—"the weapon of treachery and treason," his supporters would note, because Russia could not kill him with bombers and tanks.[38] The poison made Khattab nauseated and dizzy, and within a few hours he was dead.[39] According to the Russian newspaper *Argumenty i Fakty* (Arguments and Facts), the courier's body was later discovered, bound, in the outskirts of Baku. He was apparently shot (with five bullets to the head) on the personal order of Basaev.[40]

Chechnya after Khattab

In the years after Khattab's death, the tide in Chechnya steadily turned in Moscow's favor, and today, Russian domination is strong. Russia killed not only Khattab but also, in the years that followed, his successor, the Saudi Abu Walid al-Ghamidi, the interim leader Abu Qutaybah, and other key figures.[41] Chechnya became a graveyard for foreign fighters, and their aggressiveness and zealotry proved their own undoing along with that of their Chechen allies. Russia also hunted down opponents who had fled overseas. In 2004, a car bomb exploded in Qatar, killing former Chechen President Zelimkhan Yandarbiyev. These assassinations created a leadership crisis, as the foreigners lacked enough experienced and respected commanders to replace the fallen.

In July 2006, it was Basaev's turn. Basaev was with a convoy transporting explosives and mines in neighboring Ingushetia, when at some point a mine exploded. The Russian authorities claimed their agents either booby-trapped or detonated the mine, while the Chechens claimed it was simply an accident.[42] Regardless, the leading Chechen jihadist was dead, removing a key Chechen advocate of the foreigners. More mainstream rebels also fell one by one. Despite recently declaring a ceasefire and hoping to restart negotiations, in March 2005, Maskhadov died in a firefight in Tolstoy-Yurt—apparently shot by his nephew after Maskhadov was wounded and refused to be captured alive. Just over a year later, Russian and pro-Russian Chechen troops killed his successor, Abdul-Khalim Sadulayev, in another firefight. Kadyrov taunted that an informer betrayed Sadulayev for a dose of heroin.[43] The even more radical Doku Umarov became the dominant jihadist figure as these more mainstream leaders fell, declaring the struggle a regional one involving all the Caucasus, not just Chechnya.

At the recruit level, Arab and Turkish jihadists died by the dozens while defending Grozny and engaging in other battles.[44] Reliable mortality rates do not exist, but the scholar Thomas Hegghammer estimates a death rate of potentially 90 percent.[45] With death tolls like this, it is not surprising that the "alumni" of Chechnya who are admired by their fellow jihadists are few in number.[46]

Russia also further tightened border security. The route through Georgia, always tricky, became even harder as the United States joined Russia in demanding that Tbilisi crack down on any jihadist presence in its country. Many would-be jihadists tried, but failed, to join the fray.[47]

The Russian puppet Kadyrov government in Chechnya also implemented an amnesty program immediately following Basaev's death in 2006. Exact numbers are difficult to determine given the Russian propaganda to promote fighter defection, but hundreds of Chechen separatist fighters abandoned the struggle. Some even joined pro-Kadyrov militias. There had been previous unsuccessful amnesty programs, but the rebels struggled to recover from the leadership void after the deaths of prominent commanders like Basaev and Maskhadov, prompting many to join Kadyrov's militia.[48] The amnesty, however, did not include foreign fighters.

Attacks in Chechnya itself steadily fell. Chechnya suffered around a hundred attacks per year in 2000 and 2001. After that peak, the numbers plummeted to less than fifteen in 2004 and even fewer by the end of the decade and up to the present.[49] Yet even as traditional attacks decreased, suicide bombing became a problem. Suicide bombings, a tactic imported by the foreign fighters into Chechnya, began in Chechnya in 2000 and peaked in the 2003–2004 period, after Khattab's death, which allowed his successors to introduce more radical tactics.[50] In 2010, suicide bombers detonated bombs on Moscow's rail system during rush hour, killing thirty-nine people; in 2011, a suicide attacker killed thirty-five people at Moscow airport. Followers of Umarov orchestrated suicide bombings in Volgograd in 2013 that killed thirty-four people. Suicide bombing, hostage taking, and other terrorist tactics enabled the Chechen rebels to escape the deadly attrition battles they faced with Russian forces. The hope was to shock Russia into abandoning its support for Chechnya.[51] In some ways, however, terrorism was also a sign of desperation, showing that the rebels had lost on the traditional battlefield.[52]

As Russia steadily crushed the Chechen resistance, Arab donors and other supporters saw it as "folly," putting their money toward other causes.[53] Financial problems became even worse after 9/11, when the Saudis began a crackdown on jihadist financing, and this crackdown became far more intense after 2003, when Al Qaeda began attacking the kingdom itself.[54]

The 2003 Iraq war also proved a blow to the Chechen cause. The war generated outrage around the Muslim world. Like fighting the Russians in Chechnya, fighting the United States in Iraq had broad popular support. But unlike Chechnya, it was relatively easy to get to Iraq. Chechnya's high mortality rate and general image of failure scared off volunteers, while conflict in Iraq seemed newer and more promising.[55] Khattab's successor complained that his money was being diverted.[56] A decade later, the Syria conflict would play a similar role in siphoning off potential supporters from Chechnya.[57]

With Khattab's death, the decline in local support, and money drying up, the foreign fighters became more extreme and even less successful. In 2007, insurgents declared the establishment of the Imarat Kavkaz, the Caucasus Emirate, a grandiose claim for what was really an alliance of local jihadist groups.[58] The foreigners' new leaders abandoned Khattab's reluctance to work with Al Qaeda, and they duly called for striking the United States among other targets. These fighters wanted to exploit Al Qaeda's fundraising networks and those of Abu Musab al-Zarqawi, the fountainhead of jihad in Iraq who disseminated messages embracing the conflict in Chechnya where Zarqawi himself had once wanted to fight. They pushed an Al Qaeda–like global agenda, leading to a split with other jihadists who wanted to focus more on the region. Russia's arrests and killing of jihadist leaders continued without respite. In 2013, Russian special forces killed Umarov with a poisoned letter. His successor died a year later, and the next in line followed shortly.[59]

The brutal Russian counterinsurgency drove thousands of Chechens and their local Caucasian allies to flee Chechnya itself. As attacks in Chechnya itself plunged after 2003, they steadily grew in Dagestan and Ingushetia, with both regions suffering dozens of attacks each year as the decade wore on. Almost a thousand refugees fled to nearby Georgia—in particular, to the Pankisi Gorge area about 40 miles south of Chechnya and Ingushetia, from where the jihadis would launch guerrilla raids.[60] Arab volunteers set up charities there, building mosques and proselytizing while allowing recruiters access to the refugees.[61] In addition, Al Qaeda members fleeing Afghanistan but unable to enter Chechnya due to Khattab's opposition had also set up shop there, producing a volatile combination.[62]

Georgia, under U.S. pressure due to fears that the Pankisi Gorge would become a new Al Qaeda base, eventually cracked down, but many foreign jihadis escaped the dragnet. As a result, Russia continued to aggressively target these areas. Moscow, often working via Kadyrov and other local allies, kept a heavy hand on Chechnya. Russian forces proved particularly aggressive in the lead-up to the 2014 Sochi Winter Olympics, and many local groups sought a haven outside the region, seeing even Syria as a place of relative safety. To ensure the Olympics went smoothly, Russia even provided radicals in the Caucasus with passports, plane tickets, and assistance in their transit to Turkey, knowing from there many would go to Syria.[63] (This strategy worked and the games went off without violence.) The links that brought individuals from the Middle East to the Caucasus now were used to bring fighters from the Caucasus to the Arab world.[64]

As Russia killed jihadist leaders in Chechnya, the always-divided movement fractured further, and many joined the Islamic State and its self-declared Caucasus Province. Thousands of volunteers from the Caucasus fought in Syria for jihadist groups there, especially the Islamic State. The label "Shishani" (Chechen) is used by volunteers from the Caucasus in general, and many of those fighting are not from Chechnya but rather from the neighboring Muslim republics, such as Dagestan, Ingushetia, and even parts of Georgia. The most famous "Chechen" was the Georgian Omar al-Shishani, a veteran of the 2008 Russo-Georgian War. Shishani, who traveled to Syria in 2012, led hundreds of fellow Caucasians in service of the Islamic State and became one of its top commanders before dying in a U.S. airstrike.[65] Russia fears renewed violence if these battle-hardened Caucasian veterans are able to return home.[66]

Chechnya today is one of the most brutal and repressive places on earth. Accurate information is difficult to obtain, however, as the regime and its allies target human rights activists and journalists.[67] Nonetheless, it is clear that Chechen and Russian security forces harass, illegally detain, torture, and disappear any suspected opposition. The pervasive and ruthless Chechen security forces have successfully crushed the efforts to revive the separatist struggle. The price is fear, misery, and resentment. Terrorism, moreover, has not gone away. In 2018, the Islamic State claimed seven attacks in Chechnya, Dagestan, and other parts of Russia. The Islamic State hit not only police targets but also Sufi Muslim and Christian holy sites.[68]

The diaspora of Caucasian fighters to Syria and the regionalization of the Chechen conflict demonstrate the success and failure of Khattab and his fellow Arab jihadists. Khattab deserves credit for transforming a secular, nationalist rebellion into a jihadist fight. Khattab's fight, however, devastated Chechnya and the Chechen independence movement. As a result, the people he claimed to champion have suffered years of war and constant dictatorship.

CHAPTER 7 | The Slaughterer: Abu-Musab al-Zarqawi and the Ascendant Iraqi Jihad (2003–2006)

AHMAD FADEL AL-NAZAL al-Khalayleh, the man who would become known as Abu Musab al-Zarqawi, seemed destined to be forgotten. Yet he ranks with Azzam, Khattab, and Bin Laden—and possibly even above them—on the list of the most important jihadists of the modern era. For it was Zarqawi's vision of horrific violence directed at his fellow Muslims that would come to define the jihadist movement and inspire thousands of foreign fighters around the world.

Born poor in the impoverished city of Zarqa in Jordan, Zarqawi was a small-time thug and pimp who struggled with alcoholism. During one of his spells of freedom, his mother enrolled him in religion classes in a local mosque. Afghan commander Abdul Rasul Sayyaf (Saudi Arabia and Bin Laden's preferred warlord) visited the mosque to raise money and recruit for the anti-Soviet struggle, and he left with one more convert. Here, in Zarqawi's eyes, was a man whose deeds matched his preaching. In 1989, at the age of twenty-three, Zarqawi left Jordan for Afghanistan to join the fight against the Soviet Union, initially staying in a facility that Azzam and Bin Laden had established through the Services Bureau. Zarqawi arrived too late to fight the Soviets, but he did join the mujahedin's battles against the forces of the Communist Afghan regime that Moscow continued to prop up after its departure. Zarqawi also trained at the Sada Camp that Azzam established in the mid-1980s.[1] To mark his new identity, he took the name "the Stranger." He drew on a saying of the Prophet Mohammad that "Islam began as a stranger," which referred to how the first Muslims were essentially foreigners because they were not welcomed in the world of unbelievers. Jihadists would often portray themselves as similar "strangers." Over time, he took on the name "Zarqawi" from his hometown in Jordan, a common jihadist move.

Afghanistan transformed Zarqawi. One former comrade claimed, "Zarqawi arrived in Afghanistan as a zero," but he left "with ambitions and dreams: to carry the ideology of jihad." Zarqawi did not immediately join Al Qaeda or engage with senior Al Qaeda members; rather, he met jihadis from Syria and Lebanon,[2] areas where Al Qaeda was weak.

In Afghanistan, Zarqawi also met fellow Jordanian Abu Muhammad al-Maqdisi, who would emerge as one of the most influential theologians of jihad. Maqdisi called on Muslims to shun those not sufficiently pious, declared that the Saudi government was apostate, and rejected democracy as placing man's teaching above God's law. In contrast to Azzam, who emphasized defending Muslim lands from non-Muslims, and Bin Laden, who saw the West as the root of the region's problems, Maqdisi argued that Muslims should oppose leaders who did not enforce the true version (i.e., the jihadist interpretation) of Islamic law.[3] Thus Saudi Arabia was illegitimate, as was the Jordanian regime; Western states were deviant and enemies, but they were a lesser concern.

Zarqawi and Maqdisi returned to Jordan in 1993 and started a militant group, with Maqdisi providing inspiration and Zarqawi contributing the muscle. Their dreams were quickly dashed, however, when Jordanian intelligence, one of the best services in the Middle East, discovered their plans and imprisoned them.

Yet the transformation that began in Afghanistan continued and even accelerated in prison. In Jordan, like in Afghanistan, France, Yemen, and other countries, prison would prove a boon for jihadists, giving them a venue to proselytize and recruit among a pool of violent young males, making them more dangerous upon release. Zarqawi gave a brazen defense of jihad in court, claiming that he could only be judged under God's law and that the judge who relied on man-made law was guilty of "unbelief" and "idolatry."[4] In prison, Zarqawi's small group mixed with other small jihadist groups, forming a broader network. He tried to rally his comrades to oppose the Jordanian regime, mixing radical beliefs with a street thug's instinct for brutally enforcing his will. Zarqawi claims he was tortured there, further hardening him against the regime. He soon emerged as the leader of the jihadists in prison, the man of action eclipsing the cerebral Maqdisi. In 1999, a new king, Abdullah, took the throne in Jordan and ordered a general amnesty to celebrate his ascension.

Zarqawi was freed, though his zealotry remained undiminished. He founded the Organization of Monotheism and Jihad but quickly fled to Pakistan and then, again, to Afghanistan. Like so many foreign fighters at the time, he aspired to go to Chechnya.[5]

Zarqawi never made it to Chechnya, but in Afghanistan he did meet and gain the backing of another foreign fighter, Osama Bin Laden. The scion of one of the Arab world's richest families and the street thug didn't hit it off. According to some reports, Bin Laden, whose own mother and first wife may have been Alawi (a Shiite sect that many Sunnis and even other Shiites question as truly Muslim and that extremists like Zarqawi condemn as heretics or outright pagans),[6] was particularly put off by Zarqawi's sectarianism: "Shiites should be executed," Zarqawi declared when they met. Bin Laden nevertheless put aside sentiment and acted as a smart venture capitalist, giving Zarqawi seed money to set up his own camp in Afghanistan that would develop the jihadist presence in Jordan, Syria, Turkey, Lebanon, and elsewhere in the so-called Levant where Al Qaeda was weak. The networks formed among these jihadists would show up again and again in the years to come. One of Bin Laden's advisers recalled that the informal alliance with Zarqawi's Organization of Monotheism and Jihad was necessary because Al Qaeda wanted a presence near Israel, "since the Palestinian question is the bleeding heart of the nation."[7] Zarqawi also spread the tendrils of his network to Europe.[8] In addition, supporting Zarqawi enabled Bin Laden to undermine a rival jihadist from Syria who wanted to use the foreign fighters from that area exclusively to help the Taliban and otherwise weaken Al Qaeda's leadership.[9]

Zarqawi's horizon broadened after his return to Afghanistan, and he came to learn about other causes beyond Jordan and Chechnya.[10] Zarqawi, however, did not follow Al Qaeda's teachings. He embraced the views of Sheikh Abu Abdallah al-Muhajir, an extremist theologian even by jihadist standards. Abu Abdallah had once refused to allow Bin Laden into his training camp in Afghanistan because he saw him as too lax. He also argued that the Taliban were too permissive and thus not deserving of loyalty.[11] Of Abu Abdallah's teachings, one book, known as *The Jurisprudence of Blood*, argued that necessity trumped all else; if an attacker wanted to die for the right reason, suicide bombings, beheadings, and other horrific tactics all could be justified.[12]

At first, Zarqawi prospered. Crackdowns in Lebanon and Syria led jihadists there to flee, with some going to his camp in Afghanistan. Perhaps a hundred jihadists trained in his Herat Camp, and he encouraged them to marry family members of other fighters in order to forge tighter bonds. Zarqawi also made his peace with the Taliban, working with them to supervise the entry of foreigners into Afghanistan. Although Zarqawi himself remained apart from

Al Qaeda, he did send some of his men for additional training in Al Qaeda camps. Finally, Zarqawi also began establishing nodes of a global network with cells in Turkey and Germany.[13]

However, as for so many jihadists, the 9/11 attacks seemed like a disaster. The U.S. response led to the fall of the Taliban government and the routing of jihadist forces in Afghanistan. Zarqawi fought but eventually fled, landing first in Iran. Iran probably saw Zarqawi as a small fish and tolerated him because he was anti-Taliban and eager to go to Iraq and fight against the U.S. invaders, who were broadcasting their plans to overthrow Saddam and hinting that Iran might be next.[14] Jihadists, for their part, saw Iran as an alternative to Pakistan for transiting to and from Afghanistan and recognized that "some virtuous people in Iran" had mutual interests with Al Qaeda, in the words of one senior Al Qaeda member.[15]

Before the U.S. invasion in 2003, Zarqawi went to Iraq to prepare for the impending entrance of U.S. forces. The Organization of Monotheism and Jihad set up shop in a haven outside Saddam's control in the Kurdish north that was run by a fellow Jordanian who knew Zarqawi from Afghanistan and who had also intended to fight in Chechnya, but instead ended up in Iraqi Kurdistan.[16] Several hundred jihadists set up a mini-Islamic state in the north, where they forced women to be veiled, prohibited music, and beheaded prisoners. They even had a website, a novel feat for a terrorist group at the time, though most of their propaganda was still distributed via CDs.

Zarqawi also built a regional network, going to Damascus, to Palestinian camps in Lebanon, and even back to Jordan to secretly attend his beloved mother's funeral and plan attacks.[17] The combination of Zarqawi's charisma and his extensive contacts with jihadists across Jordan and Syria as well as with the Al Qaeda leadership, which gave him access to fundraising and recruiting networks globally, made him a natural leader. In addition, the temporary collapse after 9/11 of the Al Qaeda core and the fall of the Taliban enabled independent jihadists like Zarqawi to play a greater role.[18]

The 2003 U.S. invasion and occupation of Iraq was a textbook case of how a foreign power can foster a hostile insurgency. Iraq under Saddam Hussein was a divided society with the country's Sunni Arab minority on top, dominating the government and military forces. The toppling of Saddam and introduction of democracy reversed this hierarchy, putting the country's Shiite Muslim majority in the strongest position, much to the Sunnis' chagrin. The United States' missteps in administering Iraq—notably massive de-Baathification and the disbanding of the Iraqi military—meant that many Sunnis were expelled from Iraq's key institutions. In addition, the invasion put tens of thousands of young men on the streets who were unemployed, angry, and trained in violence.

Although many opposition groups were secular nationalists or organized along tribal lines, Saddam had pushed Islam as a way to shore up his legitimacy in the 1990s. He bombarded Iraqis with pictures of himself praying or otherwise pretending to embrace his faith. He also gave a small bit of freedom to various religious organizations as long as they remained loyal to the regime. Many Sunni Iraqis found some overlap with the jihadists ideologically, and some Sunni religious leaders already had small organizations they could build out further. The United States' efforts to stop smuggling, impose a new political system, and otherwise change society infuriated tribal leaders. This approach was, according to one Al Qaeda figure, "a huge mistake out of ignorance." In the jihadists' eyes, the U.S. approach encouraged Iraqis to give "tens of thousands of their sons to carry out jihad against the Americans."[19] American forces, too few in number and without a plan, did not provide law and order. Criminals and local fighters quickly looted Saddam's massive arms depots (the U.S. military estimated one million tons of arms and ammunition were stockpiled and free for the taking), giving them a seemingly endless supply of weapons and explosives.[20] The result, as Bin Laden argued in his call for Muslims to fight, was "a rare and golden opportunity to make America bleed in Iraq."[21]

Sowing the Wind in Iraq

Zarqawi would till this fertile ground and make his name fighting U.S. forces. He and his followers conducted hundreds of attacks on Iraqi government, Shiite Muslim, American, and other targets, causing unrest and then all-out civil war between Iraq's Sunnis and Shiites and leading to the deaths of well over a hundred thousand Iraqis.

Even before U.S. troops entered Iraq, Zarqawi's Organization of Monotheism and Jihad had built networks in the country and incorporated Iraqis into his ranks, though most of his group remained composed of foreigners. Zarqawi believed that it would be easier to operate in Iraq against Americans than against the hated regime of Saddam Hussein, as the United States, unlike Saddam, would not have informers in every house. He was even more right than he anticipated. The United States did not exercise totalitarian control as Saddam's regime had done, and U.S. intelligence initially focused on finding Iraq's weapons of mass destruction programs, not on fighting the burgeoning insurgency.[22]

Many of the initial insurgents had served in Iraq's army or paramilitary forces, and this experience complemented that of the foreign jihadists who had learned their craft in Bosnia or Afghanistan. These foreigners served as "midwives of the jihadi movement in Iraq," as Truls Tønnessen, one of the premier analysts of the Iraqi jihadist movement, put it.[23]

The Afghan war veterans tried to replicate what they had done in Afghanistan. They established a training camp called the "Lion's Den," echoing the name of Bin Laden's famous camp at Jaji. Recruits would often begin the day with prayer and then mix exercise and weapons training with lectures on Islamic law and memorizing the Quran. Iraqis and new recruits drew on the wisdom of Afghan veterans; one taught them "the science of making car-bombs" that proved vital for some of their most important initial attacks.[24] And as in Afghanistan, recruits from North Africa, Saudi Arabia, France, and other foreign countries bonded with local Iraqis and with one another. They also began to spread the war to Iraq's neighbors. In 2003, bombings rocked Istanbul, reportedly tied to the fighters Zarqawi had trained during his time in Afghanistan.[25]

Zarqawi had learned early that life in an underground terrorist group is hard, and Iraq was no exception. Zarqawi noted that, unlike Chechnya or Afghanistan, "The country has no mountains in which we can take refuge and no forests in whose thickets we can hide." The result was that "training the green newcomers [was] like wearing bonds and shackles."[26] In contrast to Afghanistan, where before 9/11 the Taliban's control ensured security for those in the training camps, in Iraq, U.S. and Iraqi government forces hunted the jihadists after Zarqawi's terrorism campaign got underway and the violence soared.[27] The Rawah Camp, the first in Iraq, was quickly bombed into oblivion two months after it was founded. As one of Zarqawi's lieutenants recalled, "We hid during the day and snuck around like rats at night . . . everyone felt a sense of total failure."[28] Zarqawi's group mostly avoided publicity at first, preferring to train its recruits and establish its networks by staying out of the spotlight.[29]

Jihadists learned to use small facilities with little infrastructure. Zarqawi even ordered that bomb-making classes be filmed so that knowledge could be transmitted if the instructor was killed. Much of the training was done indoors in safe houses in cities. Despite these efforts, many lessons could not be imparted because of the need to hide. For example, recruits learned to use a rocket-propelled grenade on paper, but they never practiced using one before battle itself. One expert speculated that training in safe houses put so much stress on indoctrination because more practical training was impossible.[30]

The City of Mosques

Zarqawi would test this training when Sunni opposition groups took over the Iraqi city of Fallujah in 2004. Fallujah, a city of several hundred thousand in central Iraq at the edge of the Sunni-populated Al Anbar province, had been a hotbed of opposition. Highly nationalistic and religious, Fallujah had earned the nickname "the city of mosques." Saddam had recruited heavily from the area for his elite forces, and although jihadists got most of the attention, the opposition consisted of a mix of Zarqawi-type jihadists and more nationalist rebels, including former military and Baathist members as well as poor Sunni men itching for a fight. They saw the U.S. invasion and subsequent occupation as a humiliation for Iraq, a view widely shared among Sunnis.[31]

The U.S.-backed Iraqi forces couldn't control the city. Right after the 2003 overthrow of Saddam, an anti-U.S. demonstration erupted in Fallujah that led to bloodshed between the mob and U.S. troops. Both sides blamed the other for starting it, but fifteen Iraqis were killed, including women and children. Multiple U.S. units quickly rotated through Fallujah, meaning that none of them developed close relations with the residents. Local preachers called for holy war against U.S. forces. Police "resigned in droves" because of jihadist attacks on police forces and facilities, one U.S. military adviser wrote.[32] On March 31, 2004, insurgents in Fallujah ambushed four American security contractors. After dragging them from the car, they stomped them to death, lit their bodies on fire, mutilated them, and then hanged them from a bridge over the Euphrates.[33] Arab media covered the attack and hangings, and images were broadcast around the world.

In the United States, political pressure to act was heavy. Conservative commentator Bill O'Reilly opined, "We should make the people of Fallujah bathe in their own blood."[34] President George W. Bush was barely less bellicose—"I want heads to roll," he declared.[35] The very name of the eventual operation, "Vigilant Resolve," indicated the U.S. desire to show how America would be tough in response to the outrage. The U.S. forces moved quickly, too quickly in hindsight, to try to retake the city. The Marine Corps commanders involved, including future national leaders such as then Brigadier General John Kelly and Major General James Mattis, sought to wait, knowing they had not built the necessary political support among moderate Sunnis and did not have enough intelligence on Fallujah or strong local allies.[36] They were ordered to go forward anyway.

Because the operation was rushed, the United States did not coordinate well with national or local Sunni officials who had been working with U.S. forces, making them seem weak or even like collaborators. In addition, there was not time to evacuate the city, virtually ensuring heavy civilian casualties as a result. Nor was the U.S. military in a gentle mood. General Ricardo Sanchez, who headed U.S. forces in Iraq, told his staff he didn't want "any fucking knock-before-search, touchy-feely stuff."[37]

Fallujah was a dream battlefield for those fighting the U.S. forces. The houses almost touched each other, and wrecks of old cars and heaps of garbage littered the narrow streets. Jihadists prepared ambushes, planted improvised bombs, and launched suicide attacks to repel the invaders. In the fierce firefights, hundreds of civilians died. Religious leaders called on Iraqis to defend the city in their sermons. Rather than fight their fellow Sunnis, one of the Iraqi battalions refused to deploy, and the other deserted. Although the two hundred or so foreigners in Fallujah initially comprised perhaps 10 percent of the total fighters, local Iraqis supported the foreign fighters, seeing them as defenders of the Sunni community. Various jihadist groups worked together against the United States, and Zarqawi's group steadily emerged as the dominant one. Outside Fallujah itself, the U.S. offensive and the significant civilian casualties it entailed convinced many hitherto fence-sitting Iraqis, Sunnis, and non-Sunnis that the United States was indeed a hostile occupying force.[38]

Insurgents had a field day in their propaganda. The Arab media exaggerated the civilian casualties, fed by insurgent disinformation. The satellite news station Al Jazeera showed images of dead babies spattered with blood and even used footage of civilian casualties from other battles, attributing it to Fallujah. Crying children talked of their dead parents. All this propaganda went unanswered. By the end of April, a whopping 89 percent of Iraqis saw the United States and its allies as an occupying force. The government's inability to stop Shia militias from killing Sunnis also increased Sunni support for insurgents.[39]

On May 1, 2004, U.S. forces withdrew, accepting a de facto truce in the area. Zarqawi's prestige soared, and the greater legitimacy gave him a more dominant position over the Sunni insurgency as a whole. General Sanchez later contended that Fallujah and the destructiveness of the U.S. offensive was the tipping point that pushed many Iraqi Sunnis into opposition.[40] In addition, as happened before in Afghanistan and Chechnya, the military victory of the jihadists made them more attractive, increasing their prestige and attracting new recruits. Making things worse, U.S. forces duly handed security off to Iraqi forces to put an Iraqi face on things. Much of the arms and equipment given to Iraqi forces to support their operations went directly to Zarqawi and other fighters.[41]

For several months, Zarqawi enjoyed a haven in Fallujah, and he made good use of it. New recruits flocked in (roughly two thousand in the first eighteen months), attracted by Zarqawi's bold persona, perceived U.S. atrocities, and the glory of fighting in Iraq.[42] In addition, they now believed they could win: fight hard and trust in God, and the Americans with all their technology would flee. The experienced trainers from the camps in Afghanistan trained a new generation in tactics like car bombing, and these new terrorists spread out across the country. The U.S. forces later found over twenty IED (improvised explosive device) factories in Fallujah.[43] Although locals pressed the jihadists to honor the truce for fear of renewed U.S. attacks, the jihadists ignored them and sent car bombs from Fallujah to Baghdad and other major cities.[44]

The foreign jihadists also tried to impose their version of Islam, killing locals who worked with the Iraqi regime, removing Sufi leaders, and otherwise fighting against what they described as the "bats of darkness" who deviated from Islam. They prohibited the sale of alcohol, shut down movie theaters, closed hairdressers, and harassed women who were not fully covered.[45]

Zarqawi's own fame skyrocketed as he spearheaded this resistance, and—in contrast to Azzam, Khattab, and Bin Laden—he glorified his own savagery. In May 2004, the jihadists released a video of Zarqawi beheading Nicholas Berg, an American radio repairman working as a contractor in Iraq, as U.S. forces departed Fallujah. Setting the standard for future jihadist executions, he dressed Berg in an orange jumpsuit, evoking the uniform of prisoners at Guantanamo Bay, and personally beheaded him with a large knife. He justified the execution as a response to the widely publicized U.S. abuse of prisoners at the Abu Ghraib prison in Iraq. Within twenty-four hours, almost half a million people downloaded the video. This mass viewership was achieved in a pre-YouTube and social media age, when mass viewership of online video was far rarer.

This public relations success led to a spate of kidnappings and beheadings of foreigners, and, taking after Zarqawi, an Al Qaeda faction in Saudi Arabia beheaded Paul Johnson, an American defense contractor working there, also dressing him in the now de rigueur orange jumpsuit.[46] Zarqawi videotaped subsequent beheadings of two Americans, a Brit, two Turks, a Bulgarian, an Egyptian, a South Korean, and a Japanese, which, along with other high-profile carnage and American outrage, cemented his reputation as "Sheikh of the Slaughters."[47] "Every Arab and Muslim who wished to go to Iraq for jihad wanted to join Al-Zarqawi and fight under his leadership," claimed one of his biographers.[48] Less prominently, but no less horribly, jihadists in Iraq also beheaded many Iraqis. Muslims from elsewhere in the Arab world and the West flocked to his banner. They often found Iraq more attractive and heroic than the grinding jihadist struggles in their own countries. Algerian jihadists, for example, flowed into Iraq, seeing the struggle there as more just and winnable than their own increasingly fruitless war against the Algerian government.[49]

Bin Laden's organization publicly embraced the resistance hero, who agreed to relabel his Organization of Monotheism and Jihad group as Al Qaeda in Iraq in 2004. One Al Qaeda leader claimed that this relationship gave Al Qaeda, still reeling from its post-9/11 losses, "a new sense of credibility" and allowed it to fight "every day and every hour." Zarqawi, in turn, got better access to Saudi Arabia and other Gulf states, increasing his recruits and fundraising as well as his overall status.[50] In private, however, Al Qaeda leaders chastised Zarqawi, calling for him to put aside his attacks on Shiitess and tone down the violence. Zawahiri argued that Afghanistan and Chechnya proved that jihadists did best when they focused on expelling infidel invaders while portraying the struggle as one of Islam against the unbelievers.[51] Yet Zarqawi ignored their pleas. His anti-Shiite sentiment was growing, and he even claimed publicly that Al Qaeda's leaders had blessed his sectarian approach.[52]

After the failure of the first battle in Fallujah, the U.S. military spent months planning and building up forces for the second assault. Unlike in the first battle, the coalition forces fully encircled the city, establishing checkpoints to control all traffic in or out, ordered all civilians to evacuate, and conducted weeks of air and artillery strikes against known insurgent positions. Finally, on November 8, U.S. forces assaulted the city, methodically clearing it house by house, block by block, in the hardest and bloodiest fighting of the war. After more than a month and a half, the city was secure, though largely destroyed, and at least a thousand insurgents were dead.[53] A few of the dead and captured were foreigners, but many of the insurgent leaders, including Zarqawi, had fled the city before the battle.[54] Battles like Fallujah gave the jihadists—or at least the ones who survived—tremendous combat experience. Their training often consisted of learning on the job and then passing on that knowledge to new recruits.[55] The battle also made it clear to most of the surviving fighters that facing the U.S. military head-to-head was a losing proposition if the United States had time to prepare and gather the necessary intelligence.

Yet even as Zarqawi's influence was peaking, local attitudes began to change, an ominous shift for jihadists. Zarqawi had warned that if there was a loss of support of Iraqi nationalists, "We will be strangled, then torn to pieces in the street."[56] But the brutality of the jihadists, both foreign fighters and native Iraqis, alienated the locals, as did their attempts to seize political control. In addition, the locals feared, correctly, that the presence of the jihadists was a magnet for U.S. forces and that if the terrorists did not quickly leave, the U.S. military would return in all its destructive power. And when U.S. forces did return, many foreigners fled, infuriating local Iraqis even further.[57] This would prove a pattern: locals welcomed foreigners when they were supporting the local fight against a perceived oppressor, but this welcome turned to bitterness when the foreigners tried to take over and became a threat in their own right.

A Magnet for Foreigners

Foreigners kept coming to Iraq after Fallujah finally fell to U.S. forces. The Iraqi jihad attracted perhaps five thousand total foreigners, likely surpassing Bosnia for the most foreign fighters since the Soviet-Afghan war. And while Afghanistan involved hundreds of thousands of Afghans, the foreign fighters in Iraq made up a far higher percentage of total fighters—almost 5 percent— and proved militarily skilled in contrast to their inept anti-Soviet forefathers.

To foreigners, Iraq seemed like a jihad out of legend. As Bin Laden and other Al Qaeda leaders had long predicted, the United States seemed bent on subjugating the Sunni Muslim world and taking its oil. Why else, they asked, would America make up stories about a nuclear program, invade a country debilitated by sanctions, and then hand over power to a Shiite government with close ties to Tehran? Although the United States did not massacre civilians or engage in constant atrocities as did the Russians and Serbs, as the war escalated it became increasingly destructive, with many Iraqi civilians dying. In addition, the spread of cheap video cameras and similar technologies enabled far more suffering to be caught on camera, and the international media saturation of Iraq led to still more images. In 2004, pictures of U.S. abuses of captured Iraqis in the Abu Ghraib prison, which included urinating on prisoners, stripping them naked and making them form human pyramids, and otherwise humiliating them, led to international outrage, seemingly confirming the jihadist propaganda.

Not surprisingly, young Muslims coming to Iraq put the United States in the same category as the Serbs and Russians. The volunteers saw themselves as defenders of the faithful, with the Christian world, represented by the United States, working with Shiite apostates in Iraq and their Iranian backers in a conspiracy against true Muslims. Abuses and the destruction of war, widely disseminated in both jihadist propaganda and the international media, reinforced their self-image as heroes. They were fighting to liberate Iraq, return power to the Sunnis there, and install a true Islamic government.

Even U.S. successes seemed to boomerang. For example, the capture of Saddam actually galvanized foreign fighter flows because Islamists no longer had to worry about being seen as helping return the Baath Party, which many Sunnis, and especially foreign jihadists, saw as an apostate regime.[58] This was especially important for Zarqawi, as he sought to recruit Iraqi Sunnis with military experience, which often meant those linked to the Baath Party. This approach later led some to label Al Qaeda in Iraq's successor, the Islamic State, as merely the Baath Party in disguise, though in reality few of those recruited had any loyalty to the Baath cause.[59]

Even better, Al Qaeda in Iraq could exploit the growing reach of the internet to spread its message. Zarqawi at first had no real media operation, but he quickly developed one that drew on past jihads for lessons. An early audio release, "Join the Line," echoed Azzam's call to "Join the Caravan" in Afghanistan. As in Chechnya, jihadists used battlefield video as well as horrific and dramatic images like beheadings. They also had cameramen trail behind suicide bombers to record gory footage of dead Shiites. Abuses, like those at Abu Ghraib prison, had proven particularly fruitful, and Iraqi jihadists often contrasted these humiliations with images of jihadists blowing up armored personnel carriers and the dead bodies of U.S. soldiers.[60]

As was true in Afghanistan, the Balkans, and Chechnya, this image of Christian powers taking Muslim lands made for powerful propaganda, and Iraq was widely considered a "defensive" jihad. The leaders of Al-Azhar University in Cairo, an ancient and conservative center of learning whose leaders had condemned the 9/11 attacks, released a fatwa calling for Muslims to fight "crusader" occupation forces: "According to Islamic law, if an enemy steps on Muslims' land, jihad becomes a duty on every male and female Muslim." Azzam couldn't have put it better. Zawahiri exulted in private, describing the war as a "blessing" that permitted "jihad in the heart of the Islamic world."[61] As opposition to the U.S. invasion grew, Al Qaeda leaders declared the anti-U.S. struggle in Iraq to be the "greatest battle of Islam in this era." These leaders also put their money and energy where their mouths were. Al Qaeda–linked websites pushed the struggle in Iraq, and the organization halved its donations to the Taliban in Afghanistan, instead using the money to facilitate jihad in Iraq.

In many ways, Iraq was even better than past jihads because foreign fighters could also take on another enemy—the Iraqi Shiites, whom the United States had put in charge of the country by installing a democratic political system that rewarded their majority status. In correspondence with senior Al Qaeda leaders, who called for fighting Jews and America, Zarqawi noted that the key to change was "targeting and hitting" the Shiites. Doing so would "show the Sunnis [Shiite] rabies and bare the teeth of the hidden rancor working in their breasts." By forcing a sectarian war, it would "awaken inattentive Sunnis as they feel immediate danger."[62] So hitting the Shiites was good in and of itself, but it also would help move Sunnis from local and nationalist identities toward a jihadist one.[63] This anti-Shiite sentiment would grow, emerging as a dominant theme for jihadists by the beginning of the Syrian civil war.

In this vein, one of Zarqawi's earliest attacks was a car bombing in the Shiite holy city of Najaf that killed eighty-four people, including Muhammad Baqir al-Hakim, a prominent Shiite leader, supposedly carried out by Zarqawi's father-in-law.[64] He also orchestrated car bombings in another Shiite holy city, Karbala, which killed almost two hundred, and a car bomb attack in Baghdad that killed the president of the Interim Governing Council, another Shiite. Preachers in Saudi Arabia, Egypt, and elsewhere declared the Shiites to be apostates and "even worse than Jews." Zarqawi often went beyond the Shiites, also lumping in Sunnis he considered traitors to their faith. He did not see them as lost sheep but rather as legitimate targets of violence.[65] He claimed even the killing of true innocents to be acceptable if it "avoided the greater evil of disrupting jihad."[66]

Al Qaeda sought to push Zarqawi to prioritize the United States, and many important religious figures, such as Zarqawi's old mentor Maqdisi, emphasized striking apostate governments over the Shiites and criticized attacks on civilians. "It is better to leave a thousand atheists than to shed the blood of one Muslim," Maqdisi would claim. Zarqawi ignored them all.[67] The United States was on the enemies list, especially in the early days of the conflict, but the Shiites were "more destructive to the Islamic nation than the Americans," according to Zarqawi. One of his initial religious advisers declared Shiism "a scheme aimed to demolish Islam."[68] Zarqawi wrote Zawahiri that U.S. forces "will disappear tomorrow or the day after" because America did not have the stomach for a long fight.[69] Al Qaeda figures privately called on Zarqawi to "mend your flaws" and pay attention to the rulings of religious leaders critical of killing Shiite and Sunni civilians. Zarqawi and his followers would ignore.[70]

In contrast to Al Qaeda, Zarqawi developed a credo that put the street thug ahead of the scholar. He criticized scholars who were "breastfed the milk of defeat" and eager to criticize the mujahedin at every turn.[71] Zarqawi argued that ideologues should join the fray, "experiencing the sweet and the sour and the pressure of the mujahedin face."[72] Brian Fishman, a leading expert on the Iraq jihad, contends the idea that scholarship without action is ill-informed and meaningless would inform jihad from then on.[73] Zarqawi's arguments convinced few religious leaders, but however many theological points Zarqawi lost due to criticism from scholars, he won far more on the battlefield.

Who Went to Iraq and How Did They Get There?

One of the biggest differences between fighting in Iraq and fighting in Afghanistan, let alone Chechnya, was that Iraq was far easier to reach. Some Sunni fighters entered Iraq from Jordan, Saudi Arabia, and even Iran, but once the war started, the Syrian route became the most popular because it was the most convenient. Syria offered long-standing smuggler networks and a sympathetic government willing to turn a blind eye to (and possibly even assist) transit across its 380-mile border. Further complicating the tracking of these already clandestine cross-border flows, many volunteers came to Syria indirectly, via Egypt, Turkey, and other countries. Even many Jordanian and Saudi fighters, despite living in neighboring countries, still entered through Syria.[74]

In the initial days of the war and occupation, fighters crossed from Syria with little interference. Local jihadist facilitators worked with criminal and tribal networks to smuggle people across the border.[75] Although both Iraq's Saddam and Syria's Bashar al-Assad were brutal dictators, they both cut deals with tribes along their borders, allowing them considerable autonomy as long as they remained loyal to the regime. Comprehensive UN sanctions after the 1991 Gulf war had led to a massive demand for smuggled goods in Iraq, and one study found that "Iraqi border security guards moved from being a security agency to a regulatory agency."[76] Local regime officials and security forces dipped their beaks into this smuggling, getting their cut in exchange for looking the other way. In one Syrian province, for example, the provincial governor, the head of a major city, and the local army and intelligence heads would all be paid off by smugglers trafficking in arms and fighters as well as consumer goods.[77] The payout could be considerable: the average Saudi payment to a Syrian travel coordinator was $2,535.[78]

For political and strategic reasons, the Syrian regime tolerated the flow of fighters. The chief mufti of Syria, Sheikh Ahmed Kaftaro, called on Muslims to fight American invaders, and sermons everywhere in Syria stressed resistance. Volunteers were feted as heroes and housed and fed by supportive Syrians, while religious and tribal leaders arranged their transport to Iraq.[79] The Syrian government stood aside; some analysts speculated that the Assad regime supported unrest in Iraq in order to dull America's post-9/11 appetite for regime change. Assad also sought to dump hundreds or even thousands of home-grown Salafists who might otherwise pose a threat to the Syrian regime.[80] As time went on, the Syrian government began to police the border more, though to the frustration of both foreign fighters and the U.S. government the regime seemed to rotate between collaboration one month and crackdown the next. Several years after the war began, dozens of foreign fighters still crossed from Syria to Iraq each month.[81]

Other neighboring countries had less of a challenge and tried harder. Jordan only had to contend with its lone border crossing, which it policed, but that still left over 100 miles of desert it did not regularly guard. The Saudi border had been officially closed since 1991, but 500 miles of largely unguarded desert separated by a sand berm offered little impediment to motivated (and paying) jihadis. By mid-2004, Riyadh responded to U.S. and internal pressures and started spending hundreds of millions of dollars a year in border enforcement and antismuggling efforts, causing the majority of Saudi militants to cross instead through Syria.[82] However, the continued disproportionate presence of Saudis from the kingdom's northern provinces, presumably benefiting from greater accessibility and cross-border tribal connections, suggests there was still movement across the border even with the increased attention of the Saudi security services.[83]

Most volunteers were in their early twenties. Many came from large, lower-income families. They often had jobs, but they were low-paying ones such as construction or driving a taxi. However, some volunteers, particularly those from the Gulf states, came from middle-class, and even prominent, well-known families. Saudis were highly sought after as they brought "enough money to support themselves and their Iraqi brothers," often tens of thousands of dollars. Perhaps unsurprisingly considering their age, many of these young men were students.[84] As most of them had been too young for Bosnia or Afghanistan, this was oftentimes their first combat experience, and no Gulf state at the time required national service. This lack of experience meant many foreign fighters were encouraged or volunteered to be suicide bombers.

Facilitation networks were robust. Previous foreign fighters who had returned to their home countries, often from a previous jihad such as Afghanistan or Chechnya, helped the next generation to go and fight. Terrorism analyst Clinton Watts estimates that between 60 and 80 percent of the foreign fighters who ended up in Iraq were recruited by former foreign fighters. These veterans had friends and relatives back home they could recruit. They knew which propaganda themes worked in their own neighborhoods: pushing the Shiites as an enemy might work in one area, while in another, anti-U.S. propaganda played better. In addition, their war stories gave them credibility among the young Muslims who were potential recruits. Perhaps most important, former foreign fighters could be trusted by groups like Al Qaeda in Iraq, enabling them to play a key role as facilitators, helping a volunteer smoothly leave his home and travel far away to a war zone without the group worrying that the volunteer was really a spy.[85] Groups of friends and relatives often traveled together to fight. As a result, networks at a certain point would become self-sustaining, and certain towns and mosques were hotspots for recruitment.[86]

The internet, for all its hype, was not a major source for recruiting according to a West Point study on foreign fighters in Iraq—less than 4 percent met a jihadist coordinator that way. In many neighborhoods in the Middle East, internet penetration was low, and there are limits to virtual intimacy. After all, it might be a government spy, not a true believer, on the other end of an email. Instead, the internet's role was to help lay the groundwork and reinforce interest. Jihad in Iraq was breaking out as broadband internet was spreading, allowing video to be distributed online rather than using more cumbersome DVDs. These videos and associated propaganda excited Muslims around the world, making them sympathetic when recruiters came knocking and leading some to seek out ways to become part of the Iraq struggle. It also meant that when young men decided to take up arms, they wanted to be under Zarqawi's glamorous command rather than that of other commanders.

Al Qaeda in Iraq made an effort to put an Iraqi face on its activities, but it began as an organization that was about 70 percent foreign (though this percentage would decline over time). As with prior jihads, it was effectively impossible to accurately track the number of fighters traveling to Iraq, much less by country of origin. All estimates were extrapolated from isolated and often small snapshot samples, including the bodies recovered and identified by U.S. forces, insurgents in U.S. detention, propaganda videos of suicide bombers, or captured Al Qaeda in Iraq personnel files. Although Saudi Arabia seemingly contributed the most (only the data provided by Riyadh unsurprisingly disputed this), there are serious disparities in the estimated percentages for other Arab countries.[87] There are significant numbers from Egypt, Syria, Yemen, Libya, Algeria, Sudan, Morocco, and Kuwait in different estimates but not in consistent patterns.[88] Of Western countries, France led the way in providing foreign fighters. However, only some dozens of Frenchmen went, followed by even smaller numbers from Belgium, Italy, the United Kingdom, Germany, Sweden, the Netherlands, and Spain. There were perhaps only a hundred European jihadists in total in Iraq in peak years such as 2005.[89]

Saudi Arabia contributed the most fighters, in part because sectarian animus there is high, but also due to preexisting networks of mobilization established during the Afghan jihad. In addition, as Zarqawi was taking off in Iraq, the Al Qaeda branch in Saudi Arabia was suffering blow after blow with the population turning against it. Faced with a choice between a dynamic group with considerable popular legitimacy in Iraq and an increasingly despised one under siege at home, many Saudis preferred to fight next door.[90] The Saudi branch of Al Qaeda criticized the Al Qaeda leadership for focusing too much on Iraq and not on the holier land of Saudi Arabia itself.[91]

Libya also proved fertile ground, contributing more than twice as many fighters per capita than any other country. The Libyan government had encouraged suspected Islamist radicals to go fight the Soviets, but when they returned home they rebelled, trying to replace Qaddafi's regime with an Islamist one. Qaddafi crushed them, but jihadist ideas remained popular, giving the Iraq cause a natural recruiting base. Moreover, the regime's persecution—Qaddafi cut off water and electricity to the jihadist hub in Darnah, declaring that the people there "deserve to die without trial, like dogs"[92]—made Iraq seem a haven where jihad still had a chance of success.

A West Point study found that more than half of the foreign volunteers were designated as suicide bombers, by far the most lethal tool the jihadists had, with most of the remainder being traditional fighters. Libyans, Saudis, and Moroccans were particularly likely to be chosen to be suicide bombers. The concurrent use of suicide attacks against Israel by Palestinians during the second intifada, which peaked in 2002 and 2003, transformed suicide bombing from a rare but dramatic form of terrorism to a common method involving regular, near-constant attacks rather than the occasional spectacular strike.

The foreigners appeared more eager for martyrdom than native Iraqis. Colonel James Brown, who commanded one coalition detention facility, noted, "There are two kinds of suicide bombers—those handcuffed to the steering wheel and those not . . . foreigners are never found handcuffed."[93] *How* recruits ended up in Iraq appears to matter considerably. If you came to Iraq via a relative, you were less likely to end up as a suicide bomber. On the other hand, if the coordinator was simply an acquaintance, and especially if you were one of the few who came solely via the internet, you were more likely to be slotted into the suicide bomber slot.[94]

This network spilled over into contacts and often close relationships with jihadists elsewhere in the region. Fighters trained in Iraq went to Algeria, where they stood out for their zealotry. The local Al Qaeda–linked group noted in captured documents that the students of Zarqawi "would not be satisfied with anything less than the VBIEDs [car bombs] and the suicide attacks."[95] Al Qaeda in Iraq assisted local groups elsewhere, and fighters from these areas relied on their Iraqi brethren. Fatah al-Islam, for example, was founded after Al Qaeda in Iraq suffered setbacks and it became too dangerous to operate in Iraq. Many fighters returned to Lebanon and Syria, where they would again take up arms with this new gruop. Notably, however, Al Qaeda in Iraq did not prioritize terrorist attacks in the United States or Europe; rather, it maintained a geographically circumscribed outlook, focusing instead first and foremost on Iraq, then on its neighborhood, and then on the greater Middle East.

Funding the Jihad

Waging a bloody campaign against the United States, the Shiite government of Iraq, and rival Sunni groups does not come cheap. Most of Al Qaeda in Iraq's money came from taxing and extorting money from those under its sway. Oil smuggling, kidnapping, and theft from the local population provided as much as $200 million a year at the group's peak strength. A senior Treasury Department official, Daniel Glaser, testified in 2005 that the Iraqi insurgency drew its financing from two principal sources: criminal activities and foreign donations. Foreign donations, most from Saudi Arabia and other Arab states, made up perhaps 5 percent of overall revenue.[96] These states saw Sunni militants as a bulwark against Iran's influence in Iraq and often tolerated recruitment and fundraising as a result.[97] Since 9/11, the United States had been working with Riyadh and other Gulf state governments on countering terrorist financing, but it was difficult to block and dismantle long-standing individual donor networks and charities that held widespread popular legitimacy.

The millions the jihadists raised helped pay for bombs, safe houses, the care for fighters' families, ransom to get fighters out of jail, and other necessities. Much of this money, however, went back into the foreign fighters' pipeline. A military study estimated that almost 40 percent of Al Qaeda in Iraq's spending (roughly the same amount it spent on weapons) went to bringing fighters to Iraq and supporting them there.[98] For a while, Al Qaeda in Iraq was awash in money. The Al Qaeda core, which traditionally funded other groups, now requested money from its Iraqi affiliate.[99]

Al Qaeda in Iraq's fundraising drew heavily on its propaganda machine. Following the tradition of Khattab, Al Qaeda in Iraq filmed its attacks (often from more than one angle) and sent out videos to potential supporters. Videos seemed like vivid proof of the group's validity. As one jihadist noted, many groups claimed to fight in Iraq but were "just stealing money" from potential donors. When wealthy people from Kuwait, Qatar, and Saudi Arabia saw these videos, they had proof of the group's operations, and money poured in freely.[100]

To manage the large sums of money in its treasury and the foreign recruits from dozens of countries, Al Qaeda in Iraq developed a large bureaucratic infrastructure. The group had forms for everything. When you joined up, you filled out a form, and if you wanted to leave the organization, you signed a written pledge, filled out a questionnaire, took a security course, and otherwise staggered through a bureaucratic gauntlet.[101]

Zarqawi's End

On February 22, 2006, five foreign fighters and three Iraqis from Al Qaeda in Iraq donned Iraqi military uniforms and infiltrated the historic Askariya mosque in Samarra, the resting place of several revered figures among Shiites worldwide. The massive bomb they set off damaged the mosque's beautiful golden dome and devastated the mosque itself. The blast killed no one, but by damaging the historic mosque, it enraged Shiites; perhaps a thousand people died in revenge attacks on the first day after the bombing. Even more consequential, the bombing led to widespread calls for Shiites to take up arms, with recruits flooding popular militias known for using power drills to kill their victims.

Terrorism was working, and such revenge attacks were part of Zarqawi's plan. For fearful Sunnis, Al Qaeda in Iraq would step into the void as the defender of the faithful. The violence would also demonstrate the jihadists' power in areas where they already held sway, allowing them to coerce the Sunni community and impose their version of Islamic law on the population.

Yet as Zarqawi's power and notoriety peaked, so too did U.S. efforts to stop him. After the capture of Saddam in December 2003, the highest priority of the U.S. Joint Special Operations Command (JSOC), then operating in Iraq as Task Force 145, was to kill or capture Zarqawi, above even finding Bin Laden.[102] The U.S. government put a price on Zarqawi's head ($25 million) equal to the bounties offered for Bin Laden and Saddam Hussein.[103] Several times the coalition thought they might have killed him, but each time he reemerged. Under the command of Lieutenant General Stanley McChrystal, Task Force 145 brought intelligence collectors, analysts, and the special operators together as one team, in what was colloquially called an "unblinking eye" intended to "find, fix, finish, exploit, and analyze."[104] To oversimplify, Task Force 145 regularly conducted raids, sometimes multiple ones in a single day, based on new intelligence regarding Zarqawi's whereabouts or those of his associates, which would then generate more intelligence that the analysts would exploit to restart the loop.

The relentless U.S. hunt paid off in June 2006. Intelligence reported the general area where Zarqawi was operating and also a safe house where he often stayed. An intense and now focused surveillance campaign began, and an American F-16 bombed the house when Zarqawi was reported to be visiting, killing him along with his "spiritual advisor," Sheikh Abdel al-Rahman, and some family members.[105]

Over ten years after his death, Zarqawi remains a hero to jihadists. His legacy is more like Khattab's than Bin Laden's: a young and hardened warrior, who fought in battle after battle against Islam's enemies, and went out in a flame of glory. Unlike Khattab, however, Zarqawi's legacy glorified brutality, such as his beheading of hostages and his group's public killing of Muslim civilians. He also disdained theologians who were far from the front, emphasizing a credo of action over theological niceties. Groups like the Islamic State would embrace this heritage, raising it to new and even more horrific heights. At the time of his death, however, it seemed that the worst of the worst among jihadists was now in the grave.

CHAPTER 8 | The Dreamer: Abu Ayyub al-Masri and the Self-Destruction of the Iraqi Jihad

ZARQAWI WAS DEAD, but Al Qaeda in Iraq seemed ascendant. The sectarian civil war between Iraq's Shiites and Sunnis would consume around 30,000 civilian lives in 2006 alone. Polls in the United States showed more than half of Americans supported a troop withdrawal within a year, if not immediately.[1] A National Intelligence Estimate in April found that Iraq was "the cause célèbre for Jihadis" and that it was "shaping a new generation of terrorist leaders and operators."[2] Zawahiri gloated that "the Americans are between two fires. If they stay, they will bleed to death, and if they retreat, they will lose everything."[3] Ironically, at the time Al Qaeda was concerned that America would leave too quickly and, as had happened in Afghanistan when the Soviets left, the jihadists would not be positioned to take over after a U.S. departure. "The secularists and traitors" would end up "holding sway over us," Zawahiri warned.[4]

Yet 2006 would prove a turning point. Zarqawi's replacement, Abu Ayyub al-Masri, and the foreign fighters he commanded would charge down the road to disaster. In November of that year, Al Qaeda in Iraq claimed over three hundred operations; a year later, that figure dropped to twenty-five. By 2010, the organization was in total disarray, its leaders dead or hunted, and the United States and its Iraqi allies seemingly on the verge of victory.

Just as Bin Laden originally imagined, foreign fighters had shown themselves to be the tip of the jihadi spear. Zarqawi's ability to use foreign fighters as suicide bombers on an industrial scale was one of the keys to his success. Yet the very characteristics that made the foreign fighters so formidable also brought the jihadist project in Iraq crashing down. Their brutality and fervor alienated many Muslims, leading to such widespread revulsion that Bin Laden considered severing organizational ties to Al Qaeda's Iraqi affiliate and denouncing its attacks. To manage the fighters, Al Qaeda in Iraq created an absurd bureaucracy that insisted on intricate record-keeping but also made messianic demands on the population. This mix of paperwork and fanaticism that would prove lethal.

At the center of the jihadist disaster in Iraq is another foreigner who, unlike Zarqawi, is largely unknown to Western audiences: Abu Ayyub al-Masri, who also went by Abu Hamza al-Muhajir. Masri took the helm of Al Qaeda in Iraq after Zarqawi's death and proceeded to make mistake after mistake. Indeed, it was lucky for Al Qaeda in Iraq that U.S. forces killed him in 2010, paving the way for a far more competent leader, Abu Bakr al-Baghdadi, to take the helm and eventually establish the Islamic State.

As his nom de guerre implies, Masri was an Egyptian (*misr* means "Egypt" in Arabic). On paper, he seemed a perfect leader to take Zarqawi's place. He began his militant career as a member of the Muslim Brotherhood in Egypt. In 1982, after that organization became more mainstream, Masri joined the Egyptian Islamic Jihad, the organization Zawahiri himself helped found as a teenager. Like many Egyptian jihadists, he fled the country in response to the Mubarak regime's fierce counterterrorism campaign, training in an Al Qaeda camp in Afghanistan and setting up shop in Yemen in the 1990s. Masri may have met Zarqawi in Afghanistan in 1999, and he also made contacts with Al Qaeda leaders when he trained on how to make explosives.[5]

Like Zarqawi, Masri went to Iraq before the U.S. invasion, helping prepare the ground for the jihadist resistance. He soon began to run major Al Qaeda operations there, establishing cells in Baghdad, helping organize the flow of foreign fighters from Syria, and encouraging local groups to fight under Al Qaeda's banner. Masri built the bombs that destroyed the United Nations headquarters and the Jordanian embassy in Iraq, two of Zarqawi's biggest initial blows against the United States and its allies. A jihadist website claimed that Masri was personally responsible for ambushing and killing two U.S. soldiers whose bodies were mutilated and then booby-trapped. Furthermore, like Zarqawi before him, he issued videos that featured him killing hostages, in this case, shooting Turkish hostage Murat Yuce, a truck driver who delivered supplies for coalition forces. Topping off his bloody record, Masri also helped lead Iraqi jihadists in the first battle of Fallujah in 2004.[6]

To give Al Qaeda in Iraq a local flavor and to counter American efforts to discredit the group, Masri and the other senior leaders symbolically chose an Iraqi, Abu Umar al-Baghdadi, as Zarqawi's successor, but the Egyptian was its true head. Prior to the U.S. invasion, Baghdadi, whose real name was Hamid Dawud Mohamed Khalil al-Zawi, was a police officer under Saddam until his long-held Salafi views led to his dismissal.[7] During the occupation, Baghdadi became involved in the insurgency. His Salafist sympathies brought him to Al Qaeda in Iraq, and he began by sheltering Zarqawi in his hometown of Haditha. Baghdadi steadily rose through the ranks, supposedly a talented organizer and ideologue.[8] In addition to simply being an Iraqi, Baghdadi was also a member of the Qureshi tribe, the same as the Prophet Muhammad. Thus, in choosing Baghdadi, Masri seemingly picked a skilled administrator and sufficiently legitimate local figurehead without seriously compromising his own authority.[9] Baghdadi's sudden rise from a relatively anonymous bureaucrat to the pinnacle of senior leadership was impressive, almost to the point of incredulity, fueling debate over his identity and power.[10] Throughout his nearly four-year term, U.S. and Iraqi authorities repeatedly declared him dead, captured, or even nothing more than a fictitious propaganda ploy invented by Masri to bolster Iraqi support.[11] There remains a debate over who was the true head of Al Qaeda in Iraq, but in any event Baghdadi and Masri appeared to work well together.

Together with Baghdadi, Masri pushed sectarianism even more aggressively than Zarqawi and embraced Zarqawi's concept of creating *an* Islamic state within Iraq (not to be confused with the future iteration of this group, which would call itself *the* Islamic State). In October 2006, the group changed its name to the "Islamic State of Iraq," though most observers continued to use the term "Al Qaeda in Iraq." Baghdadi was its official head, while Masri was its minister of war. In contrast to its eventual successor, the Islamic State, the Islamic State of Iraq controlled little territory at the time.[12] One reason Masri established the state was due to his belief that the Muslim savior, known as the Mahdi, would be arriving within the year. To those who mocked the group's pretense of being a true state, Masri made the compelling point that the first Islamic state, the one established by the Prophet himself, was small and vulnerable.

In addition, Masri wasn't particular about exactly where the state's boundaries would lie: if it governed territory under a true Muslim leader, it was legitimate. And Masri meant to govern. The group spawned laws and bureaucracies. In addition to the usual media, military, and security bureaus, it even had a Ministry of Fisheries and a proliferation of local "emirs" suppos-edly in charge of the most minute details.[13] The would-be state also called on Muslims around the world, especially from neighboring areas, to emigrate. In other words, foreign fighters were welcomed.[14] Nonetheless, the group was increasingly controlled by Iraqis, with foreigners playing a more subordinate role.[15]

The very existence of the so-called state confused outsiders. Masri had declared to Bin Laden that his group was "an arrow in your quiver," but now it was demanding others to pledge loyalty to the new state. Indeed, the declara-tion of an Islamic state occurred against the counsel of Al Qaeda's leadership; behind the scenes, Zawahiri would note that Al Qaeda leaders were not "asked for permission, consulted, or even warned." Al Qaeda leaders also feared a re-prise of Afghanistan and Bosnia. These mujahedin victories, in their eyes, led to chaos or to their enemies' taking power because the mujahedin were not prepared for the next step. Publicly, however, Al Qaeda tried to hide the dis-sension in the ranks, accepting the fait accompli and claiming that it favored the decision to declare the state.

Masri also embraced an apocalyptic vision of Islam. To prepare for the savior's arrival, Masri ordered pulpits to be built in historic mosques in Damascus, Jerusalem, and Medina and called for his commanders to conquer all of Iraq. These orders had no chance of being followed, but Masri told his followers that "the Mahdi will come any day."

Reaping the Whirlwind

Foreigners often came to Iraq with strong views on what true Islam was, but they found Iraqis, including Iraqi Sunni fighters, wanting. An Al Qaeda in Iraq after-action report blamed foreigners for their "disdain for differences in opinions, arguments and exposing faults."[16] This zealotry led foreigners to charge that local fighters were ignorant of true Islam and too attached to their tribe or nationalism; these were harsh words that allowed brutal treatment. The irony is that many fighters, foreign or Iraqi, knew little about the Quran, the sayings of the prophet, or other basics of Islam beyond a few jihadi slogans. As Al Qaeda would readily admit in its own critique of the war, "They lacked understanding of the true religious doctrine and instead understand them as logos and photos."[17] There were few jihadist scholars in Iraq to guide the fighters.

Because the foreigners believed they knew Islam best, they saw other Sunni groups in Iraq as deviant, particularly those who had a tribal or nationalistic bent. They also were brutal to non-Sunnis. Unnoticed at the time by most Westerners and foreshadowing the Islamic State's 2014 massacres in the Sinjar Mountains, the group went on a bombing spree against Iraq's Yazidi villages, killing hundreds.[18] And because Masri's group was now a state—a true Islamic state, at that—Masri demanded other Sunni fighters accept his authority "before we are forced to act against them." Al Qaeda in Iraq would target Sunni groups composed of former Iraqi army officers, tribal gunmen, and Iraqi nationalists, even though they too opposed the U.S. presence and the Shiite government in Baghdad.[19] Rival Islamists were a particular target.

Masri continued most of Zarqawi's policies along with his own more apocalyptic efforts. Al Qaeda in Iraq's disastrous campaign against the Shiites, punctuated by brutality that was often spearheaded by foreign fighters, also alienated the Iraqi Sunnis over whom they ruled. In the first years of the U.S. occupation, the United States saw many Sunni tribes and more nationalist groups as enemies (often with good reason, given that they shot, bombed, and otherwise attacked Western forces) and did not initially recognize the tensions Al Qaeda in Iraq was introducing. But despite their growing resentment of the foreign jihadists, Iraqi Sunnis feared revolting because they would pay a harsh price for resistance. In Haditha in 2005, U.S. forces went in to clear the area of Al Qaeda and other rebels, most of whom fled in advance of U.S. forces. American troops soon departed, however, and the jihadists returned and took brutal revenge. They lined up local leaders in a soccer field and shot them as a warning to others who might defy their rule. But the intimidation didn't stop the anger and resentment. Iraqis, after all, had to live in the country that the foreign fighters were destroying.

The foreign jihadists of Al Qaeda in Iraq would often systematically kill tribal leaders, seeing the tribal structure and the loyalties that many Iraqis held to their tribal chiefs as a threat to their power. They also killed Sunni religious leaders who refused to submit to their authority. They were particularly vicious to ordinary Sunnis under their rule. Only a state can legitimately punish criminals, and the foreign jihadists made a point of crucifying thieves, stoning criminals, and otherwise employing the harshest traditional punishments to bolster their credentials. The jihadists did not stop at coercing leaders, and often their practices went from horrific to ludicrous. They beat men and women who did not wear traditional garb. Contending cigarettes to be against Islam, they broke the fingers of smokers. One Sunni who later worked with U.S. forces recalled watching an Al Qaeda fighter behead an eight-year-old girl. American soldiers found Iraqi civilians beheaded in a soccer field, with their genitals stuffed into their mouths. Absurdity alternated with horror. In some areas, Al Qaeda banned the sale of cucumbers and tomatoes side-by-side, believing that they resembled female and male sex organs. In another instance, they put underwear on sheep to hide their genitals. No longer were they defenders of the community. Now, they were oppressors.

Nor did terrorism elsewhere in the region work well. Al Qaeda in Iraq launched suicide bombers at three Western hotels in Jordan in November 2005, killing sixty people, the largest group of whom were celebrating a wedding at the Amman Radisson. A fourth suicide bomber, Sajida Mubarak Atrous al-Rishawi, the wife of another bomber and the sister of a dead lieutenant of Zarqawi, was captured after she failed to set off her bomb due to a malfunction with the detonator cord. Zarqawi claimed that Jewish tourists and U.S. intelligence services used the hotels, "a place of iniquity for the nation's apostate traitors." But the attacks on innocents—Muslim innocents, no less—and the use of a female suicide bomber, and a failed one at that, was a propaganda disaster for Al Qaeda. Although many Jordanians saw the group's struggle against U.S. soldiers and the Shiite government in Iraq as heroic, attacks against ordinary Muslims celebrating a wedding made them seem like thugs. The Jordanian backlash was pronounced. Mere months earlier, only 10 percent of Jordanians reported thinking Islamic extremism was a threat to their country, nearly half agreed that suicide bombings against U.S. troops in Iraq was justifiable, and even more expressed confidence in Bin Laden.[20] After the bombing, however, at least a hundred thousand people took to the streets of Amman to protest. Zarqawi's own clan, part of one of the country's most important Bedouin tribes, declared, "We disown him until judgment day."[21] Perhaps unsurprisingly, Jordanian support for suicide bombings dropped by nearly half.[22]

The strategy of sparking a sectarian conflagration to rally Sunnis was now backfiring. The sectarian backlash left Iraq's Sunnis vulnerable to Shiite retaliation, and Al Qaeda in Iraq was too weak to defend them. Its thousands of fighters could not compete with the tens of thousands the Shiite militias could muster. It took only a couple of days following the infamous Al Askariya Mosque bombing for this disparity in power to manifest itself, with Shiite militants attacking 168 Sunni mosques and killing hundreds of Sunnis throughout the country.[23] A month after the bombing, the official murder rate of Baghdad had tripled, with the majority of the victims being Sunni men.[24] As Iraq expert Brian Fishman wrote, the jihadists' "strategic sin was arrogance; the jihadist group had the power to tear society apart but was not strong enough to pull it back together in its own image." The Shiite formed or expanded their own militias and death squads, rampaging through Sunni areas, killing and torturing as they went. Groups like the Iranian-backed and -trained Badr Organization and Moktada al-Sadr's Mahdi Army began a systematic campaign of ethnic cleansing against Sunnis in mixed communities in Baghdad and elsewhere.[25] Many Sunnis blamed the jihadists for their losses.[26]

Al Qaeda in Iraq became a guerrilla organization when it was forced out of cities like Fallujah or when it lost territory in general. Although such flexibility was a headache for U.S. military planners and enabled Al Qaeda to survive, it had costs for Al Qaeda in Iraq as well. Iraqis saw retrenchment as fleeing, not as laying low. Moreover, Al Qaeda was unable to defend the ordinary people who had supported the group. Al Qaeda strategists came to believe that "continuous retreats" led to a "change in public opinion" against the group.[27]

Many in the jihadist community recognized things had gone too far. One leader sent an online video message to Bin Laden himself, appealing for him to intervene against Al Qaeda in Iraq. The writer of the video lamented the "liquidation of scholars of sharia," attacks on other Islamist groups, and the planting of bombs "in front of houses, schools, and hospitals."[28] To drive the point home, Iraqi fighters related a story to Al Qaeda leaders about how Al Qaeda in Iraq killed prisoners belonging to one anti-U.S. nationalist group; in response, that group began cooperating with the United States and the Iraqi government.[29] Masri shunned an emissary of Bin Laden, who reported back to his chief that the declared state had little support among Iraqis and that Masri was in the grip of messianic fever. Masri tried to placate critics, but his gunmen continued to take on anyone who refused to accept their rule. The soldiers issued statements— familiar to any soldier in any war feeling micromanaged by officials far from the battlefield—protesting that their leaders did not know the true situation on the ground. When they saw others not conforming to God's laws, they explained, "We took matters into our own hands."

In a private letter to Al Qaeda in Iraq leaders, Ayman al-Zawahiri warned the fighters in Iraq that by killing the Shiites and engaging in beheadings, they were alienating ordinary Iraqis and Muslims everywhere while taking their eyes off the true enemy, the United States. One account complained that a cell failed to set off an improvised explosive device (IED) when a U.S. convoy passed because they had orders to attack the Shiites instead.[30] Zawahiri called for winning over "Muslim masses," co-opting Sunni religious figures, and unifying the anti-U.S. resistance. Remembering the post-Soviet period in Afghanistan, he recalled "killing, ruin, and destruction, which remain a stigma for all those who took part in it." Bin Laden himself later weighed in publicly, urging jihadists in Iraq to unify against the United States.

In addition to angering locals, foreign fighters caused problems within the jihadists' own ranks. Al Qaeda in Iraq's propaganda created expectations of glory and martyrdom among foreigners coming to fight. The hardship of underground life, the need to go about unarmed to avoid suspicion, and the careful planning and logistics necessary for military operations did not sit well with many foreign hotheads, leading to disgruntlement among the foreign volunteers who did not "know the harsh reality of jihad" and anger from Iraqis bearing the brunt of the insurgency. Al Qaeda in Iraq was in part a victim of its own propaganda. Jihadist videos preached that the mujahedin were in "total control" and that the "US is incapable of moving out of its bases for fear of the Mujahedin." Recruits were also told they could select their own targets and bring down at least twenty "infidels" in so doing. Volunteers chafed when they learned all of this was false. Some simply became bored by sitting idle for several months, and others were disheartened when they learned that the target that would result in their martyrdom would be a police car rather than a major operation. Often, they sought to return home as their fervor dimmed.[31] Nor did the foreigners' skill match their zealotry. An Al Qaeda study of the country captured by U.S. forces observed that foreign fighters did not know how to speak the Iraqi dialect of Arabic, did not appreciate the local terrain, and, by standing out, created security risks for local forces.

Some of Masri's lieutenants recognized they were alienating the very people they were supposed to save, but they couldn't control their own fighters. Masri's own dysfunction didn't help: his chief judge later recalled he was "absent from the details of what goes on in the battlefield." The United States' efforts to kill jihadist leaders and disrupt communications forced senior officials into hiding, exacerbating the control problems and allowing the lower ranks far more autonomy.

Yet for all its inability to control local fighters, Al Qaeda in Iraq was also highly bureaucratic. It had a national-level leadership, which in turn was divided into sectors, and then districts, with each district having "emirs" for military operations, security, medicine, and so on. Each district raised its own money and controlled its own personnel. The good news for the group was that this organization allowed it to keep functioning in one area even if it was wiped out in another. The bad news was that this organization inhibited cooperation.[32]

The jihadists' personnel policy (not a topic one usually associates with terrorism) was often a disaster. Many local leaders didn't share foreign volunteers, so some had too many suicide bombers and others too few. Some feared the foreigners were spies and kept them isolated. Nor did they take advantage of the skills of foreign volunteers. One skilled counterfeiter who spoke several European languages and held a European passport—natural skills for an international terrorist or at least a major money-maker—was used for regular operations because the local cell where he was assigned was not short on money.[33] Some local leaders kept sending out suicide bombers against well-defended targets, even though such attacks were not effective, simply so they could tell their bosses that they remained active fighters. One Al Qaeda after-action report concluded the foreign volunteer "wasn't appropriately used, neglected and ended up getting killed or he left and returned to his country of origin."[34] The result was disaster, "where everyone starts doing his own thing without anyone to manage or to control him; the young men disrespect the elders; the soldiers don't listen to their Amir, and the Amir is not taking care of his soldiers, everyone is blaming the other."[35]

The problems extended beyond the battlefield. Al Qaeda in Iraq members regularly stole money from the organization or otherwise misused it. A West Point study found that local cells systematically exaggerated the number of family members they had in order to pad their payrolls because fighters earned more if they had children or other dependents.[36] In addition, the jihadists relied on networks in Syria to bring in new foreign fighters, and the smugglers often kept the money the fighters sought to bring with them. As one Al Qaeda in Iraq document noted, the volunteer is asked "to surrender any amount of money and belongings he has on his person" when he is with smugglers, who assure him that the Islamic state will "secure all his needs while he is in Iraq."[37] When a local cell found itself short of funds, it often stole or extorted money from local Iraqis, creating more ill will.

To guard against theft and abuses, Al Qaeda in Iraq created intricate personnel records complete with spreadsheets and expense report forms, which included names, pseudonyms, family information, salary, and other personal information.[38] It also listed the "work" the individual would do, such as whether he would be a fighter or a suicide bomber. When a local group received money from the core organization, it had to give a receipt for the money and provide an accounting for how the money was spent. At times it had to have the signatures notarized. As terrorism scholar Jacob Shapiro points out, "This is a sensible requirement for most organizations, but not one that is ostensibly covert."[39] When these documents ended up in the hands of U.S. forces, they proved a counterterrorism gold mine.

Funding was a constant concern. The group paid its fighters poorly, but with thousands of men under arms, even these low salaries added up. Local commanders, moreover, might be desperate for funds to pay fighters and prevent desertions—or simply want to steal—leading to constant tension.[40] Al Qaeda in Iraq also took care of dependents and, when a fighter died or was captured, continued to pay wages to his family. Such a move helped them recruit as dying would not deprive a family, especially a poor one, of much-needed income, making it easier for young men to choose martyrdom.

These policies, however, imposed a spiraling financial burden in bad times. As the group lost territory, it lost the ability to extort the populace and thus pay its fighters, leading to defections. And when the group lost fighters in combat, its costs often rose because it continued to pay their families—a double loss. Over time this was not sustainable, and the group dropped families of martyrs from their payrolls, no doubt increasing local anger.[41]

The Tide Turns

The outrage of ordinary Iraqis at Al Qaeda in Iraq's arrogance and missteps, when combined with a more effective U.S. counterinsurgency campaign, proved a disaster for the jihadists in Iraq and the jihadist cause in general. Moreover, the failure of Al Qaeda in Iraq and other groups to protect Sunnis against the rising power of Shiite militias and their Iranian backers led many Sunnis to seek alternatives. In addition, Al Qaeda in Iraq's Iraqi members sought to dominate the Sunni community as a whole, making a bid for power that tribal leaders rejected.

On September 17, 2006, several tribes in western Iraq held a "Day of Awakening," and the "Awakening" label would later be used by other Sunnis who turned against the jihadists. As one tribal leader declared, "A Muslim is a brother of another Muslim; he neither oppresses him nor does he lie to him nor does he look down on him or humiliate him." "We all say to the terrorists," leaders warned, "leave now or you will be killed in an ugly way."[42] They explained that the jihadists started off by defending Sunnis but over time waged war without concern for the daily lives of the locals: "They planted bombs in front of homes, schools, and hospitals, and under electric generators."[43] On the Syrian side of the border, many tribes had family ties to Iraqi tribes, so violence in Iraq led to a decline of support there too.[44]

Commanders of the U.S. forces took advantage of Al Qaeda in Iraq's missteps, reaching out more to the tribes and pushing for a more inclusive government in Baghdad. The Bush administration embraced "the Surge," deploying five additional brigades to Iraq in 2007 at a time when many Americans thought it was time to cut U.S. losses. In addition to the additional troop strength, General David Petraeus adopted a more traditional counterinsurgency strategy, with troops staying in areas after they cleared them of insurgents to protect locals from reprisals, trying to work with and bolster local authorities who stood up to Al Qaeda in Iraq and build up the capacity of the Iraqi government. The Surge and the associated strategy change helped enable the Awakening, ensuring that those who stood against Al Qaeda in Iraq would have a powerful protector in their corner. A key to the Surge's success (and one often overlooked by those who called for a similar strategy in other theaters) was the heavy U.S. military presence, which enabled the tribes who rose up to survive and eventually triumph.

One key to U.S. success, however, was the blundering of Masri and other foreign fighters. As Fishman argues, "It is mostly a story of local tribes getting fed up with outsiders dictating to them." Perhaps a hundred thousand tribal fighters were part of the fight against Al Qaeda in Iraq.[45] Al Qaeda in Iraq would agree, noting in its internal records that "renegade tribes" were "the most dangerous and intense" of their enemies.[46] Nor did the tribes have to fear a repeat of Haditha and other reprisals because now the United States, especially during the 2007 troop surge, was providing them with firepower and protection. If Al Qaeda returned after U.S. forces initially cleared an area, the tribes would fight back with U.S. support.

Before the Awakening, the United States lacked consistent intelligence on where the jihadists were, leading to mass imprisonment of young men, fruitless searches of houses that humiliated the owners, and other self-defeating measures that swelled support for the insurgency. With Iraqi tribes now pointing out strangers in their midst, the United States was able to find and kill Al Qaeda members on a massive scale. Led by Lieutenant General Stanley McChrystal, U.S. special operations forces conducted dozens of raids per night, exploiting the intelligence they received from now-sympathetic tribesmen and using the raids to gather still more information from the jihadists' meticulous files.[47]

The pace of operations took its toll. The first generation of jihadists, trained in Afghanistan and accustomed to an underground life, were skilled fighters and their deaths depleted a precious core of hardened professionals. The second generation rode the wave of anti-U.S. sentiment, but they too suffered steady losses. Over time, new leaders came in but with disastrous results.[48] One local Al Qaeda leader, in captured internal correspondence, decried his status. He had six hundred fighters before the tribal awakening; a year later, he had fewer than twenty.[49] Another leader noted that after "the apostates and Americans began launching operations," the group "began clearly a series of continuous retreats." Over time, he said, "We lost the cities, and after that the villages, and then the desert became a dangerous sanctuary."[50] Even when locals might have supported Al Qaeda in Iraq, the ferocious counterterrorism pressure meant that aid was risky, with the government and U.S. forces arresting young men or otherwise bringing "misfortunes and tribulations" to ordinary Sunnis.[51]

Al Qaeda in Iraq complained that "we exchanged roles." The Americans became stealthy "guerrillas," carried out assassinations and ambushes, and became "glorified in the media," while the jihadists became a paper-pushing regular army whose activities were known to everyone. Everything was bureaucratic, with a petty leader for every activity. There was an "Emir of the Kitchen" and an "Emir of Tents," as one wry jihadist put it in internal correspondence. Even Al Qaeda in Iraq's foreign smuggling networks proved a vulnerability. Some jihadists fled to Syria because they were afraid of fighting or being killed. One Al Qaeda in Iraq study criticized those in Syria who enjoyed "safety, refrigeration, and modern cars," while fighters in Iraq fought and died.[52]

The United States also made it harder for Masri and other leaders to rein in their fighters, exacerbating the problem of command and leading to dissension in the ranks. By monitoring emails and phone calls—and using this knowledge to conduct arrests and lethal operations—the United States forced the jihadists to use couriers. These were slow-moving and subject to interception, and Al Qaeda in Iraq had to give its ground commanders substantial autonomy in order to keep operations moving. In one captured letter, a local commander complains to his boss that he is writing a letter for the fourth time because the first three were not delivered.[53] As a result, some commanders didn't know the group's overall strategy at the moment, including whether or not to attack or make nice with rival groups.[54] Paranoia, often deserved, paralyzed cells. In one Al Qaeda in Iraq exchange, a local commander warned of several possible spies in his network but concluded, "I am not sure whose story is true," urging suspicion of all those involved.[55]

Facing constant U.S. military strikes, pressure from rival Iraqi groups, resentment from ordinary Sunnis, and demands for change from his nominal bosses in Pakistan, Masri doubled down. He demanded obedience from all factions, ignoring increasingly shrill warnings from Bin Laden and Zawahiri and refusing to rein in his fighters. Failure built on failure. As Al Qaeda in Iraq suffered setbacks on the battlefield and criticism in the airwaves, the number of volunteers plummeted and foreign wallets started to close. However, to attract fighters to a losing cause, the group now had to pay them more, putting the group in an impossible situation. As money from abroad dried up and as they lost territory, Iraqi jihadists relied more on kidnapping, extortion, and smuggling, and they also increased assassination attempts against tribal leaders and other Sunnis, all of which further alienated the locals. The locals turned even more to U.S. forces and even welcomed cooperation with the Shiite-led Iraqi government.

The United States also developed a crude but effective way of countering Al Qaeda in Iraq's media wing: killing the propagandists. The United States' surveillance of internet cafes in Baghdad, which included inserting a virus into local computers to track who was uploading what, led to the death of the group's official spokesman and senior media official. Coalition raids also targeted at least eight media centers, seizing their computers and materials and disrupting their operations.[56]

Political measures helped the United States further divide Iraq's Sunnis from the foreign jihadist-dominated groups. The United States was able to encourage Iraqis to participate in elections, join the Iraqi security forces, and form local self-defense units against Al Qaeda in Iraq. Such measures both gave them a stake in the new Iraqi system and helped them better defend themselves against the jihadists.

The group's dependence on Syria for the transit of foreign fighters also became more difficult as the Syrian regime tightened the screws in response to U.S. pressure. A key Syrian Salafist who worked closely with Syrian intelligence, known as Abu al-Qa'qaa, died mysteriously from a bullet to the head, with most fingers pointing at his former friends in the regime.[57] In revenge, jihadists now turned their guns on Syria. On September 29, 2008, seventeen people died in a car bomb explosion near the Syrian intelligence headquarters in Damascus in an attack supposedly orchestrated by Fatah al-Islam, the Lebanese group with close ties to Al Qaeda in Iraq. Damascus further cracked down on jihadists in Syria.[58]

Recruiting began to dry up. One Kuwaiti recruiter declared that the fight was "between the mujehedin and the Sunnis there" and thus was no longer a legitimate jihad. In January 2007, around ninety foreign fighters crossed over from Syria; by June of the following year, this figure had fallen to approximately twenty. By the end of 2008, Al Qaeda in Iraq had gone from the jihadists' greatest victory to their worst nightmare. According to captured documents, Al Qaeda in Iraq no longer welcomed foreign fighters unless they agreed to become suicide bombers or had special qualifications.[59] Foreign fighters, for their part, now stayed home or considered other causes, as Iraq was seen as sullied and lost.[60]

In the years that followed, Al Qaeda in Iraq went from disaster to disaster. The U.S. and Iraqi forces killed perhaps three-quarters of its senior leaders and drove the rest underground. In 2010, U.S. and Iraqi forces killed Masri and Abu Umar al-Baghdadi in a firefight near Lake Therthar. They also found leadership rosters, financial information, and other vital intelligence that led to further raids that decimated the senior leadership.

Al Qaeda in Iraq focused on domestic terrorism as a way to stay relevant and to intimidate its enemies. In an audio statement, Masri had called for "blowing up the filthiest house, which is the White House" and claimed that jihad would not stop at Iraq. Several Al Qaeda members even had links to a few averted plots in Europe. However, after the disastrous Amman hotel attacks, the group appeared to put little effort into international terrorism in general, and those few plots that occurred had only tenuous links to the leadership of Al Qaeda in Iraq itself.[61] Instead, Al Qaeda went on a killing spree in Iraq. In 2009 and 2010, it killed hundreds of Iraqis in attacks—in 2010, it conducted seventy-five suicide bombings alone in Iraq.[62] It also waged a campaign of assassination against tribal and other Sunni leaders who opposed it, killing over 1,300 people from 2009 through 2013.[63] Because of this mayhem, many Iraqis did not trust their own government to secure the peace. In addition, by decimating local leaders, the group would prepare for its resurgence several years later.

Yet still, compared to the civil war Al Qaeda in Iraq had fomented only a few years earlier, these attacks seemed more like a last gasp than a new lease on life. By the end of 2009, an average of only five foreign fighters a month entered Iraq, down from more than ten times that a few years back.[64] In June 2010, the commander of U.S. forces in Iraq, General Ray Odierno, noted that, in the previous ninety days, U.S. and Iraqi forces had "either picked up or killed 34 of the top 42 Al Qaeda in Iraq leaders," and this included the two top figures. The end seemed near. In 2011, CIA director Leon Panetta would declare, "We're within reach of strategically defeating al-Qaeda."

A Defeat for the Cause

The unraveling of jihad in Iraq hit hard at the Al Qaeda core itself. Not only did its Iraqi affiliate lose recruits and money, but so too did the movement in Pakistan, Algeria, and other countries. Some recruits in Iraq went to neighboring states, but overall, the problems in Iraq and the decline in conflict there and in other areas led to a plunge in recruiting.

Just as Zarqawi used the internet to attract foreign fighters, disgust at their methods had gone viral, displaying the infighting within Iraq to the worldwide jihadist community. Other Sunnis accused Al Qaeda in Iraq's leaders of "transgressing Islamic law" because of their constant killings and accusations that other Muslims were apostates. Abdullah Anas, one of the first volunteers in Afghanistan, criticized Zawahiri's record in Afghanistan and noted that jihad in Iraq, with its emphasis on kidnapping and killing civilians, had moved far from Azzam's teachings.[65] All lamented the "splurge in blood" that was leading the resistance to consume itself.[66]

Salman al-Awda, an influential Saudi preacher whose criticism of the Saudi royal family in the 1990s and subsequent imprisonment had made him a hero to Bin Laden, lashed out at Al Qaeda: "My brother Osama, how much blood has been spilt? How many innocent people, children, elderly, and women have been killed ... in the name of Al Qaeda? Will you be happy to meet God Almighty carrying the burden of these hundreds of thousands or millions of victims on your back?" Dr. Fadl, one of the founders of Al Qaeda and the chief ideologue of Zawahiri and Masri's original Egyptian organization, also blasted Al Qaeda, condemning 9/11 and calling for Muslims in the West to respect the hospitality they received from their host countries. Abu Muhammad al-Maqdisi, perhaps the most influential jihadist theologian alive today and originally a mentor to Zarqawi, declared Al Qaeda in Iraq to be "deviant" and against Islam. He also blasted the group for wasting "the life of its youth" because it lacked any plan other than endless violence.[67] Other jihadist groups disparaged Al Qaeda for the orgy of violence in Iraq. When I was in Libya in 2010, former jihadists who had fought in Iraq told me that their cause in Iraq was just because they were fighting American occupiers but that they had returned because of the killing of civilians.[68] Just as Communist attacks against other left-wing groups had alienated idealistic foreigners like George Orwell during the Spanish civil war and turned them against Communism in general, jihadist depravity against Muslims in Iraq would scar many former supporters, transforming them into compelling critics.

To counter the criticism, Zawahiri attempted a public "web chat" with jihadists worldwide. The criticism was scorching. One would-be jihadist wrote in to ask who was killing "the innocents in Baghdad, Morocco and Algeria? Do you consider the killing of women and children to be jihad? ... Why have you—to this day—not carried out any strike in Israel? Or is it easier to kill Muslims in the markets?"[69]

Bin Laden increasingly seemed desperate to find a new grievance on which to hang Al Qaeda's hat. He even tried to lambaste the United States for not signing the Kyoto Protocol and for its election laws that favored wealthy donors, criticisms that seem better designed to attract liberal college students than would-be jihadists.

Yet for all its image problems in Iraq and around the world, the group often succeeded in its propaganda even as it failed on the ground. Technology helped. YouTube, Facebook, and Twitter all emerged during Al Qaeda in Iraq's struggle in Iraq, and the group employed social media to spread its cause. It also developed videos (some poorly produced, but many professionally done) that it spread throughout the internet. As Fishman points out, the group's media strength enabled it to appear formidable around the world even as it suffered operationally. When Masri and Baghdadi died, jihadists throughout the Muslim world expressed condolences, and some, loyalty, to the would-be state.[70]

The Iraq war also spread violence around the Muslim world. Improved explosive device technology honed in Iraq, involving remote detonators and better bomb designs, spread to other war zones. One Taliban commander told Al Jazeera, "We have 'give and take' relations with the mujahedin in Iraq."[71] The Iraq conflict also spurred more jihadist attacks around the world, convincing at least some Muslims that violence was necessary.[72]

Al Qaeda in Iraq's collapse shapes the views of U.S. counterterrorism officials, the Al Qaeda leadership, and the Islamic State to this day.

The United States learned that ordinary Muslims would reject the jihadists when they had an alternative. If the United States would push an inclusive government, respect local tribal authority, and try to win over ordinary Iraqis, it seemed, then the jihadists could be defeated. Indeed, with their foreign ways, penchant for record-keeping, and mindless brutality, the jihadists were often their own worst enemies. Yet ironically, the United States forgot the role of its own forces. Ordinary Sunnis might resist Al Qaeda, but only if there was someone there to protect them from the jihadists' wrath. In addition, a McChrystal-type campaign to kill and arrest jihadists required an integrated and massive intelligence and military effort that could not easily be duplicated or applied on a smaller scale.

For Al Qaeda leader Ayman al-Zawahiri, the Iraq experience showed the need to work with local Sunnis, persuade rather than kill Shiites, avoid declaring a state, cooperate with other fighting groups, and otherwise be a benign team player (exactly the approach its formidable affiliate, Jabhat al-Nusra, would take in Syria). Too much fervor could backfire. In a lesson that could have been taken from a U.S. counterinsurgency training manual, an Al Qaeda "lessons learned" study counseled that jihadists must collect information on "income per capita" and "the nature of existing clans" before going to war. Similarly, the Al Qaeda leadership's lesson was that declaring an Islamic state was premature. Declaring the state was a failed attempt to hide military weaknesses. Popular support was often lacking, and in any event, the United States would be there to oppose it. Bin Laden counseled jihadists in Yemen and elsewhere to avoid declaring a state because the United States "continues to possess the ability to topple any state we established."[73] With these lessons learned, Al Qaeda itself was not likely to repeat its mistakes in Iraq.

Al Qaeda's leaders had criticized their Iraqi affiliate for slaughtering locals who refused to cooperate, igniting a sectarian war, disseminating horrific images on the internet, and relying on foreign fighters who alienated Iraqis.

Those fighters in Iraq who would go on to form the Islamic State, however, believed these methods worked. Indeed, they believed the problem was that they had not been brutal enough. This lesson seemed absurd in 2010 when Masri was killed and the jihadist flame seemed extinguished. But Iraq's embers still smoldered and would soon roar back to life.

CHAPTER 9 | The Gadfly: Omar Hammami

OMAR SHAFIK HAMMAMI'S murder in 2013 by his fellow jihadists capped one of the most bizarre terrorist careers in modern history. His life story would be funny if its protagonist was not an eager murderer. Hammami rightly described himself as a "walking contradiction," a man "seriously passionate" about jihad but also one who commits it "while laughing at almost everything."[1] While this laughing foreign fighter's story began in Alabama, with stopovers in Canada and Egypt, he would make his mark—and meet his fate—in Somalia, one of the most important theaters of jihad before the Syria conflict and emergence of the Islamic State.

The conflict in Somalia illustrates the problems foreign fighters face and the weaknesses their presence engenders. The key jihadist group there, the Shebaab, was a less-publicized forerunner to the Islamic State. It would eventually succeed in controlling an area roughly the size of Denmark within Somalia and imposing Islamic law. However, as it grew stronger, the Shebaab's own divisions and operational limits would become more apparent.

Omar's childhood home in Daphne, Alabama is the antithesis of Somalia. Hammami's father, Shafik, moved from Syria to Daphne and settled there in 1972. Shafik's path represented an immigrant success story. He became a civil engineer and married a local American woman who taught elementary school. His son Omar's cousins included Hispanics and Hawaiians, reflecting America's broad diversity.[2]

Omar Hammami looked back fondly on his childhood. Born in 1984, he enjoyed a "privileged" upbringing, as he recalls in his memoir, and his parents loved him. Even after he turned to jihad and became estranged, he insisted that he loved his family dearly. Behind the back of his father, his mother raised Omar as a Southern Baptist. He even attended church and Bible camp, and his family celebrated Christmas. He would go "deer hunting like good old boys" with his grandfather, who "used to drink six packs of Budweiser like water."[3] He loved Shakespeare, Kurt Cobain, soccer, debate, and Nintendo—an almost perfect combination for a high school student. He was president of his sophomore class and a strong student. "You knew he was going to be a leader," explained one friend to *New York Times* reporter Andrea Elliott, who wrote a superb profile of Hammami.[4] A review of Hammami's own memoir and other sources suggests a boy always striving to make his mark. At age twelve, he wrote a poem titled, "I've Got a Taste of Glory, the Ticket, but Where Is My Train?" One classmate compared his mix of troublemaking and leadership to the winsome Matthew Broderick character Ferris Bueller.[5]

But Hammami never completely abandoned his Muslim heritage. At home, his family abstained from eating pork, left their shoes at the door, and otherwise respected Muslim culture. "It was like two schools of thought under one roof," his sister would later say.[6] As a youth, Hammami also traveled several times to visit family in Syria, where one uncle "spent over 20 years in a tormenting hell of a prison" because of his ties to the Islamist resistance against the Hafez al-Assad regime, which was crushed in the early 1980s.[7]

The cultural clash became particularly pronounced as Hammami's sister entered her teen years with a fondness for marijuana and boys, outraging her father and eventually leading her to leave home at sixteen. By his high school years, Hammami followed his father's lead as the elder Hammami returned to Islam. A visit to his relatives in Syria bolstered his convictions, and indeed, on a second visit, he became more religious than his Syrian cousins. In high school, he began to pray at school while starting to shun non-Muslims, and he even convinced a friend (and future jihadist volunteer), Bernie Culveyhouse, to convert. Culveyhouse would later say, "I had a fucked up childhood," noting the prevalence of drugs and violence in his life growing up.[8] Hammami's support for violence and intolerance grew too. He praised Bin Laden when the 1998 embassy bombings occurred and swore at his onetime favorite teacher, deriding her for being Jewish.[9] He also began to think about jihad, using the computer of his school library to follow the stories of fighters in Chechnya like Khattab.[10]

After graduation, Hammami attended the University of South Alabama, where he became a Salafi and, again showing his leadership potential, headed the Muslim Students' Association. His strong Salafi views led to tension with his father (many immigrant Muslims like his father disdained Salafi converts).

Hammami and his friends left the local mosque, becoming more and more puritanical in their behavior. In his actions, he sought to provoke. For example, he went to the local Walmart in a traditional robe, and his car had a bumper sticker that read, "As Muslims we believe in one God. We don't worship rocks, trees, or men." In 2002, Hammami refused to pose for a family photograph (some Muslims question being photographed, believing it smacks of idolatry), resulting in a blowup with his father. He then left home and dropped out of college.[11]

Hammami and his high school buddy Culveyhouse moved to Toronto to join the Muslim community there, working a series of dead-end jobs. He recalled an increase in harassment after 9/11 due to being a Muslim wearing traditional dress. However, he also noted (mocking the language of analysts like me), "But 9/11 itself didn't 'radicalize' me as they say." Hammami long eschewed politics as corrupting, but now the U.S. invasion of Iraq focused Hammami on jihad. He felt obliged to join the fray with "Americans attacking my brothers, at home and abroad." On the internet, he obsessively watched a video documentary of Khattab. Hammami, however, still rejected attacks on civilians and perceived the initial fighting in Iraq as too linked to secular groups. He wanted only to defend Muslim lands and create an Islamic state. Hammami also noted that he avoided supposed FBI attempts to entrap him, claiming that "the FBI was trying to send me reformed crack heads as spies."[12]

Hammami became familiar with the Somali immigrant community in Toronto when he delivered milk to residents (he also deplored their habit of urinating in the elevators).[13] In 2005, he married a Somali refugee in Canada, the sister of Culveyhouse's wife, which gave him a personal connection that led to his focus on the conflict in Somalia.

He continued his peripatetic existence, moving with his family and that of his friend Culveyhouse to Egypt, hoping to study at the famous Al-Azhar University. Both were rejected. Hammami blamed Egypt's legendary bureaucracy, noting that "to enroll in Azhar you have to chop down the largest tree in Cairo with a Falaafel." Culveyhouse gave up and returned to the United States. Hammami stayed in Egypt and studied with a Salafi sheikh, who introduced him to the writings of jihadist ideologues such as Abu Mohammad al-Maqdisi. He made the final plunge: "Jihad is truly an individual obligation upon all of us," he wrote.[14] In Cairo, Hammami also met Daniel Maldonado, an American convert to Islam who had connections to the jihadist world.

A movement called the Islamic Courts Union (ICU) in Somalia attracted the duo's attention. At the time, the ICU was attempting to establish a government based on Islamic law—an accomplishment that would attract thousands of foreigners to Syria a decade later. The ICU had begun in 2000 as local clans set up courts to deliver justice, and these merged and spread among a population hungry for law and order. As the ICU spread, it lifted roadblocks, reopened schools, cleared debris, and otherwise brought a modicum of peace and stability to a country ravaged by seemingly endless war.[15] Bin Laden praised the ICU in July 2006: "You have no other means for salvation unless you commit to Islam, put your hands in the hands of the Islamic Courts to build an Islamic state in Somalia."[16] Both Hammami and Maldonado secretly left for Somalia in November 2006.

Although Hammami used visiting in-laws as a cover story to explain his trip, his Somali-born wife refused to join him and would later return to Toronto and divorce him. "There's going to be an Islamic State," he excitedly declared to his wife, attempting to convince her to join him.[17] It didn't work. Although he claimed he missed her and especially his daughter, he defended his actions as other jihadists have before him. "I'm sure my daughter will grow up being told how selfish her father is, but it was exactly my selflessness that caused me to make my decision. If everyone stayed behind with their loved ones, who would be left to help those who had their loved ones murdered?" Khattab had uttered the same mantra. He would stay in Somalia despite pressure from his father and other family members, who questioned his activities in "God Forsaken Somalia (with some expletives)," Hammami said.[18]

Jihadism Emerges in Somalia

The Somalia that Hammami entered was not an obvious breeding ground for jihadism. All Somalis are Sunni Muslims, but, until recently, very few identified as Salafis, let alone as jihadists, following instead less austere forms of Islam. In the 1960s and 1970s, small groups in Somalia formed to advance the role of Islam in politics, but they primarily focused on Sufi or Muslim Brotherhood teachings—interpretations of Islam that the Shebaab would later consider as anathema.

In the 1970s, however, Saudi Arabia expanded its proselytizing mission worldwide, and this had a profound impact on nearby and poor Somalia. Riyadh brought hundreds of Somalis to study in the Kingdom and simultaneously supported schools, mosques, and other institutions in cities and rural areas across Somalia, aiming to spread its intolerant version of Wahhabi Islam. As the International Crisis Group argued, old-fashioned Sufi schools "where students wrote on wooden slabs (*loh*) and often sat under trees were no match for the well-funded modern Wahhabi *madrasas*," which also often provided food and clothing.[19] Saudi Arabia itself was increasingly looking outward, as its embrace of the Afghan war in the 1980s suggested. Decades of such proselytizing would fundamentally transform the nature of Islam in Somalia.[20] For example, Ahmad Godane, the future leader of the Shebaab, received a Saudi scholarship to study in Pakistan, where he first entered the world of militant Islam.[21]

Although only a few Somalis went to fight, the Soviet invasion of Afghanistan proved another important milestone for the future Shebaab. In Afghanistan, they imbibed the idea of jihad as a response to attacks against Muslims and learned that borders among Muslim states represent false colonial creations that a caliphate should replace.[22] On their return, they formed a loose network, linking small groups together in a society otherwise divided by clan and geography. They circulated propaganda, such as videos by Abdullah Azzam, and worked with local jihadist groups such as Al-Itihaad al-Islamiya (AIAI, translated as Islamic Unity), a small jihadist organization formed in the early 1980s, many of whose members would play an important role in the Shebaab.

Civil war erupted in Somalia in 1991, and Somalia has remained a failed state ever since, which is perhaps the longest stretch of any country in the world, though Afghanistan gives it a run for its money. The civil war began as a reaction to the dictatorship of Siad Barre, whose authoritarianism and ineptness prompted widespread resentment. The country had always faced difficulties with governance, as it suffered from fierce clan divisions among its six major and numerous minor or sub-clans. A coalition of anti-Barre clans and other opposition figures toppled him from power but soon turned their guns against each other. In this environment, Islamist organizations, often suppressed under Barre's dictatorship, began to multiply.[23]

Jihadists like AIAI played little role in the initial civil war, but their impact increased as the decade continued. The AIAI group sought to recruit Somalis who had gone to Afghanistan and a few foreign fighters showed up to train its new members.[24] In 1992, AIAI tried to form a mini Islamic emirate in the northeast of Somalia, where it banned smoking, forced women to veil, and otherwise tried to impose its will. Local clans working with the dominant warlords of the area quickly crushed jihadists, killing hundreds of their members and forcing the rest of the organization to flee.[25]

When U.S. forces intervened in 1992 in Operation Restore Hope in response to widespread famine, a few jihadists fought American troops on the streets of Mogadishu alongside the forces of Somali militias, and they also laid mines targeting the United Nations Operation in Somalia (UNISOM). After the downing of a Black Hawk helicopter and the deaths of eighteen

Americans, the United States withdrew from Somalia. Al Qaeda leaders later exaggerated their minor role, however, to portray themselves as the drivers of the U.S. withdrawal.[26] (One Al Qaeda figure was frustrated with the portrayal of what happened in the film *Black Hawk Down*—not the first person to find Hollywood's depictions of reality inaccurate.) The AIAI group also struck at Ethiopia, bombing hotels and trying to assassinate ministers, as it tried to create a "greater Somalia" that drew on Ethiopia's own restive ethnic Somali population. Ethiopia launched cross-border attacks to wipe out AIAI in 1996 and 1997, killing much of its personnel and fragmenting the group.[27]

Yet AIAI's legacy would endure. Its members included figures like Sheikh Hassan Dahir Aweys and Aden Hashi Farah Ayro, both of whom became prominent Shebaab figures. As one U.S. official described it, the group would transform from a "noun" to an "adjective," becoming more of an idea than an actual entity. The network that developed issued Somali- and Arabic-language newspapers and videos, and it fielded representatives to neighboring states, Saudi Arabia, and countries with a large Somali diaspora like the United Kingdom.[28]

Nor did Al Qaeda forget about Somalia. Bin Laden considered relocating to Somalia when the group felt pressure to leave Afghanistan and Pakistan in the early 1990s, hoping to "find a location for military operations that would replace Afghanistan." Other jihadists looked to Somalia as a place to fight after being expelled from Bosnia.[29] Al Qaeda also feared that the U.S. famine relief effort in the area in 1992–1993 was a means to "spread US hegemony over the region" and hoped that a base in Somalia would give Al Qaeda a means to counter this as well as increase its influence in the region and nearby Yemen and Saudi Arabia.[30] Bin Laden appointed one of his senior military officials in charge of Somali operations, and several senior members traveled to Somalia to instruct the locals.[31] Al Qaeda, however, failed to establish a significant presence in Somalia in the 1990s, and the country never became a base for international terrorism. Al Qaeda's version of jihadism lacked appeal there. Locals preferred to focus on the threat from other clans, not the United States or other enemies, and tribal loyalty trumped religious solidarity. Furthermore, warlords extorted jihadists at every turn rather than welcoming them as brothers-in-arms.[32]

Even though the Soviets were long gone, Afghanistan continued to hold its allure for Somalis in the late 1990s, this time to provide training for would-be fighters. Many key figures in the Shebaab would spend time there, soaking up more global ideas from Al Qaeda and like-minded groups as well as gaining valuable instruction. Future Shebaab leaders like Ahmed Godane and 'Ayro, for example, learned how to use explosives in Afghanistan and, upon their return, taught the techniques to other Somalis.[33] Also in the late 1990s, a new phenomenon emerged: clan-based ad-hoc courts that used Islamic law (*sharia*) for their judgments. Those who spent time in Afghanistan often joined these courts, drawing on the "learning" they received in the Afghan training camps. By joining these courts, they also became integrated with various Somali clan networks who provided protection.[34]

As a result, global jihad and the associated networks took root. When the United States invaded Afghanistan after the 9/11 attacks, more than a hundred Somalis traveled to Afghanistan to fight, strengthening existing linkages.[35] Al Qaeda's cell in East Africa conducted an attack in Mombasa, Kenya, in 2002 on an Israeli-owned hotel there, killing six, and tried to shoot down an Israeli passenger airplane with surface-to-air missiles. Jihadists in Somalia protected them.

Fearing more attacks, the United States tried to disrupt this network, and Somalis bore the brunt of the massive U.S. response. Economic punishments targeted at various groups linked to terrorism hit many ordinary Somalis hard. The United States even blocked the assets of Somalia's largest remittance program, which was responsible for a huge portion of Somalia's economy and services such as water purification, because it feared Al Qaeda–linked terrorists were exploiting it (the United States would later admit that it had found no serious links).[36] Some militias captured and tried to sell innocent Arabs to Western intelligence services, claiming they were Al Qaeda. Under pressure, Somali jihadists united for self-defense and to protect their own commercial and clan interests and retaliate against the warlords targeting them.[37] Some small groups of jihadists also began to attack Western aid workers, government security forces, and even peace activists.[38]

Over time, Islamist ideology would continue to gain credibility, particularly because it promised a solution to the biggest problem facing Somalis: law and order. In 2005–2006, the ICU expanded quickly using the promise of law and order under Islam to spread their influence and counter the Transitional Federal Government, the nominal internationally recognized regime. Perhaps even more important, they also subdued many of Somalia's warlords, including the hilariously named Alliance for the Restoration of Peace and Counter-Terrorism, which was widely seen as a front for the United States. They seized control of Mogadishu in June, earning Bin Laden's praise. By the end of 2006, the ICU controlled most of southern Somalia and the majority of the population. The United States reacted with alarm. The senior U.S. diplomat for Africa, Jendayi Frazer, declared the ICU "extremist to the core" and "controlled by al-Qaeda."[39]

The Rise of the Shebaab

The leaders who would form the Shebaab emerged from the broader jihadist network several years before Hammami would enter Somalia.[40] The Shebaab was an element within the ICU that often had considerable autonomy. It acted as an enforcer for the ICU, assassinating government supporters and other opponents. All four of its founders had trained in Afghanistan, including Aden Hashi Ayro, who led the group when it was first part of the ICU, and Ahmed Abdi Godane, its first official leader when the Shebaab emerged as an independent group.[41] The Shebaab leaders had extreme beliefs alien to most Somalis. They believed they could declare Muslims apostates for failing to embrace jihadist ideas, opposed Somali cultural practices, and supported traditional Islamic punishments, all of which were unpopular.

The Shebaab received a major boost in December 2006, when over 10,000 Ethiopian troops invaded Somalia. To the alarm of the Ethiopian regime, voices within the ICU had called for jihad against Ethiopia, claimed territory inhabited by ethnic Somalis, aided insurgencies there, and forged links to Eritrea, Ethiopia's archenemy. The transitional government of President Abdullahi Yusuf, widely seen as Ethiopia's man, had appealed for neighboring countries to help defend his regime from the ascendant ICU.[42] Ethiopian troops ostensibly were there to bolster transitional government forces, but in reality they took the lead in the fighting, quickly conquering large parts of the country and retaking Mogadishu in the name of the Somali government.

At first, the Ethiopian invasion seemed disastrous for the Islamist cause. Far better armed and trained, the Ethiopians devastated the ICU and other Islamist groups, and some Somalis blamed extremists for giving the Ethiopians an excuse to invade.[43] The United States tacitly blessed the Ethiopian invasion and provided Ethiopian troops with intelligence, logistical support, and money in the name of counterterrorism. The United States also used bases in Ethiopia to try to kill and capture Al Qaeda figures in Somalia on the heels of Ethiopian troops.[44]

Yet the intervention set the stage for the Shebaab's emergence as one of Somalia's strongest players. Somalia and Ethiopia have a history of war and rivalry, and the invasion enraged many Somalis. Under colonial rule, Ethiopia controlled several Somali-populated areas, and Somali nationalists often talked about unifying all Somalis under one state. Ethiopia is also a majority Christian population, although a third of the population is Muslim, enabling jihadists to portray Ethiopia as the latest successor to Serbia, Russia, and America as the infidel enemy of the faith.

For many of the Shebaab's foreign volunteers, the group's appeal mixed nationalism and religion. A senior Somali Islamist asked for Muslims around the world to join their fight in Somalia, and a number of volunteers from the Somali diaspora in Minnesota later testified that they felt an obligation to fight "invaders."[45] At the same time, volunteers like Hammami felt inspired by the Shebaab's attempt to create an Islamic state. As jihadists successfully did in Afghanistan, Bosnia, Chechnya, and Iraq, the Shebaab could now fuse religion and nationalism, labeling Ethiopia, and by association all international forces, as "crusaders" and claiming their collaborators betray God as well as the Somali nation.[46]

The Ethiopian military, following a similar doctrine to the Russians in Chechnya, indiscriminately shelled cities and otherwise failed to distinguish fighters from civilians, leading to a surge of anger and a desire for revenge. Covertly, the secular dictatorship of neighboring Eritrea provided hundreds of thousands of dollars in support to the Shebaab to weaken its Ethiopian archenemy.[47] Perhaps most important, the Ethiopians, like the Americans in Iraq after 2003, toppled their enemy without a credible replacement government, and the population widely viewed the Ethiopian-backed transitional government as a puppet. The Ethiopian invasion also devastated the ICU, a double-edged sword, allowing even more radical factions like the Shebaab to gain influence. In addition, transitional government leaders stole all they could without paying the police and soldiers, increasing the contrast with the law and order imposed by the Islamists. Many police and soldiers simply deserted, leaving large parts of the country in chaos.[48]

Somali recruits joined the Shebaab for many reasons beyond outrage at the Ethiopian invasion: anger at abuse from the transitional government, a paying job, clan politics, antiforeign sentiment, and an embrace of the ideology with its constant message that Islam was under siege. The Shebaab also represented one of Somalia's more competent fighting groups, and its prowess attracted local youths. When the group advanced, some Somalis wanted to side with a winner. When it declined, the group often coerced young men to join. Few recruits knew much about Islam or the Shebaab leaders' ideology.[49]

Given its ties to foreign groups and causes, the Shebaab was more open to working with foreigners than most Somali groups, which often had a pronounced xenophobia. "We are in need for Somalia's Zarqawi, Khattab, and Abu-al-Layth [a senior Al Qaeda figure]," Shebaab propaganda noted.[50] So it is not surprising that Hammami ended up with this group (law enforcement would arrest his traveling companion Maldonado near the Somalia-Kenya border and send him to jail in America). However, Hammami was an exception among the Shebaab's foreign fighters. Of the thousands of foreigners who fought in Somalia, the vast majority came from ethnic-Somali diaspora communities in Kenya, Ethiopia, and other Horn of Africa countries or from the hundreds of thousands in the Somali diaspora in the West. Only a few hundred foreign fighters did not have Somali heritage.[51] The Shebaab also attracted Al Qaeda–affiliated fighters from Yemen, just across the narrow straits, who sought shelter from the Yemeni and U.S. counterterrorism campaign.[52]

In many parts of Europe and the United States, the Somali community was poor and not well integrated, making its members more susceptible to Shebaab calls for help. Of the 1,500 to 2,000 or so foreign fighters the Shebaab attracted, roughly 200 or so were from the European Union. Perhaps 40 Americans joined the Shebaab, and almost 100 traveled from the United Kingdom; Sweden also began to see members of its Somali community leave, and a Somali with Danish residency tried to murder a cartoonist there who had mocked the Prophet. Numbers of foreign fighters would fall as the outrage over the 2006 Ethiopian invasion faded and the Shebaab's brutality against its fellow Somalis became widely known.[53]

In the Western world, the Shebaab also gained a powerful champion: the U.S.-born Anwar al-Awlaki, who was emerging as a top propagandist for the jihadist movement. Awlaki, like Hammami, was particularly skilled at selling jihadist themes to a Western audience, and he had serious religious credentials that gave him credibility. In late 2008, Awlaki posted "Salutations to al-Shabab of Somalia," praising the group for "implementing the sharia and giving us a living example of how we as Muslims should proceed to change our situation." Awlaki crowed, "The ballot has failed us but the bullet has not."[54]

The Shebaab initially avoided pitched battles, relying on guerrilla war and terrorism to undermine enemy morale. Its targets included transitional government officials, such as civil servants and members of the police; businessmen with connections to the regime; and indeed anyone working with its myriad enemies, including women who sold tea to soldiers.[55] Foreigners brought guerrilla tactics, improved roadside bomb designs, suicide bombings, and other tactics and procedures with them. In urban areas, Shebaab fighters dug tunnels to hide and surprise the attackers—a technique borrowed from Chechnya. Suicide bombing did not occur in Somalia before the rise of the Shebaab in 2006, and even then it remained rare until 2010, when more foreigners came in. In addition, foreigners trained Shebaab recruits in sniping, leading to a dramatic rise in sniper attacks on outside forces.

Foreigners also transformed the Shebaab's media and propaganda. For years, the group relied on word of mouth or older technologies to recruit and share information, but as foreigners streamed in, the Shebaab used video and the internet far more extensively, becoming the best media user among jihadists until the emergence of the Islamic State. In its propaganda, the Shebaab would glorify its dead as martyrs while offering visceral footage of its fighters desecrating the bodies of dead Ethiopian soldiers. More prosaically, Shebaab propaganda also urged foreign fighters to come to Somalia to find wives. The Shebaab also integrated propaganda into its operations, issuing videotapes of its more dramatic killings, such as the beheading of a rival military leader.[56] Over time, the propaganda internationalized, with messages in Arabic, English, and Somali. Propaganda included the images and words of Azzam, Bin Laden, and others in an effort to court Al Qaeda and become recognized by it. Attracted by this propaganda, many foreign fighters came to Somalia with no relevant skills and unable to operate in the harsh environment. Shebaab found it had to babysit them, to its dismay.

Hammami played an important role in the Shebaab, acting as an articulate and charismatic English-language spokesman for the group. In October 2007, Hammami's popularity surged from local curiosity to international terrorist superstar. He gave an interview to *Al Jazeera* as "Abu Mansoor al-Amriki" (the American). Tech-savvy and a natural leader, Hammami became a prominent spokesman for the Shebaab as it tried to expand its role outside the region. In 2009, the group chose Hammami to respond to President Obama's June 2009 speech in Cairo, which was meant as a rhetorical olive branch extended to the Muslim world embittered by the U.S. invasion of Iraq and other unpopular actions in the Bush presidency. In April 2011, Hammami released two truly awful rap music songs, and in 2013, he praised the Boston Marathon bombers: "These brothers are making history. Let them shine." Perhaps most important, Hammami was a pioneer in the jihadists' use of social media. His Twitter account had thousands of followers, and his calls for action and personal redemption (themes the Islamic State would use on social media) blended well with his sense of humor. Hammami also recruited nearly twenty Americans to join the cause. As he wrote in the introduction to his memoir, "The war of narratives has become even more important than the war of navies, napalm, and knives."[57]

Throughout his jihad, Hammami retained his sense of humor and even a sense of romance. Reading his 2012 autobiography (with the intro noting that he is "still alive and well"), one is struck by his willingness to mock himself and those around him, an attitude in short supply among zealous jihadists. He laments his addiction to Tim Horton's coffee while in Canada and offers shout-outs to his favorite teachers and high school buddies. At the same time, he glorifies his time in Somalia, noting, "I would even pretend that I was watching myself on a TV screen, as though this were some form of Chechen Jihaadi flick!"[58]

Hammami had found his own way to Somalia, but over time, an extensive apparatus grew to recruit foreigners through mosques or religious schools, help them travel to Kenya, and then channel them into training camps in Somalia.[59] Some, like Al Qaeda operative Fazul Abdallah Mohammad, posed as aid workers to get through to Somalia. Because the Shebaab drew on recruits from neighboring states, from the broader Somali diaspora, and those like Hammami with only a loose connection at best, they needed different networks and structures to recruit them and bring them in. In Kenya, for example, a network of radical preachers helped pull in volunteers for the Shebaab. In the West, in contrast, the Shebaab relied more on blanket propaganda to lure recruits, with a few local sympathizers at times playing a facilitating role.[60]

Funding supported the Shebaab's success. In 2007, fighters received $20 for a hand grenade attack, $30 for killing a soldier, and $100 for a roadside bomb or mortar attack. The police and army, in contrast, often went unpaid. Over time, the group paid regular fighters $60 a month and officers $200 or more; this salary made their fighters less likely to loot to survive, reducing the risk of a popular backlash against the group. The Shebaab would also pay the families of its "martyrs." The Shebaab gained a reputation for consistency that its rivals lacked.[61]

The Frustrations of Jihad

On entering Somalia, Hammami embraced the Shebaab, but over time he became more critical. He struggled with the transition from a wealthy and comfortable Western existence to a war zone in a developing country, an experience similar to other Westerners who found themselves on the front lines of jihad. He recalled eating maggots and daydreaming about Krispy Kreme. He and his fellow jihadists warred against "the Red Army," ferocious army ants that plagued their campsites. At another point, Hammami recalls praying for the enemy to hurry up and make him a martyr so he could "leave the mosquitoes to the less fortunate."[62]

Somalia's nonexistent infrastructure stunned Hammami: "There are times when the Bedouins (carrying their stick with the classic 3 liter jug) can outpace the car on the road." Going to the bathroom often became a nightmare, requiring hiding from planes and enemy forces while clutching a gun and avoiding losing "an eye from thorns." The language problems exacerbated the culture shock. Hammami recalls trying to ask local Bedouins for some bread in Somali; his Arab companions thought he asked for slave girls, while the Bedouins gave him cooked meat instead. "I don't remember having one joke, one suggestion, or one idea properly understood for the greater portion of a year," he wrote.[63]

The reality of battle proved tough for the foreigners. Hammami recalls that some fighters had to fend for themselves with no supplies or support. Some ran out of water and had to drink urine. He also had to dismiss his initial fantasies about divine intervention, inspired by the works of Azzam and others: "I had to come to terms with the fact that the angels don't come down and save the day for every battle."[64] Recruits also chaffed at the boredom and tedium common to soldiers in war. When asked to stand down when the Shebaab sought a break in the fighting, Hammami and others considered trying to find another place to fight.

Not surprisingly, many recruits deserted. Hammami related that during training, hundreds would flee the daily beatings and other petty abuses. One of his fellow jihadists quipped, "The true blessing is not to make it to Jihaad . . . the true blessing is *staying* in Jihaad." Many people, Hammami noted, "come here on a hype" but quickly became exhausted. He criticized jihadi films as making battles look glamorous and easy, but he said, "Everyone must know that this is not a movie." Some would even join the other side. Hammami explained that he missed ice cream, Chinese food, gourmet coffee, and his family, especially his little daughter. However, when asked why he would not ever return to America, he retorted, "The 'why not' would have to be [Attorney General] Eric Holder, war ships, most wanted pictures, and kangaroo courts!"[65]

Hammami's class of recruits suffered a high mortality rate. He noted that out of five volunteers in his group, one was captured and three were killed (Hammami, the fifth, would also later be killed). The foreigners' zealotry in combat and eagerness for martyrdom is one reason for the high casualty count, but arrest or death by rival forces was also more likely because of their foreign looks and ways. Hammami recalls passing through hostile checkpoints hidden with other foreigners amid a pile of petrol (which produced noxious fumes) because "the slightest glimpse of our whiteness will lead to a show down." He also wryly complained, in reference to the U.S.-led program to kill foreign fighters suspected of being terrorists, "Drones on Somalia are racist. They only shoot at white people!"[66]

To better assimilate, Hammami tried to find a second wife among the Somalis. After a few trials and tribulations, and with the support of senior Shebaab figures, he found one, giving him local connections. He joked that he could "now live in a mud hut and eat fish until my heart was content," but, in reality, he gained considerable benefits through a local marriage. Locals would protect him as long as he adhered to the rules and norms of the clan, provide him with food and shelter, and hide him from prying enemy eyes, tremendous benefits for a member of a group on the run.[67]

The Shebaab's High-Water Mark—A Mini Islamic State

The Shebaab continued to gain strength. Ethiopia's initial successes bogged it down into an expensive guerrilla war, and it failed to build a more moderate Islamist alternative to the Shebaab. In the January 2009 Djibouti agreement, Addis Ababa agreed to completely withdraw its forces, and the Shebaab filled the resulting vacuum. The UN considered sending more forces to Somalia, but the Shebaab's suicide attacks and assassinations helped deter both international and regional powers.[68] The Shebaab had a healthy 2,000 or so fighters in 2008, and by 2011, it had almost 10,000 men under arms.[69]

The Shebaab began to control more and more territory. At its peak, the Shebaab would control an area the size of Denmark, ruling over five million Somalis. To administer this territory, it appointed regional governors, who then oversaw local administrators, Islamic courts, financial offices, and armed forces.[70] As the Islamic State would later learn, such control is a source of strength but also a tremendous vulnerability.

On one hand, control of territory meant money, and money provided more power. The Shebaab provided a degree of much-needed stability and law and order to Somalia, allowing trade to revive, though hardly flourish, and it even rebuilt bridges, roads, and irrigation canals.[71] As one Somali commented, "You cannot be robbed in the street in Mogadishu, actually, the part they control. You cannot be robbed. You can walk openly with a lot of money." Shebaab courts had long queues, as they were often the only justice system available.

Claiming their taxes were really just the collection of the religious tithes that devout Muslims must pay, the Shebaab would take up to 15 percent of a business or construction project, taxed employees at 5 percent (especially if they had links to an international NGO), taxed imports and exports from the ports, and took a share of property ranging from homes to goats. If the Somalis in question moved from place to place, herding goats and camels, they took a portion of the herd. In some cases, they forced people to pay a fixed dollar amount each month as a business tax or for rent if they lived in a public building. The sugar and charcoal trades brought in hundreds of thousands of dollars.[72] The Shebaab generated as much as $100 million a year from taxation and extortion of areas under its control.[73] The group also kidnapped foreigners for ransom, generating millions of dollars.[74] Some of this money went to help poor Somalis, but most of it went to pay soldiers, policemen, and administrators. The Shebaab also set up an elaborate system of surveillance to ensure that those who collected money were carefully monitored for corruption.[75]

The Shebaab maintained control through a mix of fear, belief, and co-optation. In addition to paying salaries, it also created the Amniyat, a secret police, that targeted the families of defectors and deserters, and the Shebaab would use the organization to instill fear whenever its more gentle means failed. The Shebaab introduced a ministry for promoting Islam, using schools and preaching to spread its teachings. It pushed religious leaders to teach the Shebaab's interpretation of Islam and took over or set up radio and TV stations as well.

Gaining territory also allowed the Shebaab to expand its training camps. Recruits like Hammami received some practical training, learning how to use AK-47s and other small arms as well as the occasional more specialized weapon, like a Draganov sniper rifle. They also learned how to build a booby trap and a bomb.[76] But, as Hammami would note, "It's not exactly the Faaruuq training camp of Afghanistan." When foreign fighter veterans of Afghanistan, Chechnya, or other conflicts provided the training, it usually exceeded the quality of that provided by local forces. One of Hammami's trainers fought with Khattab in Chechnya, and he recalls reenacting one of the master jihadist's battles as he learned the basics of guerrilla war.[77] The particular camp mattered. Hammami's camp, Nabhan, was the most international and worked with many East Africans, trying to indoctrinate them on global jihadist teachings and paint the world as a struggle between Bin Laden's knights and the forces of darkness led by Bush and then Obama. Other camps, however, only helped the Shebaab train local clan fighters, with little ideological indoctrination.[78]

Often the recruits received bizarre training. Designed to toughen them up, it was a caricature of military conditioning. Hammami notes that his "trainer believed that beating the muscles with a stick would hasten the workout process." In one instance, recruits were instructed to dig their own graves with their hands; they then laid in their graves while the trainer jumped from grave to grave, stepping on their stomachs. Trainers also instructed recruits to walk on their hands while someone carried their feet (the "wheelbarrow" familiar to American elementary school kids) but over broken glass.

The Shebaab's leadership drew on a cross-section of Somali clans, at times enabling it to rise above or at least contain these endemic disputes. It would also imprison or kill the leaders of clans who opposed it while trying to work with clans or subclans that felt they received an unfair share of the spoils.[79] The Shebaab established a local council of clan elders whom it would consult. They also respected clan custom, allowing locals to be ruled by clan leaders, unless it directly opposed Islamic law. At the same time, the group tried to recruit orphans or teenagers away from their families, drawing on those enrolled in religious schools with some degree of indoctrination.[80] Clans are the bane of Somalia's politics, however, and many of their new recruits and subjects still put the clan first. One Shebaab defector recalled that fighters might only care for fellow clan members who got injured, abandoning others on the battlefield.[81]

In addition to its problem with clan politics, the Shebaab governed poorly and alienated locals initially attracted to the Shebaab's promise of law and order. When it took over new areas, the Shebaab would purge Sufi religious leaders and destroy their shrines. Sufis believe that holy men can intercede with God, which the Shebaab views as attributing to the holy men divine powers that only God posseses. The Shebaab would also proselytize and force girls to wear a veil. It enacted other unpopular policies, such as forbidding Somalis to watch soccer and slashing women who did not dress with appropriate modesty. In some areas, it forced families to give their daughters to fighters as wives, and its forces at times kidnapped and gang-raped as they advanced.[82] The wrong haircut, "indecent" clothing, playing music, or sitting with a member of the opposite sex could merit a whipping or other punishment.[83] The foreign fighters made the humanitarian crisis in Somalia worse, driving out international aid workers, whom many jihadists saw as spies, covert missionaries, and agents of Western influence.[84] The International Crisis Group summed up the Shebaab's record of governance as "disastrous."[85]

Although Al Qaeda operative Fazul Abdallah Mohammad boasted that in Somalia, unlike Iraq, the jihadists did not harm Muslims, they still had trouble winning over locals. As one expert reported, "Somalis are committed xenophobes," and they distrust people from other tribes, let alone true foreigners.[86] Foreigners like Hammami also grated on the local leaders when the foreigners told them what to do. One leader suggested they leave if they didn't like how the locals planned their campaign; Hammami replied by saying that Somalia is not for Somalis, but rather belongs to all Muslims.[87] Many Somalis probably disagreed. Furthermore, Somalis resented some of the suicide bombings on civilian targets, a tactic widely seen as tied to the foreigners. Some foreign fighters complained that even the Shebaab treated them as second-class citizens.[88]

On the battlefield, the Shebaab could easily defeat the small transitional government forces, and guerrilla war had worked against Ethiopian troops. But the Shebaab was unable to make progress against the Ugandan and other national contingents of the African Union Mission in Somalia (AMISOM), which came into being in 2007. The mission of AMISOM was to support the transitional Somali government and help facilitate humanitarian aid. Its forces, which usually numbered more than 10,000 troops, came from Kenya, Ethiopia, Uganda, and other neighboring countries, and most troops had better training and equipment than any of the Somali groups. The Shebaab tried to combat these more powerful forces directly, leading to huge losses that the relatively small group could ill afford.

In 2010, the group commenced the massive "Ramadan offensive," losing roughly one-tenth of its total forces, including many top leaders. As Hammami would note, "Unfortunately, it would take many failures for the Mujaahidiin to realize that ambushes and irregular urban warfare were the true keys to success against a much stronger occupier."[89] In 2011, the group lost control over Mogadishu, a huge symbolic blow as well as the loss of a source of taxation and recruitment. In the same year, drought struck much of Somalia, leading to over 200,000 deaths. The vast majority died in Shebaab-controlled areas because it refused to allow in international support, believing the aid workers to be spies.[90] Such failures discredited Godane's leadership, with Shebaab cofounder Hassan Dahir Aweys describing Godane as "Machiavelli" and unfit to lead.[91] The Shebaab reached out more and more to Al Qaeda, which generated more opposition internally by those who feared the Shebaab would come to be seen as foreign puppets.

Others appealed to Al Qaeda to push aside Godane. Godane, however, successfully weathered the storm, purging the organization of rivals to stay on top and building up a formidable internal security force.[92] The Shebaab engaged in a campaign of assassination to intimidate its opponents in Somalia. It attacked government officials and supporters, members of the media, and even a comedian who mocked the group.[93]

As the Shebaab lost territory and suffered military defeats, it increased taxation and forced recruits to join, both of which decreased its popularity. Its fickle Eritrean patron began to have its own Islamist problem and cut back on funding.[94] Over time, it lost recruits. The Somali government also tried to encourage defections among locals in particular. It established a program to provide defectors with an education, job skills, and religious classes if they abandoned the Shebaab.[95] Part of the hope was to separate the foreigners from local Somalis, enabling the arrest or killing of the foreigners or forcing them to flee the country.

Hammami's Fall

The Shebaab's problems were not lost on Hammami, and in characteristic fashion, he decided to say something about it, leading to a sudden, and eventually terminal, falling out with other Shebaab leaders. In a 2012 video, he rejected the Shebaab's focus on Somalia and the nearby region, advocating instead a more internationalist approach. Along with a small group of fighters, he split from the group. Perhaps more worrying to the Shebaab leadership, other disgruntled foreign fighters supported Hammami as did rivals to Godane, who used the foreigners' status as an excuse in their power struggle and even sent an open letter critical of Godane to Zawahiri.[96] The whole drama also played out on Twitter for all to see. "War booty is eaten by the top dogs," Hammami tweeted, "but the guys who won it are jailed for touching it. A gun, bullets, some beans is their lot." He later even declared Godane an apostate.[97] The Shebaab responded by publicly criticizing Hammami's "narcissistic pursuit of fame." Hammami eventually rejected both the Shebaab and Al Qaeda itself when it lined up behind the Somali group, though his fans were no doubt pleased to know he still considered himself, in his own words, a terrorist.[98]

Hammami found refuge with local tribes that had turned against the Shebaab.[99] He survived at least one assassination attempt (and, of course, immediately tweeted out that he had been shot in the neck and survived), but his luck did not hold out. On September 12, 2013, gunmen from the Shebaab's intelligence service loyal to Godane ambushed Hammami and his small group of followers, where they were hiding out in a village in central Somalia.[100] His clan had relinquished him, allowing him to be assassinated. The Shebaab became more skeptical of foreign fighters from the West, believing they were spies or likely to turn against the group like Hammami had done.[101]

The Shebaab as a Terrorist Group

For the Shebaab, many attacks often labeled "terrorism" are part of military campaigns against its various enemies. The Shebaab attacked government officials, launched bombings, and otherwise tried to intimidate its enemies, but it did not engage in global terrorism. The vast majority of the Shebaab's attacks are in Somalia, where it has hit military facilities, government buildings, hotels, ports, and Somalia's national airline. It also struck at United Nations facilities in Somalia and those of the government's foreign backers, such as countries like Uganda and Kenya. Nevertheless, the presence of many foreigners among the Shebaab's ranks, including Americans like Hammami, generated fears among Western officials that the foreigners would orchestrate terrorist attacks in their home countries.[102]

These fears were compounded when the Shebaab began making noises about openly joining Al Qaeda. One faction declared allegiance in 2009, and the group's central core sought an affiliation in 2010. However, while he was alive, Bin Laden offered the Shebaab guidance but opposed a public merger with the Somali group, fearing that it would be another Al Qaeda in Iraq, bad at governing but skilled at alienating locals.[103] After Bin Laden's death, however, Zawahiri welcomed ties to the Shebaab, which was particularly eager for a merger given the disaster of the Ramadan offensive and other setbacks. Godane asked Zawahiri to "lead us to the path of jihad and martyrdom that was drawn by our imam, the martyr Osama," and pledged his allegiance openly on February 14, 2012. This helped it gain worldwide attention, but its terrorism continued to focus primarily on its immediate region, not globally.

Yet terrorism did go beyond Somalia, just not in the global way that Al Qaeda favored. As with many groups that recruit foreign fighters, the Shebaab expanded to attack regionally. Just as many Chechen jihadists viewed the cause as fighting for Islam in the Caucasus, not just Chechnya, important parts of the Islamist movement in Somalia believe all areas where Somalis live (including parts of Ethiopia, Kenya, and Djibouti) should become a single caliphate.[104]

Revenge also played a role in the Shebaab's internationalism. The group warned in a press release that countries like Uganda and Burundi must "take out your forces, or face blasts in your capital cities."[105] In 2010, the group launched two massive bombings in Uganda at a restaurant and club where people had gathered to watch the World Cup final, killing over seventy people. Uganda represented a logical target, as its military forces had prevented the Shebaab from securing southern Somalia. The Shebaab encouraged jihadists around the world to attack Uganda and Burundi because of their support for the transitional government.[106]

The Shebaab had long worked with ethnic Somalis in Kenya, but after 2009, it extended its efforts to non-Somali Muslims there, taking advantage of Muslim-Christian tension and Kenya's widespread economic problems. Refugee camps in Kenya became rear bases for the Shebaab and a place for it to recruit. Kenyans soon became the largest foreign element within the Shebaab. The Shebaab also worked with extremist organizations in Kenya like al-Hijra that proselytized and recruited in the name of radical Islam. As a result, those trained in Somalia conducted attacks in Kenya, and the Shebaab infiltrated parts of the country.[107]

Attacks against Kenya increased. Many attacks were near Kenya's border with Somalia, but in 2013, the Shebaab struck the Westgate mall in Nairobi, killing sixty-seven people, and in 2015, it hit a university there and killed more than one hundred twenty more. In January 2016, its fighters killed over one hundred Kenyan troops, taking their armored personnel carriers, artillery, and other equipment. [108] In 2017, Shebaab fighters beheaded nine Kenyans.

Yet terrorism was a sideshow for the Shebaab. Terrorism allowed the Shebaab to retaliate against its enemies and served as a distraction when the group suffered setbacks. However, almost all members of the Shebaab, including those with close ties to Al Qaeda, prioritized establishing Islamic governance and primacy among the warring factions in Somalia over conducting international attacks.[109]

Foreigners Fighting the Shebaab

Although the Shebaab hoped to use terrorism to frighten intervening states into leaving, in reality, terrorism usually backfired, convincing Somalia's neighbors that the group must be defeated. The AMISOM presence since 2007 helped stiffen the transitional government, enabling it to survive the Shebaab's offensives and, over time, push it back. Burundi, Ethiopia, Kenya, and Uganda—all bolstered by the United States—led the fight against the Shebaab, many focusing on areas near their own borders. Uganda has had a presence in Somalia for a decade, with its forces in 2017 exceeding six thousand, many of them deployed around the capital Mogadishu.[110] In 2011, Kenya and Ethiopia deployed military forces in Somalia to protect their borders, with Kenya occupying much of southern Somalia. Burundi deployed over five thousand troops to AMISOM.[111] Ethiopia's presence has waxed and waned, though it maintains that it is still a staunch AMISOM supporter.[112]

The United States also played a considerable role. After 9/11, the U.S. focus on all jihadist groups increased, including the Shebaab. At first, the United States tried, largely unsuccessfully, to arm and finance Somali warlords to fight jihadists.[113] However, the warlords had at best limited popularity because of their tolerance of plunder and corruption. The United States also aided AMISOM, paying troops and providing logistical support and stepped-up aid to the anti-Shebaab transitional government. By 2014, the United States had given approximately $500 million to AMISOM and almost $200 million to the nominal Somali government.[114]

Over time, the United States became more directly involved. United States Navy ships have bombed Shebaab areas, blockaded the port of Kismayo to stop arms shipments to the Shebaab, and conducted cruise missile attacks.[115] By 2017, the United States maintained makeshift bases in Somalia, and several hundred U.S. special operations forces worked with Somali, Kenyan, and Ugandan soldiers to conduct raids, often providing them with surveillance assistance and intelligence. United States forces have trained a small military unit, Danab ("lightning" in Somali), to carry out operations rather than trying to build up large forces to control territory. The Trump administration also expanded authority for carrying out offensive air strikes against the Shebaab.

The United States killed Shebaab fighters and leaders with between thirty-two and thirty-six airstrikes from 2001 to 2016. Some of the dead included Shebaab founders.[116] In 2008, the United States killed Ayro with a cruise missile strike, and in 2014 the United States killed Godane, another blow to the group.[117] In subsequent years, drone strikes have taken out several top Shebaab commanders. In 2016, a U.S. airstrike killed more than 150 Shebaab fighters at what the United States described as a "graduation ceremony."[118] To avoid drones and U.S. strikes in general, Shebaab leaders have tried to avoid using phones and the internet, fearing U.S. monitoring, but this strategy has also prevented the group from exercising control over its members.[119]

The Shebaab Settles in for a Long War

The Shebaab has persisted in the face of this broad set of enemies. By 2017, the Shebaab still controlled many rural areas of central and southern Somalia and had the ability to launch attacks elsewhere, including Mogadishu.[120] Although losing territory hurt the Shebaab's prestige, it also means less administrative overhead, though the group still has to pay its fighters. In the end, the Shebaab's enemies "mow the lawn"—reduce the Shebaab's presence—but do not solve the deeper problems of poor governance in Somalia.[121]

Militarily, the Shebaab's fight against the transitional government and AMISOM forces has devolved to a predictable back and forth. When AMISOM attacks, Shebaab forces typically offer only limited opposition. They then wait for AMISOM to stretch its forces, attacking its supply routes and trying to intimidate the locals. Most foreign forces have little or no training in counterinsurgency.[122] Meanwhile, the Somali army remains in poor shape aside from special units like Danab; soldiers are untrained, poorly equipped, and often unpaid.[123]

Transitional government forces continue to steal and abuse power, alienating local Somalis. They also often employ fighters from specific parts of Somalia. When these soldiers deploy to areas where they do not have kin, they often steal, kidnap for ransom, and otherwise abuse power.[124] In addition, the Shebaab controls key prisons; thus, incarceration does not mean members truly leave the group.[125] The government is also too weak to protect its citizens in many areas, leaving them vulnerable to Shebaab retribution, and thus making them reluctant to support the government in any way.[126] The Shebaab also kept its finances in order, not only collecting taxes on areas it controlled but also extorting money from businesses in Mogadishu and other cities, where merchants feared the Shebaab was still strong enough to punish them. The Shebaab even kept administrators on its payroll in areas where its rivals ruled, maintaining a shadow government to keep its influence alive.[127]

Somalia, however, fell out of fashion among foreign jihadists. Just as Bosnia eclipsed post-Soviet Afghanistan and Iraq grabbed jihadist attention in 2003, the 2011 Arab spring, which led to civil wars in Libya, Syria, and Yemen, drew foreign fighters back to their home countries. The subsequent wars and power struggles provided an alternative to Somalia's messy conflict.[128] Syria in particular would prove a magnet for European and Arab foreign fighters. Even ethnic Somalis in Minneapolis chose to go to Syria, not Somalia, to fight after 2014, leaving the Shebaab as an afterthought.

Hammami himself was unique, but his experience highlighted many aspects of the foreign fighter experience that both would-be recruits and terrorism analysts often miss. Foreign fighters struggle with the transition from the West to the war zone, and the foreigners' zealotry often creates tensions with the locals and the native jihadists. Just as we can read Hammami's tale as a story of radicalization and violence, it also acts as a cautionary tale for would-be fighters, who can easily get lost on the path to jihad.

CHAPTER 10 | John the Beatle and the Syrian Civil War

W ITH HIS FACE covered by a balaclava, the man in the video is dressed all in black and brandishes a knife. Fluent in English with a British accent, he denounces the "arrogant foreign policy" of President Barack Obama and intones, "Just as your missiles continue to strike our people, our knife will continue to strike the necks of your people."[1] The man then proceeds to behead the American journalist Steven Sotloff. In other videos, he beheaded American journalist James Foley, American aid worker Peter Kassig, Japanese journalists Kenji Goto and Huruna Yukawa, and British aid workers David Haines and Alan Henning. He also led a group that beheaded more than twenty Syrian soldiers on video. Hostages lucky enough to have been ransomed tell of this English-speaking man and his comrades torturing his prisoners with electric shocks or waterboarding them. They dubbed him "John," after John Lennon of the Beatles, with his three fellow British fighters of the hostage-taking cell receiving the names Paul, George, and Ringo. The British media would call him "Jihadi John," a name he hated.[2]

John was born Mohammed Emzawi, and in 2013 he joined the Islamic State—a descendant of Zarqawi's Al Qaeda in Iraq that would attract more foreign fighters than any jihadist group in modern history. As with so many foreign fighters, John did not fit the terrorist stereotype of a violent, poor, and uneducated person, motivated to take up arms out of anger or desperation. Born in Kuwait, he moved to Britain at age six. He attended a good high school in a posh neighborhood of London (where two of his classmates also became foreign fighters).[3] Later, he studied information systems at the University of Westminster and worked as a salesman for an IT company in Kuwait after receiving his degree. His schoolmates remember him as a "nice guy" who loved soccer and the pop band S Club 7.[4] The other members of "the Beatles" had different backgrounds, united only by their admiration for the Islamic State. El Shafee Elsheikh came as a child to the United Kingdom from Sudan and dreamed of joining his local soccer team but fell in with local gangs. Alexanda Kotey is a half-Ghanaian, half-Cypriot former drug dealer who converted to Islam. Aine Davis, the last of the Beatles, was a convert and drug dealer.[5]

John's interest in jihad predated the Islamic State. An Islamic State hagiography would later claim that it was the 2005 Al Qaeda attacks in London that awoke John's jihadi spirit.[6] Later, obsessed with Somalia and the emergence of a proto-state under Islamic law there, he sought to fight for the Shebaab as Hammami did before him. He never arrived. After traveling to Tanzania in order to transit to Somalia, British intelligence disrupted him. If they had a crystal ball, the British probably would have let him travel to Somalia, if only to avoid his future horrors in Syria. (John claimed he traveled to Tanzania only for safari and that British intelligence officers roughed him up.) John later tried to go to Kuwait, but again British intelligence prevented him from traveling. John lamented in an email, "I had a job waiting for me and marriage to get started, but now I feel like a prisoner, only not in a cage, in London." John claims that harassment by British intelligence turned him against his home country, though his early obsession with Somalia seems to contradict this claim.[7] Even in Syria, he would retain his obsession with Somalia, forcing hostages to watch Shebaab videos.

Traveling to Syria proved easier than going to Somalia. John traveled by boat to Belgium, from where he flew to Albania. From Albania, smugglers took him to Greece, where he was briefly detained, before proceeding on to Turkey.[8] Once in Turkey, it was a hop, skip, and a jump to cross the border, and the Islamic State maintained robust networks there to help foreign fighters travel into Syria. There, he joined the fray.

Syria gave John fifteen grisly minutes of fame. Emzawi's 2014 beheading of American photojournalist James Foley, titled "A Message to America," went viral. In the video, the Islamic State created a sense of foreshadowing, showing the next beheading victim so viewers could linger over his horrific fate in the intervening days. The brutality dramatized the group's claims of victory and, as a form of theater, captured world attention. The beheadings reached 94 percent of Americans—a staggering figure, higher than any major news event in the five years preceding the killing, according to one study.[9]

On November 12, 2015, a drone strike killed John outside the Islamic State's capital in Raqqa. The U.S. and British officials worked "hand in glove" on the strike, according to British Prime Minister David Cameron. Although U.S. military officials admitted that John "wasn't a major tactical figure or an operational figure," they also pointed out that "this guy was a human animal and killing him is probably making the world a little bit better place."[10] The Islamic State praised his "sincerity" and his "mercy, kindness, and generosity toward the believers," contrasting it with his hatred of infidels.[11]

Other members of the Beatles fared only slightly better. Turkish forces arrested Davis and sentenced him to seven years in jail. Syrian Kurdish allies of the United States captured Kotey and Elsheikh as they routed Islamic State forces in 2017. After capture, in interviews, the surviving Beatles called the beheadings "regrettable," but only because they believed Foley, Sotloff, Kassing, and others might have been worth more as prisoners. In 2018, the Kurds and the British negotiated over where to try the two— neither country wanted the burden—and the United Kingdom revoked their citizenship.[12] In a CNN interview, one declared that losing his citizenship "would be a very black day for international law," a remarkable claim for a man who seemed to delight in beheading people.[13] Perhaps their only contribution was informing on fellow jihadists, leading to the death or capture of additional militants.[14]

John's deeds were unusually chilling, but his decision to join the jihad in Syria was one many other Muslims embraced. More than 40,000 foreigners fought in Iraq and Syria, most on behalf of the Islamic State. The Islamic State shattered records for European participation in particular, making figures like the Beatles more than just curiosities. Indeed, it is in Syria that the global jihadist movement reached its height (so far) and proved as attractive as international Communism did in the past, ranking alongside the Spanish and Russian civil wars in terms of its attractiveness to foreign volunteers.[15] Syria represented the perfect jihadist storm. In addition to being easy to access, it combined powerful jihadist recruiting pitches (notably, sectarianism and the desire to live under Islamic law) with an impressive record, having been allowed to expand with little interference. In addition to attracting an unprecedented number of foreign fighters, the Islamic State proved unusually scary. Through a combination of gruesome attacks and relentless propaganda, the Islamic State wedged itself deep in the popular imagination. A survey from the summer of 2017 found the fear of an Islamic State attack to be the number-one global concern, even as the group was actively collapsing.[16]

The Rise of the Islamic State

To much of the world, the Islamic State seemed new when it proclaimed a caliphate in the parts of Iraq and Syria it controlled in 2014. However, it merely represented the latest incarnation of Zarqawi's decade-old group once known as Al Qaeda in Iraq, which had gone through numerous name changes over the years.

The United States had left Al Qaeda in Iraq (or, as the group called itself at this time, the Islamic State of Iraq) close to dead as U.S. forces departed in 2011. Much of the success against Al Qaeda in Iraq occurred because Sunni tribes and militias had turned against the group and worked with U.S. forces and the Washington-backed Iraqi government in Baghdad. When U.S. Navy SEALs killed Bin Laden in 2011, it seemed like the final nail in the coffin.

However, as U.S. forces drew down, Prime Minister Nouri al-Maliki's rhetoric became increasingly sectarian, and he tried to woo Iraqi Shiites by excluding Iraq's Sunnis from power. Sunni tribal leaders, who had worked with the Maliki government against Al Qaeda in Iraq, lost their salaries. Maliki broke promises to integrate local militias into the Iraqi security forces and arrested many militia members. When protests erupted, Iraqi forces tried to crush them, with Maliki declaring that all who opposed him were terrorists.[17] In 2013, Iraqi security forces killed fifty peaceful protesters during demonstrations in the city of Hawija.[18] Al Qaeda in Iraq (under the moniker of the Islamic State in Iraq) slowly came back. It conducted a massive assassination campaign in Sunni parts of Iraq, killing leaders who cooperated with the Baghdad government. In 2013, it attacked two prisons, allowing nearly six hundred inmates to break free, including many of its senior leaders.

Although the group originated in Iraq and began to renew itself there, the Syrian civil war also proved vital to its rebirth. Since the 1960s, religious minorities ruled Syria, despite the country having a Sunni Muslim majority. In particular, Alawites, an offshoot of Shiite Islam that many Sunnis consider to be heretics, dominated the country. Hafiz al-Assad, who assumed power in 1970, and his heir and son Bashar, who took over following his father's death in 2000, were both Alawites. Father and son ruthlessly suppressed any dissent, while favoring other religious minorities, including Kurds, Christians, Shiite Muslims, and Druze. The regime was in essence a coalition of minorities who worked with the co-opted Sunni elite, leaving most Sunnis out of the magic circle.

In 2011, inspired by successful revolutions in Egypt and Tunisia earlier that year, brave Syrians gathered to protest this dictatorship that ruled the country for decades. Protests led to demonstrations, which the regime met with its usual toolkit of killings, jailing, and torture. Rather than be cowed, Syrians continued to march. Demonstrations, however, slowly morphed into violence and then civil war, in which well over 500,000 people would die by the end of 2017 and eleven million more would become refugees or internally displaced persons. As of 2018, the war continues.

Although jihadist groups opposed the Assad government, the regime's policies helped them rise—a surprise only if you don't know how diabolical the Assad regime is. When unrest broke out, the regime feared that its coalition of minorities would unravel and other religious communities would join the Sunni rebels. Assad sought to paint the mainly Sunni Muslim opposition as fanatic jihadists. This was a false characterization when the war began and jihadists were few and far between in Syria, but one that became truer over time. During peaceful protests in 2011, the regime arrested thousands of demonstrators and, at the same time, let violent jihadists out of the notorious Sidnaya prison. Several of those released became leaders in the subsequent fighting. The regime also created Alawite militias that raped and brutalized Sunni Muslims, knowing this would prompt a backlash against other minorities by the Sunnis. When it did, the regime was quick to publicize these and foster an us-versus-them divide.

As the civil war dragged on, the jihadist role in Syria became more and more prominent as the violence intensified and more moderate groups split or suffered setbacks. Yet the Assad regime concentrated its military efforts on the far larger, nonjihadist Sunni opposition, recognizing that this sector posed a greater threat to its rule both politically and militarily than the jihadists. In 2014, when the Islamic State battled other rebel groups, the Assad regime bombed them too, and the Islamic State's forces largely refrained from shooting at the Syrian army. Similarly, the regime's allies like Russia often concentrated their firepower more on the Syria regime's more moderate opponents than on the jihadists. The regime also cut deals with the Islamic State over the city of Palmyra, traded oil with it, and otherwise engaged in limited cooperation.[19] Neither considered the other an ally. Indeed, they would happily kill each other and eventually did. However, both saw the nonjihadists as the greatest danger in the early years of the war.[20] As one Islamic State leader declared, "All that will be left in Syria is two camps," the jihadists and the regime.[21]

The war in Syria also injected new energy into the jihadist landscape on the Iraqi side of the border. Iraqi Sunnis identified with the Sunni-dominated, antiregime opposition and shared their optimism that Assad would soon fall. Maliki feared that chaos in Syria would lead to the rise of a hostile Sunni regime in Iraq, and this fear pushed him closer to Iran.[22] Iraqi jihadist leaders themselves feared losing members to Syria and, at the same time, wanted to exploit the excitement over the fighting there. To channel this energy (and to attract new recruits), Al Qaeda in Iraq sent Abu Muhammad al-Jolani, a Syrian, and several others in 2011 to form an organization to extend its reach. When it announced its presence in Syria in 2012, the offshoot had taken the name Jabhat al-Nusra.[23]

Syria soon proved a brilliant jihadist success as recruits flocked to fight, and the cause gained support from Muslims around the world. In March 2013, Syrian jihadists, working with other Syrian opposition forces, captured Raqqa, the first provincial capital to fall to the anti-Assad forces. Not surprisingly, quarrels emerged over who should get credit. Al Qaeda in Iraq wanted the group in Syria to be subordinate. Jabhat al-Nusra's leaders, however, preferred to maintain autonomy from their Iraqi parent organization and take orders from the Al Qaeda core, which had long rejected Al Qaeda in Iraq's beheadings, sectarianism, and terrorizing of civilians.

On April 9, 2013, this led to an open split, with Abu Bakr al-Baghdadi, the leader of Al Qaeda in Iraq (going by the name the Islamic State of Iraq), declaring control of Jabhat al-Nusra and, eventually, contending that Al Qaeda in Iraq and Jabhat al-Nusra now represented one group, which it now called the Islamic State of Iraq and Syria—ISIS.[24] Jabhat al-Nusra's leaders rejected this claim and maintained their own group identity, but many of its fighters shifted allegiance to ISIS. They found the Zarqawi legacy of sectarianism, Islamic rule, and atrocity more appealing than Al Qaeda's call to focus on the West and work as supporters of the local population. The split became violent. The group that now called itself ISIS hit Nusra strongholds in several parts of Syria, seizing its territory and also taking the important Koniko gas field. In addition, ISIS rhetorically blasted Al Qaeda and, by implication, its loyal servant Nusra, for working with Iran, increasingly the bogeyman in this sectarian war. It shamed Zawahiri personally for being "distant from the battlefield" while the Islamic State's leader Baghdadi was on the front line.[25]

Beyond their struggle over power and control of the movement, Nusra and the Islamic State differed on many fundamental issues, showcasing the divisions within the jihadist movement. Nusra embraced Azzam's legacy. It sought to avoid becoming entangled with issues related to morality and religious doctrine. Muslim blood, for the most part, was declared to be sacred (though Nusra was far from pure on this score, killing civilians from Syria's Druze and Alawite minorities as well as some Sunni enemies). They also followed different strategies. Nusra opposed establishing a caliphate immediately and, as with Azzam, it favored removing infidels from Muslim lands. In the case of Syria, the infidels comprised the supposedly fake-Muslim Alawite regime.[26] ISIS favored the opposite. Taking the "state" in its name seriously, it argued all local factions should be subordinate, and if you did not live by its extreme code, you were a false Muslim. This included not only supposed apostates like the Alawites and Shiites but also the many Sunnis who in one way or another had worked with the Syrian government over the years.

At the beginning of 2014, ISIS shifted back from Syria to Iraq, ramping up its operations. Yet even as ISIS reemerged, the world underestimated how dangerous it might become. Indeed, the group's own brutality seemed to ensure its demise. William McCants, a former State Department official and leading scholar of jihadist groups, noted that at the time there was "a strong belief that brutal insurgencies fail" and, as a result, the group "would destroy itself."[27]

These illusions ended later in 2014, when ISIS grabbed world attention after its rapid military campaign culminated in the capture of Iraq's second-largest city, Mosul, and its depredations against the Yazidi minority, whom ISIS saw as apostates who could be enslaved, killed, and raped. Because of the abuse and mistreatment of Iraqi Sunnis at the hands of the Maliki government, many of the tribes and local militias that fought with U.S. forces against Al Qaeda in Iraq as part of the Surge now allied with the jihadist cause. This created a snowball effect where the Islamic State's strength made other local groups less likely to resist it. The group's forces kept rolling and seemed to threaten Baghdad, as it menacingly warned Iraqi Shiites that "we have a score to settle."[28] In triumph, ISIS declared a caliphate in June 2014 with Raqqa as its capital, and its leader, Abu Bakr al-Baghdadi, as the Caliph. It also changed its name yet again, going from the Islamic State in Iraq and Syria to simply the Islamic State, as a way to show that its claims now were no longer bound by geography. (To reduce confusion, I will refer to the post–June 2014 group as the Islamic State and the previous period as Al Qaeda in Iraq, despite the numerous name changes in between.)

The first months of the Caliphate seemed like a brilliant success. The Islamic State remained on the offensive in parts of Iraq and Syria, and its foes seemed lackluster and ineffective. The group also maintained perhaps a hundred thousand fighters, although exact figures depend heavily on what constitutes a fighter and the role of Iraqi and Syrian groups that cooperated with the Islamic State.[29] Globally, a range of existing local groups and new ones pledged their allegiance to Baghdadi and became "Provinces" in the Caliphate. Important ones emerged in Afghanistan, Sinai, and Libya, and existing groups like Boko Haram in Nigeria offered their fealty. The Islamic State seemed unstoppable.

The Appeal of Jihad in Syria

Foreign fighters shifted from a sideshow to center stage as the Syrian jihad progressed. Indeed, Syria attracted a record number of foreign fighters—over 40,000 from more than 110 countries.[30] These foreign fighters began to define the conflict, shaping the nature of the violence in Syria, the threat to neighboring states, and how the United States and its European allies approached the war.

The Syria conflict attracted so many foreigners for two reasons: the war there featured many powerful motifs that appealed directly to Muslims' sense of victimization, and the Islamic State proved a master of recruitment. Altruism, sectarian anger, boredom, a desire to live under an Islamic government, and group bonding all played a role as well. The Islamic State also benefited because the previous Iraq war had already brought many of these issues to the fore and created personal networks that endured even as the fighting there had died down. As one Danish government official told me, "Syria was worse than Iraq because there was an Iraq."[31]

Many of the first volunteers to Syria joined in solidarity with their fellow Muslims against a brutal dictator, seeing the conflict as an extension of the "Arab Spring," when dictators seemed to fall like dominoes. They sought to defend Muslims against Assad's depredations and remove him from power. Indeed, the actions of these initial volunteers matched the words of Western leaders, who called for Assad's downfall and supported the opposition in words if not in deeds. Despite their rhetoric, however, Western leaders warily watched the foreign fighters flooding into Syria: "A man leaves his home to fight for the oppressed people . . . sounds heroic until you add in 'Muslim man.' Then he's a terrorist/extremist," tweeted one young British volunteer who died in 2013.[32]

As the Syrian conflict morphed from its beginning state as a rebellion against a brutal dictator, the motivations of volunteers shifted as well. The conflict became more sectarian in 2012 and 2013.[33] Historically, jihadist causes had gained more support when they fought against a foreign occupier, such as Russia in Afghanistan and Chechnya, the United States in Iraq, and so on. Syria seemed to lack this foreign element, but jihadists compensated by seeing the conflict as an Iranian-led Shiite occupation that encompassed the Shiite regime in Baghdad, the Alawite regime of Assad in Damascus, and the Lebanese Hezbollah. These fighters saw their community, fellow Sunni Muslims, as being under attack. Given the Assad regime's near-genocidal brutality against Sunni communities, this perception was well-founded.[34] As such, they harvested the seeds planted by Al Qaeda in Iraq almost a decade earlier, which promoted the anti-Shiite struggle above the fight against the United

States. More than fifty Saudi clerics called for Arab and Muslim countries to provide military aid to fight the Assad government.[35] Indeed, the anti-Shiite and anti-Alawite sentiment became the dominant discourse in the region.

After Baghdadi declared a caliphate in 2014, another goal emerged: the desire to live in a true Islamic state. Baghdadi declared "migration to the Abode of Islam is obligatory."[36] In the eyes of many volunteers, they had a duty to support the state and live in accordance with God's law.[37] Perhaps equally important, the new Caliphate seemed to be winning. The Islamic State carved out territory in Syria, and then in mid-2014, as the Caliphate was declared, it surged in Iraq, seizing Mosul, its second largest city, and eventually ruling over 10 million people and land the size of Britain.

Islamic State volunteers maintained a complex relationship with Islam. Serving their faith and sacrificing, even dying, in Islam's name was a popular idea among recruits. In addition, they tried to root their actions in the Quran and the sayings of the Prophet, with some members, especially propagandists, delving into Islamic history and a range of scholarly interpretations of their faith to justify their actions.[38] However, most paid little attention to doctrinal particulars. One European intelligence official lamented the time he spent studying various jihadist teachings, pointing out that "only one percent know of a theologian." Data from captured Islamic State records showed that 70 percent of foreign recruits claimed they had only a basic knowledge of Islam,[39] and a UN-sponsored study found that "religious belief seems to have played a minimal role" for the fighters it examined.[40] A former French hostage noted that the European recruits spent more time watching horror movies than reading the Quran.[41]

On the other hand, many recruits drew genuine faith and inspiration from Islam. Recruits might not know the jurisprudence behind the law, but they knew the law mattered. In their in-depth interviews with foreign fighters, the scholars Amarnath Amarasingam and Lorne Dawson find that fighters used faith, not socioeconomic marginalization, to explain their decisions. In particular, *hijrah* (migration) to an Islamic-ruled land gave their lives a meaning that it lacked, and they came to view jihad as obligatory. Similarly, the fighters noted that "the status of a Shaheed [martyr] is one of the highest."[42]

In many parts of the world, the Salafi communities that Saudi funding helped to establish became the bedrock for the next generation of foreign fighters.[43] In Albania and Kosovo, Saudi Arabia and other Gulf states built hundreds of mosques and religious schools and funded extremist clerics and organizations that helped lead to a massive flow of foreign fighters from these countries. To promote Kosovar Salafism, the Saudis rewarded families that attended sermons with stipends.[44] One Saudi-funded preacher would disrupt more moderate rivals while issuing bloodcurdling rhetoric calling for all Muslims to join the jihad: "The blood of infidels is the best drink for us Muslims."[45] The linkage was not always direct. As the head of Kosovo's counterterrorism police noted, the foreign organizations did not directly fund travel to Syria. Instead, "They supported thinkers who promote violence and jihad in the name of protecting Islam."[46]

When wars break out in the Muslim world, these radical preachers and organizations try to exploit them to increase their own popularity. Images from the war zone, a mix of propaganda and real pictures of the horrors of war, inflame popular sentiment. These images compel communities to action, and organizations can increase their fundraising and recruitment by linking themselves to the wars overseas.[47] Some of these radical figures had tremendous influence over militant groups. From his base in Germany, Abu Walaa not only arranged for his followers to travel to Syria to fight with the Islamic State, but he also helped some gain prominent positions, such as in the Islamic State secret police.[48] Often various networks overlapped. Criminal groups interacted with extreme Salafi organizations, with a former foreign fighter or radical preacher serving as the charismatic glue.

For all its emphasis on religion, the Islamic State's extreme violence and its declaration of a caliphate angered many Islamic scholars, including many who embraced the jihadist ideology. One prominent jihadist theologian who had inspired foreign fighters to join other jihads, Abu Qatada, declared the Caliphate "null and void," proclaiming that no one should fight under the Islamic State's banner.[49] Instead, the Islamic State relied on Abu Abdullah al-Muhajir's so-called "The Jurisprudence of Blood." Al-Muhajir argued that all governments, Muslim and non-Muslim alike, are enemies as they all reject true Islam. As a result, jihadists had the right to "desecrate the blood and property of infidels as they please."[50]

These ideological concerns mixed with more personal ones. Many volunteers simply wanted to escape their own situations, feeling marginalized in their home countries.[51] "No future" summarized why Belgians became foreign fighters, according to one report.[52] In Bosnia, youth unemployment is more than 60 percent, and many of the fighters, at best, had jobs on the black market.[53] Poor Central Asian Muslims appreciated the salaries and the housing that the Islamic State provided both them and their families.[54] Still others felt the pull of adventure and meaning, using the above reasons to justify following their restless spirit.[55] Yet, for many fighters, a salary or material rewards, such as luxury goods and cars, supplied the more important incentive.[56]

In the Middle East, the Islamic State also gained recruits as other ideological and political alternatives collapsed. Communism had long lost its allure, and pan-Arabism declined as a political force since its peak in the 1960s. For many Muslims, political Islamist groups like the Muslim Brotherhood, which promised to govern under Islamic principles but eschewed violence in most countries, offered a new lodestar. The rise of Islamist governments in Egypt and Tunisia after dictators fell in the 2011 revolutions seemed to offer the peaceful alternative the Arab world lacked. However, jihadists argued that the compromises inherent in democratic politics would corrupt Islam, and regardless, the infidel powers would never agree to a true Islamic government—it must be imposed. As if on cue, the Muslim Brotherhood, which in Egypt offered an authoritarian but peaceful Islamist alternative, fell victim to a coup in 2013. Concurrently, jihadist violence in Tunisia led to a massive crackdown on Salafis there.

Many European foreign fighters attracted to jihad had criminal backgrounds, and this percentage grew as the conflict progressed and the Islamic State emerged as the dominant group. The specifics vary by country, but common figures cite one-third or one-half of volunteers as having a criminal background.[57] Anis Amri, who killed eleven when he hijacked a truck, shot its driver, and drove it through a Christmas market in Berlin, had dropped out of school at fifteen and was on a path to nowhere. "My son Anis drank and stole," recalled his father.[58] Fighting in Syria would allow criminals to become respected members of their communities and to wash away their past sins, while continuing to kill and wreak havoc and even gaining divine goodwill for doing so. One scholar of recruits from Belgium concluded that the Islamic State was simply a "super gang," which conveyed status to its members.[59] In contrast, far fewer Middle Eastern recruits had a criminal background.

Some veteran foreign fighters, however, lamented how jihad was manifesting in Syria. Abdullah Anas, who was Azzam's son-in-law, contends that those who went to Afghanistan sought to liberate the country, not just achieve martyrdom, and he criticized kidnapping and suicide bombing. Anas also claimed, with considerable exaggeration, that the prisoners taken in Afghanistan "enjoyed full rights," while those in Syria were beheaded. Azzam, he noted, had welcomed Western reporters and aid workers who might be sympathetic to the regime and did not pick fights with Western governments.[60]

Rape and sex played an important role in Islamic State selling points. The group boasted that it parceled out Yazidi women and other sex slaves as "war spoils" for its fighters. It developed a massive apparatus for this; its propaganda explained that enslavement makes a woman more likely to choose Islam, its human resources department parceled out slaves by rank, its financial offices gave additional money to fighters who had a child with the slave they raped, and its doctors and nurses administered medical exams.[61] Buildings next to training camps would house women for fighters to "party" with before going out to face death.[62] Not surprisingly, it attracted many recruits with a history, and thirst for, sexual violence.[63]

Regardless of the ideological motivations and demographic data, however, the role of groups and personal ties may explain the most important factor for recruitment. Friends and families often gathered at mosques, schools, and neighborhoods, and these communal locations provided the ideal space to radicalize and introduce the ideology and mission of the Islamic State. Those that became radicalized made the decision to travel to Syria together.[64] One early volunteer for Iraq called for "all my mates" back in his home neighborhood to "come and defend Islam."[65] In the United Kingdom, 30 percent of the fighters had a sibling or another family member who also joined.

Propaganda, Social Media, and Recruitment

Azzam used magazines to educate the faithful, Bin Laden used satellite television to denounce the West, Zarqawi used the Internet to highlight his gory campaign, and Hammami publicized the Shebaab via Twitter. But even more so than its predecessors, the Islamic State employed a massive propaganda apparatus. From the traditional side, its *Al-Furqan* media wing included dozens of outlets that published in Arabic, English, Russian, and other languages.[66] Composed mainly of young people, the Islamic State used the technology of the time: Ask.fm, Facebook, WhatsApp, Kik, Tumblr, Facebook, and Telegram, among many others, with Twitter as its most popular application for many years.[67] Much of its media output was of impressive quality. The *New York Times* media critic, for example, highlighted the "remarkable drone camera work" of the beheading videos when noting the Islamic State's "sophisticated" productions.[68] The group had tighter narration, with more action scenes and fewer monologues on Islam, than Al Qaeda.[69]

As with every foreign fighter–linked jihad, the Islamic State uses its military operations for propaganda. The more than fifty-part series "Messages from the Battleground" offered images of the group's military operations, proving the group's strength and success to potential supporters around the world.[70] The propaganda reflected the recruits' preferences; most wanted to be warriors, fighting on behalf of the Islamic State, not terrorists.[71] Similarly, as in past jihadi propaganda, that of the Islamic State emphasized the miraculous aspects of the fighting such as the beautiful smell of the bodies of those who fell as martyrs.[72]

Unlike much of the propaganda generated from past jihads, however, the Islamic State's most watched and compelling propaganda often glorified brutality in addition to war. Propaganda included images of beheadings, crucifixions, slow drownings, throwing homosexuals off rooftops, burning captives to death, and other grisly punishments. One video showed a toddler kicking the head of a decapitated victim, and, in another, a child playing in a playpen is given a gun and directed to shoot someone in the head.[73] Brutality as a form of propaganda is not new—Bosnian foreign fighters at times recorded brutal videos, and Zarqawi vaulted to jihadist stardom when he videotaped the beheadings of captives in Iraq—but social media enabled far wider and easier distribution.

Symbolism pervaded the execution videos. Islamic State executioners, like Zarqawi before them, forced captives to don an orange jumpsuit, echoing the garb of jihadist prisoners at the U.S. Guantanamo Bay facility. Videos of Westerners' executions often had English narrations, tied to the hostage's government's policies. An infamous video of burning a caged Jordanian pilot alive was preceded in Islamic State propaganda with images of coalition airstrikes and dead and dying children. Just as they burned in airstrikes carried out by the pilot and other Islamic State enemies, so too would enemies of Islam burn.[74] To justify these tactics, the Islamic State cites sayings of the Prophet or verses in the Quran. The group instructs Muslims to strike unbelievers "upon their necks," for example, and cites the Prophet's beheading of hundreds of Jews who betrayed a pact.[75]

Through its propaganda, the Islamic State linked being a foreign fighter to glamorous, movie-style violence and made jihad seem fun and cool. Some social media posts referred to murdered Tupac Shakur, an icon of gangsta rap. Others referenced popular films: "They've watched too many Rambo movies," noted one Syrian activist. One British foreign fighter tweeted, "It's better than that game Call of Duty. It's like that but it's in 3D where everything is happening in front of you."[76] A British prosecutor invoked the (actual) Beatles, noting that "the boys want to be like them and the girls want to be with them."[77]

In sharp contrast to its shocking snuff films, Islamic State propaganda also emphasized the beauty and meaning of life under its rule. As jihadist propaganda expert Charlie Winter indicates, the Islamic State sought to prove that the Caliphate existed as a true Islamic State. As such, videos showed schools where children learned the Quran, courts that implemented traditional Islamic punishments, and the giving of charity in accordance with scripture.[78] Images of fun and brotherhood also proved compelling. Clips showed fighters drinking tea, singing together, and embracing. Tweeting pictures of cats was quite popular. One French fighter shared a picture of himself holding a container of Nutella. "Being a radical is fun," claimed one Belgian foreign fighter.[79] The Islamic State tried to encourage families to come as a unit and offered volunteers a new family (complete with an unwilling bride) if they lacked one.[80]

Islam, of course, extends past state borders, and propaganda emphasized the universal claims of the Caliphate. One of the Islamic State's first videos after declaring the Caliphate, entitled "Breaking the Borders," showed Islamic State bulldozers demolishing barriers along the Iraq-Syria border, with fighters cheering and leaders denouncing "the borders of humiliation." Predictably, and tragically, the video ends with Islamic State fighters shooting border guards.

The Islamic State has also played up apocalyptic rhetoric, taking advantage of the Prophet Mohammad's frequent references to Syria and the belief among many Muslims that the messiah's return and end of times are near.[81] Good Muslims are engaged in a cosmic battle against an array of enemies with Syria as the battleground. Volunteers will act the vanguard who will achieve the victory of Islam in the final battles. The title of one of the Islamic State's early leading English-language journals, *Dabiq,* originates from a town in Syria where, according to a Muslim apocalyptic tradition, the believers and Christians will fight the last battle.

To promulgate these various messages, the Islamic State's official media outlets produced around a thousand products a month at their peak.[82] Videos are far more compelling than text, and the images provided evidence for the Islamic State's arguments that the West, the Shiites, and other foes slaughter Muslims. Some Islamic State users tweeted hundreds of times per day. Their propaganda not only appeared in Arabic and English, but also in French, Russian, and even Uyghur and Bengali.[83] The Islamic State provided ideas and raw video, allowing "fanboys" or "jihobbyists," in Winter's turn of phrase, to tailor content to best fit the propaganda they promoted.[84] In one of its offerings targeting the Balkans, it featured mostly Bosnian foreign fighters and portrayed the history of the Balkans as a fight between Muslims and Christians and atheists trying to take Muslim land and slaughter innocents; in France, it stressed France's crimes against Muslims, and so on.[85]

The recruitment process encouraged individuals to disseminate propaganda, and this dissemination further committed them to the group.[86] In addition, as radicalization scholars Tim Stevens and Peter Neumann indicate, the internet offers a relatively risk-free way to recruit and network; if the online recruiter is discovered, he is usually still safely away in Syria or another country.

Social media feeds, however, do not simply reflect the view of the individual volunteer. The Islamic State understood this, and thus made many new recruits turn over their cell phones and punished any unauthorized contact. As a result, much of the "spontaneous" communication was actually well-orchestrated.[87]

Jihadist group recruiters often stalked different Islamic-oriented accounts that promote radical views—for example, that Islamic law should be imposed on society—but that do not directly endorse violence and are otherwise protected as free speech. They then solicited individuals who frequented these accounts, making themselves available, sharing propaganda, and otherwise trying to influence and befriend them.[88] In one case, a young American woman received money, chocolate, books, and other gifts from Islamic State recruiters and supporters, moving her steadily into their embrace.[89] After identifying a likely suspect, the recruiters often shifted to one-on-one communication in order to proselytize further among promising recruits and determine if they were spies. As they wormed their way in, they encouraged the individual to separate from non-Muslims and, over time, non-radicals. Radicals created a virtual "echo chamber" where ideas became more extreme with little contradiction.[90] The next step was to use encrypted platforms to give specific instructions on how to travel to Syria or use violence.[91]

The virtual and real worlds interacted. In many countries, face-to-face and small group meetings with recruiters, often former foreign fighters themselves, proved the most valuable.[92] In radical mosques, Salafi community organizations, or simply small groups of friends, individuals sought out like-minded people, reinforcing the divisions fostered online. To isolate the "believers" from the non-believers (i.e. family, friends, and other Muslims who did not embrace extreme views), the radicalization process disparaged the non-believers as "coconuts," white on the inside even if they looked brown on the outside.[93] The jihadist community offered new friends and a community to replace the old.[94] As Winter contends, "There must always be an external human influencer to spark and sustain the radicalisation process."[95]

Over time, however, the Islamic State became more cautious with social media. In 2015, the group warned its soldiers not to post updates from their social media platforms, and in 2017 it issued a strict ban on all social media unless authorized from the top. The group feared that its Western enemies and rival groups were posing as group members and discrediting the group. In addition, some of its soldiers jeopardized the group's security. For example, one took a selfie in front of an Islamic State headquarters building, enabling U.S. intelligence to locate the facility and destroy it in an airstrike.[96]

Twitter, Facebook, and other platforms became more restrictive, and the Islamic State adapted by creating new accounts and taking other steps, but this adaptation usually fell short. Although the Islamic State had tens of thousands of accounts on Twitter, it relied heavily on a small fraction of these for much of its social media presence.[97] A study by radicalization specialists J. M. Berger and Heather Perez found that the number of Islamic State Twitter accounts fell from 2014 to 2016, in part because of more aggressive efforts to shut down their accounts: "Over time, individual users who repeatedly created new accounts after being suspended suffered devastating reductions in their follower counts."[98] Because of such crackdowns, the Islamic State now uses more peer-to-peer methods that are harder to detect, but they reach far fewer people and require more time on the part of Islamic State operatives. Even Telegram, the Islamic State's preferred communication application as of 2018, initially even mocked calls to stop usage by the Islamic State ("I propose banning words," its founder said, "there's evidence that they're being used by terrorists to communicate") but began to remove some Islamic State channels after the Paris attacks.[99]

With some irony, the Islamic State uses social media to disseminate information on how to avoid detection from services monitoring social media. "Try to make it so that even if the idolatrous dogs intercept and decrypt your messages . . . the only information they will be able to find is your username and password," advised one of the group's propaganda outlets.[100] As the group suffered defeat after defeat in 2017, it also banned members from being on social media without permission.[101]

This diminishment represents a U.S. victory, as it is far harder to recruit on Telegram than on a more popular and open platform like Twitter. However, the Islamic State generated enough images and has enough real accomplishments to feed future propaganda for years, including for successors. If jihadists could cherish Afghanistan for decades despite their minimal role, the far more dramatic accomplishments of the Islamic State will endure and prove powerful even though the Caliphate failed.

A Five-Star Jihad

The Syria conflict in general, and the Islamic State's emergence in particular, electrified Muslims around the world (in separate chapters, I discuss the reaction in Europe and the United States). In response, the foreign fighter movement that began in Afghanistan and ebbed and flowed ever since would reach its peak: more fighters traveled to fight in Iraq and Syria than went to all recent modern jihads combined.

As Table 10.1 indicates, the foreign fighter numbers are staggering. France and the United Kingdom together saw almost three thousand fighters travel to the Islamic State, while almost four hundred fighters left from tiny Bosnia

TABLE 10.1 Foreign fighters to Iraq and Syria per country

Source: The Soufan Group, "Beyond the Caliphate," unless otherwise noted. See also the ICCT report and the CIA World Factbook for population estimates.

and Macedonia. Saudi Arabian foreign fighters represent the largest contribution, and the Maldives represented the largest contingent per capita.[102] Many fighters originated from Central Asia and other parts of the former Soviet Union—more, in fact, than the entire Middle East, according to some studies.[103] Recruits hailed from an incredibly broad number of regions. China, for example, saw significant numbers of recruits, as did Trinidad and Tobago.[104]

The numbers can be sliced in multiple ways. Although foreign fighter statistics are usually reported as total numbers from a country, often the rate of recruitment per capita provides a better description of overall risk; the United Kingdom, after all, has a much larger Muslim population than Belgium, yet the numbers are comparable, suggesting a much bigger problem for Belgium. Jordan, Kosovo, and Lebanon have high numbers as a percent of total population. If we consider the number of foreign fighters relative to the size of the Sunni Muslim population, then the scale of the flows from outside the Middle East is staggering, with Trinidad and Belgium leading the pack.[105] Tables 10.2 and 10.3 present the top ten countries as a percent of total population and as a percent of total *Muslim* population, respectively.

Unfortunately for counterterrorism officials, no uniform volunteer profile existed. The age range of foreign fighters varied tremendously with the oldest revealed in one cache of documents was sixty-nine, while the youngest was

TABLE 10.2 Top ten countries as a percentage of total population

Country of Origin	% of Population (rounded to one millionth)
Maldives	≈ 0.050928%
Jordan	≈ 0.029274%
Tunisia	≈ 0.025658%
Kosovo	≈ 0.016726%
Tajikistan	≈ 0.015351%
Lebanon	> 0.014447%
Saudi Arabia	≈ 0.011354%
Trinidad	> 0.010671%
Azerbaijan	> 0.009035%
Libya	≈ 0.009018%

Source: The Soufan Group, "Beyond the Caliphate," unless otherwise noted. See also the ICCT report and the CIA World Factbook for population estimates.

TABLE 10.3 Top ten countries as a percentage of the Muslim population

Country of Origin	Percentage of Muslim Populations
Trinidad	0.21343%
Belgium	0.091895%
Austria	0.080504%
Sweden	0.065476%
Denmark	0.064652%
Norway	0.060418%
Finland	0.053693%
Maldives	0.051756%
Georgia	0.037942%
France	0.035578%

Source: The Soufan Group, "Beyond the Caliphate," unless otherwise noted. See also the ICCT report and the CIA World Factbook for population estimates.

only twelve. The average age was between twenty-six and twenty-seven.[106] Roughly 30 percent were married.[107]Although the education of the fighters varied widely, many appeared to be well-educated when compared with the average education level in their country. In Saudi Arabia, perhaps the single biggest supplier of foreign fighters, many had a university education and were well-off, while those from many cities in North Africa, which often had the highest concentration of fighters for their overall population, were often poorer and less educated.[108] Foreign fighters from Kosovo, which had huge flows as a percentage of population, were more educated than the average Kosovar.[109]

Many individuals were involved with peaceful groups that espoused radical ideas, such as calling for Islamic law to be the law of the land, or existing local terrorist groups. Ansar al-Sharia, a Tunisian group that openly promoted jihad, often helped Tunisians and Libyans join the Islamic State. The Islamic State regularly recruited from these groups and trawled websites associated with them, looking for volunteers.

As in all jihads except Afghanistan, former veterans formed a key part of the volunteers. Dernah, which is in eastern Libya, had perhaps the largest concentration of fighters volunteer for an area its size. It had also supplied many fighters to Iraq and Afghanistan in the past.[110] Approximately 10 percent of the volunteers had prior experience in jihad, a healthy number given the overall size of the Islamic State's foreign forces.[111]

Unusual for any jihad, large numbers of women signed up, almost five thousand in all.[112] Initial reporting tended to portray them as subservient or brainwashed, with jihadist recruiters luring unsuspecting innocents to a life of bondage. Some (especially the younger teens who joined up) fit this description, but many found the promise of living in a true Islamic State compelling and felt that only there could they and their families be true Muslims. "I came for the Jihad, for Sharia and the Islamic State," recalled one Tunisian woman.[113] Islamic State hagiographies of dead women describe a wide range or roles, including some who prepared food for fighters, others who joined their ministries to enforce Islamic behavior, and some who wrote religious decrees; all played an active role in supporting the group.[114] Almost a thousand women from Europe traveled to the Islamic State and even more from the Muslim world and Central Asia. The records left by over a thousand women from an Islamic State guesthouse show they came from sixty-six countries and almost 80 percent were married.[115]

Although Europe gets much of the attention (indeed, I devote a separate chapter to it), Russia and nearby Central Asia represented a huge source of recruits to Iraq and Syria with nearly five thousand going, and the former Soviet Republics in total generated almost nine thousand recruits according to one study. Dagestan, in fact, sent the largest number of women.[116] Similar to recruits from other countries, many initial volunteers simply sought to defend their brothers as part of a religious obligation. "They went there as if it were the *hajj,*" recalled one fighter's brother. The supposed religious obligation of migrating to, and living in, the true Caliphate became a dominant theme, with bringing your whole family as an added bonus.[117]

Yet much of the explanation for the prominence of Central Asians foreign fighters has little to do with ideology and rather derives from Russian counterterrorism efforts. By 2013, Russia had crushed the once-formidable Chechen jihadist movement and others at home.[118] Russian intelligence carried out hundreds of operations, hounding any suspects, further incentivizing them to leave for Syria. They even poisoned food sent to fighters in the forests. Russian officials also cracked down on a range of peaceful Salafi groups, preventing them from preaching, arresting leaders, and at times even torturing them. "We are treated like cattle," complained one local.[119] For many Central Asians, joining jihad or even being a Salafi in their home countries meant only arrest, torture, and death. One supporter commented that jihad in Central Asia was now "a 1,000 times harder than in Syria."[120] The Islamic State emphasized this contrast, comparing "eating leaves in the parochial backwaters of Dagestan" with the "five star jihad" in Syria.

Russian officials happily allowed jihadists to leave. "We thought they'd just get killed," noted one Russian officer.[121] Ironically, Moscow was making the same mistake that Arab regimes made about their citizens going to fight Russian soldiers in Afghanistan. Indeed, before the 2014 Sochi Olympics, Russia sought to drive potential jihadists out of the region and used Syria as a convenient dumping ground. "They have turned the green light on and opened the road," said one activist. A security official privately admitted, "We opened borders, helped them all out and closed the border behind them." He wryly elaborated, "Everyone's happy: They are dying on the path of Allah, and we have no terrorist acts here."[122]

Many suspected jihadists fled to nearby Turkey, which maintains cultural and historic ties to Central Asia. Dozens of Central Asians who relocated to Turkey served as facilitators for the Islamic State, and Syria, which was a ferocious war zone for most volunteers but for several years became a refuge when compared with life for Salafists in Central Asia.[123] Although Central Asians often received the label "Chechens," many originated from Dagestan, Ingushetia, and nearby areas, and even those of Chechen origin often grew up in Georgia or other neighboring states as refugees. The label "Chechen," however, lent street cred, and many happily adopted it.[124]

As disturbing as it might be, the Russian approach seems to have worked— in a limited way, and perhaps for a limited time. Terrorism-related violence in the North Caucasus fell in the years after 2013, though there were still attacks in Dagestan and elsewhere from time to time.[125] After Sochi, and after Russia's involvement in Syria, its permissive transit policy ended, and by late 2014, Russia tried to stop fighters from going to Syria, perhaps fearing violence on return.[126]

The Turkish Highway

More than other modern jihad, Syria offered easy access, especially for Arabs, Russians, and Europeans, a simple and unexciting fact that explains much of the Islamic State's recruiting success. The trip usually involved a drive or short flight to Turkey and then a quick trip across the border to the war zone, which was far simpler than going to Afghanistan or Iraq, let alone Chechnya. Flying from Bosnia to Turkey, for example, cost a little more than $100.[127]

In the Arab world, transit became easier due to the outbreak of the Arab Spring in 2011 and the subsequent collapse of many governments and weakening of others. Libya's civil war never really ended, taking on new forms after Qaddafi died in the fighting. In Yemen, the collapse of the old regime of Ali Abdallah Saleh in 2012 ushered in more violence, eventually leading to major interventions by Iran, Saudi Arabia, and the United Arab Emirates, in a conflict that continues as of 2018. In Tunisia, a new and more democratic government came into power, but it was weak and oscillated between tolerating Salafi jihadist groups and brutally cracking down on anything Salafi-related, with both approaches causing problems. As a result, many governments could not or would not police their own borders, enabling recruits to travel to Syria.

For several years, the Islamic State controlled the Syrian side of the border and Turkish officials did little to interfere. One analysis found that in 2013 and 2014, more than 90 percent of foreign fighters entered Syria via six border towns in Turkey, with Istanbul as a staging area from which Islamic State facilitators helped fighters cross.[128] Befitting its aspirations and status as a quasi-government, the Islamic State operated multiple crossing points into the war zone.[129]

Here too, social media and the internet helped. Often recruits and recruiters communicated clandestinely about how to travel to Turkey, whom to contact on arrival, and other practical information, using encrypted communications in one-on-one settings. The final assistance was often given by a friend who already joined the group or someone known from the individual's neighborhood.[130] As with past jihads, a small number of facilitators helped facilitate a large number of recruits. One facilitator along the border with Turkey, for example, personally helped more than one thousand foreigners pass through in just over a year.[131]

Turkish policies deserve particular explanation in part because the United States and its allies had long counted on Turkey as a pillar in their counterterrorism campaign. By one account, Turkey had arrested more than three thousand Al Qaeda-linked suspects between 2003 and 2010, working closely with the United States. After the Syrian civil war broke out, however, Turkish officials turned a blind eye as volunteers came from Europe, Chechnya, Arab countries, and other places and traveled into Syria. When U.S. and European officials complained, Turkey instead blamed the West for not cooperating on Kurdish terrorists, who had long opposed the Turkish government; claimed Western governments did not share intelligence; and argued that it was impossible to sort out western foreign fighters from ordinary tourists.[132] However, none of this explains why Turkey could act decisively against jihadists in the past but not against those fighting in Syria.

Despite its claims to be fighting terrorism, the Turkish government thought it could channel and exploit the jihadists. Although the government had little sympathy for the jihadists, it feared, correctly, that the

Syrian civil war empowered Syria's Kurdish rebels, whom Kurdish rebels in Turkey supported. Ankara encouraged jihadist units to attack Kurdish rebel-controlled cities in Syria. In addition to undermining the Kurds, Turkish leaders also hoped jihadist operations would lead to Assad's downfall. Assad had supported anti-Turkish Kurds in the past. Moreover, the Turkish leadership embraced Islamism (not jihadism); accordingly, they also favored anti-Assad Sunni forces. Jihadists were seen as an instrument. They would weaken Assad and the Kurds, but in the end, Ankara wanted other opposition forces to triumph. Former U.S. ambassador Francis Ricciardone declared that "the Turks frankly worked with [jihadist] groups for a period, including [Al Qaeda-linked] al-Nusra."[133]

At the same time, however, popular support for radicalism in Turkey grew, raising the political cost of any crackdown. The Turkish government legitimized the anti-Assad struggle, and thus the jihadists looked good simply because they opposed the Syrian dictator. In addition, President Erdogan and other Islamist leaders wanted "to raise up a religious generation." The majority of Turks came to believe there was a Western "Crusade" against Islam, and support for terrorist attacks against Western targets grew, with 20 percent of Turks approving of political violence in the name of Islam.[134]

In 2015, Turkey began to become more restrictive. Ankara allowed the United States and other coalition countries to base aircraft out of Incirlik and Diyabakir airbases in southern Turkey for strikes on the Islamic State. In that same year, Turkey began to crack down on travel and on the jihadist infrastructure in Turkey, arresting recruiters and travel facilitators.[135] In addition, other states improved their intelligence sharing, providing names of suspected travelers to Turkey—a list that would total more than 50,000 names by 2017.[136] Jihadists felt the impact. One smuggler noted the shift taking place in 2015, "Two months ago, you could get in whatever you liked," including explosives and foreign fighters. Now, he said, "Turkish snipers shoot any moving object."[137]

The Islamic State responded with a terrorism campaign to punish the Turkish government and increase tensions between the country's Kurdish and Turkish citizens.[138] Terrorists attacked Diyarbakir and Gaziantep as well as major nightclubs, the airport, and other targets in Istanbul and Ankara. By July 2017, Turkey had suffered fourteen Islamic State attacks and disrupted far more.[139] Foreigners, many originally from Central Asia, carried out many of these attacks.[140] Turkey offered a relatively easy target. In addition to the vast foreign fighter networks on Turkish soil (the Islamic State had recruited 1,500 native Turks to fight) the group could easily direct operations from neighboring Syria. In addition to larger public attacks, the Islamic State shot and beheaded activists linked to groups like "Raqqa Is Being Silently Slaughtered," a non-government organization providing information and video footage of the brutal life in areas controlled by the jihadists.[141] As in Pakistan, the jihadist tool would slip from its master's grasp.

Although the Islamic State made Turkey bleed, such bloodshed resulted in further disaster for the group. The violence led Turkey to extend its crackdown, and additional Islamic State retaliatory attacks only pushed Turkey to police its border and try to uproot the jihadist infrastructure more aggressively. In 2014, Turkish officials claimed to capture 15,000 people trying to cross the border illegally; in 2016, this number increased to almost 400,000 people.[142] Turkey used tanks and artillery to strike the Islamic State after 2016 bombings in Istanbul and shelled Islamic State positions in response to Islamic State cross-border shelling.[143] They also backed rival Syrian opposition groups, pushing the Islamic State away from the Turkish border by September 2016. Turkey also gradually abandoned its hope that Assad would fall, further decreasing the utility of jihadists.

As the Islamic State lost territory, the foreign fighter flow further diminished. Foreign fighters could no longer simply hop across the border into the Caliphate. They now had to travel through territory controlled by the Syrian government, hostile Kurds, or other foes, hindering their efforts to join the fray.[144] In addition, states' measures to stop fighters from leaving in the first place became more effective. By 2017, the flow of fighters slowed to a trickle.[145]

Training Camps and Hard Fighting

As would be true when entering any country, travelers entering the Caliphate had to present passports, fill out forms, get their documents stamped, and be interviewed by border officials. To prove their bona fides, often recruits had letters of reference from former volunteers, mosques, or recruitment networks back home. Volunteers had to give standard information such as their names and family histories, but also their blood type, level of religious knowledge, occupation, and name of a facilitator and recommender, if available. They were also asked whether they wanted to be fighters, suicide bombers, or suicide fighters and if they had other special skills. The Islamic State was particularly interested in volunteers with military experience and hackers.[146] (Conveniently, the form also had an entry for "date and location of death."[147]) The Islamic State used the forms to find those in their ranks with rare skills and to take advantage of those who had fought in their home countries' militaries or in previous jihads.[148]

After screening, recruits then received training. Some had trained in other countries. Libya proved a stopping ground for the many North Africans en route to Syria, with one U.S. defense official calling it "the I-95 for foreign fighters [pouring] into Syria from Africa."[149] For others, the Islamic State ran training camps in both Syria and Iraq. Training camps, often named after heroes of jihad like Bin Laden or Zarqawi, varied in their length and content. Some recruits received only two weeks of training, while others trained for up to a year. Recruits also learned the basics of Arabic to ensure that foreigners could communicate with the Arab core of the Islamic State. Much of the training for recruits was straightforward, such as learning firing positions for various weapons along with their ranges. However, as with Al Qaeda previously, some individuals were selected for more advanced training, ranging from combat in difficult conditions to diving courses.[150] Some recruits found the training inadequate. "Frankly, the course prepares you for nothing," recalled one defector.[151]

Training camps also imbued recruits with the Islamic State's worldview and mission. "By proselytization and sword," one Islamic State cleric explained, "they cleanse you." A sign declaring, "remember that we didn't come for this life, we came for the afterlife" hung at one camp.[152] Many of the religious leaders themselves had little religious education and used sayings of the prophet and other sources, often out of context, to justify their choice of enemies and tactics. This indoctrination changed many recruits. Chinese volunteers, for example, fled China because of harsh state repression and anger at Beijing, but while in Syria imbibed the broader, more global vision of the Islamic State.[153] The indoctrination also focused on the Islamic State's jihadist enemies. One recruit for the Islamic State's chief rival in Syria, the Al Qaeda-linked Jabhat al-Nusra, noted that much of the indoctrination he received "focuses on the danger of ISIS." The Islamic State returned the favor in its rhetoric.[154] They also tried to implicate recruits, making them commit atrocities and thus be unable to return home or leave the group without fear of punishment. One defector claimed that you had to cut the throat of a prisoner to graduate.[155]

As recruits became more trained, they slowly integrated into Islamic State operations. Recruits at first manned checkpoints as they finished their training, and over time many were incorporated into a formal military structure. Each sector had three battalions of three hundred to four hundred fighters per battalion, with each battalion divided into small units of fifty to sixty fighters. At a more senior level, the Islamic State had officials responsible for logistics and military operations. Officials also oversaw commandos, suicide bombers, and ambush forces.[156]

Experienced fighters who had fought in Afghanistan, Chechnya, Iraq, and elsewhere showed up in Syria to fight with the Islamic State.[157] Foreign fighters often did "the hardest fighting," explained one U.S. official.[158] Veteran foreign fighters served as snipers, planted roadside bombs, or manned more sophisticated weaponry. U.S. officials claimed that Chechens taught some of the most sophisticated fighting methods.[159] For many years, Omar al-Shishani ("the Chechen"), who despite his name, served in the Georgian Army before joining the jihad, acted as the Islamic State's operational commander in Syria.[160] Shishani would earn the moniker "Abu Myaso" (the Father of Meat) because so many of his followers died in the fighting.[161]

The battle for western Mosul between Islamic State foreign fighters and Iraqi Security Forces in the first half of 2017 demonstrates the resolve of foreign fighters. At the end of January 2017, Iraqi security forces captured eastern Mosul, pushing the foreigners across the river that bisects the city to the western part. Most local Islamic State fighters fled, as they could blend in with the exodus of civilians leaving the city, but the foreign fighters lacked this exit option. Many also preferred to fight and die rather than surrender. The remaining 1,500-2,000 fighters in west Mosul originated from Russia, Saudi Arabia, Yemen, China, and Tajikistan and organized into ten-man teams, using sniper positions on rooftops and suicide car and truck bombs to attack the encircling Iraqi security forces. With their "dying breath" efforts, the Islamic State continued sending suicide bombers against Iraqi police-held areas. Despite being backed by massive U.S. air power, Iraqi security forces only ultimately liberated Mosul from the Islamic State in July 2017.[162]

The Islamic State used suicide bombers on an industrial scale, and many of these were foreigners. The Islamic State used more than a thousand suicide attacks in 2016; in contrast, there was a total of fifty-four suicide attacks globally in 2001. Only 16 percent of Islamic State suicide bombings targeted civilians, with most of the strikes being part of its military operations. Suicide bombers in cars were a favorite method. In its 2015 surge into the Iraqi city of Ramadi, the Islamic State used a swarm of armored four-wheel drive vehicles to breach the city's defenses. The drivers exploded their vehicles, and killed themselves, in built-up, defended areas, bringing down fortified positions and obliterating the defenders. Once the way was open, a second swarm of lighter vehicles zoomed in to attack positions previously thought to be invulnerable. The vehicles targeted command positions, groups of enemy fighters held in reserve, and otherwise sowed chaos and fear. During intense fighting in Mosul at the end of 2016, the Islamic State averaged more than twenty-five suicide bombings a week.[163]

For many foreign fighters, the most glamorous role was not traditional suicide bombing but rather fighting in highly dangerous situations. This might include attacking fortified positions or leadership targets, often shooting until they ran out of ammunition. Sometimes they sought to neutralize an enemy position, while in other attacks they sought to spread fear, demonstrating to their enemies that no position was safe.

Yet for all their military accomplishments, foreign fighters, especially those from the West, often struggled to adapt and fit in. Weak or non-existent Arabic language skills, lack of knowledge about the local culture, and little to no experience living in demanding conditions plagued the new recruits. As such, new fighters often leaned heavily on the groups they joined. Foreign fighters may all claim to share one Muslim identity, but they still often congregated based on language, ethnicity, and country of origin. As terrorism expert Clint Watts points out, "Recruits are drawn to jihadi leaders that talk like them and look like them."[164] Communication, of course, was particularly important on the battlefield. Often the units formed on the basis of language groups, leading French-speakers from Belgium, France, and North Africa to operate in one unit while Bosnians served with Muslims from Serbia, Montenegro, Macedonia, and Kosovo, often under the command of Chechens.[165]

Although Islamic State propaganda glorified the role of foreign fighters, the tough conditions did not match the mix of heroism and Nutella promised in the propaganda. "It was totally different," recalled one volunteer.[166] Volunteers testified that some foreign units had no medical personnel or facilities, leading many to bleed to death or otherwise die from treatable wounds.[167] The Islamic State seized the passports and often the phones of new recruits, hindering efforts to escape, should they become disillusioned. Even after completing the training, the omnipresent Islamic State security services monitored them to prevent any defections.[168]

Life in the Islamic State

When the Syrian city of Raqqa first fell to anti-Assad rebels in March 2013, the opposition groups now in charge established representative institutions, such as a city council with local doctors and lawyers, and women's groups. Jihadists, however, sought not just to defeat Assad but also to rule directly. In mid-May, they murdered the head of the city council, the first in a string of murders of rebel leaders and intellectuals that numbered hundreds in all. A suicide car bomb took out the local rebel military leadership. Other opposition members fled, while, after the Islamic State declared itself, local clans gave a public oath swearing loyalty to Baghdadi.[169] Then the Islamic State forced locals to go through reeducation camps, "repenting" for their willingness to work with the regime or rival groups and promising to follow the Caliph.[170]

As the fall of Raqqa suggests, the Islamic State's operations often proceeded in stages, and other key cities like Mosul were often systematically infiltrated before the Islamic State attacked.[171] At first, group members might open a missionary center to try to spread their version of Islam. Of those who attended, a few would be chosen as spies to report on key families and their leaders, the size of rebel forces in the area and their officers, and any compromising information that could be used to blackmail locals. Key "brothers" would also marry into influential families to "ensure penetration of these families without their knowledge." The Islamic State also used locals to do the wet work of intelligence. These individuals murdered and kidnapped to intimidate or eliminate what their security chief referred to as "hostile individuals" who opposed their expansion and to prevent cracks in the group's own ranks. Former intelligence and military officers in Saddam Hussein's regime in Iraq came to play important roles in the Islamic State, bringing with them expertise in intimidation.[172]

The Islamic State, like most jihadist groups, had an almost pathological fear of spies in its ranks, which is why they asked recruits to give the name of someone who could vouch for them.[173] Beyond this basic measure, the Islamic State created multiple spy services to ensure that all key figures watched each other.[174] The first intelligence and secret police service had both internal functions (rooting out spies and traitors) and external ones, including launching attacks overseas and behind enemy lines in Iraq and Syria.[175] Another service conducted ordinary law enforcement. The third service handled religious enforcement, closing stores during prayer times, stopping alcohol use, and so on.[176]

As is also true for jihadists governing in other countries, law and order was at the heart of the Islamic State's appeal to those under its rule. Prior to the group's rise, both Syria and Iraq had rampant corruption as well as government brutality. One Islamic State supporter declared the Iraqi government members as "the best thieves in the world"—a depiction many ordinary Iraqis would voice as well. Records found at an Islamic State police station in Iraq show that the group helped local citizens resolve disputes, forced people to pay back debts, and punished even small infractions of the law. One resident, successfully, went to the Islamic State's police after a soldier took one of his chickens without paying. The head of the police station claimed, "If we succeeded in delivering justice, we knew we would win the hearts of the people."[177] Even many Islamic State critics admit that the group's legal system offered a more efficient and less corrupt model than its predecessors and won it considerable goodwill. "The Islamic State was a terrorist state, but it was also a modern state," noted one engineer who worked under its rule.[178] Residents of Mosul recall that basic services like water, sanitation, and power ran better under the Islamic State than when the Iraqi government was in charge, in part because corrupt or lazy civil servants faced a prison sentence or worse under the jihadists.[179] In addition, the Islamic State punished its own members, including commanders, who abused civilians without cause (though, of course, the group tolerated many low-level abuses of power). One resident claimed his city's crime rate was "near zero" under the Islamic State.

The Islamic State, of course, defined law in religious terms. It argued that man-made laws represent a deviation from God's commandments and thus are a form of heresy. In Aleppo, the group hung a sign in its courthouse declaring "No dogs or lawyers allowed," and it has executed judges for apostasy. By necessity, this required the group to adapt and interpret Islamic law to cover issues such as traffic violations.[180] Still, even one defector claimed that the Islamic State's harsh rule "made the country better."[181]

The Islamic State established its own version of a bureaucracy to run the land it conquered. In an excellent study based on captured Islamic State documents, *New York Times* reporter Rukmini Callimachi describes how the group issued birth certificates and ran its own DMV. It set up a morality police that ensured women were completely covered and men wore garb similar to that supposedly worn by the Prophet's companions at the dawn of Islam. To describe its bureaucracies, it used the term *diwan*, an Arabic word conjuring up images of the courts of the early Caliphs. In reality, however, the bureaucracies served modern functions such as health and education. The Islamic State required Sunni male civil servants to continue to work: "We did the same job as before," one official in Mosul noted, "except we were now serving a terrorist group."[182]

Most Christians sensibly fled the Islamic State's onslaught, but those unable to leave had to be openly subordinate, could not build or repair churches, and paid a special tax in exchange for protection. In Mosul, the Arabic letter "N" (for Nazarene) was put on the homes and stores belonging to Christians. In addition, as part of a religion tied to Western powers, Christians were subjects of constant scrutiny for disloyalty. However, other non-Muslim minorities did not even receive this recognized status. Yazidis, whose faith combines aspects of Islam with teachings from Christianity, Judaism, and Zoroastrianism, were declared as apostates and "can only be given an ultimatum to repent or face the sword," according to the Islamic State's magazine *Dabiq*. During the 2014 attack on the Yazidi homeland around Mount Sinjar in northern Iraq, the Islamic State executed perhaps five thousand Yazidi males and enslaved seven thousand Yazidi women. Young boys were kidnapped, converted, and then sent to fight for the Islamic State. The Islamic State also operated a slave market, selling children and women it captured, many of whom were repeatedly raped in their captivity. Beyond religious minorities, the Islamic State also claimed that anyone who worked with its enemies, including those who played minor roles with the Iraqi or Syrian state, were apostates. They could be killed and their property would be seized.[183]

True to its teachings, the group also expropriated and sold or redistributed the property of Shiites, Christians, and others who had fled, often to the delight of other locals. It had a *diwan* for distributing what it called "war spoils" and another for pillaging the antiquities in areas it conquered. Locals, many bitter about how the Shiite government in Baghdad had treated them, would phone in the addresses of Shiites and others so their property would become available. Kahina el-Hadra, the wife of one of the suicide bombers who blew himself up in the Paris attacks, wrote back to her teacher in France, "I have an apartment that is fully furnished. I pay no rent nor even electricity or water lol. It's the good life!!!" When her teacher expressed concern that the apartment was taken from another family, el-Hadra replied, "Serves them right, dirty Shia!!!"[184] Although better off than the Yazidis, many local women were treated as de facto property because they had "collaborated" with (i.e., lived under) the regime or with rival opposition groups. Being parceled out as a wife to an Islamic State fighter was both a punishment and a form of protection.

Small transgressions, such as playing dominoes and smoking, led to prison. Blasphemy was punished by death, armed robbery by cutting off the right hand and the left leg, and drinking alcohol by eighty lashes.[185] Islamic State officials dropped a stone on the head of a teenage girl accused of adultery.[186] Even worse were atrocities committed as part of the Islamic State's war. It is difficult to walk the line between conveying the horror of the Islamic State's rule properly and yet not overwhelming the other facets of the group, but a few examples seem necessary. Mehdi Nemmouche, who killed four people at the Jewish museum in Brussels—the first significant Islamic State attack in Europe—also held captured Westerners in Syria. He delighted in torturing them, and he claimed he had raped and killed a young woman and then beheaded her baby.[187] Foreign fighters detained and then tortured Kurdish children.[188]

Even minor crimes deserved punishment. The Islamic State put a cage in the middle of the Syrian city of al-Bab where citizens who sold cigarettes or otherwise sinned were imprisoned for all to see their shame.[189] Smoking also could be punished by amputating fingers or worse. Captured prisoners were often beheaded by the dozens or even hundreds to spread fear among the locals. "The human blood from the executions ran like a river," recalled one defector."[190] As horrific as these punishments were, populations that had known the misery of civil war and chaos often welcomed some form of law and order and government services that worked.

Wealthy Arabs in Saudi Arabia, the United Arab Emierates (UAE), Qatar, and Kuwait donated to the group. In addition, the group kidnapped Western journalists and businessmen and held hostage women (with the threat of sexual violence hanging over every transaction) in exchange for massive ransoms.[191] In addition, the Islamic State also controlled many minor oil and gas fields when it held vast territory, generating millions of dollars a month. But taxation offered the most lucrative source of revenue, and it required a bureaucracy to implement and sustain. The group required, as any government would, that the farmers, businessmen, and others under its control pay taxes.[192] Agriculture was its most important resource. The Islamic State collected rent for fields it had seized, taxed the harvest, collected tolls as grain was transported, and then taxed the final sale. It earned as much as $800 million from taxation.[193] The French government estimates that the Islamic State took in $2.5 billion in total between 2014 and 2016.[194]

Because losing locals' support had decimated the Islamic State's predecessor in Iraq, the group was both careful and brutal toward any residents who might not be fully loyal. As a result, the group "cleansed" (in its words) territories in its control, with Shiites and other supposed apostates fleeing along with any Sunnis who might be accused of disloyalty. Its maxim was "Nine Bullets in the heads of the apostates (from among Muslim factions) and one bullet in the head of Crusaders"—a fair summary of how the group prioritized its violence.[195] Local women were often pressed to marry Islamic State fighters to erase suspicion if a family member served in the Syrian regime or was otherwise on the Islamic State's enemies list.

As in other jihadist war zones, locals had mixed attitudes toward the foreign fighters. Some locals admired the foreigners' bravery and military prowess and were grateful for their role in defending Sunnis against a murderous regime. One local noted, "These foreigners left their families, their houses, their lands and traveled all the way to help us here in Syria. So to support us they are truly sacrificing everything they have." Yet he also noted the "crazies" who arrived; young men who knew little of Islam and cared even less, but simply sought to repent for their past sins, to seek adventure, or to use violence.[196]

When it came to killing or torturing, the Islamic State often valued foreigners more than locals. The locals often feared that if they acted brutally, then the victims or their families would retaliate against themselves and their loved ones. The foreigners, without families nearby, had no such inhibitions.[197]

The foreigners' preferred status alienated many Syrians and Iraqis, including those who otherwise supported the group. One report said that foreigners usually made around $200 compared with the locals' $130, and another claimed that foreigners received two or even three times as much as the locals. European foreign fighters received free electricity for their houses (which were often stolen from locals who fled or were killed), while locals had to pay for it. Foreigners could purchase an iPhone, while the locals could not.[198] In the hospital, the foreigners, along with other Islamic State cadre, had better treatment and more access to medicine than locals.[199] Some fighters also enjoyed lording it over the locals. One Syrian under the Islamic State's rule complained that the foreign fighters "act as if they are masters and the people of Raqqa are their slaves."[200] Locals joined for many reasons, but these usually differed substantially from those of foreign fighters. Locals' reasons were practical; they often wanted law and order in the war zone or joined due to economic desperation or fear of reprisal due to family links to the regime.

Leaving the Islamic State

Many Islamic State volunteers died on the battlefield. Some of the bravest fought to the death, but hundreds also surrendered. Local Kurdish or Iraqi units often summarily executed foreigners or gave them at best a sham trial, and locals who had suffered at the hands of the Islamic State were quick to identify them to security officials.[201]

Yet most volunteers did not die. In the first years of the conflict, many recruits went to and fro. In addition to leaving to conduct terrorist attacks outside Iraq and Syria, foreign fighters returned from Islamic State territory to visit family, to recruit, or simply because they became tired of jihad. By some estimates, almost half of the Europeans who came in 2013 and 2014 returned home.[202] As the Islamic State began to lose territory in 2015, however, many left simply because they feared for their lives and felt the cause was too risky. When the Caliphate neared total collapse in 2018, some defected to other groups, others tried to go underground in Syria and Iraq or nearby states like Turkey, while still others fled home.

Numbers are constantly changing, but roughly 30 percent of the European fighters have returned to their home countries, and overall, almost six thousand fighters from thirty-three countries have gone home. The number is probably much larger in countries with weak border and security services, which hinder them from tracking returnees.[203] Information from 2017 suggests that around 400 returned to Russia (slightly more than 10 percent), 760 to Saudi Arabia (roughly 20 percent), 271 to France (around 15 percent), and a whopping 800 to

Tunisia (over 25 percent).[204] Some of these returnees conduct terrorist attacks, encourage others to become foreign fighters, or are otherwise a security threat.

To dissuade deserters, the Islamic State killed and imprisoned anyone even talking about leaving. In characteristic fashion, it burned some and let others freeze to death.[205] However, as the group lost control, its ability to enforce its will plummeted. Many fighters did not return. The loss of territory on the Turkish border hindered not only fighters trying to join the Islamic State but also those attempting to leave it. To escape, fighters must pass through areas controlled by the Syrian government or territory controlled by Syrian allies of the United States, such as Syrian Kurdish forces. Foreigners and other Islamic State fighters often tried to bribe security officials or worked with smugglers to evade detection as they tried to escape the charnel house that Syria had become.[206] Often the bribes cost well above $10,000, which most fighters could not afford. Nevertheless, many volunteers ended up caught or trapped in Turkey. Yet Turkey, once a place where ex-fighters could lay low, is no longer a safe haven; Turkish police now search buses and raid homes to try to find those escaping. Deportation represents the biggest fear for those who make it to Turkey, particularly those from Russia, Turkmenistan, and Uzbekistan. Many of those deported faced torture in their home country and were never heard from again.[207]

Judging why recruits leave the Islamic State often proves difficult because much of the information originates from arrested deserters' interviews. Not surprisingly, the vast majority of those arrested on return claim that the Islamic State misled them, denying personal involvement in any of its atrocities.[208] A Danish government study found that some fighters returned because the frequent killing of other Muslims disillusioned them. "Muslims are fighting Muslims. I didn't come for that," one British militant stated.[209] In addition, many of those who returned may have resented being relegated to a role in the organization and became bitter for *not* being used as they expected. For some fighters, living in a caliphate always at war and steadily shrinking proved too dangerous. Others simply missed their families and homes and felt that they had fulfilled their duty. Mothers proved particularly influential; after mothers contact and press their foreign fighter sons to return, many do.[210]

The Islamic State had long proffered its provinces as an alternative destination for foreign fighters who could not make it to the Caliphate or sought to leave it. Libya emerged as the fourth-biggest destination for foreign fighters, following Afghanistan, Iraq, and Syria, with perhaps three thousand foreigners traveling there (mostly from neighboring states, but a handful from more faraway lands, including nine from the United States). Some Tunisians went to Libya in order to have a rear base from which to train and plan attacks in their home country.[211] The group's Libyan organization was linked to the Manchester attack in the United Kingdom in 2017, where a suicide bomber killed twenty-two people at an Ariana Grande concert, and the December 19, 2016 attack in Germany. Salman Abedi, the perpetrator of the Manchester bombing, met with members of Katibat al-Battar al-Libi in Libya, where he had family, prior to the attack and trained with mid-level operators there. However, the Islamic State in Libya has not exercised full command and control over any plot in the West.[212]

Many of the Islamic State fighters who returned home eluded arrest. As of 2017, of the roughly 15,000 known to have left, 36 percent were in prison, while 46 percent were not (the fate of many is not known, accounting for almost 20 percent of returnees).[213]

The Terrorism Threat

Of those who have escaped arrest, many simply returned home and did nothing, resting on their laurels, disillusioned by the fight, or otherwise ending their jihadist career. A small but important minority, however, sought to conduct terrorist attacks. Others may not launch attacks, but they act as recruiters for the next wave of fighters.[214]

The Islamic State's use of terrorism globally was prolific. Between the declaration of the Caliphate in 2014 and the beginning of 2017, it conducted or inspired more than 140 terrorist attacks in twenty-nine countries, killing more than two thousand people. In Europe, in addition to the Paris attacks, foreign fighters who had fought for the Islamic State in Syria killed thirty-two in suicide attacks at the Brussels airport and metro in 2016. Islamic State foreign fighters did not attack the United States, but the group did inspire bloody attacks, such as the 2016 shooting at the Pulse nightclub that killed forty-nine people, the deadliest jihadist attack in American since 9/11.[215] Russia, which had driven many radicals out of its country, also paid a price when the Islamic State affiliate in Sinai brought down a Russian passenger jet in 2015, killing all 224 people aboard.

For the first years of the Syrian war, easy transit also played a role after a terrorist attack. The coordinator of the Paris attack in November 2015, Abdelhamid Abaaoud, traveled to Syria at least three times, the second time to drag his thirteen-year-old brother to become a foreign fighter and the third, to avoid detection by authorities.[216] The Islamic State also exploited its access to captured Syrian passport equipment, using it to manufacture new passports for its fighters, who could then pose as refugees.[217]

Although attacks in Europe and the United States got much of the attention, Iraq, Syria, and other Middle Eastern countries suffered far more. Islamic State operatives, affiliates, and sympathizers bombed Shiite mosques and Sufi shrines in Saudi Arabia, Yemen, and Pakistan; beheaded Christians in Libya; struck neighborhoods in Lebanon where Hezbollah was popular; and attacked military recruits and hospitals in Afghanistan. Many attacks involved strikes behind enemy lines in Iraq and Syria, with terrorism incorporated into a broader military campaign.

Until his death in 2016, Abu Muhammad al-Adnani, a Syrian who first joined the jihadists after the U.S. invasion of Iraq, had overall responsibility for planning terrorist attacks outside of the Caliphate, but Abu Sulayman al-Faransi, the Frenchman, played a key day-to-day leadership role. Foreign fighters also played a key role as Faransi's lieutenants, with an Indonesian heading external operations in Southeast Asia, another Frenchman responsible for operations in Europe, and so on.[218]

The Islamic State also offered general principles to its followers for targeting in the West. The group emphasized acting on "symbolic dates," though many dates have some symbolism given Islam's long history and the many special days in the West. They also called for capitalizing on violence by neo-Nazis and other right-wing groups to align jihadists with ordinary Muslims, who will seek protection and revenge—a variant of how the Islamic State promoted sectarian attacks in Iraq and tried to position itself to capitalize on the backlash.[219]

For those preparing to operate in Europe and the United States, the Islamic State created guides such as "How to Survive in the West." Advice ranged from how to deal with border security to what clothes to pack. "A secret agent always lives a double life," they admonished, explaining how to form a "sleeper cell" that will activate when needed. Jihadists were advised to keep their real identities secret from each other and to choose false names that would not arouse suspicion. They were told to regularly change their phones, speak in code, and use Tor rather than more mainstream browsers like Google. Recruits were warned against growing a beard and urged to seem "normal" to avoid showing up on the radar screen of security officials. And, of course, "Before any real Jihad can be fought, Muslims require money." Jihadists were advised on conducting credit card fraud, embezzling from their bosses, or otherwise scamming the system.[220]

The Global Response

The Islamic State's flame outshone all its rivals. The caliphate the group established for several years is perhaps the most impressive accomplishment of any jihadist group in modern history. But the flame that burns twice as bright burns half as long. By early 2015, the Islamic State controlled territory the size of Britain, ruling farmlands and oil-producing areas in Syria as well as major cities like Mosul. In Sinai, Libya, Nigeria, and other Muslim areas, jihadist groups had declared themselves provinces of the Caliphate. But by 2018, these accomplishments were in ruins. A global coalition had shattered the Caliphate and forced its leaders and soldiers to go underground, while around the world, regional governments pushed back against the group's provinces and tightened defenses at home. The Islamic State's prestige, and its ability to recruit foreign fighters, plunged.

When the Syrian civil war broke out, most major powers outside the region sought to avoid involvement in Syria and dismissed the threat of the Islamic State. President Obama went against the advice of his CIA director and secretaries of state and defense, rejecting a significant program to aid the anti-Assad resistance. He notoriously walked back from his "red line" after promising to bomb the Syrian regime for its use of chemical weapons. He feared U.S. intervention in the Middle East would inevitably fail or even backfire. As Obama explained, "I am not haunted by my decision not to engage in another Middle Eastern war. It is very difficult to imagine a scenario in which our involvement in Syria would have led to a better outcome, short of us being willing to undertake an effort in size and scope similar to what we did in Iraq." As for the Islamic State, "The analogy we use around here sometimes, and I think is accurate, is if a jayvee team puts on Lakers uniforms that doesn't make them Kobe Bryant. . . . I think there is a distinction between the capacity and reach of a bin Laden and a network that is actively planning major terrorist plots against the homeland versus jihadists who are engaged in various local power struggles and disputes, often sectarian."[221] Understandably, Western powers did not view the group as a major threat; although its Iraqi incarnations had fought hard against coalition forces in Iraq itself, the group did not mount an aggressive campaign against Europe or the U.S. homeland.

Neighboring governments might have been expected to be more concerned about the rise of jihadists in Syria, but they did not prioritize it as a top enemy, especially before 2014. Jordan, Turkey, and the Gulf states had focused first on ousting Assad, and the Gulf states then shifted to opposing the Iranian role. Meanwhile, Turkey was concerned about Kurdish rebels and how they might exacerbate Kurdish separatism domestically. Indeed, many U.S. allies in the Middle East fanned the flames. The State Department noted that "entities and individuals within Qatar" provided money to terrorists, including Al Qaeda's affiliate in Syria. Turkey allowed jihadists to use its soil as a logistics base. Former U.S. Treasury Department Under Secretary David Cohen called Kuwait "the epicenter of fundraising for terrorist groups in Syria."[222]

Less illegally but even more dangerously, allies whipped up a sectarian frenzy against the Assad regime and its Iranian and Hezbollah allies. A number of prominent Saudi preachers regularly condemned Shiite Muslims and praised those fighting this supposed scourge, thus validating the Islamic State's sectarian campaign and increasing its legitimacy among ordinary Sunni Muslims. The city of Qassim in Saudi Arabia has a long history of anti-Shiite sentiment and became one of the centers of Islamic State recruitment in the Kingdom.[223]

The West's blasé attitude changed in 2014 when the Islamic State's power seemed to surge with its conquest of Mosul. The group took sex slaves and otherwise outraged Western audiences. On August 9, U.S. and allied airstrikes commenced on Islamic State positions in Iraq, and a month later the United States began targeting jihadist forces in Syria. As the United States and its allies intervened, the Islamic State also began to systematically behead Western hostages and disseminate videos, claiming it was a response to foreign aggression. Such barbarism further alarmed, and inflamed, world opinion.

The initial campaign moved slowly, but under U.S. leadership, the coalition steadily pushed back the Islamic State from its strongholds in Iraq and Syria. In Iraq, a mix of Shiite militias, Kurdish forces, and Iraqi government troops rallied to fight the Islamic State. In Syria, the United States found fewer allies but managed to work with Syrian Kurdish forces who proved effective on the battlefield. In April 2015, Iraqi forces regained the city of Tikrit. The United States and its allies conducted thousands of airstrikes on Islamic State targets in Iraq and Syria, devastating its ranks, putting it on the defensive, and hindering it when it tried to maneuver its forces. The U.S. military estimates these strikes killed tens of thousands of Islamic State fighters.[224] In October 2015, the United States also deployed special operations forces to northern Syria.

The battle of Kobani, where the Islamic State's foreign fighters fought and perished in droves, illustrates the problems the Islamic State faced as the coalition kicked operations into high gear. Starting in September 2014, Islamic State forces approached the city of Kobani, which had around 400,000 residents, on the Syrian-Turkish border. Using tanks and artillery along with suicide truck bombers to defeat Syrian opposition forces, the Islamic State steadily captured nearby towns and villages and began to encircle Kobani, leading hundreds of thousands of Kurds to flee into Turkey. Observers in Turkey could see the Islamic State's black flag fluttering across the border, and the group boasted about Kobani's imminent "liberation" and how the failure of U.S.-backed forces would lead regional allies to abandon Washington.[225]

The People's Protection Units (YPG), a Syrian Kurdish group that worked closely with U.S. forces opposing the Islamic State, and other Syrian opposition forces pushed back against the Islamic State. The Islamic State sent waves of foreign fighters on kamikaze missions against Kurdish defenders.[226] The fighting was intense, with much of the city destroyed in house-to-house battles or aerial bombardment. The Kurds even used a female fighter as a suicide bomber against the Islamic State. When the Islamic State captured Kurds, torture, beheading, and mutilation were common. At first, the Islamic State continued to make headway against Kurdish forces, and by November 2015, Kobani's capture seemed imminent.

But the bombing and Kurdish resistance steadily took its toll. To aid its local allies, the U.S. Air Force dropped ammunition and medicine to them directly, as Turkey was leery of supporting Kurdish groups, fearing their ties to antiregime militants at home.[227] The coalition bombed Islamic State fighters and also targeted their ammunition, supplies, and reinforcements, making it hard for the group to sustain the fight. The United States and Kurdish forces developed procedures to coordinate U.S. airstrikes, greatly improving their precision and impact. "Planes did not leave the air, day and night; they did airstrikes all day and night," reported one Islamic State fighter.[228] Another lamented, "They bombarded everything, even motorcycles."[229] The Islamic State lost around a thousand fighters, with the Kurdish forces losing over three hundred.[230] The Islamic State proved unable to sustain these losses, with one fighter admitting, "We had to withdraw and the rats advanced."

Fights like Kobani were repeated throughout Iraq and Syria, with the Islamic State's forces pushed back by local militias and government troops, usually backed by U.S. and allied airpower. As the war heated up on all fronts, the group cut training because it desperately needed its fighters to go to the front lines, making its military operations less and less effective. The Islamic State also began to cut pay as its revenues shrank, never a popular decision. Many locals deserted as a consequence.[231] Foreign fighter flows, which peaked in 2014–2015, declined as the Islamic State declined.[232]

In addition to attacking the group directly, the United States went after its finance sources. The United States' pressure on Kuwait, Qatar, and other countries led to tighter controls that diminished the group's ability to fundraise globally. Air strikes on the oil infrastructure and on trucks transporting oil in Islamic State areas also hit the group hard. Most important, conquering territory and attacking finance went together. The group relied heavily on taxing locals in the territory it controlled. As its territory shrank, so did its tax base and ability to loot or extort money.[233]

In July 2017, the Islamic State lost its Iraqi capital, Mosul, after months of hard fighting, and in October 2017, its Syrian capital, Raqqa, fell. By the end of 2017, the United States and its allies had killed as many as 70,000 Islamic State fighters, including much of its leadership. Some fell into the hands of Iraqi or Syrian governments, where many were dispatched with a show trial, at best.[234] The Caliphate, for now at least, was over.

Part of the group's appeal once it grabbed the world's attention in 2014 was its "winning" identity. "Winners attract winners," noted one terrorism expert when explaining why foreigners joined the group.[235] As the group went from dramatic success to steady failure, propaganda could only succeed so much. In addition, it's harder to maintain a massive propaganda effort when bombs destroy your television studios and kill your propagandists. Both the quality and the quantity of its propaganda fell.[236]

The United States also tried to work with its allies to step up the fight against Islamic State "provinces" in Afghanistan, Egypt, Libya, and elsewhere. In 2016, the United States worked with local militias and deployed special operations forces to Libya, where the Islamic State had thousands of fighters, striking Islamic State leaders and military forces and pushing the group back from the territory it controlled around Sirte. Israel worked with Egypt to hit Islamic State forces in the Sinai, conducting dozens of strikes with unmarked aircraft to maintain the illusion that Egypt could handle its security on its own. In Afghanistan, where the Islamic State branch emerged as a major threat, U.S. military forces and those of the Afghan government targeted the group, and so too did the Taliban, which considers the group a rival.[237]

The world also made more aggressive efforts to stop foreigners from going to Syria to fight and to monitor them on return. In September 2014, the United Nations Security Council passed resolution 2178—the first resolution specifically targeting foreign fighters. It demanded that states

> prevent and suppress the recruiting, organizing, transporting or equipping of individuals who travel to a State other than their States of residence or nationality for the purpose of the perpetration, planning, or preparation of, or participation in, terrorist acts or the providing or receiving of terrorist training, and the financing of their travel and of their activities.

In addition, the resolution called on all states to cooperate with one another to stop recruitment, transit, and other foreign fighter essentials.[238] Although UN resolutions are often dismissed as wishful thinking, this one had a profound effect. A number of states link their domestic laws to UN resolutions, particularly in Europe, and this resolution gave states the impetus to crack down at home and cooperate more abroad.

In 2017, the UN Security Council passed resolution 2396. It focused on terrorist travel, requiring member states to collect and record names of passengers in order to prevent terrorists from returning home indirectly—for example, by going back to Europe via Latin America. Member states are also required to gather biometrics, improve data sharing, and otherwise improve efforts to undermine foreign fighters' ability to travel.

The Islamic State's loss of its territory aided these efforts. Coalition forces captured the Islamic State's meticulous membership records, and this was shared widely. Interpol received almost 20,000 names.[239] The list made it easier to identify potential returnees and disrupt their travel. Some recruits did return home, and still others found their way to Turkey, where they went into hiding from security forces. Although world governments rightly worry about the terrorism threat these individuals pose, the danger is far less than it was when the Islamic State seemed triumphant.

The Islamic State recognized its pitiful position. As the group lost more of its strongholds, its rhetoric shifted to dismiss the importance of territorial control. Instead, the Islamic State emphasized the concept of a caliphate, as opposed to its reality, as the driving force behind the group's success. Abu Mohammad al-Adnani, then the Islamic State's spokesman and senior operational figure, stated in a May 2016 recorded message, "O America, would we be defeated and you be victorious if you were to take Mosul or Sirte or Raqqa?. . . Certainly not! We would be defeated and you victorious only if you were able to remove the Quran from Muslims' hearts."[240] Like so many other Islamic State leaders, Adnani is now dead.

Just as every past jihad spawned new movements and networks that made long-term victory elusive, the Syrian struggle will likely do the same. The sheer volume of foreign fighters encompasses part of the problem. Even if only a fraction of a fraction of the 40,000 or so foreign fighters become dangerous, their existence still poses difficulties for governments globally. Poor governance in both Iraq and Syria may allow opportunities for the Islamic State or another group to again rise and plague the region.

Most troubling for the long term, the Islamic State has nurtured the flame of jihad around the world. Even as the group declines, the ideas it champions—the necessity of a caliphate, the glory of brutality, and the evil of Western states—have spread further, as the staggering volume of foreign fighters suggests. The Islamic State's propaganda is extensive and almost ubiquitous. Successor organizations will no doubt try to harvest what the Islamic State planted.

CHAPTER 11 | The Facilitator: Amer Azizi and the Rise of Jihadist Terrorism in Europe

E UROPE's 9/11" OCCURRED on March 11, 2004, when Al Qaeda–linked terrorists set off ten bombs on four trains in and near Madrid, killing 191 people and injuring almost 1,800. The terrorists packed 10 kilograms of dynamite and half a kilogram of shrapnel, screws, and nails in each bomb and placed them into backpacks and sling bags. Then they detonated the bombs during a ten-minute span on the morning commute into Madrid. Middle- and working-class people and university students accounted for most of the casualties.[1] Dubbed "3/11" to highlight the similarities to the September 11, 2001 attacks in the United States, the event showed how, once again, foreign networks proved crucial to launching a deadly, highly coordinated attack.

Both before and after the 3/11 attacks, Europe struggled with the threat of jihadist foreign fighters. Roughly 90 percent of cells in Western Europe in the pre-9/11 era involved a foreign fighter; this number fell to 70 percent through 2007 and 50 percent from 2008 to 2013, but even that was a sizable figure.[2] Foreign fighters also played leading roles in several of the Islamic State's bloodiest attacks on Europe, notably the 2015 attacks in Paris that killed 130 people and the 2016 suicide bombings in Brussels that killed 32 more.

The Spanish government quickly blamed Basque terrorists, who had long plagued Spain, for the 3/11 attacks. When this proved false, the conventional wisdom shifted to describing the attack as a bottom-up plot of local jihadists enraged by Spain's support for the war in Iraq. Indeed, the Spanish public came to believe that the bombing was retaliation for the government's unpopular decision to join the U.S.-led invasion of Iraq. The government's popularity plunged, and it lost the next election to the Socialist Party, which campaigned on the promise of removing Spanish troops from Iraq.

Over time, however, it became clear that Al Qaeda played a leading role in planning the attack from its base in Pakistan and that the planning began well before the Iraq war. In his magisterial study of the bombings, the Spanish scholar Fernando Reinares describes the plotters as a mix of three groups: the survivors of an Al Qaeda cell formed in 1994 in Spain, members of a Moroccan terrorist group that also had a presence in the country, and a gang of thugs with holy warrior aspirations.[3] Ironically, the key figures' ability and decision to go abroad enabled them to work together better at home.

Amer Azizi sat at the center of this nexus. Born in Morocco, Azizi moved to Spain, where "he became a different Amer," according to a friend. He attended meetings of Tablighi Jamaat, an ostensibly peaceful Salafi group that preached a strict interpretation of the faith and served as an incubator for violence in several European countries. Azizi became even more extreme after joining the "Abu Dahdah cell," named after the Syrian who led the cell in 1995. The cell sent Azizi to Bosnia to train with fighters there, and then later he went to Afghanistan. Azizi trained alongside another 3/11 bomber, Said Berraj, in an Al Qaeda camp, where the latter learned to use cell phones to detonate bombs.[4] An Al Qaeda hagiography published after Azizi's "martyrdom" declared him "noble, at the service of his brothers" as well as "of great intelligence" and "filled with fervor for this religion."[5]

Azizi's experience abroad gave him tremendous prestige among local jihadists when he returned to Spain, making him an effective recruiter. He recruited Serhane ben Abdelmajid Fakhet, another Tablighi Jamaat member who later became the local leader of the 3/11 attacks. Fakhet and other cell members would watch videos on the fighting in Chechnya, Bosnia, and other countries. Inspired by Azzam's references to "Al-Andalus," the name of a Muslim-controlled kingdom in Spain that ruled from the eighth through fifteeth centuries, cell members sought to "reclaim" the country for Islam, a position Al Qaeda leaders repeatedly endorsed.[6] Indeed, when abroad, Azizi took the name "al-Andalusi."

Spanish authorities cracked down on jihadist networks in Spain after 9/11. Fatefully, several cell members escaped the dragnet. Azizi had fled Spain earlier and gone to Iran to work on building up transit routes that would enable jihadists to go to and from Afghanistan. He then traveled to Pakistan and fought with Al Qaeda, attacking U.S. forces and their allies in Afghanistan. Initial plans for an attack in Spain may have predated the 9/11 attacks, but regardless, planning escalated once Azizi became more involved with Al Qaeda. Hungry for revenge after Spanish law enforcement officers arrested his fellow jihadists, at first Azizi drew on his own networks and knowledge. He steadily integrated into the Al Qaeda core and convinced his superiors to support the plan, serving as an intermediary between them and local cell members in Spain.[7] Azizi probably returned temporarily to Spain, meeting with cell leaders and otherwise trying to move the plot along.

Azizi found other allies upon returning to Spain. The post-9/11, U.S.-led counterterrorism campaign swept up jihadists of all stripes. The U.S. officials targeted Al Qaeda members, separate groups that at times cooperated with Al Qaeda, and individuals who had trained in a jihadist camp in Afghanistan. Although these differences mattered tremendously in the jihadist world before 9/11, a common foe and crushing pressure led jihadists around the world to join forces out of desperation. In early 2002, representatives from Moroccan, Libyan, and Tunisian jihadist groups met in Turkey, a far safer location for them than their home countries. According to Spanish security services, they agreed that no longer would a "good Muslim have to leave and go to a war zone like Chechnya or Iraq," but rather, "jihad should happen in those places where they reside."[8] Thus, a Spanish-based cell linked to a Moroccan group also joined Azizi's network, connected by a friend whom he met in Madrid. Others in the cell had fought or trained in Afghanistan or other theaters.

Although based in Spain, the outlook of Azizi and his comrades crossed borders. The cell initially focused on proselytizing and raising money, with financial sources ranging from credit card fraud to charitable donations for victims of the fighting in Bosnia and Chechnya. The cell channeled some of this money to Abu Qatada in London. Qatada, a Jordanian of Palestinian origin, was one of a number of radical preachers who had set up shop in the British capitol. In addition, the cell leader known as Abu Dahdah had extensive contacts, including to Mohamed Atta, the Egyptian who led the 9/11 attacks. Abu Dahdah was one of the few who had advance knowledge of the 9/11 plot.[9]

The cell also found local allies via a gang leader, Jamal Ahmidan, known as "El Chino" (the Chinese). Many members of his gang had spent time in jail in Spain, Morocco, or France, but Ahmidan had done all three. He became radicalized during his time in prison, perhaps in France, but certainly by the time he served time in a Moroccan jail from 2000 to 2003. Ahmidan met Fakhet through friends and coordinated much of the plot's logistics. He arranged a safe house, acquired false documents, raised or stole money, and stole explosives from a quarry in northern Spain.[10]

Al Qaeda later claimed it tasked Azizi with instructing foreign fighters and local attackers "for the purpose of transforming the tranquility of the crusaders into a hell." Bin Laden declared, "These are your goods returned to you," citing Palestine as one justification. Propaganda also played up revenge for Spain's support for the Iraq war, but this only amounted to window dressing; the decision to attack and the plot had been in motion for years.[11] Azizi paid a high price for his new friends. In 2005, a U.S. drone strike targeted Hamza Rabia, a senior Al Qaeda figure responsible for terrorist operations in the West, in a remote village in Pakistan. Azizi died in the same drone strike.[12]

The attack in Spain illustrates one of the most important dangers posed by foreign fighters: connections. Fighting in Bosnia and training in Afghanistan gave Azizi and foreign fighters like him a broader mindset and network, transforming them from local troublemakers to global dangers. As a foreign fighter, Azizi could tap into Spanish militants, a range of North African groups, and the Al Qaeda core. In addition, he had more credibility back home, enabling him to recruit more effectively, with radical Islamist organizations, like Tablighi Jamaat, and prisons proving particularly rich hunting grounds. Azizi also illustrates how foreign fighters can boomerang, starting their radical activity in Europe, going abroad to fight, and then launching or orchestrating attacks at home.

Europe, of course, is no stranger to foreign fighting, having sent thousands of volunteers to fight in Spain, the Russian revolution, and various nationalist struggles. In the past, governments worried that returnees would prove Soviet agents or otherwise act as radical catalysts. Now, however, they worry that foreign fighters will bring the war home through terrorism and that the interconnectedness of Europe and its open borders means that even a vigilant government will pay for the lax policies of its neighbor.

Although the Madrid attack offers the bloodiest example of the growing connectedness of European jihadists, it is far from the only one. In his survey of jihadist attacks in Europe, terrorism scholar Petter Nesser finds that foreign fighters who returned home acted as entrepreneurs, creating and leading new cells and using their authority and credibility to bring together local radicals, misfits, and others under their wing. Foreign fighters then link these local cells to armed groups in war zones, both fueling the journey of new foreign fighters and bringing foreign-directed terrorism home to Europe.[13] One European expert put it to me more bluntly: "It becomes a totally fucked-up mix."[14]

The Origins of Europe as a Jihadist Battlefield

Europe played a role in the jihadist struggle long before the attacks in Spain, but the Madrid attack highlighted how Europe moved from sideshow to center stage. Outside of Bosnia, jihadism in Europe originated as a spinoff of the Algerian civil war in the 1990s. Jihadist networks in Europe steadily strengthened after that, but they served primarily to support conflicts abroad with fundraising, propaganda, and foreign fighters. This changed after 9/11, and especially after the 2003 Iraq war, with European cells increasingly seeking to strike in Europe and drawing on resources from foreign groups to do so.

More than a century of colonization, followed by a brutal war of independence, wove French and Algerian history together in a frayed and often bloody pattern. Islamists mobilized, largely peacefully, in the 1980s in Algeria, with their hopes set on winning at the polls in long-promised free elections. They scored a strong victory in the first round of elections in 1991, but the military intervened with a coup, dashing their hopes of peacefully gaining power. Protests quickly led to violence, and more than 100,000 Algerians died in the civil war that erupted. The regime slowly turned the tide, but the conflict dragged on throughout the 1990s and continues sporadically today, as Algerian militants now reside in neighboring countries. Horrific violence characterized the war, with one group, the Armed Islamic Group (GIA), standing out for its brutality.

The GIA emerged from the fires of Afghanistan as much as it did from the violence in Algeria. Regime crackdowns on Islamists in the 1980s had led some Algerians to flee to Afghanistan and Pakistan, where they had a de-gree of safety as well as access to training camps. The strife resulting from the coup in Algeria began as the Afghan war ended, and many veterans returned. Several of the GIA's initial leaders were Arab Afghans, including Qari Said, one of the GIA's founders, and these returnees had prestige and fighting skills that enhanced their influence. Bin Laden and others also gave them money. The GIA proclaimed it would "purge the land of the ungodly." Unlike other groups that wanted concessions and would negotiate with the government, the GIA declared, "no agreement, no truce, no dialogue." To defeat the gov-ernment, it sought to destabilize the country, and to this end it assassinated government employees, detonated car bombs in civilian areas, and kidnapped the families of its enemies.[15]

Foreshadowing the Islamic State's tactics and problems, the GIA not only fought the regime but also determined that rival groups and civilians who did not actively aid the jihadists were apostates who deserved death. They slaughtered children, pregnant women, and of course any stalwart of the other side, which included supposed collaborators like schoolteachers and religious leaders who opposed jihadism. One of its Arab Afghan leaders declared war on journalists, contending, "he who fights us with the pen, we will fight with the sword."[16] The GIA also beheaded enemies and took women as war booty, methods later popularized by the Islamic State. The jihadists were particularly hostile to France, given that country's colonial history in Algeria and support for the Algerian regime.

Group leaders rejected Bin Laden's attempts to send foreign fighters to Algeria, and GIA fanatics murdered Libyan jihadists who came to offer support, believing they were not zealous enough and probably spies. Indeed, lecturers in Afghan training camps later cited the GIA example as a case where jihad went off the rails. However, given the large number of Algerians already in Europe, especially France, the war consumed the Algerian diaspora community. The rebels raised money, scrounged arms, and distributed propaganda in Europe, using it as a rear base. Although initially France did not crack down as harshly as it would later, its support for the Algerian regime and effort to counter the GIA at home led the GIA to try to expand the battlefield. In December 1994, GIA fighters hijacked an Air France flight. French authorities tricked the hijackers into allowing the plane to land in Marseilles for a supposed fuel stop, where French commandos successfully stormed it. In 1995, the GIA murdered a rival Islamist leader in Paris, killed eight and injured dozens more in attacks on metro stations in Paris, and injured fourteen in a bombing attack on a Jewish school. The GIA members saw killing in France as an extension of the war in Algeria, with the French government's support for the regime justifying the attacks. More ominously for the future, jihadists saw France as deserving of attacks because the French government oppressed Muslims at home, Jews there supposedly conspired against Islam, and society itself was impious. Many other attacks failed, but the pace of the strikes and the numerous targets led to a massive crackdown in France and, over time, led France to develop one of the best and most aggressive intelligence services focused on the jihadist movement.

The Algerian networks also showed up beyond France. Christophe Caze, a Belgian convert who fought in Bosnia, forged ties to the GIA. He emerged as a leader of the "Roubaix Gang," which tried to bomb the G-7 meeting in nearby Lille along the French-Belgian border. French police tracked down the gang members, killing Caze and his fellow conspirators. The end of the Roubaix Gang, the crackdown on GIA networks in France, and the decline in GIA networks throughout Europe and in Algeria led to a decline in Algeria-related terrorism. However, the broader idea that Europe itself was impious did not die.

As France fought GIA terrorism, a number of radical preachers set up shop in Europe, especially in London—dubbed "Londonistan" by critics. These included the aforementioned Abu Qatada, the Syrian Omar Bakri, and the Egyptian Abu Hamza. Abu Hamza fought in Bosnia and also fought (or at least trained) in Afghanistan. He was the imam of the Finsbury Park Mosque in London in the late 1990s and led a Salafi group that called for the imposition of Islamic law. In both these capacities he served as a recruiter for jihad, emphasizing the war in Chechnya among other causes. Abu Hamza would be arrested several years after 9/11 and eventually deported to the United States, where he was tried and imprisoned for his support for terrorism.

Abu Qatada arrived in Great Britain in the early 1990s on a forged United Arab Emirates passport, claiming asylum for himself and his family because Jordanian authorities tortured him.[17] He had fought in the Afghan jihad and proved an inspirational figure, eventually linked to numerous foreign fighters and terrorists. In his journal and preaching, he would even highlight the actions of obscure jihadists in the Middle East, including the trial of a young Abu Musab al-Zarqawi, the Jordanian who would later become the leader of the Iraqi jihad.[18] Qatada sent money to various jihadists around the world, while the rest helped build networks in Europe and the Middle East. Jordan sentenced him in absentia for his involvement in the bombings at the American School and a Jerusalem hotel in Amman, and a Spanish court named him as one of the British contacts for a Spanish cell involved in the 9/11 attacks. The Spanish judge in the trial referred to Qatada as "the spiritual leader of mojahedins across Europe."[19]

Bakri led Al Muhajiroun, which was founded in 1986 and not banned until 2005. British authorities linked the group to dozens of individuals who became terrorists. It sought to raise awareness of Islam and called for the establishment of a caliphate, a radical but nonetheless ostensibly peaceful goal. Al Muhajiroun, however, expressed support for an array of jihadist causes. In 2002, it held a conference on "The Magnificent 19," in praise of the 9/11 attackers. Bakri himself declared that "there is no such thing as an 'innocent' unbeliever."[20] Bakri sent hundreds of recruits to Pakistan to train, usually to fight in Kashmir (Bakri also claims to have sent some British Muslims to the United States for training as guns are legal in America and private companies provide weapons training).[21]

From London, these leaders issued propaganda, brought recruits into radical mosques, and helped mobilize to support jihad. Acolytes attended lectures, heard stories of former foreign fighters, raised money to train, and participated in the jihadi world. They sang jihadi hymns and learned Arabic, all the while trying to dress the part in military fatigues or Afghan-style dress. The preachers supported causes in Algeria, Egypt, and Libya, but they also embraced wars in Bosnia, Chechnya, and other countries. The camps in Afghanistan that Al Qaeda and other groups built proved useful for their struggles and often acted as gatekeepers for recruits.[22] A leading jihadist declared London "the new

'Peshawar' of the Islamic Awakening," noting the Arabic and jihadist media presence thriving in the city. A subculture of jihadi hymns, poetry, and images began to spread.[23]

As in the real Peshawar, militants in Europe competed with each other as much as they worked together. In London, Arab and Pakistani militants battled each other for control of several mosques.[24] Some preachers favored national struggles over Al Qaeda's global approach, and they all competed for resources. A few endorsed attacks on Europe. One magazine published out of London devoted an entire issue celebrating the GIA attacks in France, and a leading jihadist argued that the attacks would "unify the Islamic Nation" as the anti-Soviet jihad united Muslims. Some jihadist organizations, however, were reluctant to strike in Europe during the 1990s because of its importance as a logistics hub and the considerable freedoms awarded to radical preachers in London and other countries due to speech protections. These organizations argued that they had entered a "covenant of security." By accepting visas voluntarily from a Western government, they had accepted its protection and authority and could not in turn attack it.[25]

Jihadism in Europe Post-9/11

The shift toward more international targets accelerated after the 9/11 attacks and, especially, after the 2003 Iraq war. European Muslims played a tiny role in the anti-Soviet struggle, and only a handful trained in Afghan camps in the 1990s.[26] As preachers sent young men to camps in Afghanistan, Bin Laden began tapping into the emerging networks, giving fighters money to conduct attacks on their return. In 2000, Al Qaeda tried to bomb a Christmas market in Strasbourg and several U.S. targets in Europe. Many of the attacks that occurred in the next several years involved individuals who had gone to Afghanistan (or in one notable case the Caucasus) where Al Qaeda indoctrinated them and then helped them network with other jihadists. European cells, which initially developed as support networks to assist foreign fighters seeking to go to Afghanistan and Chechnya, now helped terrorists championing other jihadist causes, shared personnel and expertise, and assisted in attacks on Europe itself.[27] The wars in Bosnia and Chechnya and the training camps in Afghanistan had accomplished their goals. Multiple nationalities now worked together and broadened their horizons, posing a threat well beyond the war zone.

European Muslims were falling under the sway of Al Qaeda and its teachings. Having trained in Afghanistan or learning from those who did, they believed Europe, in alliance with the United States, was behind many of the Muslim world's problems and that they were striking blows in defense of their community. Indeed, many were going beyond Al Qaeda, which focused on the foreign policies of Western states. Jihadists also criticized Europe for the personal and sexual freedom women enjoyed, tolerance of homosexuality, and other supposedly un-Islamic values.

Since several European states participated in the 2003 invasion of Iraq, Al Qaeda members and other foreign fighters gained a new cause to radicalize the next generation. The radical preacher Bakri annulled the supposed "covenant of security," accusing Britain of going to war with Islam because of its involvement in the Iraq war and its crackdown on jihadists at home.[28] However, many foreign fighters focused first and foremost on the Iraq struggle. Those who sought to attack at home often involved individuals on the network's periphery or those who had unsuccessfully tried to travel to fight.[29]

European states and extremist Muslims entered a cycle of hostility. The post-9/11 crackdown, along with many European states' involvement in the Afghanistan and Iraq wars, led many extremists, who previously enjoyed a relative haven, to become more hostile to their host governments. More terrorist plots and acts led to greater popular hostility toward Muslims and greater government crackdowns, exacerbating the anger. The United Kingdom saw a surge in attacks linked to its citizens of Pakistani origin. Before 2004, Pakistanis in the United Kingdom or elsewhere in Europe might have joined groups in Pakistan, but there they focused on either fighting in Kashmir or supporting other causes in South Asia. As Al Qaeda increased its ties to Pakistani groups after 9/11, and as European Muslims became enraged with the Iraq war and European government mistreatment of them, they began to attack at home.

One of Europe's biggest attacks after Madrid occurred on July 7, 2005, when terrorists who trained in Pakistan with Al Qaeda and Pakistani groups bombed three London Underground trains and a bus, killing fifty-two people. As with the Madrid attacks, the London bombings illustrate how radical preachers and networks in Europe connected with foreign fighter–associated groups abroad with the result being terrorism back in Europe. Officials initially described the attack as homegrown by Muslims with no prior jihadist history who were enraged by Britain's role in the Iraq war. This anti-war narrative fit into the political debate of the time, similar to the early depiction of the Madrid attack as a strike motivated by the Iraq war. However, Al Qaeda played a key role, facilitated, of course, by foreign fighters who could bridge the gap between locals and the core group in Pakistan. As terrorism scholar Bruce Hoffman found, the bombers came from a mix of backgrounds, several of which seemed stereotypically British. All four were born in the United

Kingdom, and they lived near one another. The leader, Mohammed Siddique Khan, who committed the suicide bombing of the Edgware Road tube station that killed six innocent people, seemed a model citizen; he had a job and university degree and even worked with special needs children. A parliamentary investigation noted that "he had a real talent and vocation for working with young people." In a note to his family, he claimed that leaving his baby daughter "was the most difficult thing in his life."[30] In contrast, Jermaine Lindsay, who bombed the Russell Square metro, converted to Islam and came from a broken home.[31] The youngest, Hasib Hussain, was born in Leeds and a member of the local cricket team, and he also spent time in Pakistan. The fourth, Shehzad Tanweer, worked in a fish and chips shop and was radicalized completely at home. Khan led the group and recruited the others. He even established a gym supposedly to get young men off the street—a gym, officials later learned, that he used as a recruitment center.

Rashid Rauf, an Al Qaeda recruiter and fellow British national of Pakistani origin, recruited Khan himself and arranged for him and his right-hand man Shehzad Tanweer to travel to Pakistan (Khan likely traveled to Pakistan multiple times and probably also went to Afghanistan). Rauf, a dual national of Pakistan and the United Kingdom, fled the United Kingdom in 2002 to hide out with Al Qaeda in Pakistan and was deeply involved in European operations from his haven there. Khan was ripe for recruitment. The preaching of Abu Hamza, the American jihadist preacher Anwar al-Awlaki, and sermons from Tablighi Jamaat (the same group that put Azizi on the road to radicalism) inspired him. Pakistani militant groups hosted Khan and Tanweer, and they trained in an Al Qaeda camp. At the camp, they met the head of Al Qaeda's external operations who instructed them to hide their intentions by behaving in an "un-Islamic" way by going to movies and trying to lay low. On return, both men came on the radar screen of British intelligence, but the overworked service saw them as "petty fraudsters" and focused its efforts elsewhere. Up to the moment of the bombing, Khan stayed in touch with Al Qaeda, whose experts provided technical advice on constructing the bombs as well as other assistance. After the attacks, Al Qaeda released martyrdom videos of Khan and Tanweer that they filmed while in Pakistan, in which they blamed British forces for "atrocities around the world"; lauded Bin Laden; spoke of Palestine, Chechnya, Afghanistan, and Iraq; and otherwise peddled the Al Qaeda line.[32]

Later investigations revealed that Khan participated in a broader network of British recruits who would attack their home on Al Qaeda's behalf. As part of this network, while in Pakistan he met Muktar Said Ibrahim, who came as a child to the United Kingdom when his Eritrean family sought asylum. Ibrahim was the leader of another terrorist campaign launched on July 21,

2005 that involved three bombs on Underground tube stops in London and one on a double-decker bus. Fortunately, the bombs were poorly constructed. Only the detonator caps fired with the bombs themselves not going off, resulting in no deaths. Khan also met one of the leaders of the August 2006 plan to bomb multiple airlines as they crossed the Atlantic. This plot involved liquid explosives and led to changes in airline security that banned bringing fluids past security screening.[33] Rauf, operating from his haven in Pakistan, had his hand in orchestrating all these plots.

In addition to terrorist attacks and plots, culture wars brought the "war on Islam" from Iraq and the Muslim world into the heart of Europe. Extremists retaliated against art criticizing Islam, and European governments took actions to ban Islamic practices. In 2004, a local militant cell stabbed Dutch filmmaker Theo Van Gogh to death after he made a film highly critical of the treatment of women under Islam. In 2005, a Danish newspaper published cartoons mocking the Prophet Mohammad, igniting widespread rage and numerous plots against the newspaper and others who reprinted the cartoons. Swedish artist Lars Vilks drew the Prophet as a roundabout dog (it's a thing in Sweden) in 2007, leading to several attempts on his life. Supposedly in response to attacks like these, in 2009, Switzerland banned the construction of new minarets. In 2010, France banned women from wearing garments that covered their face, the so-called veil ban, igniting widespread protests. To score political points, European politicians at times blasted Islam, with Brtisih Prime Minister David Cameron referring to the "poisonous ideology of Islamist extremism." The mayor of Rotterdam said that Muslims who don't want to integrate should "piss off."[34]

These culture wars became intertwined with broader social and economic problems related to integration, with problems including poverty, unemployment, drug use, and tensions with the police. A study of Spanish jihadists, for example, found that the second generation of Muslim immigrants was particularly vulnerable, with 60 percent of Spain's recruits coming from this community. A resident of Moroccan origin in Spain was over seven times more likely to be arrested for jihadist activity in Spain than a resident of Morocco; Spaniards of Moroccan origin were also far more likely to become foreign fighters.[35] In 2005, Paris and other French cities erupted in riots for three weeks, with young men of African and Middle Eastern descent usually in the lead. One European expert I interviewed described the 2005 riots as involving "the older brothers of today's foreign fighters."[36] The same European terrorism analyst noted that the French veil ban was "stupid" as it gave the radicals more fodder. [37]

Because Islam and Muslim integration has entered the political debate, people "look differently at a Muslim guy with a backpack," noted one official.[38] The lack of integration, combined with terrorism, created a dangerous circle. Muslims in Europe complain, correctly, that they are systematically profiled and suffer discrimination.[39] The communities are often hostile to or suspicious of the police. Some British Muslims feared sharing relevant information with the police for fear of being branded as collaborators or getting in trouble with law enforcement as a terrorist sympathizer.[40] This lack of integration and suspicion of law enforcement facilitates the spread of militant Islam. The jihadists offer European Muslims an explanation for the discrimination against them and provide a course of action to respond.[41] To non-Muslim Europeans, violence seemed like proof of the problem, and calls for more police pressure grew.

As the London and Madrid bombings suggested, after 9/11, jihadists conducted a range of indiscriminate attacks in Europe that targeted civilians randomly. As the decade wore on, however, more attacks focused on military personnel, Jews, and those seen as anti-Islam. This shift in targets, which lasted several years, from the population as a whole to particular enemies suggested that Al Qaeda deprioritized Europe.[42] Although Europe received considerable attention from those concerned with terrorism, Al Qaeda focused on Iraq, Afghanistan, and its own survival. This extended to financial support as well, a few cells received money from abroad, but the vast majority had to generate all or most of it by themselves.[43]

Europe also developed a prison problem (and this will get worse, as the rise of the Islamic State and the huge European foreign fighter numbers have led to large numbers of prisoners). In France, 60 percent of prisoners are Muslims, although they represent only 8 percent of the total population. In Italy, Muslims are almost 20 percent of the prison population though only 2.5 percent of the total population.[44] Many inmates become more pious in jail, growing a long beard, fasting during Ramadan, and otherwise embracing their faith. Prison officials often confused piety and radicalism, harassing all Muslims and driving them toward extremism. Mixing ordinary Muslim criminals with radicals allowed militants to expand their networks, as prisons are filled with troubled young men open to a new identity and supposedly noble cause.[45] Some of Europe's worst terrorist attacks involved jihadists who went to prison and became more radicalized. Europe's jails are teeming with Muslims.

Despite all these problems, the jihadist foreign fighter threat looked less ominous by the ten-year anniversary of the 3/11 attacks. Europe had avoided a massive jihadist terrorist attack since the London bombings. Plots fell dramatically, Bin Laden was dead, and successful revolutions in Egypt and Tunisia had created a sense that jihadism had declined. Al Qaeda was hunted in Pakistan and around the world, and in Iraq, it looked like the Al Qaeda branch was on the ropes with the war in the rear-view mirror. Indeed, the worst attack Europe suffered in the years after 3/11 was not perpetrated by a jihadist but by Anders Breivik, a self-identified Norwegian fascist who in 2011 set off a bomb in downtown Oslo that killed eight; he then shot sixty-nine people, mostly teenagers, at a Labor Party youth camp on the island of Utøya.

The Islamic State in Europe

In hindsight, the end of the last decade was the calm before the storm. Europe's terrorism problem surged as the Islamic State emerged from the Syrian civil war. In 2011, when the war began, European states arrested 122 people for jihadist-linked terrorism; by 2015, that number soared to almost 700. From June 2014, when the Islamic State declared a caliphate, through June 2017, Europe saw thirty-four attacks, half of which were carried out in France. Europe averaged roughly five terror plots or attacks per month by 2017, the vast majority linked to the Islamic State.[46] Islamic State supporters also pioneered a simple but lethal new terrorist tactic, using vehicles to run down pedestrians. In Nice, France, an Islamic State supporter drove a truck through a crowd celebrating Bastille Day, killing eighty-six people. In 2017, terrorists in the United Kingdom and Stockholm perpetrated similar attacks, though thankfully far less bloody. In all, more than three hundred people died. Beyond attacks, Europeans often played an important role in sustaining groups overseas. In Germany, for example, the Islamic State network collected donations and engaged in burglaries to fund both overseas and domestic cells, all justified as plunder from unbelievers.[47]

The biggest shift, however, was the massive increase in European Islamic State foreign fighters compared with previous conflicts—over five thousand in total. For the first time in history, Europe supplied a major portion of the total foreign fighters to a jihadi conflict. Sweden alone provided more foreign fighters to Syria (over three hundred) than had gone from all of Europe to Somalia (just two hundred or so); France's over 1,900 volunteers numbered more than the 1,500 European Muslims who had gone to Afghanistan in total. If Europe's approximately forty-five million Muslims (roughly twenty million of whom live within the European Union) acted as members of a single country, it would have a greater percentage of volunteers fighting in Syria than any country in the Arab world.

Foreign fighter rates varied tremendously across Europe, and the size of the Muslim population did little to explain this. European countries with large Muslim populations like France, Germany, and the United Kingdom sent almost four thousand volunteers, but others with relatively small populations like Belgium, Denmark, and the Netherlands also had large numbers.[48] Indeed, Belgium had the largest number of fighters per capita, as more than four hundred of its citizens traveled successfully to Syria and Iraq.[49] Spain and Italy saw far fewer foreign fighters than many northern European countries and France.[50] A handful of German residents went to Chechnya and Bosnia, a few dozen to Somalia, and perhaps 220 to Afghanistan; yet nearly 1,000 individuals traveled from Germany to Iraq and Syria, most of whom went to fight.[51] For some European states, their citizens leaving for a conflict represented a new problem, yet for all European countries, the scale of the exodus was unprecedented.

As these figures suggest, Syria put the jihadist movement in Europe on steroids. Europe's foreign fighter flows to Syria were 600 percent higher than in the Iraq conflict a decade prior.[52] And of course the terrorism problem extends past foreign fighters, also including extremists who never left for Syria. In 2017, for example, France incarcerated more than 300 jihadi terrorists, surveilled nearly 6,000 more suspected jihadi terrorists, and viewed another 17,000 as a possible threat. France's president Emmanuel Macron declared fighting Islamic terrorism France's "top priority."[53] As one French official told me, the scale is "totally unprecedented."

There is no single profile for European foreign fighters who went to the Islamic State, and many of the general factors that motivated recruits for the Islamic State in the Arab world or from Central Asia inspired European Muslims as well. The average foreign fighter from Europe was a young man between the ages of eighteen and twenty-nine. Most were not well educated. Their marital and family status varied; roughly a third had no job while many others were low-paid, but in some countries, many foreign fighters were far better off. Many of these fighters found meaning and dignity in the conflict that they lacked at home. Many European volunteers had converted to Islam— roughly 15 percent in all, but higher in some countries (almost a quarter, in France, for example). Women comprised 17 percent of foreign fighters from Europe. A similar ratio of women committed attacks in Europe.[54] Like Islamic State fighters in general, some Europeans welcomed the free houses, sex slaves, and other perks of being an Islamic State fighter. Some joined to search for adventure. Criminality was a common background factor among Europeans, and, like many Islamic State recruits, few had a serious knowledge of Islam. Many simply followed friends and family, inspired more by camaraderie than ideology. As before, returned foreign fighters often proved the best recruiters.

Many of the first foreign fighters who traveled to Syria before the Islamic State declared a caliphate subsequently returned to Europe, and some helped to recruit for later waves.[55]

As a demographic, one common problem among the foreign fighters was the role of segregated Muslim neighborhoods and banlieus (suburbs) in Europe, in contrast to the United States and Canada.[56] These neighborhoods hinder integration and also foster an us-versus-them mentality within European countries. Residents there suffer discrimination and are less likely to cooperate with the police and security services, enabling radicals to operate and hide with less risk. As the 2005 riots in Paris suggest, many of their problems are not religious, but hostility to Islam adds extra fuel to an already combustible mix.

Many European recruits had ties to nonviolent but extreme organizations or preachers before they embraced violence. In addition to Tablighi Jamaat, these organizations include Islam4UK and its predecessor Al-Muhajiroun, Sharia4Belgium, Profetens Ummah in Norway, Forsane Alizza in France, and Millatu Ibrahim in Germany, among others. Many of these groups claim that democracy and Islam are incompatible and that Muslims in the West should resist social integration.[57] A British study found that two-thirds of the British foreign fighters had ties to only six preachers or recruiters in the United Kingdom, while almost 80 percent had some sort of connection to an extreme, but nonviolent, Islamist group.

Anjem Choudary, sentenced to jail in 2016 for his support for the Islamic State, inspired over a hundred British recruits to carry out violence. Choudary was released in 2018 after a short stay in prison. Terrorism scholar Assaf Moghadam relates that Choudary was a protégé of Omar Bakri Mohammad, who founded Al-Muhajiroun, the first significant radical Salafi organization in the United Kingdom, which was banned after the July 2005 bombings there. Choudary formed spinoff organizations that all pushed the idea that Western values and Islam were incompatible. He also helped inspire and coordinate various "Sharia4" organizations in Belgium, Holland, and other countries as far away as South Africa and Australia. They maintain a strong internet presence but also engage in street protests and otherwise try to push action on the ground. Many of these organizations facilitated the flow of foreign fighters to Syria and other battlefields.[58] In contrast, Italy lacks such groups, which hinders an individual from connecting with a jihadist facilitator and traveling overseas.[59]

Many radicals were part of a second generation of European Muslims, unable or unwilling to fully assimilate. Countries with larger first-generation Muslim populations, like Italy and Spain, had a far smaller foreign fighter problem than countries with more established Muslim communities like

France or the United Kingdom.[60] Born in Europe, the second generation of Muslim immigrants often face an identity crisis. Some of the most important recruits felt caught between two cultures, a far more important predictor than economic status or educational background. European jihadist-turned-spy of Moroccan origin Omar Nasiri (not his real name) writes, "Because I'm part Arab, part European, my home is nowhere."[61] European states have tried different policies to address this identity crisis. In France, for example, the government pushes Muslim immigrants to assimilate, while the United Kingdom embraces multiculturalism. Both policies, however, have failed to solve second-generation isolation.

Jihad Returns to Europe

Many of those who fought will never return. The numbers vary by country, but many European officials claimed a body count of 25 percent or more for their citizens. Many jihadis remained in the war zone, tried to travel to another one nearby, or remain stuck in Turkey. However, roughly a third of the five thousand or so European fighters in Syria returned, producing a major counterterrorism concern.[62] Belgium, which has the highest foreign fighter per capita rate in Western Europe, released detailed figures. As of November 2017, it had a total of 611 attempted and actual foreign fighters: 288, or almost half, remained in Iraq and Syria; 125 returned, 85 tried to go and failed, and 113 are candidates to travel. Although some came back due to disillusionment and others for their family and friends, most did not want to abandon jihad and simply returned because the Caliphate was collapsing.[63]

Few of the initial European recruits joined the Islamic State out of animus toward their own countries' policies, instead seeing themselves as heroic defenders of Muslims in the sectarian war in Syria and the pioneers who would establish true Islamic rule there. However, the anti-Western ideas percolating in jihadist circles made them open to attacking at home and eager to embrace the Islamic State's call for violence in Europe when the group began to emphasize attacks there.

Determining exactly when the Islamic State set its sights on Europe is difficult. On the one hand, the group's Iraqi history predisposed it toward anti-Americanism and anti-Westernism in general, and Zarqawi helped support a cell in Germany. Even when the Islamic State urged its fighters to come defend and expand the Caliphate in Syria, many of those fighters promised to attack the West in their personal social media accounts.[64] In February 2014, months before the Western military intervention in Syria, French officials arrested a man who fought with both Jabhat al-Nusra and the Islamic State in Syria. In his possession was a manual titled "How to Make Artisanal Bombs in the Name of Allah," and he acquired TATP, a volatile explosive that the Islamic State often uses in its bombs. The French believe he planned to attack the French Riviera.[65] A few months later, Mehdi Nemmouche shot four people at a Jewish museum in Belgium. Nemmouche was radical before going to Syria, but while in Syria, he gained a set of contacts who helped him carry out his attack.[66] From these examples, it appears that the Islamic State targeted Europe even before the Europeans intervened militarily against the group.

On the other hand, the decision by the United States and several of its closest European allies, including Belgium, Denmark, France, the Netherlands, and the United Kingdom, to bomb the Islamic State led to a fundamental change in the group's priorities. Before August 2014, when the bombing began, most of the group's attention focused on Iraq and Syria or immediate neighbors, even though some members harbored ambitions to attack the West. Even the group's 2015 guide on how jihadists should operate in the West noted in its foreword that God's promised victory in Europe will only come after jihadists have taken Persia.[67] After the U.S.-led bombing began, its spokesman charged that "the Islamic State did not initiate a war against you," but rather, "it is you who started the transgression against us." He then warned that "you will pay the price" in the form of dead soldiers and violence "as you walk on your streets." The spokesman singled out "the spiteful and filthy French" for particular attention.[68] However, the Islamic State also went after European states that had not joined the coalition. Germany, for example, did not participate in the military coalition, yet the Islamic State carried out attacks there.[69]

Foreign fighters posed a danger beyond their numbers, and they led or participated in several of the deadliest attacks. Of the thirty suspects that investigators believed participated in the 2015 Paris attacks, sixteen had fought in Syria or Iraq, which included the majority of the most important figures. These sixteen also played a major role in recruiting nonfighters to join the plot.[70] In 2016, surviving members of the cell launched three suicide bombings in Brussels, killing thirty-two people. At least two of the five main attackers had fought in Syria.

The Islamic State harvested recruits from Europe's fertile soil, taking advantage of the weak integration of many Muslims there. Even when they could not bring a recruit to the Caliphate itself, the Islamic State tried to coach its recruits from afar. Anis Amri, who killed eleven when he drove a truck through a Christmas market in Berlin in December 2016, was in regular contact with an Islamic State contact via Telegram. Amri had not fought in Syria, but jihadists abroad worked with him virtually to carry out an attack at home.

As travel to Syria became harder due to better intelligence efforts and a Turkish crackdown, many jihadists shifted their focus to attacks at home. As one French jihadist noted, "We believe that even a small attack in the land of the infidels is better than a big attack in Syria. As the door of migration closes, the door of jihad opens."[71]

The Islamic State's indoctrination was a particular concern. As one French official put it, the Islamic State "ran a brainwashing machine—and as a result they come back fucked up." The problems may not manifest in an immediate terrorist attack, but European officials fear foreign fighters will be important nodes in larger networks that will plague their countries for years.

The European Response to Foreign Fighters

European governments, like the United States, took few actions when their citizens left to fight in Afghanistan or support the Afghan war, seeing it as a remote issue that did not rise to the level of a serious threat. As violence linked to jihadism grew in the 1990s, however, the European response steadily evolved, with each major wave of jihad—Bosnia, Iraq, and Syria—provoking changes.

Still, until jihad came home to Europe with attacks in Madrid and London, most countries devoted few resources to the issue, and their laws were permissive. Only a few countries, notably France, took the problem seriously. Europeans captured in Afghanistan after 9/11 often did not face legal charges or were detained outside the law because their home countries lacked laws criminalizing their actions in Afghanistan.[72] Even the first returnees from Syria did not face systematic prosecution, and the vague or restrictive criminal codes in many countries hindered efforts to jail would-be or returning fighters.[73] More decisive action earlier would have saved lives, but for most states, it took a major attack, often on their own soil, to prompt action.

With open borders, individual European states struggled to prevent jihadis from leaving and to monitor their transit. The abolishment of passport and other border controls in the European Union's (EU) Schengen Area made travel and commerce much easier for all states involved, but it also facilitated terrorists' travels. This ease of travel allowed networks to broaden rather than confining them to local communities. One network disrupted in 2001 involved members who trained in Afghanistan and had a presence in France, the Netherlands, and Spain with links to radical preachers like Qatada in London.[74]

When the Syria conflict broke out, most volunteers felt little need to hide their activities. The Dutch intelligence service, for example, at first believed the Netherlands had few radicals and only in hindsight realized that 2013 represented a banner year for recruitment, when almost a hundred volunteers went to Syria. In The Hague, Islamic State supporters, often affiliated with groups like Sharia4Holland, brandished the Caliphate's black flag in demonstrations and discussed the call to jihad openly on Twitter and Facebook.[75] Belgian officials worried that if they criminalized foreign fighter participation it would lead to communities not reporting suspected radicals. Still other European government officials worried that jailing foreign fighters would signal that the government supported the Assad government.[76] Many local authorities secretly smiled as these volunteers, many troublemakers or criminals, left for the Caliphate. Their departure led to a fall in crime and, some officials hoped, would remove a potential source of radicalism.[77] French officials made it clear to me in 2014 that "it is not a concern if they die there—only if they come back."

Yet when the European governments focused more attention on foreign fighters, they achieved considerable success. Especially after the Paris and Brussels attacks, foreign fighters played only a limited role in Islamic State attacks on Europe, a surprising finding given the huge numbers of Europeans who have gone off to fight in Syria, their bloody record in the past, and the repeated fears expressed about the danger they posed. Most of those who attacked in the name of the Islamic State were not trained operatives from Syria, and less than 20 percent were foreign fighters, which was a much smaller percentage than for previous terrorist campaigns. A French analysis found that only 3 percent of French returnees planned or committed an attack in the 2013–2016 period.[78] Foreign fighters failed to conduct a successful attack in Europe after the March 2016 attack in Brussels through August 2018, when this book went to press.[79] As a Danish intelligence report notes, "Attacks in Europe are overwhelmingly committed by lone individuals who have not been to a conflict zone."[80]

Europe-wide efforts bore some fruit in preventing and detecting foreign fighters. Across Europe, intelligence services created or improved databases and conducted more joint operations, making it harder for the Islamic State or other groups to maintain large networks. If terrorist organizations tried to amass a large network, a mistake by one member would allow a more comprehensive crackdown.[81] A Danish intelligence assessment argued that increased control over EU borders and better information sharing have made it far riskier for foreign fighters to return to Europe.[82]

The overall security bar in Europe rose, making it harder for terrorists to operate from countries where security services had once paid little attention. In October 2014, the EU adopted a joint counterterrorism strategy for Iraq and

Syria, emphasizing the danger of foreign fighters.[83] United Nations resolution 2178, passed in 2014, expanded the definition of what constituted terrorism and mandated that states track the travel of their citizens joining terrorist groups—the first such international legislation. In response, Germany revised its criminal code to allow the prosecution of those planning and preparing to travel abroad, rather than waiting until they were actually in the process of leaving.[84] Many European governments, especially after the Paris attacks, devoted far more resources to counterterrorism.

Once European police and intelligence services began looking, they easily gathered information on foreign fighters going to Syria. Often the travelers were voluble on social media, especially in the conflict's early years. Going to war boosted an individual's status at home, and many volunteers bragged about their accomplishments on Facebook or Twitter. Indeed, many did not turn off the location functions on their phone even when they went to the war zone, enabling outsiders to track their movement in real time.[85] Friends and family might tell police an individual left or others in the war zone might tweet about it. Some volunteers might receive welfare or other support from the state; when they failed to cash their checks, officials began to ask why.[86]

Volunteers often left a financial or even criminal trail that clued law enforcement about their intended actions. In addition to the obvious, such as purchasing plane tickets or sending money to Turkey, many made unusually large cash withdrawals, took out a wide variety of loans (never intended to be repaid), purchased a prepaid phone card or outdoor equipment suitable for living the rugged life of a foreign fighter, or otherwise put their money where their feet were going, but, in so doing, raised flags for investigators.[87] One Al Qaeda–linked cell, for example, used impressive operational security to hide members' true names and otherwise evade detection, but law enforcement learned of it because of credit card fraud and other crimes designed to raise money.[88] One estimate found that police knew roughly half of the foreign fighters already due to the fighters' involvement in crime.[89]

As discussed in the chapter on the Islamic State, changes in Turkish policy proved crucial to reducing the jihadist threat. In addition to not policing its border and otherwise allowing jihadists a relative haven in the country in the Syrian civil war's first years, Turkey often refused to execute European arrest warrants or extradite suspects. Even when Turkish security services did send suspects back home, they often did not notify local authorities, allowing the individual to hide once he or she arrived (this happened with one of the bombers involved in the Paris and Brussels attacks). Over time, however, as Turkey began to seal its borders and uproot networks, it also worked more closely with European governments.[90]

In contrast to the United States, jihadis struggled to acquire weapons in Europe. The Islamic State's handy-dandy "How to Survive in the West" manual, for example, spends considerable time on how to get weapons via drug dealers and gangs. These elaborate efforts are not necessary in America.[91] Militants do take advantage of arms markets in the Balkans, but security services regularly monitor and disrupt these attempts. Indeed, one reason that jihadists in Europe called for vehicle attacks and knifings likely arose due to limited access to firearms. "If you are not able to find an IED or a bullet," the Islamic State's spokesman had counseled, "smash his head with a rock, or slaughter him with a knife, or run him over with your car, or throw him down from a high place," continuing all the way down to "if you are unable to do so, then spit in his face."[92] One European official told the head of U.S. counterterrorism: "If we faced our terror threat with your level of access to firearms, we'd be in big trouble."[93]

Despite these considerable successes, European states struggled to handle gateway groups like Al Muhajiroun, the Sharia4 organizations, and the Tablighi Jamaat. Some states aggressively prosecuted these groups, seeking to disrupt the networks they created.[94] In response, these groups learned discretion, adjusting their propaganda to decrease the level of violence and instead to focus on less prosecutable themes, such as the good life in a jihadi state and the moral and religious necessity of jihad.[95] Often, officials looked on helplessly as radical preachers and leaders of sympathetic organizations recruited without explicitly breaking the laws of many countries, such as sending supporters abroad for "religious education" (but, in reality, sending them to a foreign fighter camp). However, these nefarious efforts became harder as European states tightened their laws and broadened the scope of what was prosecutable.

European officials disagreed on whether to allow foreign fighters to return, kill them overseas, bring them home and put them in jail, or use deradicalization programs to reintegrate them into society. It is expensive to try suspects and put them in prison, and security officials fear they will be further radicalized, or will radicalize others, there. Moreover, many, like Anjem Chaudary, serve only a short sentence and pose a potential threat upon release.

Overall, as one report noted, in general European governments "prefer that foreign fighters do not come back," though most do not prevent them from doing so.[96] Prime Minister Mark Rutte of the Netherlands said that he preferred that foreign fighters be killed overseas than come home.[97] Rory Stewart, a British government minister, warned of the danger of returning foreign fighters and declared, "Unfortunately the only way of dealing with them will be, in almost every case, to kill them."[98] British special forces reportedly have a list of two hundred British combatants for the Islamic

State that they have orders to kill or capture to prevent their return to the United Kingdom.[99] France deployed its special forces to Iraq to work with Iraqi government forces to hunt down and kill French nationals who joined the Islamic State.[100] In contrast, other governments, such as Germany, do not target their nationals.[101] At times, these different policies create tension. For example, France favors killing its jihadist citizens, while Belgium opposes it. The Islamic State, however, put citizens from the two countries into the same units because they speak the same language. Thus, French efforts often resulted in Belgian deaths.[102]

To avoid the return of their citizens captured fighting for the Islamic State, many European states hide behind the lack of extradition treaties with the Iraqi government or with Iraqi or Syrian Kurdish groups, whose fighters hold many foreign prisoners. France even works with Syrian Kurdish forces to conduct local trials for French nationals, which will usually result in the fighter's execution, shamelessly claiming this is a form of due process.[103] Germany, in contrast, seeks to bring its nationals captured abroad home for trial. From an American perspective, which involves more global interests, denying a European fighter the right to return risks dispersing them, thus endangering other U.S. allies or the United States itself by forcing the United States to rely on less competent intelligence and law enforcement services than Europe's. A French fighter who cannot return to Paris, for example, may show up in Tunis or Istanbul, where the security services are less capable than those in France.

European countries' laws and policies towards returnees vary considerably. The United Kingdom allows the government to monitor individuals suspected of terrorism, confiscate their computers and bank accounts, and even move them from their homes. France employs an extensive intelligence and police network to monitor and disrupt suspected terrorists and uses its broad terrorism laws to arrest and jail all returnees.[104] Germany, in contrast, has a high bar for evidence, at times even excluding documents captured from the group from being used in court and prohibiting the use of social media posts because the alleged perpetrators might have been simply boasting.

Italy, unusually for Europe, has a tough deportation law on the books. Most Muslims in Italy are classified as noncitizen legal migrants, as it is hard to get Italian citizenship. Using a 2005 law, Italy deported almost a hundred suspected jihadists to Tunisia, Morocco, Albania, and other states, often with little evidence. This included not only suspected terrorists but also ostensibly peaceful Islamists. For example, four residents demonstrated to create a "Sharia4Italy" modeled after "Sharia4Belgium"—three were deported and the fourth arrested.[105] Such measures proved effective, but they raise civil liberties issues that would make them a nonstarter in other European countries and the United States.

Prison both offers an answer to terrorism and is part of the problem. As noted earlier, some of Europe's worst terrorist attacks involved jihadists who went to prison, where they became more radicalized and developed networks with other jihadists. Many incarcerated European Muslims are often released after a few years, at an age when they are still likely to join a violent group. In the United States, the average person's sentence for jihadist-linked terrorism is almost fifteen years; France, with an average of just over seven years, maintains Europe's highest prison sentence average for jihadi-linked terrorism; and the Netherlands only sentences three years for the same crime.[106] In some European countries, a jihadist defendant might claim to have changed his or her heart or express contrition to receive a lighter sentence.[107] Alain Grignard, an expert on radicalism in Europe, warned, "Rarely do people come out of prison better than when they went in," while a former French intelligence official claimed, "We have to have the same attitude towards those leaving prison as we do toward those coming back from Syria."[108]

Officials are trapped in a catch-22. Incarcerating individuals may lead to more radicalized prisoners, but permitting their freedom may lead to more terrorist attacks. European states, however, have made progress since the Paris attacks on how to link prison and counterterrorism. France created an intelligence unit within its prisons. Belgium has "satellite prisons" for convicted jihadists with more monitoring and better-trained staff. Prison staff also receive more extensive training on identifying radicalization, and specialized personnel are present to focus on terrorists.[109]

Some European states experimented with restrictions short of jail. The Netherlands arrests and questions all returnees. The government monitors some returnees, requires them to seek psychological counseling, bans their contact with radicals, or otherwise limits their activities without jailing them.[110]

Denmark has one of the most comprehensive programs. The Danish government tries to work with families, employers, and others to dissuade an identified at-risk person from traveling. They present alternatives to fighting, such as helping refugees, and also note the consequences of leaving.[111] If they leave, officials quickly identify most individuals on returning—some because they were on an intelligence radar screen all along, others because they reach out to known networks in Denmark or even because their family reaches out to the government for help. Schools, social services, and police work together to assess the risk of returnees and individually counsel them along with their families. The government provides a personal adviser to those willing to leave the jihadist world who helps with jobs and housing as well as psychological treatment. The police, meanwhile, constantly assess risks and prepare to step in if violence seems likely. The Danish program boasts near 100 percent success.[112] Such programs to rehabilitate and deradicalize suspected terrorists, however, both require intensive resources and political capital to sustain. It is easier to try to look tough and imprison everyone than take a risk on a program that might not work.

In some countries, the deradicalization programs often make the problem worse. In Britain, in the name of deradicalization the government required institutions to promote "Britishness" and vet for extremists, alienating many Muslims. Some states also restrict speech to counter radical views. In Germany, for example, some Salafi teachings are outlawed because they run counter to the country's constitutional guarantees regarding human rights and seek to abolish the political system.[113]

Because deradicalization programs require both resources and political will, European governments often talk a bigger game than the reality. Belgium, for example, has a prevention unit that works with social workers and communities, but one government official told me that the country still mainly focuses on police and intelligence. Only a few municipalities have these prevention units, and even those are small.[114] The programs that exist often overlap or are uncoordinated: "The organizations are fighting over radicals," claimed one official. Interagency infighting often exacerbates the problem. Understandably, social services do not want to be seen as arms of an intelligence service, so often they withhold relevant information. The combination of few resources, bureaucratic roadblocks, and the public's low tolerance for risking potential attacks causes governments to calculate that deradicalization programs offer more risk than reward.

Policies toward women involved in jihad have also moved forward. At first, officials treated women solely as victims, puppets of men with no volition of their own, despite the important role many women played in the Islamic State and the terrorism risk some pose. For example, a group of women attempted to carry out an attack near Notre Dame in Paris in 2016, and other women have served as recruiters. Over time, judges and intelligence services have recognized women jihadists as important actors on their own.

European governments still must also develop policies to address the children of foreign fighters. Many European children traveled to the Islamic State with their parents, and hundreds of babies were born there to foreign volunteers.[115] Sweden, Belgium, France, the United Kingdom, and other countries have dozens or even hundreds of child citizens born or raised in the Caliphate.[116] These children saw constant violence and hardship, and the Islamic State indoctrinated many into its ideology. In addition, teenagers often received at least some military training. All European states accepted that the youngest children should be repatriated, but some are highly restrictive. France treats children as young as thirteen through a law enforcement mechanism rather than through social services.

The daunting numbers of European radicals make the resource question paramount. To follow one person twenty-four hours a day requires perhaps fifteen policemen—a personnel load that grows far too heavy when the returnee figure reaches the hundreds. Monitoring social media is also labor-intensive. In an interview I conducted before the 2015 Paris attacks, one French expert foretold that France could handle dozens of returnees, as it did from Iraq, but it could not handle hundreds like Syria. British security services knew of the ringleader of the 2005 transportation bombings before the attacks but did not scrutinize him due to limited resources. By 2017, the United Kingdom had an overwhelming 23,000 terrorist suspects it sought to monitor.[117] In response, many states had to dramatically increase spending. Germany, for example, hired hundreds of new officers to man its intelligence and police services as the Islamic State threat emerged.[118]

Overall, the European experience shows both the high risk Europe faces and how counterterrorism improvements can mitigate the threat. Europe faced many jihadist plots since the Madrid attack, including some horrific jihadist successes such as in Paris in 2015, but overall terrorism levels have not soared despite the huge numbers of volunteers for the Islamic State and the return of many to Europe. Although only a fraction of European returnees are involved in terrorism, the sheer number of returning fighters makes even this number of concern. As French security officials put it, "Statistically it is impossible that an attack won't happen." When it does, however, Europeans should recognize the many successes as well as the continued level of danger.

Despite these qualified successes, Europe is seeing a terrorism boomerang effect. For many years, European preachers and religious organizations generated foreign fighters and propaganda, creating networks with foreign organizations in Algeria, with Al Qaeda, and later with the Islamic State. Over time, the more international agenda of the foreign groups found its way into Europe itself, creating violence there. Now home and abroad are intertwined, with groups and causes abroad stirring up violence in Europe, while Europe itself risks being a major exporter of terrorism if massive foreign fighter flows like the ones that occurred to Syria resume.

CHAPTER 12

The Pied Piper: Anwar al-Awlaki
and the Limits of Jihad in America

B Y ITS VERY name, the Hellfire missile promises to visit biblical wrath
upon those on its receiving end. On September 30, 2011, it delivered just
that to Anwar al-Awlaki, a U.S.-born preacher and an operational leader of Al
Qaeda in the Arabian Peninsula, who had plotted repeated attacks from his
hideout in Yemen. The same strike also took out Samir Khan, another U.S. national and propagandist for Awlaki's organization. A separate strike a few weeks
later killed Awlaki's teenaged son, also an American citizen. The latter two appear to have been collateral damage in strikes aimed at others. Awlaki, by contrast, was not. He was specifically targeted with lethal force by a government,
his own government. The Obama administration had semipublicly sought his
death for months, tracking him across Yemen even as it fended off litigation by
his family to remove him from the U.S. government's targeting list.

Much of the jihadist activity in America shows the domestic side-effects
of transnational jihadism. The American foreign fighters and the groups they
joined shaped not just the American volunteers but also American terrorists
who never left home at all. Their impact ranged from being an inspiration to
providing detailed help on where and how to launch an attack. Over time, it
became hard to separate "domestic" terrorists from global jihadists.

Awlaki himself was a U.S. citizen and traveled between the United States
and his family home in Yemen, getting a U.S. university degree and eventually
becoming an imam, preaching first in Denver, then in San Diego, and then in
Virginia. Before beginning to preach, however, he traveled to Afghanistan in

1991, and the trip transformed him; he returned spouting Azzam and wearing Afghan garb. Awlaki then fought alongside Al Qaeda's Yemen branch and had linkages to several of the 9/11 hijackers.

Awlaki harnessed the power of the internet to recruit for Al Qaeda, translating the group's rather dry rhetoric into a compelling message for English speakers. He emerged as global jihadism's top English-language propagandist, described as the "pied piper" of jihad for his role in luring so many youths to the battlefield.[1] Awlaki was one of the founders of *Inspire* magazine, the first major jihadist publication in English, which terrorism expert Bruce Hoffman described as "the *Vanity Fair* of jihadist publications. It is glossy and snarky and designed to appeal to Generation Z."[2] Impressionable Americans could easily grasp Awlaki's straightforward teachings that unbelievers will be "stamped out," that "Islam will rule the world," and so on.[3] In a precursor to foreign fighters using social media in an interactive and user-friendly way, Awlaki also ran a blog where he offered answers in response to posted questions. For many Westerners, Awlaki served as a guide to which causes mattered. Zachary Chesser, who became prominent in his own right with the Shebaab, recalls that Awlaki "simply put the Shabaab on the radar for me" (Chesser, like his fellow volunteer to Somalia, Hammami, was also very funny, wryly threatening a congressional committee to do as he said, "or else I will publicly endorse them in their bids for re-election").[4]

Long before the Awlaki killing, the Obama administration had put the Bush administration's drone program on steroids, killing hundreds of suspected militants with near-constant strikes in the tribal areas of Pakistan. Awlaki, however, was not just another dead terrorist. Because of his U.S. citizenship, his killing moved the Obama administration into an uncharted realm for counterterrorism. Once upon a time, Attorney General Janet Reno had fretted about whether the United States had the legal authority to kill the Saudi terrorist Osama bin Laden, who had never set foot in the United States, but who had publicly declared war on it and demonstrated his grim intentions by planning the bombings of U.S. embassies in Africa and the USS *Cole*. By contrast, in killing Awlaki, the Obama administration targeted a U.S. citizen, one who had never been proven in any court to have been directly responsible for actual deaths and had actively resisted judicial supervision.

Yemen itself, meanwhile, was both ally and enemy, helping the United States fight terrorism at times, while at other times tolerating, or even directly aiding, jihadists bent on killing Americans. And while the killing led to lawsuits and condemnation from human rights groups that it "violates both U.S. and international law,"[5] it barely caused a ripple of protest among the American people. More Americans agree that "terror suspects who are

U.S. citizens" should "be deliberately killed by U.S. forces" than favor granting these suspects "the constitutional right given to U.S. citizens to be tried in a court of law."[6]

For the Islamic State, Al Qaeda, and associated movements, however, American volunteers present both a blessing and a risk. For propaganda purposes, they underscore their claim to be a global organization. And the cultural and personal connections these Americans have to their home make them more effective propagandists and recruiters as well as operators. However, Americans often do not fit in neatly with the locals, not understanding the language and culture. In addition, there is always the chance that an American might be uncommitted and thus easily suborned upon his return or perhaps even a spy from the start.

Awlaki lived on after his death. Many self-professed American supporters of the Islamic State claimed that hearing Anwar al-Awlaki's sermons on the internet led them to jihad. By reaching English-speaking audiences, Awlaki could improve the reach of jihadist groups not only in the United States, Canada, and the United Kingdom but also in a host of countries like India, where English is widely spoken. In addition to inspiring foreign fighters, more than ninety U.S. attacks or plots had links directly or (usually) indirectly to Awlaki, including such major killings as the Orlando and Fort Hood shootings and the Boston Marathon bombings. Fort Hood shooter Nidal Hassan, who shot thirteen people in 2009, repeatedly e-mailed Awlaki asking for religious guidance and advice on the permissibility of suicide attacks. In radicalization expert Seamus Hughes's words, Awlaki provided the "mood music" that helped recruits embrace militancy.[7]

Jihadist propaganda didn't die with Awlaki. Junaid Hussain, a British hacker who led a band of a dozen or so jihadist computer specialists, also lived by and died by the virtual sword in trying to fill Awlaki's shoes. Hussain acted as one of the Islamic State's most prolific English-language propagandist, and he lured recruits to Syria while directing, advising, and inspiring perhaps thirty plots around the world from the Islamic State's haven there.[8] The FBI dubbed Hussain and his group "the Legion" and the "Raqqa 12," and Legion members tried to recruit and direct fighters in countries with many English speakers, ranging from America to India.[9] Roughly a fifth of the plots between the Islamic State's declaration in 2014 and March 1, 2017 involved such members. The FBI officials found that these "cybercoaches" often did not direct the plot but rather motivated an individual, presented him with a menu of targets, and otherwise facilitated the attack.[10]

Hussain, a second-generation British citizen whose parents came from Pakistani Kashmir, always seemed to prefer online activism. He learned to hack at the age of eleven, and by fifteen had embraced politics. "I started from watching videos of children getting killed in countries like Kashmir and Palestine," he recalled. Often working with other hackers, he spent much of his time opposing the English Defense League, a right-wing British group that is violently anti-Muslim. Although an activist for Muslim causes, or more accurately a hacktivist—an individual who hacks for political or social motivations—Hussain was not particularly religious. However, his hacking got him into trouble, particularly when he and his colleagues launched a denial-of-service attack on a British counterterrorism hotline. After Hussain boasted that law enforcement could never find him, officials quickly arrested him. As with so many European terrorists, prison marked a turning point; there, he became more religious, and his radical views took on a jihadist dimension.

Attracted to the call of jihad, Hussain traveled to Syria in late 2013 and joined the Islamic State, taking the nom de guerre Abu Hussain al-Britani. His Twitter avatar shows him with an intimidating look, his face partly obscured as he takes aim with a rifle. Adding to his celebrity, Hussain's wife, Sally Jones, was a former singer and guitarist for the punk rock band Krunch. Eventually dubbed the "White Widow" and "Mrs. Terror" by the British press, she met Hussain online and converted to Islam when she and her son from a previous relationship arrived in Syria.

Other groups too employed cybercoaches like Hussain that tried from afar to recruit Americans to commit terrorism at home. One such coach, Mohamed Abdullahi Miski, a Somali American from Minnesota, radicalized other Somali Americans and served as a conduit to the Shebaab. Yet Hussain was especially prolific. While in Syria, he tweeted regularly, encouraging Muslims to migrate to the Islamic State and calling for terrorism in the United States and the United Kingdom. Officials suspect that he attempted to hack the U.S. Central Command's (the regional military command responsible for operations in the Middle East) Twitter and YouTube accounts. He publicly posted the names and addresses of more than 1,300 American military and government employees, instructing his followers: "Kill them in their own lands, behead them in their own homes, stab them to death as they walk their streets thinking they are safe." Hussain also directed an effort to kill Pamela Geller, a bigot and self-proclaimed anti-Muslim activist; helped a British recruit target a high-speed train with an improvised bomb; encouraged an Australian teenager to conduct bombings in Melbourne; and worked with Ohio college student Munir Abdulkader to kidnap and behead a U.S. soldier and record it on video. Hussain and other members of the Legion initially urged Americans to travel to Syria, but as U.S. counterterrorism pressure grew, they instead encouraged attacks in the United States because they believed "it simply had gotten too dangerous to go to the airport."[11]

Hussain became number three on the U.S. military's targeting list—quite an honor for a man who did little fighting.[12]

One by one, however, the United States and its allies hunted down the jihadists' virtual warriors. In 2015, Hussain met his fate. Reports on his death vary. Some say that a drone killed him when he finally stopped using his stepson as a human shield; another source argues that Western security agencies tracked him while deciphering his encrypted messages; and still others have him clicking on a compromised hyperlink sent by a double agent.[13] To find Hussain and those he inspired, the FBI sifted through thousands of his followers on social media to identify those who might be plotting on behalf of the Islamic State, leading to almost a hundred arrests. Indeed, these connections between followers and recruiters identified hitherto unknown suspects, according to the FBI. Unbeknownst to the would-be jihadists, they found themselves in contact not only with an Islamic State virtual coach but also with the FBI, who tracked the progress of various plots and swooped in to make arrests once violence looked imminent.

Between May and September 2015, drones killed at least four Legion members, in addition to Hussain. Another Brit, Siful Sujan, succeeded Hussain as "Director of the Islamic State's computer operations," and a coalition airstrike killed him in December 2015.[14] Similar fates befell most cybercoaches; security services in the West often quickly identified their recruits, and the coaches became targets. As the Islamic State lost territory, the group began to rely on cybercoaches living outside of Iraq and Syria. But it turns out that location matters even on the internet. These new coaches found their jobs harder, as they lacked the legitimacy Hussain and others gained from living in the Caliphate.[15]

The campaign against the Legion represents only one part of the broader U.S. campaign against jihadist groups in the post-9/11 era, a top priority of the Bush, Obama, and Trump administrations. These efforts involved aggressive FBI investigations and monitoring at home, tighter borders, tracking militants in a war zone, disrupting safe havens, and working with allies to arrest foreign fighters around the world, among other measures. Although imperfect, this counterterrorism campaign proved remarkably effective in diminishing the threat of foreign fighter terrorism and of terrorism in general against the United States, despite the emergence of dangerous groups like the Islamic State.

Who Are the American Foreign Fighters?

The United States is a nation of immigrants, and Americans have long remained involved in the battles of their countries of origin. Irish rebels, fleeing persecution at home, founded the Fenian Brotherhood in the United States in 1858. They organized and bought arms and even invaded British-ruled Canada in the hope of trading the territory they conquered to the British for Ireland. In the late nineteenth and early twentieth centuries, American anarchists, drawing on and adapting ideas imported from Europe, attacked American industrialists and financiers; and in 1901 the Polish American anarchist Leon Czolgosz assassinated President William McKinley. Almost fifty years later, several hundred American Jews would fight in Israel's War of Independence.

The ideas of global jihad began to swirl around in America during the anti-Soviet struggle. These ideas gained a small toehold in the years that followed, and Azzam's propaganda found an avid audience in the United States. Experts estimate around 150 Americans went to fight in Afghanistan and, in the post-9/11 era, at least 37 people went to Pakistan and 34 to Somalia to join Al Qaeda and the Shebaab, respectively.[16] A few, like Awlaki, traveled to Yemen. Some of these volunteers stayed abroad, while others returned to America and led ordinary lives. Table 12.1 gives numbers for different groups and conflicts as well as how many fighters actually made it to the war zone.

The Syria conflict in particular grabbed the attention of Americans. One 2018 study found that sixty-four Americans successfully traveled to fight in Iraq and Syria with the Islamic State or (less frequently) the Al Qaeda–linked Jabhat al-Nusra, with the government stopping at least fifty others. Of the sixty-four who traveled, twelve returned to the United States (in comparison, Europe has more than 1,500 returnees), where officials arrested the vast majority. Although an early volunteer to Syria could slip into and out of the United States in 2012, greater security afterward made this far harder. The few that managed to make it to Syria had a high death toll; more than 30 percent died there.[17]

Many Americans decided to fight in Syria for similar reasons to foreign fighters from other countries. At first, American volunteers fighting in Syria saw themselves as defenders of fellow Muslims against the barbaric Assad regime. Over time, as the Islamic State emerged and declared a caliphate, the obligation to perform *hijrah,* the migration from an infidel world to a Muslim one, rose to the fore. Indeed, the majority of would-be foreign fighters from the United States wanted to live in a caliphate. Not surprisingly, the American fighter numbers plummeted in 2017 when the United States and its allies overran the group and drove it underground. As with the Europeans, the American fighters wanted to belong to a cause bigger than themselves, engaging in a search for meaning.[18] Moner Abu Salha, a young Floridian and the first American suicide bomber in the Syrian war, released a video where he told his fellow American Muslims, "You have all the fancy amusement parks and

TABLE 12.1 U.S. foreign fighters, 1980–2017

GROUP	UNSUCCESSFULLY ATTEMPTED (Arrested during or before attempt or otherwise failed to reach conflict zone)	SUCCESSFULLY TRAVELED (Did not return)	SUCCESSFULLY TRAVELED (Returned to the U.S.)	TOTAL
Islamic State	>50	48	8	>106
Al Qaeda core	16	10	17	43
Al-Shebaab	7	24	5	36
Taliban	16	5	2	23
Al Qaeda in the Arabian Peninsula (AQAP)	7	3	1	11
Jabhat al Nusra	4	4	4	12
Lashkar-e-Taiba (Pakistan)	0	2	9	11
Al Qaeda in Iraq	6	0	0	6
Afghan Mujahedin	0	0	6	6

Source: For the Islamic State, numbers are from Meleagrou-Hitchens, Hughes, and Clifford, "The Travelers." Data for all other conflicts taken from James, Jensen, and Tinsley, "Understanding the Threat."

the restaurants and the food and all this crap and the cards. You think you're happy. You're not happy." Life in Syria, in contrast, is "the best I've ever lived."[19] Manliness mattered too. One female jihadist taunted those not yet committed, comparing the fighting jihadists as "true real men fighting for Allah" to the "wimps in Detroit good for nothing thugs."[20]

Unlike the Europeans, however, the United States lacked geographically concentrated recruitment. There is no American "hotspot." Although Minnesota, Virginia, and Ohio top the list of states from which recruits originate, would-be foreign fighters came from almost a hundred American cities.[21] Because of the Muslim community's diversity in the United States and because many jihadists are converts to Islam, no ethnic profile applies to the American jihadists and foreign fighters. Indeed, with the exception of many Somali Americans going to Somalia, the pull of the homeland—whether to

Syria, Pakistan, Iraq, or another country—did not seem to exert much pressure for Syrian Americans, Pakistani Americans, Iraqi Americans, and so on.[22] This too contrasts with Europe, where French citizens of Algerian origin often became involved in the Algerian conflict and British citizens of Pakistani descent had links to groups in Pakistan.

The Somali American community offers an important exception, albeit still a limited one, to this generalization. In particular, the Ethiopian invasion of Somalia in 2006 and the emergence of the Shebaab electrified some Somali Americans. In a short period in 2007 and 2008, the Shebaab attracted more than twenty Somali Americans from Minneapolis. One recruit, Shirwa Ahmed, became the first American suicide bomber when he blew himself up as part of a Shebaab military operation. Many of the Somali American recruits grew up in America but encompassed what scholars refer to as the "1.5 generation." They spent their early years in refugee camps but came to America in their teens. As in so many cases, foreign fighters not only fought themselves but also tried to recruit the next generation. For example, Caabdullahi Faarx fought in Somalia with the Shebaab and then returned to Minneapolis in 2009 to recruit fighters. Using the credibility he gained from fighting in Somalia and self-reported personal bravery, Faarx held secret meetings at a local mosque, gathering local boys to listen to Shebaab leaders calling in from Somalia. Suggesting how jihadist ideas can become embedded, this high rate of recruitment continued as Somali Americans quickly substituted the Islamic State for the Shebaab.[23]

Notably, American jihadists have surprisingly normal backgrounds, and their profiles often do not vary from the American average. Unsurprisingly, typical American recruits encompassed young men in their early to mid-twenties, though the average age of would-be Islamic State members was slightly higher at twenty-seven.[24] Although 10 percent of American jihadists have mental health issues, this is lower than the U.S. average. Jail time was slightly more common for jihadists than for the average American (12 percent vs. 9 percent), but again, not a dramatic departure from the American norm. Many recruits attended college, had respectable if not high-paying jobs, but nevertheless felt the pull of jihad. "They are, on average, as well educated and emotionally stable as the typical citizen. They are ordinary Americans," noted terrorism analyst Peter Bergen. "'Who becomes a terrorist?' turns out, in many cases, to be much like asking, 'Who owns a Volvo?'"[25] The Islamic State, however, seemed to attract less impressive American recruits. Many seemed caught up in the badass nature of the group but knew little about its goals or theology. One recruit, for example, had his back tattooed with a large Islamic State flag, a questionable symbol of loyalty given that many Sunni Muslims consider tattoos impious.

The United States diverges from other countries in its disproportionate number of converts who become foreign fighters, particularly with regard to the Islamic State. Of Americans arrested for ties to the Islamic State, converts accounted for a whopping 40 percent.[26] Islamic State operative guidance encourages recruiting converts; they present ideal operatives since they more easily pass as non-Muslims.[27] In addition, converts commonly act as the most zealous members of the group. "Their need to prove their religious convictions to their companions often makes them the most aggressive," noted an assessment made by New York City Police Department analysts.[28] Converts also have fewer ties to local Muslim communities and, at first, are less knowledgeable about their faith, both of which facilitated the Islamic State's efforts to woo them. The group offered its members both an instant community and access to "true" Islam, which conversant believers would more likely find objectionable. Further, in some circles, conversion represented a counterculture, the modern equivalent of joining a commune, which meant that the individuals involved already identified as antiestablishment rebels.

Most Americans who made it to Syria played at best minor roles in the jihadist drama, but a few stood out. Zulfi Hoxha, the son of Albanian Americans, featured in a video beheading captured Kurdish soldiers under the name "Abu Hamza al-Amriki." In the video, he encouraged believers in the United States to attack in any way possible, ranging from throwing people off buildings to running them over with cars. Several other Americans used the internet to make new contacts at home, pass on propaganda videos and issues of the Islamic State's magazine *Dabiq*, and encourage new recruits.[29]

The Limits of the Internet

As Hoxha's efforts suggest, jihadist groups like the Islamic State seeking recruits in the United States relied on the internet to recruit because they had a problem: a lack of face-to-face recruiters. In Europe and in the Middle East, hardline but openly peaceful Salafi groups like Tablighi Jamaat or the various Sharia4 organizations radicalized locals and facilitated their path toward jihad. At times, Al Qaeda or Islamic State cells based in-country served as recruiters, with large numbers of returned foreign fighters playing an important role. In the United States, however, the Islamic State and other groups had no large-scale militant Salafi groups on which to draw, and they never established a deep bench of former jihadists who could recruit the next generation. What few groups existed, such as "Revolution Muslim," were smaller and less powerful, though they did spawn a number of important U.S. jihadists. As a result, groups like Al Qaeda and especially the Islamic State tried to use the internet to recruit followers or hoped their internet-based propaganda would motivate attacks independently.[30]

The internet-dominated approach frequently failed. As political scientist John Mueller points out, it is hard for a cybercoach to judge the quality of recruits from afar. One recruit shot himself in the leg, while another tasked to run people down with a car lacked a driving permit. Security is also a constant problem. The cybercoach and the recruit must find each other on the open internet, and if the government is watching (and it is), they are vulnerable, as the Legion members regularly learned. One of the few Americans the Islamic State succeeded in recruiting for an attack at home, Emanuel Lutchman, was a mentally ill panhandler. After converting to Islam, Lutchman posted inflammatory statements on Facebook (a constant security problem for would-be Islamic State recruits in the United States). He soon found himself in what he thought was a terrorist cell of four people, but the other three members were all FBI informants.[31]

Because of the importance of the internet, the United States explored online countermessaging programs. Given the global nature of the internet, these programs often meant that foreign-oriented bureaucracies, like the State Department, ended up supporting messaging overseas that reached American audiences. The State Department, for example, created "Think Again, Turn Away" to engage and dissuade potential jihadists. A number of American jihadists, however, trolled the account and tried to discredit and exploit it. For the most part, would-be jihadists ignore such government efforts.[32]

Attacks in America

Many early jihadist attacks in the United States included foreign fighters in instrumental roles, but over time U.S. authorities improved at countering the threat posed by the foreign fighters. Indeed, it is hard to imagine a discussion of the worst terrorist attack in history, the 9/11 attacks, without recognizing the role of foreign fighters. The story of 9/11 has been told and retold, so it doesn't need to be discussed in depth here. But the following points briefly highlight the range of foreign fighter–related issues:

- Of the nineteen hijackers, the conflict in Chechnya initially motivated many to become foreign fighters and, like so many who aspired to fight there, they ended up in Afghanistan as a way station. In Afghanistan,

Al Qaeda redirected these hijackers for an operation against the United States.

- At least nine of the low-level "muscle" hijackers did basic training in Afghanistan.[33]
- Khalid al-Midhar and Nawaf al-Hazmi, two of the key leaders, fought in Bosnia. Hazmi also fought with the Taliban in Afghanistan.
- Osama bin Laden, the head of Al Qaeda, was a Saudi foreign fighter. Based in Afghanistan, he funded and approved the plot.
- Khalid Sheikh Mohammad, the plot's creator and coordinator, also fought in Bosnia and, like many of the hijackers, once aspired to fight in Chechnya with Khattab.

In the 9/11 attacks, all of the dangers that foreign fighters represent came together. When individuals went to fight, they radicalized and gained skills. They also joined a dangerous group that could redirect them from their original intent and use them for its own purposes. Leaders stayed behind, using the haven they enjoyed to organize, fundraise for, plan, and orchestrate the attack in another country. Indeed, the 9/11 attacks defined the U.S. response to foreign fighters ever since.

In contrast to Europe, the Middle East, and other parts of the world, however, foreign fighters have played an insignificant role in post-9/11 attacks in the United States. Notably, in the post-9/11 era, every significant terrorist attack in the United States involved individuals who have not traveled abroad to fight, even though American foreign fighters traveled to Iraq, Somalia, Syria, and other war zones. Rather, some preferred to stay in the war zone or feared that law enforcement would apprehend them on their return. Others decided not to become foreign fighters but found the Islamic State or other groups' appeals to strike at home more convincing than fighting abroad.[34] Indeed, would-be fighters who did *not* travel posed a greater danger. Of the plots in the United States, a staggering 60 percent of the attacks involved those who considered travel but did not ultimately attempt it.[35]

This absence of post-9/11 foreign fighter attacks in the United States is remarkable. A RAND study found that most American jihadists were arrested at home, arrested overseas, or killed. Of the post-9/11 fighters they studied, only 9 of 124 returned to the United States to conduct an attack, and none of those succeeded.[36] Let's repeat that: in the post-9/11 era through the end of 2018, when this book went to press, foreign fighters committed *zero* attacks in the United States. A George Washington University study found that of the twelve travelers who returned from Syria, only one intended to carry out an attack. That fighter had joined the Al Qaeda–linked Jabhat al-Nusra, not the

Islamic State. The overwhelming majority of would-be jihadists in the United States went abroad to join a group, not to return and conduct attacks.[37]

The Islamic State inspired several bloody attacks in the United States, however, and the FBI disrupted numerous other plots. Individuals that the Islamic State inspired or who claimed to act in the group's name attacked police officers with a hatchet, shot a seventy-four-year-old man, and hacked at random people at a restaurant with a machete. Often the plots involved a heavy dose of personal grievance with a dusting of Islamic State rhetoric. One of the first attacks perhaps inspired by the Islamic State occurred in September 2014 when Alton Nolen beheaded an employee at the Vaughan Foods processing plant, which recently fired him. In San Bernardino, California, in 2015, a husband and wife team shot up the husband's coworkers at a holiday party, which supposedly aimed to strike a blow for Islam. In 2016, in the worst single attack since 9/11, Omar Mateen killed forty-nine people at the Pulse Night Club in Orlando, Florida. Mateen once claimed to support Hezbollah, a Shiite group and one of the Islamic State's archenemies, suggesting that being seen as hardcore was more motivational than any particular ideology.[38] Yet even in those cases, no foreign fighters had direct involvement. Although many of the U.S. attackers read Islamic State material online and some attackers had cybercoaches like Hussain, the cybercoaches did not play a major operational role.

Mohamed Elshinawy represents perhaps the only Islamic State plot involving a transfer of resources. Elshinawy, a Maryland resident, considered joining the Caliphate in 2015 but decided instead to attack at home. The Islamic State provided him with several thousand dollars as well as instructions for building a peroxide bomb. The FBI, however, was following the money and seems to have known about the plot early on, efficiently disrupting the plot and arresting Elshinawy.[39]

As Nicholas Rasmussen, then director of the National Counterterrorism Center, noted, his first thought after an attack in the United States would be to attribute it to a homegrown perpetrator—so-called Lone Wolves— rather than a foreign fighter.[40] A Lone Wolf is traditionally described as someone who operates on his or her own and lacks a group, network, or direction from an outside organization. Lone Wolf attacks became more attractive as would-be travelers found themselves quickly arrested. In 2016, the Islamic State's spokesman and external operations leader Muhammad al-Adnani declared, "The smallest action you do in the heart of their land is dearer to us than the largest action by us and more effective and more damaging to them."[41] Islamic State supporters listened. Both the United States and Europe saw roughly (much depends on exactly what is counted) twice as many successful Lone Wolf attacks in 2015 and 2016 as they did in the 2011–2014 period.[42]

These attackers hated the United States for many reasons. Some consumed the steady diet of sermons by Awlaki, Adnani, and others that argued that America was at war with Islam throughout the Middle East and good Muslims needed to fight back. Some pointed to anti-Muslim rhetoric at home, such as Pamela Geller's campaign to block the construction of a mosque near the Twin Towers site in New York and her sponsorship of a "Draw the Prophet Mohammad" contest designed to mock Islam. Islam, in their eyes, is under attack and their violence is a form of both defense and revenge.

Technology helps enable a Lone Wolf credo. A young Muslim in Billings or Boston can read the words of ideologues like Adnani or Awlaki with just a quick Google search. Perhaps most worrisome, Lone Wolf shootings have become part of the terrorist zeitgeist and, as such, feed on themselves. A similar phenomenon developed with school shootings in the United States. Columbine High School killers Eric Harris and Dylan Klebold created a model for other violent teen misfits. In the United States, an idea of terrorist violence hangs in the air and attracts a small group of individuals who might otherwise have turned their thoughts in another direction.[43]

Fortunately, Lone Wolves often fail. The Pulse nightclub shooting in Orlando represents a rare incidence of a high death toll—indeed off the charts—compared with the vast majority of Lone Wolves, who usually kill only a small number, if any, before being killed or arrested. Although they inspire fear, we should remember that for Al Qaeda, and then for the Islamic State, Lone Wolves signal the group's weakness. The Islamic State once urged its sympathizers to fight in Syria in defense of the fledging state and expand it. Only those who could not travel to the Islamic State would conduct Lone Wolf attacks. Necessity, not choice, led them to embrace this tactic.

For all their operational deficiencies, Lone Wolves have a real, indeed a strategic, impact in the United States by helping to change American political rhetoric and government policies. After San Bernardino, terrorism fears in the United States spiked.[44] As a result, U.S. policymakers prioritized the Lone Wolves threat, with many political voices condoning law enforcement profiling of Muslim Americans, intrusive surveillance, and other tactics. This rhetoric also invaded American attitudes. Hate crimes against Muslims in 2015 rose to the post-9/11 peak. In so doing, such actions risked shattering the good relations between Muslim and non-Muslim communities so vital to counter-terrorism and to democracy in general.

Stopping American Foreign Fighters

The failure of the Islamic State to use foreign fighters to attack America shows how U.S. counterterrorism has advanced. Prior to 9/11, jihadis could fundraise for, recruit for, and travel to conflicts with little U.S. interference. The Services Office, which Azzam founded to handle logistics for foreign fighters in the anti-Soviet struggle, had offices in Brooklyn, among other locations, with the tacit blessing of the U.S. government. Early foreign fighters like Ali Mohammad flew below the radar screen, going to Pakistan and Afghanistan with little government awareness or interference. Ayman Zawahiri, who became the head of Al Qaeda, did a fundraising tour in the United States in the early 1990s. A jihadist fundraising cell in Chicago raised money for the foreign fighters in Bosnia. At the CIA, only a handful of analysts focused on Al Qaeda; the FBI and other agencies had fewer officers working on the case. Agencies often failed to gather, let alone share, vital information.[45]

All this changed after 9/11, when the United States began spending massively more money on counterterrorism. From 9/11 through the end of the 2017 fiscal year, the United States spent $2.8 trillion on counterterrorism. In 2017, the annual total was $175 billion. Much was spent on the wars in Iraq and Afghanistan as well as Syria, but almost a trillion went to homeland security in the years since 9/11 (the figure for 2017 alone was $71 billion). Spending on intelligence and warning went up over 300 percent between 9/11 and 2017.[46] These spending increases showed up in many ways. The FBI task force in New York and the New York police intelligence unit have a combined force of two thousand people dedicated to counterterrorism. In 1980 there were twenty.[47]

In addition to spending money, the United States made huge organizational and policy changes. The United States upped aviation security, mandated more intelligence sharing between agencies, and created or reorganized dozens of offices, agencies, and departments. Some of today's core counterterrorism institutions like the Department of Homeland Security and the National Counterterrorism Center did not exist prior to 9/11. Before 9/11, the United States had sixteen people on its no-fly list. By 2015, the list included more than 40,000 names. These changes permeated the justice system as well. Since 9/11, prosecutors have aggressively gone after suspected foreign fighters, and the conviction rate is close to 100 percent for those accused of supporting the Islamic State.[48]

Yet despite the post-9/11 focus on terrorism, some conflicts seemed to slip through the cracks. For example, the FBI initially devoted few resources to

Somalia as it seemed obscure and not directly tied to the broader struggle against Al Qaeda. As a result, some Americans joined the fray in 2006 with little interference. As officials became aware of the problem, however, vigilance grew, and those seeking to travel to Somalia were mostly disrupted.

For the most part, however, the United States has maintained a vigilant posture toward anything to do with jihadism. The U.S. efforts to fight foreign fighters and groups like the Islamic State can be grouped into three areas: law enforcement, military operations, and intelligence operations.

LAW ENFORCEMENT

In general, anything or anyone linked to Al Qaeda and, after 2014, the Islamic State is a magnet for U.S. intelligence and law enforcement. A review of criminal complaints against those arrested for trying to travel to join the Islamic State or other groups in Syria indicates several interesting patterns. First, the FBI arrested many at their homes or at airports, suggesting U.S. intelligence and law enforcement officials knew of their intentions to travel well in advance. Second, often family and friends stop individuals from going. Family members have persuaded would-be recruits not to travel, taken their passports, or even called the police or FBI to prevent someone close to them from joining the jihad.[49]

The United States has an advantage over Europe and most Muslim countries in that it is far from the theaters of jihad. Getting to Bosnia, let alone Chechnya, Somalia, or Afghanistan, involves a transatlantic flight and significant travel after landing. Would-be American volunteers often did not know how to reach the war zone; one volunteer posted on Instagram, "I would love to join Allah's army but I don't know how to start."[50] Syria offered an easier destination. As with other nationalities, most Americans attempting to join the Islamic State went via Turkey. "I just went online and bought a ticket," claimed one early American volunteer. "It was like booking a flight to Miami Beach."[51] However, U.S. officials quickly focused on travel to Turkey as a gateway to Syria. Further, U.S. officials benefited by narrowing their efforts on airports, while Europeans had to widen their efforts to include trains, buses, and cars.[52] As the Islamic State lost territory and as Turkey turned up the heat on Islamic State networks, Americans struggled to reach Syria. The Islamic State told one volunteer to go to Libya instead because Syria was "closed."[53]

Nor are those who seek to travel master terrorists whose brilliant tradecraft baffles investigators. More than two-thirds of Americans who aspired to become foreign fighters openly participated in radical social networks, and more than half openly expressed radical views to friends, coworkers, and others.[54]

One U.S. volunteer told a passport specialist he planned to go alone to Istanbul but could not provide hotel information or any details about his trip, before admitting he had neither money to sustain himself nor family connections in Turkey. Another had pictures of Islamic State flags and IED attacks on his cellphone. A third would-be fighter asked children at a park in his hometown of Brownsburg, Indiana, if they wanted to join the Islamic State.[55] Jaelyn Delshaun Young, a college student at Mississippi State University and former high school cheerleader, came under the Islamic State's spell. Young repeatedly told undercover FBI agents online that she wanted to help the group, bragging that she was "skilled in math and chemistry" and that she wanted to raise "cubs" for the state.[56] The list goes on.

Many leave a trail of clues all over social media, whose public content the FBI can easily monitor. One jihadist had a picture of Al-Awlaki and the Islamic State flag on his Facebook page. This is a cool way to show your colors to your jihadist-leaning friends, but a bad move if you want to avoid arrest. Another posted Tweets that praised the Caliphate and declared, "Hate the kuffars [infidels]."[57]

State or local officials are at times the first to realize that an individual plans to leave, and their approach varies. In New York City, police will knock on doors and try to dissuade potential radicals from joining the cause; in Virginia, officials will more likely simply lock someone up. Minneapolis takes a more northern European approach to deradicalization, with programs designed to offer known radicals "off ramps" to move them away from violence.

The FBI, with the support of every post-9/11 administration, aggressively pursues suspected terrorists—too aggressively, in the eyes of many civil libertarians. When the Islamic State hit its peak, the FBI opened hundreds of new terrorism cases, regularly using confidential informants and undercover operatives to monitor suspected terrorists, even though these are supposed to be tools of last resort. Hasan Edmonds, for example, gained FBI attention after he made alarming pro–Islamic State social media posts, and an undercover agent proceeded to monitor him after Edmonds accepted the agent's "friend" request. More controversially, however, civil libertarians accuse the FBI of facilitating terrorist plots in order to arrest suspects. Agents and informers have helped suspected terrorists acquire weapons, identify and surveil targets, learn how to get to Syria, and move along the road to terrorism in order to determine suspects' intentions and convict them. Critics argue that many of these suspects would not have acted illegally if left to their own devices. "They're manufacturing terrorism cases," argued one former undercover agent. Lutchman, the mentally ill Islamic State recruit whose short-lived career as a jihadist was noted earlier, illustrates this argument. He often begged for money or scrounged cigarette butts outside the local bowling alley in Rochester, and his father told reporters that "he's easily manipulated." Lutchman proposed attacking a bar that threw him out for panhandling, and his informant had to cover the $40 cost of the machete, ski masks, and other supplies for the terrorist attack he planned. Judges criticized the FBI for its handling of the case. One judge said, "I believe beyond a shadow of a doubt that there would have been no crime here, except the government instigated it." But she, and all judges, do not throw the cases out. The FBI argues, however, that such aggressive methods are necessary to prevent attacks and that all suspects had ample chances to back out.[58]

The costs of overzealousness extend beyond the individuals involved; aggressive counterterrorism efforts can also damage government relations with the Muslim community as a whole. After the 9/11 attacks, the United States arrested thousands of young Muslims, but only found one with links to Al Qaeda who had trained in Afghanistan in the 1990s.[59] One jihadist noted, "All of the West's vaunted values collapsed. What emerged were feelings of hatred and racist practices against everything Islamic."[60] As Daniel Benjamin, a former senior counterterrorism official, recalled, "Repairing the damage from that crackdown took years."[61]

The political climate in the United States has grown nastier and more hostile to Muslims. Polls show many Americans associate Islam with terrorism and have negative views of Muslims in general.[62] This Islamophobia, in turn, can begin a vicious circle. As communities become suspect, they withdraw into themselves and become less trustful of law enforcement. They provide fewer tips and are reluctant to point out the bad apples among them. Concurrently, political pressure grows for harsh policies toward the community as a whole rather than the small number of terrorists in their midst. In contrast, if a community has good relations with the police and society, terrorists have fewer grievances for terrorists to exploit and community members are more likely point out malefactors in their midst. More than 40 percent of foreign fighters involved in U.S. terror plots expressed their intentions to someone not involved in the plot.[63] Even though he was never arrested, Mateen, the Orlando shooter, came to the FBI's attention because a local Muslim found him suspicious and reported him.[64]

MILITARY OPERATIONS

In addition to more aggressive efforts at home, the United States engaged in repeated wars and military operations abroad. At times this meant massive interventions, but in others it was limited to airstrikes and support for local militias.

The U.S. military conducted counterterrorism operations in Afghanistan, Iraq, Somalia, Yemen, Libya, Niger, Pakistan, and other countries. United States forces, of course, overthrew the Taliban after 9/11 and continued to fight in Afghanistan, often focusing on remnants of Al Qaeda, the local Islamic State province, and foreigners in general. In addition, the United States deployed tens of thousands of troops to fight Al Qaeda in Iraq. After 2014, the United States also intervened decisively against the Islamic State in Iraq and Syria, pushing the group back in both countries through a mix of air strikes, support for local forces on the ground, and other measures. In Somalia, the United States usually pursued indirect operations. At times tactics involved direct U.S. airstrikes or raids by special operations forces, but mostly they meant working with neighboring governments or militias. Although public commentary usually focuses on the limits of these operations, such as the on-going Taliban insurgency in Afghanistan, in reality, they have hit hard at Al Qaeda and the Islamic State. The Al Qaeda core in Pakistan has had no real successful operations against the United States or the West in years, and its affiliates have had only a few.

Although direct targeting gathers the most attention, more common are U.S. efforts to help allies fight terrorist groups and their foreign fighters. The United States spends billions on programs to train and equip allied governments and militias to help fight the war on terrorism. Most of this money funded counterterrorism efforts, with Iraq, Jordan, and Tunisia benefiting in the Middle East, Pakistan in South Asia, and Kenya, Niger, and Ethiopia in Africa among many other countries. United States officials hope that these programs will help allies better fight terrorists, police ter-ritories they liberate from their clutches, defend their borders against enemies, and ensure the rule of law—and in so doing, diminish any need for U.S. intervention.[65]

When these train-and-equip programs work, they are far cheaper than deploying U.S. military forces. In addition, they avoid inciting a nationalistic backlash, which commonly occurs when foreign troops enter a country, even with the best of intentions. But train-and-equip programs frequently produce little progress. Painfully, the concept failed when it mattered most: fighting the Islamic State. In Iraq, the United States spent billions to build up the Iraqi army after 2003, only to see it collapse in 2014 as the Islamic State ad-vanced. The Islamic State boasted that it took Mosul, Iraq's second-largest city, with only 350 fighters, while tens of thousands of Iraqi security forces fled.[66] The United States spent less in Syria, but again, local allies received money, weapons, and training worth hundreds of millions, yet did not show up for the fight.

In addition to military efforts, much of the U.S. role involves acting as the conductor of a global intelligence orchestra. On a daily basis, the United States works with liaison services around the world to increase collection on foreign fighters and other jihadists, disseminate the information to the necessary partners, and act on it rapidly.[67] The National Counterterrorism Center and various intelligence agencies seek to gain information on all foreign fighters, not just Americans, going to Syria and other jihadist hotspots in order to coordinate a global response.[68] Similarly, the *New York Times* reported on Operation Gallant Phoenix, an intelligence operation that disseminates information gathered in commando raids in Syria and Iraq and passes it to allied security forces.[69] These and similar efforts enable allies to disrupt the transit of fighters and arrest them on return, greatly diminishing the threat they pose.

What's Next?

Successfully stopping would-be jihadists from traveling created its own problems. Although the figures for Syria are still tentative, past war zones proved lethal, with almost half of the U.S. volunteers dying in the conflict.[70] Surviving U.S. fighters who stay in the war zone rarely contribute to terrorism back home, and if they return, officials usually arrest them before they get close to launching an attack. Would-be foreign fighters prove more dangerous than returnees. According to a report released by the National Consortium for the Study of Terrorism and Responses to Terrorism, those who attempted to travel but failed to do so were five times more likely to be involved in a plot.[71]

As with Europe, the United States also must determine its legal response to would-be and returning foreign fighters, especially the role of incarceration. The United States sentences terrorists to longer jail terms than Europe. The average U.S. sentence is ten years for returnees and even longer, fourteen years, for those who try to go and fail (this puzzling disparity in sentencing between attempted and returning foreign fighters is because many returnees cooperate with authorities, informing on their comrades and thus reducing their sentence). Unlike in Europe, few Americans become radicalized in prisons, but many U.S. jihadists will be released in the coming years, and they need to be kept away from radical circles. However, the United States, in contrast to Europe, lacks deradicalization programs both for inmates in jail and after their release.[72] Such programs are necessary to prevent further radicalization or to stop others from beginning the path to radicalization.

One clear recommendation is to ensure community support, and the United States initiated several small pilot programs to this end though their funding remains uncertain. In the United States, improving community relations could include working with faith-based local organizations to ensure ties to the community. Often, building community relations also involves addressing nonterrorism-related issues, such as crime, to win over local community leaders. Indeed, framing terrorism issues in terms of public safety is more effective, as Muslim communities rightly fear being singled out on terrorism while anti-Muslim harassment is ignored. In addition, national programs can most effectively provide resources, share best practices, and coordinate, allowing local experimentation and diversity to dominate.

The lack of attacks from returnees, and the many successful efforts to disrupt those inspired by jihadists abroad, is impressive given the scope and scale of jihadist operations around the world. Americans should recognize that the post-9/11 effort against American foreign fighters has proven a remarkable success.

CHAPTER 13 | How to Stop Foreign Fighters

FROM AZZAM IN Afghanistan to John the Beatle in Syria, the story of the modern foreign fighter spans decades, continents, and cultures. Despite many differences, it is remarkable the extent to which foreign fighters learned and integrated strategies from their predecessors and then inspired their successors. Azzam's preaching later motivated Barbaros to train in Afghanistan and join the fray in Bosnia. Khattab took his military experience in Afghanistan and gained glory in Chechnya, inspiring new fighters to go to Afghanistan to train. These trained fighters not only conducted terrorist attacks but also helped seed jihad in Iraq after the 2003 U.S. invasion. Hammami consumed Chechen war propaganda, and the publicity he gave to jihad in Somalia brought other Westerners like John the Beatle into the jihadist world, with many ending up in Syria. And John the Beatle's successors will draw on the rich and brutal experience of Syria in the next war.

Jihadism is vibrant and resilient, whether you look just at terrorism or also at civil wars and the spread of the ideology. Groups like Al Qaeda and the Islamic State, their affiliates, and fellow travelers still enjoy wide support.[1] They have established proto-states or strongholds in Libya, Mali, the Sinai, and Yemen, as well as places discussed in more detail in this book. Jihadists' globalism helps. They may lose in Syria or another location, but they renew themselves elsewhere. As one European counterterrorism analyst told me, the jihadists have high morale even though they have "taken an incredible amount of shit."[2]

Because of this resilience, the foreign fighter problem will endure even with the Caliphate being forced underground at the end of 2018. They still are likely to spawn new conflicts in the Middle East and attempt acts of international terrorism. The trend line is disturbing. When the movement began in Afghanistan, a few dozen foreign fighters traveled to fight. More than thirty years later, more than 40,000 fighters went to Syria. Foreign fighters often milk their victories for many years. Decades later, the anti-Soviet period in Afghanistan endures as a jihadist success even though the foreigners themselves played no significant role. In the same vein, it is likely that jihadists will live for years to come off the success of the Caliphate in 2014 and 2015. Indeed, because foreign fighters from the previous wave often inspire and assist recruits in the next one, the networks formed in the last jihad could make the next wave even bigger.

Many jihadist teachings have moved from the fringe of Islamic discourse toward the center. For example, for most of Islamic history, there was a high bar for declaring another Muslim an unbeliever. Jihadists, however, regularly declare their enemies to be false Muslims, applying this to authoritarian Muslim regimes, Muslim governments working with Western powers, religious minorities like the Shiites or the Alawi, and even ordinary Sunni Muslims whom jihadists regard as insufficiently zealous. The ground is fertile for future groups to expand this slander.

Yet a comparison of the pre- and post-9/11 eras also shows how effective policy can diminish the foreign fighter terrorism threat. In Europe at the time of 9/11, foreign fighters represented around 80 percent of the terrorism danger, with those who trained in Afghanistan proving a particular risk. In the United States, of course, this danger manifested in the worst terrorist attack in history. Figures like Ali Mohamed and Awlaki could train in Afghanistan in the early 1990s as could minor players, like a group of Yemeni Americans from a suburb of Buffalo, New York.[3] U.S. intelligence services did not know most of these individuals. Similarly, Bin Laden, Barbaros, and Khattab all traveled abroad to fight, and the Saudi government did not recognize them as a threat for years. Indeed, it often lauded their activities. Only states with a long history of jihadist radicalism at home, like Egypt or Algeria, focused on the problem.

As is true today, intelligence collection involved coordinating a country's internal and external services—the FBI and the CIA, in the case of the United States—as well as police. This seemingly mundane challenge proved surprisingly hard, with key information on suspects not shared due to bureaucratic barriers and incompetence. Sharing information with foreign countries proved a greater challenge, as many domestic intelligence services lacked long-standing partners overseas and a culture of international action and coordination.

Perhaps most important, no one put the pieces together. The Algerian service might know of an Algerian who traveled to Bosnia to fight, while Saudi Arabia might know of its own citizens. The United States might have focused on a few individuals with known links to Al Qaeda. However, states shared information at best on an ad hoc basis and, as a result, much of what was known did not translate into effective policy.

Many of the key ideologues for jihad in the Muslim world resided in Europe, where free speech and even overall policy protected them. In the 1990s, the jihadist preacher Abu Qatada justified a gruesome jihad in Algeria, called for killing family members of Muslims he deemed apostates, and praised the actions of an aspiring Jordanian jihadist, Abu Musab al-Zarqawi, in his sermons and writings. He also encouraged European Muslims to go to Chechnya and Afghanistan, leveraging his network to fundraise, facilitate travel, and introduce them to jihadist groups overseas. British law gave his preaching considerable latitude, and British policy in the 1990s preferred him to operate openly, so authorities could monitor him.

The United States and many of its allies did not know what happened to volunteers once they went to a war zone or to training camps in Afghanistan. Government analysts at best knew many of the groups superficially, and important nuances dividing them were often missed or misunderstood. The training camps were intelligence black holes, with little understanding of who was there, what they learned, and what, if anything, these individuals intended to do upon return.

Travel, both to and from the war zone, was often unimpeded. Future Al Qaeda leader Ayman al-Zawahiri traveled to the United States to raise money before 9/11. Key figures like Barbaros found it easy to enter war zones like Bosnia. Some countries like Saudi Arabia were even complicit, encouraging jihad abroad to please important domestic voices or at least hoping to get troublemakers out of their own countries to somewhere, anywhere, else.

Today, Europe, the United States, and many countries in the Muslim world are far more effective at disrupting foreign fighter plots, and it is homegrown extremists who pose the bigger threat. Despite the massive flows to Syria, only 20 percent of Europe's terrorism problem today has immediate links to foreign fighters. In the United States, where the foreign fighter role in 9/11 will always remain a scar, this success is even more marked; no former foreign fighters from the more recent jihads in Somalia and Syria have returned and attacked the United States (so far).

Much remains to be done. Some countries fail to adequately fund their security services or otherwise prioritize intelligence gathering on potential foreign fighters. Many countries should bolster information sharing with the

United States, INTERPOL, or international databases to disrupt travel and identify terrorists operating on their soil.[4] Other states struggle to gather information from community leaders and civic organizations that might first detect a potential wave of radicalization. For this book, I interviewed numerous foreign intelligence officials, and all criticized their own performance or those of their partners, including the United States. Nevertheless, they all agreed the trend is in the right direction.

No silver bullet exists to stop foreign fighters, but plenty of useful weapons, collectively, can limit their impact. Officials can take some steps before potential fighters even leave their countries, while other measures involve stopping transit to and from a war zone. States can hinder fighters in the war zone with military force, covert action, and a foreign policy that tries to reduce the violence and the jihadist role in it. Finally, officials can disrupt the violence when fighters return or persuade returnees to turn away from terrorist acts. At almost every stage, intelligence collection and sharing are vital. Together, these can profoundly reduce the threat foreign fighters pose. The foreign fighter lifecycle depicted in Figure 13.1 shows how to conceptualize the foreign fighter production process as a way of illustrating how to better disrupt it.

Halting the Foreign Fighter Production Process

Figure 13.1 illustrates the process of becoming a foreign fighter from the initial stage of radicalization to travel to the war zone to eventual return.

THE RADICALIZATION STAGE

As the earlier chapters make clear, no single factor explains why someone radicalizes and becomes a foreign fighter. Some are idealists, while others are motivated by a sense of adventure. For the Islamic State, many recruits had brushes (or worse) with law enforcement. In Europe in particular, poor integration made radicalization more likely, and many recruits had ties to ostensibly peaceful but radical organizations like Al Muhajiroun. The goal at this stage is to identify and dissuade individuals before they take illegal actions. As Zachary Chesser, an American volunteer for the Shebaab, later wrote, "There is no stage between someone saying 'I like the Taliban' for the first time and a sting operation."[5]

Using resources to focus on certain at-risk elements, such as those in prison or those who have expressed support for jihadist ideas on social media, is a sensible approach that does not target a community as a whole. In addition,

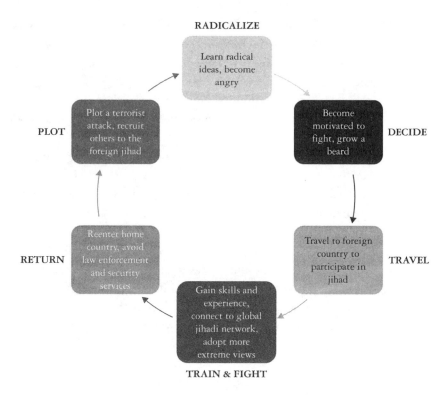

RADICALIZE

Learn radical ideas, become angry

DECIDE

Become motivated to fight, grow a beard

PLOT

Plot a terrorist attack, recruit others to the foreign jihad

TRAVEL

Travel to foreign country to participate in jihad

RETURN

Reenter home country, avoid law enforcement and security services

TRAIN & FIGHT

Gain skills and experience, connect to global jihadi network, adopt more extreme views

FIGURE 13.1 The foreign fighter production process. (Created by author.)

European allies must address ostensibly peaceful groups like Al Muhajiroun and the various Sharia4 organizations it spawned that promote jihadist-type teachings. Some of these groups control important mosques or humanitarian organizations with connections to theaters of jihad. Such organizations often require more monitoring, and governments and social organizations should try to supplant their place in Muslim communities.

Counternarratives offer another tactic to diminish the groups' appeal to potential recruits and contest the groups' online messaging. Common themes reappear for recruits traveling to jihad theaters only to become disenchanted: difficulty in adjusting, disgust with Muslim infighting, and shock at the brutality of the conflict. A Tunisian lawyer who represents returnees noted that the majority of those returning express disappointment at the fighting between the Islamic State and groups like Jabhat al-Nusra: "They never thought there would be a fight between Muslims. They find that they have been deceived and sold like mercenaries."[6] Pragmatic arguments may illustrate the consequences of leaving for the individual's safety, family, and friends. Failing to develop a counternarrative cedes the information battlefield to the jihadist groups. After the first battle of Fallujah, for example, the United States and its allies largely stayed silent as fighters issued torrents of propaganda detailing supposed U.S. atrocities and the heroic resistance of jihadists, leading to a surge in recruits.

It's easy to call for developing a counternarrative but hard to do so in practice, as the limitations inherent in government hinder the quantity and quality of the resulting messages. Government social media efforts are often slow at responding and limited in number. One French official admitted to me, "We are not good at this."[7] The U.S. State Department's Center for Strategic Counterterrorism Communications (replaced in 2016 by the Global Engagement Center) seeks to undermine terrorist propaganda and has produced tens of thousands of online "engagements" in multiple languages. However, it has few employees and a small budget. As a result, it could not compete with the thousands of Islamic State accounts operating twenty-four hours each day. Further, governments struggle to put out compelling content with the right message, while also appropriate for all audiences. The content is often derided as amateurish. Ambassador Alberto Fernandez, who headed U.S. efforts until 2015, admitted that the U.S. government lacks a counternarrative. "What we have is half a message: 'Don't do this.' But we lack the 'do this instead,'" he explained.[8] Part of the difficulty stems from the lowest-common-denominator effect that occurs when different bureaucracies and countries work together to find a single message that satisfies everyone. Perhaps most important, government messages are simply uncool to a disaffected twenty-five-year-old looking for adventure.[9]

Unsuccessful attempts at counternarratives cause more harm than good. Harmful counternarratives may obviously target a specific community, suggesting that the government associates all community members with terrorism. For example, the British government's efforts to win over British Muslims since 9/11 often backfired, angering the community and convincing Muslims that law enforcement singles them out.

When done well, however, counternarratives can foster community support for government efforts. Western countries have found that communities and particularly families often assist in discouraging potential recruits from traveling to fight but will flag authorities only if they trust the government.[10] In addition, if communities see volunteers as deluded or worse, the stature of foreign fighters would diminish, reducing the allure of becoming a jihadist in the first place.

Counternarratives tend to work best when the government supports local religious, community, and neighborhood groups that promote their own messages of moderation. Another option is to amplify "turned" jihadists and their stories to highlight a jihadist's negative experiences in the war zone. The Saudi government sought to discourage its citizens from traveling to Syria to fight by running interviews with returned and disillusioned jihadists on Saudi state television.[11] In the West, former jihadists like Jesse Morton in the United States and Mubin Shaikh in Canada offer a message about their own experiences and disillusionment that could be amplified. These interviews also send a message to those who want to come in from the jihadist cold that society will welcome them back.

All jihadist groups used the technology of their times, and today much of the information battle will be on the internet. Fortunately, Twitter, Facebook, and other social media sites slowly but steadily became more aggressive in disrupting the Islamic State's attempts to use their platforms, greatly reducing the group's online presence. Sometimes more destructive measures may offer a more effective approach to reduce a group's online presence. As territory was taken from the Islamic State, the group struggled to maintain media centers and otherwise keep the infrastructure of communication. Governments can also attack the group directly online through denial of service attacks or by infiltrating and monitoring. The head of GCHQ, the British equivalent of the NSA, revealed that his agency had gone after Islamic State propaganda, so that the group "found it almost impossible to spread their hate online, to use their normal channels to spread their rhetoric, or trust their publications."[12]

Furthermore, government officials must recognize the impact of their words on inflaming foreign fighter grievances and alienating potentially sympathetic communities. Increasingly, politicians in the West demonize Muslims, risking backlash and legitimating right-wing violence. This mix of violence and demonization not only leads to a back-and-forth cycle of radicalization as extremes react to each other but also scares ordinary people, leading to distrust of their neighbors, their governments, or both.

THE DECISION STAGE

If someone cannot be prevented from embracing a radical agenda, the next opportunity to disrupt the person is when he or she decides to go fight. Azzam's preaching convinced Barbaros to fight in Afghanistan, Masri fled Egypt when the government there cracked down, while Hammami sought to live under the Shebaab's rule. Intercepting an individual before he or she leaves would reduce the numbers of foreign fighters in a conflict zone and the long-term risk of terrorism.

Security services play an important role. This may involve confiscating passports, instructing internet companies to remove websites that provide travel guidance, and detaining or imprisoning recruiters linked to terrorist groups. Egypt, for example, required young males to apply for security approval before transiting Turkey, the most common gateway to Syria.[13]

In the post-9/11 era, many states—some suddenly fearful of the threat, others eager to appease a vengeful America—began to look for radical networks on their own soil. The resulting disruption to Al Qaeda and other groups was tremendous. The recruitment and logistics networks the groups enjoyed came under siege, while those who fought or traveled abroad became prime suspects. At times, as in the Azizi case in Spain, the crackdown led to a desire for revenge. But overall, disrupting cells proved a huge blow to Al Qaeda and similar groups.

Many recruits originate from a few flashpoint sites. Darnah in Libya proved a leading source of recruits for Syria, and half of Germany's recruits for Syria came from just eleven cities.[14] Narrowing the target set further, many emerged from a small number of mosques in these cities. As terrorism expert Clinton Watts points out, "The call for jihad may be global, but the recruitment is extremely *local.*"[15] Focusing efforts on key nodes offers security services a more effective and efficient means to target recruits, while also avoiding angering the community as a whole.

As the Syria conflict heated up, European governments developed programs to dissuade those on the cusp of deciding to go to Syria. These programs recognize that families and friends often provide vital sources of information as they desperately try to prevent their loved ones from joining terrorist groups, and many family members are less likely to cooperate if they believe that involving authorities will result in sending a loved one to years in jail.[16] The Danish government maintains an extensive program to talk to potential volunteers before they go to Syria, working with families and local authorities. They stress the dangers of fighting and the consequences, such as losing welfare benefits. France has hotlines for family and community members to alert authorities that someone might travel to Syria. In the United Kingdom, the British government appealed to Muslim women to persuade their sons and brothers not to join the fray.[17]

Diplomatically, the international community should ban becoming a foreign fighter regardless of the legitimacy of the cause. UN Security Council Resolution 2178 focuses on those traveling "for the purpose of the perpetration, planning of, or participation in terrorist acts" and singles out groups like the Islamic State and the Al Qaeda affiliate in Syria. This ban, however, should apply more broadly as often individuals travel to train or to fight in a civil war, both of which are dangerous. A ban should apply to those joining the Kurds to fight against the Islamic State, Russian "volunteers" in Ukraine, and so on. Private wars, in other words, would be illegal. Even small steps can help. When Bosnia began to criminalize becoming a foreign fighter and to stop departures to Syria, it required volunteers to use new routes, often forcing them to travel via other cities like Rome or Vienna. This made the trip far more expensive and thus unaffordable for many.[18]

On a broader scale, developing peaceful alternatives to help people affected by the conflicts in the Middle East will also discourage potential recruits during the decision stage. A genuine desire to defend their fellow Muslims against brutal regimes originally motivated some fighters who went to Afghanistan, Bosnia, Chechnya, and Syria. Indeed, the rhetoric of Western leaders embraced this goal as well. Encouraging charitable activities, identifying legitimate channels for assistance, and highlighting ways concerned individuals can help alleviate suffering may siphon off some of the supply of foreign fighters, especially at a critical early stage. Although these actions will not solve the bleeding wound that is today's Middle East, offering opportunities to assist peacefully may resolve feelings of helplessness that push individuals to travel abroad to fight.

THE TRAVEL STAGE

Deciding to fight is not enough: the volunteer must get to the war, and this is another opportunity for disruption. Terrorist groups, at least, recognized the importance of travel. Facilitating travel was one of the primary purposes of Azzam's and Bin Laden's Services Bureau. Al Qaeda had a "passport office" and trained operatives in forging documents, identifying corrupt border officials, and otherwise developing broad networks to send operatives to and from war zones.[19] Some of its affiliates established nonaggression pacts with states to ensure easy transit. The Mauritanian government, for example, paid Al Qaeda in the Islamic Maghreb between ten to twenty million Euros a year and promised that it would not interfere with jihadist travel if, in exchange, the group agreed not to kidnap tourists or otherwise attack in Mauritania.[20]

The transit route to Syria via Turkey illustrates the danger of easy travel. For several years, the Turkish government knowingly turned a blind eye as volunteers flew or drove into Turkey and then traveled across the border into Syria to fight. Once Turkey began to crack down and changed its policies in 2015, and military force removed the Islamic State along the border, reaching Syria became far harder. The foreign fighter stream slowed to a trickle, becoming more like Bosnia and Chechnya, where jihadists had to traverse carefully guarded borders. In response, the Islamic State began encouraging would-be volunteers to wreak havoc at home instead.

Effective intelligence gathering can detect and disrupt those who plan to travel. A Canadian intelligence report found that individuals who travel often maxed out their credit cards, sold their belongings, improved their fitness, and otherwise revealed clues as they tried to be financially and physically ready for the fight. What they sold varied, ranging from cars for an older person or a video game console for someone younger. Usually individuals mobilized in groups, not as individuals, with group members helping one another. A richer member might give a poorer one money for a plane ticket, for example. Travel preparation often involved what the Canadian service labeled "leakage," with knowledge of the forthcoming travel dribbling out and friends and family becoming aware.[21] If intelligence can work with communities and access the leakage, dangerous travel can be better prevented.

Deploying more border security personnel, improving training and procedures for detecting fraudulent passports, and better sharing of information on suspected travelers all make a marked difference in the ability of potential fighters to reach a war zone or return undetected. Before 9/11, no U.S. government agency systematically analyzed terrorist travel, "thus missing critical opportunities to disrupt their plans," in the words of the 9/11 Commission staff. Most U.S. allies, if anything, paid even less attention. After 9/11, the CIA, the State Department, the FBI, and other agencies began to focus on disrupting travel.[22]

In addition to blocking transit routes, governments must target jihadist travel agents. Timothy Holman, in his excellent article on travel facilitation, conveys the wide range of roles that former foreign fighters, jihadist nongovernmental organizations, and social media platforms can play as facilitators. They help fighters leave their country of origin, find transit into war zones, and house fighters and new recruits joining the jihad. In addition, facilitators can help vet recruits to ensure they are not spies, often by asking an established fighter or a respected religious leader to vouch for them. A facilitator often influences which group an individual joins and where an individual fights. Facilitators' networks are often personal and hard to replace, so removing a prolific facilitator through arrest or from the battlefield may lead to fewer foreign fighters later on.

TRAINING AND FIGHTING IN THE WAR ZONE

Some fighters will not be dissuaded or detected before leaving their homes and will successfully evade any travel restrictions, arriving safely in the war zone and into the arms of a jihadist group. In such war zones, Barbaros developed his skill with the Russian-made "Hound" rockets in Afghanistan, Azizi trained and networked with other jihadis also in Afghanistan and Pakistan, and John the Beatle beheaded numerous Americans for propaganda in Syria. Other jihadis met one another, learned new skills, and disseminated propaganda to convince the next wave of recruits to join.

In these war zones, terrorists seem out of reach from American or allied influence. Indeed, counterterrorism officials in the pre-9/11 era constantly lamented that as long as Al Qaeda enjoyed a haven in Afghanistan, its leadership could freely arm, train, organize, and build a mini-army. The group could plot attack after attack and only needed to evade U.S. counterterrorism once to succeed in striking terror.

In the post-9/11 era, with the danger of the Afghanistan sanctuary seared into the American consciousness, the United States has prioritized preventing and disrupting terrorist havens. The United States overthrew the Taliban in Afghanistan following the 9/11 attacks and worked with governments in Asia, Africa, and the Middle East to decrease Al Qaeda's operational freedom in other potential havens. The invasion of Iraq after 2003 and the collapse of the Iraqi regime helped create a sanctuary for jihadis, but after 2006, an effective U.S.-led counterinsurgency campaign drove jihadis into hiding. The Obama administration hesitated to become embroiled in the Syrian civil war after 2011, but as the Islamic State emerged and developed a sanctuary, the United States belatedly deployed troops, supported local forces, and launched airstrikes. President Trump continued this approach, and the campaign steadily shrank the Islamic State–controlled territory, eventually driving the Caliphate underground. Although experts rightly note that the line between battlefield success and preventing external terrorist attacks is not direct, there is a relationship.[23] As terrorism analyst Clinton Watts pointed out, "Despite all their macho bravado, no foreign fighter wants to join a fight where al-Qaeda is getting its ass kicked."[24]

The United States also uses drone and other airstrikes as well as raids by special operations forces to keep terrorists off balance and in hiding in potential safe havens. In Pakistan's tribal areas, Somalia, and Libya, the United States struck Al Qaeda, the Islamic State, and associated jihadist groups repeatedly, driving these groups further underground and impeding their operations. Hammami's joke that drones in Somalia are "racist" because they only attack white people (i.e., nonnative Somalis) suggests that these campaigns focus on foreign fighters and those tied to groups that employ them.

Many of those killed are "cannon fodder" (and at times innocents), but casualties also include dozens of these organizations' senior leaders and top figures whom groups cannot easily replace. In addition to a drone attack killing 3/11 mastermind Amer Azizi, Rashid Rauf, one of the Al Qaeda architects behind the July 7, 2005 bombings in London and other attacks, died in a drone strike. Before his death, Atiyah Abd al-Rahman, a senior leader of Al Qaeda who was himself killed in 2011 by a drone strike in Waziristan, warned that the death of experienced leaders leads to "the rise of lower leaders who are not as experienced as the former leaders and . . . the repeat of mistakes." Likewise, terrorist organizations suffer when they lose skilled operatives, such as passport forgers, bomb makers, recruiters, and fundraisers. Drone strikes have also undercut terrorists' ability to communicate with far-flung followers and train new recruits. A tip sheet found among jihadists in Mali advised militants to maintain "complete silence of all wireless contacts" and avoid "gathering in open areas." Incommunicado leaders, however, cannot give orders, and training on a large scale is nearly impossible when a drone strike could wipe out an entire group of new recruits. Drones and associated surveillance turn the terrorists' command and training structure into a liability, forcing the group to choose between having no leaders or risking dead leaders.[25] Groups like Al Qaeda in the Arabian Peninsula have moved away from working with foreigners, fearing their zealotry, hostility toward local communities, and the risk of attracting American drones against their own operatives and any locals who might otherwise work with them.[26]

Particularly in the Middle East, jihadist groups are often involved in civil wars or insurgencies that pose a serious threat to regional stability as well as a risk of terrorism. For the United States, working with and through allies is a way to avoid large-scale deployments. Train-and-equip programs and embedding U.S. special operations forces are crucial to combating safe havens. Local forces know the conditions, geographic area, leadership, and population in ways that foreign forces will not. Local forces will also have more of a stake in the outcome as it is their homeland.

As its experiences in Iraq and Syria suggest, however, the United States often wastes years of effort and billions of dollars on incompetent and venal allies.[27] Part of the problem is that the United States often starts with damaged goods. Countries facing a major terrorism problem or insurgency often suffer from problems that allow violence to flourish, and the resulting violence can exacerbate these problems.[28] Societal divisions prove a particular problem. Weak national identity in Iraq, Somalia, Syria, and other countries pushed populations to instead identify with tribes, sects, or other smaller groups. Citizens only wanted to fight for their own communities and distrusted others, while the national army was viewed as a tool of the dominant community rather than an impartial force. Some of the Iraqi army forces fighting to retake Mosul, for example, hung Shiite religious imagery from their vehicles, hardly a reassuring sight to the mostly Sunni inhabitants of Mosul.[29] Rampant corruption at all levels also hinders efforts to work with partners in the developing world. For instance, the Iraqi army had tens of thousands of "ghost soldiers," phantom troops who only existed on paper so their superiors could collect additional salaries.[30]

Further, rulers often lack legitimacy among rival communities and, at times, even among their own. With the exception of Tunisia, all of the Arab governments in the Middle East lack democratic legitimacy, and some fail to provide even the most basic of services. For many Iraqis in Mosul, Islamic State rule was an improvement over that of the Iraqi government. In Somalia, the Shebaab often gained support because it was less corrupt than the nominal government in Mogadishu and provided a modicum of law and order.

The lack of unity and weak governmental legitimacy often leads rulers to politicize their militaries and exacerbates this problem. Fearing a coup, they put loyalists in senior positions. By placing loyalty over competence, the rank-and-file soldiers are even less likely to fight, as they believe their officers do not deserve their loyalty.[31] This incompetence feeds into the societal divisions, as citizens who may have relied on the military view it as incapable of protecting the community. Instead, these citizens turn to militias, further feeding the societal divisions.

In addition to being a place to fight jihadists, war zones abroad also provide an opportunity for intelligence collection. A fighter's presence in the war zone now might lead to his discovery, information about training camps and command locations, and the identification of comrades back at home. Governments regularly intercept communications to and from suspected fighters and leaders, revealing broader networks, including individuals who previously may have gone unnoticed in their home countries. The fighters' love affair with social media makes their security even more precarious, as government monitoring of "friends" and "followers" reveals entire networks and aspirational fighters. As one security expert noted, "A lot of their members are just teenagers, and teenagers have bad impulse control."[32]

Acting as a conductor of global liaison services around the world represents a key role for U.S. intelligence. The U.S. intelligence agencies share names, biometrics, and other basic information with state and local partners and also with foreign countries.[33] For example, the 2004 arrest of the Al Qaeda operative and key Jemaah Islamiyya leader "Hambali," who went to Afghanistan in the 1980s to fight the Soviets and became close to Osama bin Laden, involved U.S. coordination of information and action from Indonesia, Malaysia, the Philippines, Singapore, and Thailand.[34] The countries in question often did not cooperate well with each other, but the United States assisted with overall coordination, facilitating the eventual success.

Beyond military measures and gathering intelligence, there are more subtle ways of interfering with foreign fighters in a terrorist sanctuary. On the most basic level, governments can enlist concerned family members to guilt their loved ones to return. As one defector recalled, "The sound of my mother or father crying over the phone made me break down and immediately led to my decision to leave Syria."[35] Furthermore, the Islamic State and other jihadist groups in Iraq and Syria are highly vulnerable to offensive counterintelligence. By relying on large numbers of foreign volunteers, they left the door open to spies—and they knew it.[36] Suspicion of foreigners led the Islamic State to reject many genuine candidates, conduct purges, and reduce the value of foreign volunteers, all of which negatively affected the group's cohesion and effectiveness. Security agencies should take all measures to sow doubt in extremist leaders' minds about the true loyalties of their volunteers. Highlighting information gained from captured recruits and even spreading disinformation about the degree of infiltration by security services can heighten fears.

The United States has spent trillions on intervention in Afghanistan, Iraq, and Syria.[37] If just one one-hundredth of this figure funded conflict prevention programs, it would represent a dramatic and welcome policy change. Violence related to the Syrian civil war touched Dhaka, Melbourne, Orlando, Paris, and almost every country in the Middle East. Allocating this funding between train-and-equip programs, targeted development, and cushioning the impact of necessary economic reforms offers a great first step to mitigate the breakout of civil wars. Vigorous diplomacy would complement this effort to resolve grievances before they break out into massive war. All of this might prevent the next war, and thus break the cycle where yesterday's returnees recruit tomorrow's volunteers.

If military force successfully removes a group or diplomacy resolves a conflict, the state must improve governance to prevent the jihadists' return. Bosnia did not become a jihadist sanctuary after the 1995 war ended in part because the Bosnian government became strong enough to expel most of the remaining jihadists. In contrast, although the U.S.-led campaign helped drive Al Qaeda in Iraq to the brink of defeat, the Iraqi government's corruption, discrimination against Sunni groups, and other problems allowed jihadists to regain their footing.

THE RETURN STAGE

Some volunteers not only make it to the war zone and survive the fighting but also manage to return home. Once at home, it is critical to arrest returnees or use rehabilitation programs to turn them away from future violence and jihad.

Without such programs, returnees can leverage their skills and networks to launch deadly attacks.

The good news, however, is that returning foreign fighters pose less long-term danger than regularly assumed if the right policies are in place. Although foreign fighters played a role in many terrorist attacks, their relative importance has fallen since the heyday of training camps in Afghanistan, when perhaps one in eleven foreign fighters later had a role in terrorism. The scholars Thomas Hegghammer and Petter Nesser suggest that one in 360 returned Islamic State foreign fighters is involved in terrorism. This is not a tiny number given the large overall numbers of returnees, but a far lower ratio than many feared.[38] Two other scholars, David Malet and Rachel Hayes, found that most returnees' attacks occurred within the first few months after coming home and that the threat fell sharply after six months. Despite claims to the contrary, Malet and Hayes found no evidence of Islamic State or other sleeper cells.[39]

As a first step toward minimizing the threat, security services in countries with large numbers of fighters identify which ones deserve the most attention and which are less dangerous. More dangerous returnees may include individuals who have been on security services' radar for many years or individuals with known connections to jihadist leaders. These returnees may require constant surveillance, ranging from traditional wiretapping or tailing to social media infiltration. For less dangerous returnees, enrolling the individual in a rehabilitation program that helps reintegrate him or her into society may offer a helpful avenue. Regardless, the state must know of the returnees' whereabouts, activities, and connections to ensure that he or she will not plot an attack at home. Communities play an especially strong role at this stage, as the state must rely on them to report suspicious actions.

Even though a relatively small number of returning foreign fighters may launch attacks, tracking suspects is exceptionally resource-intensive, particularly if it involves full-time surveillance. The Australian security services estimated that to monitor just one returning jihadist around the clock cost eight million Australian dollars (US$7.4 million) per year.[40] Yet intelligence services see surveillance of all suspects as necessary because the public equates success with no attacks. After an attack, officials struggle to justify failing to have monitored a known suspect. As one intelligence official explained to me, "This is what gets directors fired." Beyond surveillance, intelligence officials must analyze the massive amount of data they collect, which proves even more difficult. "The data are buried in a mountain of data," noted the same European analyst.[41]

The security services' own effectiveness can work against them. By successfully disrupting terrorists, they decrease the danger, thereby creating the impression that they need fewer resources. However, if fewer attacks results in fewer dedicated resources, the danger may grow.

In addition, the counterterrorism process should integrate prisons rather than simply using them as the final stage of justice. Incarceration presents a double-edged sword. On one hand, prison prevents violence by removing dangerous people from society. Politically, it is easier to take harsh steps than to create counternarratives, disengagement programs, and other measures that supplement law enforcement and jail. A terrorist who acted after security services passed on a chance to arrest him would embarrass the service and enrage the public. In most countries, however, prison officers need better training. They need to recognize that prisoners have a right to practice their religion and that religiosity and militancy are not the same thing.[42] Furthermore, sending potential and actual fighters to jail may radicalize them further, particularly if they share prisons with large numbers of jihadists. Several important foreign fighters—Zarqawi, Zawahiri, and Awlaki, among others—became more hardened and committed to jihad in jail.[43] In states with large numbers of volunteers, particularly in Europe and the Middle East, prison radicalization poses a greater problem.[44] Further, the short length of many prison sentences, often only a few years, does not remove many potential fighters from the pool of potential terrorists.

Ultimately, incarceration is necessary for more dangerous jihadists, but if it is applied too broadly it can backfire. When an individual on the fence knows he or she will face imprisonment upon return, that person may feel he or she has less to lose by moving toward terrorism at home. As radicalization expert Shiraz Maher put it, "This makes the decision for you."[45] Many foreign fighters simply fade away, but if they have no way to put the past behind them, then they become professional jihadists.[46] Coercive measures can also create "suspect communities" where radicalization is more likely and where community members are less likely to work with the police and government in general.[47] As one expert told me, in these communities, young Muslims "hear they are different and dangerous" and thus are more prone to leave and become jihadists.[48]

The state should also work side-by-side with religious leaders, families, and local organizations to monitor the individual's progress as well as to assist him or her in finding employment. A Saudi program put in place during the mid-2000s seeks to reeducate foreign fighters, countering the ideology they learned in foreign training camps that calls for fighting Muslim regimes and denigrates nonjihadists.[49] Saudi Arabia's program has reportedly achieved some success; the government claims that only roughly 12 percent of those who participated in the program returned to terrorism—a percentage that can be considered low or high depending on a country's risk tolerance. Programs in Indonesia, Yemen, and other countries have also tried to turn convicted terrorists from violence with, at best, mixed success.[50]

A number of European countries also initiated disengagement and deradicalization programs. The experiences of Denmark and France make a useful contrast. France systematically prosecutes returnees on charges of terrorism. According to former Interior Minister Bernard Cazeneuve, the formula is straightforward: "I'm often asked what happens to people who leave to wage jihad in Syria when they return to France. It's simple: They're connected with a terrorist enterprise, [so they're] arrested and handed over to justice."[51] True to that view, French officials arrested two underage boys from Toulouse who went to Syria and returned to France after the fighting disillusioned them, much to the consternation of their parents.[52] In Denmark, in contrast, officials carefully evaluated returnees for risk. Those who are considered traumatized are sometimes recruited as informants, and in general, officials push for returnees to enroll in school or seek employment and otherwise remove them from a dangerous milieu. Danish observers fear that being more coercive might strengthen "the victim discourse" within the Muslim community and thereby exacerbate the social conditions that can lead some individuals to participate in jihad.[53]

Countries like Russia and China, with harsh policies that drove many Muslims to flee, face a different challenge. On the one hand, they have tough border controls and aggressive intelligence services, enabling them to track returnees effectively. On the other hand, their returnees cannot return and live normal lives or otehwise "drop out," like their Western counterparts. For those that decide to return home, some may join or form radical groups as a result of lacking nonviolent alternatives. As one analyst of China noted, "It's become a self-fulfilling prophecy."[54]

Unlike the other stages in the foreign fighter cycle, the return stage entails the greatest number of competing agendas, requiring a state to adopt an array of policy options. For a successful policy in the return stage, a state must follow through on the public expectation to prevent any and all terrorist attacks, engage communities but not inflame or exacerbate community tensions, determine a realistic allocation of resources that allows for a sustainable and long-term policy, offer an exit ramp for those jihadists that become disillusioned with the conflict and seek to reintegrate peacefully, protect civil liberties, and maintain a cohesive society overall. All this must be done, moreover, on a reasonable budget. Achieving some of these goals at the expense of others would be self-defeating. A smorgasbord of incarceration, rehabilitation programs, and surveillance based on the risk assessment of each returnee is complex but necessary.

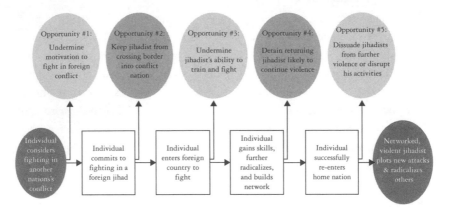

FIGURE 13.2 Model of foreign fighter radicalization with opportunities for disruption. (Created by author.)

Finally, the international community also must address a new problem that emerged in the Syria conflict, namely the large number of children re-turning from jihadist-controlled territory—a problem that will likely recur in future conflicts. Thousands of family members of foreign fighters are in camps or orphanages in areas controlled by anti-Assad militias or the Iraqi govern-ment. Germany's domestic intelligence director warned that the children were "brainwashed" and "living time bombs."[55] On the other hand, children did not go to the war zone willingly, and they still can become peaceful and produc-tive citizens. Indeed, as the most vulnerable, they are owed the most support.

The policy responses for each stage of the foreign fighter production cycle are illustrated next. As Figure 13.2 shows, governments have many opportunities to disrupt, dissuade, or otherwise hinder foreign fighters, greatly reducing the overall number of attacks.

THINKING BEYOND THE PLOT STAGE

Terrorism, unfortunately, has become a feature of modern life. Yet it is im-portant not to panic and to recognize that many countries have dealt with this problem before, instituted effective measures to reduce the threat of ter-rorism from jihadist returnees, and developed policies to limit the scale of any attacks that might occur. States can and should improve these measures, but the public cannot expect perfection as the standard of success. If they do, we are doomed to failure and overreaction.

A culture of resilience would help. Despite the relatively low number of deaths on U.S. soil since 9/11, and roughly comparable figures of attacks in

Europe for the pre- and post-9/11 periods, public fear of terrorism remains high. Highlighting counterterrorism successes, including the more effective efforts against foreign fighters, and emphasizing the low risk most Westerners have of dying from terrorism would hinder groups like the Islamic State from using terrorist attacks to instill fear in their enemies.

From a resource point of view, the United States and its allies must determine the acceptable threat level given the inevitability of a future attack. Given the greater money spent and the lower threat facing the U.S. homeland when compared with Europe, the answers will vary among countries. For the United States, the threat posed by right-wing violence might be greater than that of returnees. The spread of a new infectious disease might be far more perilous.

Finally, rhetoric after an attack must try to ensure community support and rally people together—a seemingly obvious point that seems increasingly elusive in the United States and many European countries. With emotions running high, leaders should not conflate Muslims and terrorists, enact draconian surveillance measures or travel restrictions, or otherwise worsen interreligious relations and exacerbate fear. Such measures may help politicians, but they also help the terrorists. These measures give extremists evidence to back up the narrative that the United States and its allies are hostile to Muslims and discourages the vast majority of Muslims who would otherwise loath the group from working against it (because doing so means working with what they see as a hostile government). Unfortunately, such a recommendation is the one least likely to be heeded in the aftermath of a terrorist attack.

It is often difficult for Western leaders to fight radicalism at home, but they can at least try to do no harm. Discriminatory policies against Muslims serve jihadist recruiters and make it harder to gather information from the community. Similarly, the harsh anti-Muslim rhetoric is common fodder for jihadist propagandists.

As this book makes clear, the transnational jihadist movement has evolved from its early days with Azzam in Afghanistan to the bloody prominence it enjoyed under the Islamic State. Fortunately, counterterrorism too has improved. Governments are far more aware of the problem, and they are better at sharing information, disrupting attacks, preventing havens, and otherwise making the lives of foreign fighters and the groups they support more difficult and dangerous.

The long-term hope is that transnational jihadism, like international anarchism and communism before it, will burn itself out or at least move from center stage to a sideshow. The movement is highly divided, and its local and regional concerns have in the past and may again overwhelm its global ambitions. Additionally, when in power, its successes are limited, with the movement unable to sustain a state. When the movement might decline is not clear: no one predicted in 1985 that the global jihadist movement would take off, and no one predicted that in a few years Communism would collapse. For now, governments must assume the movement will endure, try to counter it, and limit the damage that can be done by foreign fighters and the terrorists they inspire.

NOTES

Chapter 1

1. Greene, "Video Shows ISIS Thugs Planning Paris Terror Attacks"; Bayoumi, "ISIS Urges More Attacks on Western Disbelievers."
2. "What Happened at the Bataclan?"
3. Gartenstein-Ross and Barr, *Recent Attacks Illuminate the Islamic State's Europe Attack Network.*
4. Miller and Mekhennet, "One Woman Helped the Mastermind of the Paris Attacks."
5. Holley, "Paris Suspect Bragged of Eluding Bloated Crusader Intelligence."
6. Miller and Mekhennet, "One Woman Helped the Mastermind of the Paris Attacks."
7. Rayner, "Who Is Abdelhamid Abaaoud?"
8. Miller and Mekhennet, "One Woman Helped the Mastermind of the Paris Attacks."
9. Lawler, Fraser, Akkoc, and Millward, "Paris Attacks: Police Warn of EU Border Failures—As It Happened on Thursday Nov 19."
10. Goldman and Miller, "American Suicide Bomber's Travels in U.S., Middle East Went Unmonitored."
11. Goldberg and Bekiempis, "Bronx Man Who Got 'Terrorist Propaganda' from Chelsea Bomber Laughs during Court Appearance."
12. Lafitte, "How the Planners of the 2015 Paris Attacks Were Systematically Eliminated."
13. Malet, "The European Experience with Foreign Fighters and Returnees"; and Malet, *Foreign Fighters.*
14. Iley, "Vidal Sassoon Interview."

15. MI5 Security Service, "Foreign Fighters."

16. Horwitz and Goldman, "FBI Director: Number of Americans Traveling to Fight in Syria Increasing."

17. Susman, "Islamic State Presence in U.S. Is 'the New Normal,' FBI Director Says."

18. The White House, "Statement by the President on ISIL."

19. For a discussion, see Bonner, *Jihad in Islamic History.*

20. Malet, *Foreign Fighters,* 9.

21. See United Nations Security Council, *Resolution 2178.*

22. Meleagrou-Hitchens, Hughes, and Clifford, "The Travelers: American Jihadists in Syria and Iraq," 5–6.

23. Van Ginkel and Entenmann, *The Foreign Fighters Phenomenon in the European Union,* 3.

24. Interview with European counterterrorism official, June 2016.

25. Chu and Braithwaite, "The Impact of Foreign Fighters on Civil Conflict Outcomes." The study, however, included many nonjihadist conflicts.

26. Hegghammer, "Should I Stay or Should I Go?," 11.

27. Bakke, "Help Wanted?"

28. Fishman, *The Master Plan,* 43

29. Arntsen, "Yemen's Al-Qaida."

30. See Mansour, "Mum, I'm Fighting for Allah Now."

31. Filiu, "Ansar al-Fatah and 'Iraqi' Networks in France," 358.

Chapter 2

1. "Abdullah Azzam Documentary."

2. McGregor, "'Jihad and the Rifle Alone.'"

3. Hegghammer, "Abdallah Azzam and Palestine."

4. Ibid.

5. Brown, "Foreign Fighters in Historical Perspective," 18.

6. Central Intelligence Agency Directorate of Intelligence, "Afghanistan: Goals and Prospects for the Insurgents," 1.

7. See Riedel, *Deadly Embrace,* for a history.

8. Muhammad, *Safahat Min Sijill An-Ansar Al-Aarb Fi Afghanistan,* 45.

9. *Militant Ideology Atlas,* 286; McGregor, "'Jihad and the Rifle Alone'"; Bergen, *The Osama Bin Laden I Know*; Coll, *Ghost Wars,* 204.

10. Muhammad, *Safahat Min Sijill An-Ansar Al-Aarb Fi Afghanistan,* 88.

11. Hegghammer, *Jihad in Saudi Arabia,* 43.

12. Azzam, *Join the Caravan.*

13. Azzam, *Join the Caravan.* For the full argument, see Azzam, *Defending Muslim Lands Is among the Most Important of an Individual's Duties.*

14. Azzam, *Join the Caravan.*

15. McGregor, "'Jihad and the Rifle Alone.'"

16. Azzam, *Join the Caravan.*

17. Aboul-Enein, "The Late Sheikh Abdullah Azzam's Books."

18. Azzam, *Defending Muslim Lands Is among the Most Important of an Individual's Duties.*

19. *Militant Ideology Atlas,* 287.

20. Wagemakers, "Revisiting Wiktorowicz," 18.

21. Faraj, *Dhikrayat Arabi Afghani: Abu Ja'far Al-Misri Al-Qandahari,* 21.

22. Aboul-Enein, "The Late Sheikh Abdullah Azzam's Books."

23. Azzam, *Join the Caravan.*

24. Bergen, *The Osama Bin Laden I Know,* 30.

25. Stenersen, *Brothers in Jihad,* 80.

26. Bergen, *The Osama Bin Laden I Know,* 85; Hyman, "The Arabs in the Afghan War," 85; Coll, *Ghost Wars;* Williams, *Counter Jihad,* 27; Hamid and Farrall, *The Arabs at War in Afghanistan,* 37; Aboul-Enein, "The Late Sheikh Abdullah Azzam's Books"; Stenersen, *Brothers in Jihad,* 78.

27. Husayn, "Al-Zarqawi."

28. McGregor, " 'Jihad and the Rifle Alone' "; Stenersen, *Brothers in Jihad,* 87–91.

29. Hamid and Farrall, *The Arabs at War in Afghanistan,* 181; Brown, "Foreign Fighters in Historical Perspective," 281.

30. Zawahiri, "Knights under the Prophet's Banner."

31. Hamid and Farrall, *The Arabs at War in Afghanistan,* 24 and 140.

32. For a discussion of the enduring influence of these and other works, see West Point Combating Terrorism Center, *Militant Ideology Atlas* (2012), https://www.ctc.usma.edu/v2/wp-content/uploads/2012/04/Atlas-ResearchCompendium1.pdf; "Bin Ladin Guard Interviewed on Saudi 'Coup' against Salafi Youth, Al-Qa'ida"; McGregor, " 'Jihad and the Rifle Alone.' "

33. Aboul-Enein, "The Late Sheikh Abdullah Azzam's Books."

34. West Point Combating Terrorism Center, *Militant Ideology Atlas,* 44; Anas, *Weladt "Al Afghan Al Arab,"* 14.

35. Azzam, *Miraculous Signs of God the Compassionate;* Aboul-Enein, "The Late Sheikh Abdullah Azzam's Books."

36. Aboul-Enein, "The Late Sheikh Abdullah Azzam's Books."

37. *Al-Bunyan Al-Marsus,* no. 6 (1986): 40–42; Bergen, *The Osama Bin Laden I Know,* 33; Hegghammer, "Azzam," 137–138; McGregor, " 'Jihad and the Rifle Alone.' "

38. Farrall, "Revisiting al-Qaida's Foundation and Early History."

39. Stenersen, *Brothers in Jihad,* 76.

40. Hamid and Farrall, *The Arabs at War in Afghanistan,* 26.

41. Bergen, *The Osama Bin Laden I Know,* 28.

42. Faraj, *Dhikrayat Arabi Afghani: Abu Ja'far Al-Misri Al-Qandahari,* 33.

43. Hamid and Farrall, *The Arabs at War in Afghanistan,* 84.

44. Bergen, *The Osama Bin Laden I Know,* 29.

45. West Point Combating Terrorism Center, *Militant Ideology Atlas,* 47.

46. Hamid and Farrall, *The Arabs at War in Afghanistan,* 83; Stenersen, *Brothers in Jihad,* 91–92; *The 9/11 Commission Report,* 156; Muhammad, *Safahat Min Sijill Al-Ansar Al-Aarb Fi Afghanistan,* 112 and 199.

47. Muhammad, *Safahat Min Sijill Al-Ansar Al-Arab Fi Afghanistan,* 31; Ahmed Rashid, *Taliban,* 131; McGregor, "'Jihad and the Rifle Alone.'"

48. Bergen, *The Osama Bin Laden I Know,* 41; Hamid and Farrall, *The Arabs at War in Afghanistan,* 86; Coll, *Ghost Wars,* 63–72.

49. Muhammad, *Safahat Min Sijill Al-Ansar Al-Aarb Fi Afghanistan,* 60.

50. Coll, *Ghost Wars,* 82–87.

51. Ibid., 60; Brown, "Foreign Fighters in Historical Perspective," 22.

52. As quoted in Coll, *Ghost Wars,* 63.

53. Hamid and Farrall, *The Arabs at War in Afghanistan,* 42.

54. Faraj, *Dhikrayat Arabi Afghani: Abu Ja'far Al-Misri Al-Qandahari,* 26.

55. "Abdullah Azzam Documentary" (Part Two).

56. Azzam, "Martyrs."

57. McGregor, "'Jihad and the Rifle Alone.'"

58. *Al-Bunyan Al-Marsus,* no. 30 (1990): 11.

59. Coll, *Ghost Wars,* 203.

60. See the introduction to Azzam, *Join the Caravan.*

61. *Al-Bunyan Al-Marsus,* 9.

62. Wilhelmsen, *When Separatists Become Islamists,* 28n93.

63. *The 9/11 Commission Report,* 56.

64. Azzam, *Join the Caravan*; Aboul-Enein, "The Late Sheikh Abdullah Azzam's Books"; Aaron, "In Their Own Words," 69.

65. Stenersen, *Brothers in Jihad,* 93; Farrall, "Revisiting al-Qaida's Foundation and Early History."

66. Hamid and Farrall, *The Arabs at War in Afghanistan,* 111; Farrall, "Revisiting al-Qaida's Foundation and Early History."

67. As quoted in Bergen, *The Osama Bin Laden I Know,* 83.

68. *The 9/11 Commission Report,* 56.

69. Muhammad, *Safahat Min Sijill Al-Ansar Al-Aarb Fi Afghanistan,* 200.

70. Farrall, "Revisiting al-Qaida's Foundation and Early History."

71. Bergen, *The Osama Bin Laden I Know,* 52, 56–59; Brown, "Foreign Fighters in Historical Perspective," 24; Hamid and Farrall, *The Arabs at War in Afghanistan,* 98.

72. Hamid and Farrall, *The Arabs at War in Afghanistan,* 116.

73. Hegghammer, *Jihad in Saudi Arabia,* 45.

74. Ibid., 47.

75. Bergen, *The Osama Bin Laden I Know,* 85.

76. Hamid and Farrall, *The Arabs at War in Afghanistan,* 152; Farrall, "Revisiting al-Qaida's Foundation and Early History."

77. Scheuer, *Osama Bin Laden,* 65.

78. Hamid and Farrall, *The Arabs at War in Afghanistan,* 155.

79. Ibid., 165; Stenersen, *Brothers in Jihad,* 98–99.

80. As quoted in Stenersen, *Brothers in Jihad,* 108.

81. Hamid and Farrall, *The Arabs at War in Afghanistan,* 179.

82. Ibid., 173.

83. Stenersen, *Al-Qaida in Afghanistan,* 47–49.

84. "Radical Arabs Use Pakistan as Base for Holy War," *New York Times,* April 8, 1993.

85. Gargan, "Radical Arabs Use Pakistan as Base for Holy War"; Hyman, "Arab Involvement in the Afghan War," 87; "Arab Veterans of Afghanistan War Lead New Islamic Holy War."

86. "Bin Ladin 'Bodyguard' Details Al-Qa'ida's Time in Sudan, Move to Afghanistan"; Zawahiri, "Knights under the Prophet's Banner."

87. Cragin, "The Challenge of Foreign Fighter Returnees," 9; Nayil Mukhaybar, Sa'id al-Quwaysi, and Muhammad al-Zahir, "Arab Afghans Declare Jihad against the World," *Al Watan Al-'Arabi,* December 1, 1995; "Former Bin Ladin 'Bodyguard' Recalls Al-Qa'ida Figures," *Al-Quds Al-'Arabi,* March 31, 2005.

88. Cragin, "The Challenge of Foreign Fighter Returnees," 9.

89. See the testimony of Saif al-Adel in Husayn, "Al-Zarqawi."

90. *The 9/11 Commission Report,* 146.

91. "Arab Veterans of Afghanistan War Lead New Islamic Holy War."

92. "Bin Ladin Guard Interviewed on Saudi 'Coup' against Salafi Youth, Al-Qa'ida."

93. Hamid and Farrall, *The Arabs at War in Afghanistan,* 313.

94. "Bin Ladin Guard Interviewed on Saudi 'Coup' against Salafi Youth, Al-Qa'ida." Hamid and Farrall, *The Arabs at War in Afghanistan,* 313.

95. See Hartman, *The Roots of Terrorism in Indonesia;* and author's email correspondence with Julie Chernov Hwang, March 10, 2018.

96. Cragin, "The Challenge of Foreign Fighter Returnees," 13.

97. Tawil, *Brothers in Arms,* 51.

98. "Arab Veterans of Afghanistan War Lead New Islamic Holy War"; Cragin, "The Challenge of Foreign Fighter Returnees," 11–12.

99. "Arab Veterans of Afghanistan War Lead New Islamic Holy War."

100. Wright, *Looming Tower,* 177.

101. Jehl, "The Twin Towers; Rahman Errors Admitted"; *The 9/11 Commission Report,* 56–57.

102. *The 9/11 Commission Report,* 108.

Chapter 3

1. Clinton, "Clinton Transcript."

2. United States of America v. Enaam N. Arnaout, 64.

3. "Interview with Commander Abu Abdel Aziz 'Barbaros' "; Kohlmann, *Al-Qaida's Jihad in Europe,* 16–17; Hogg, "Arabs Join in Bosnia Battle."

4. Hegghammer, *Jihad in Saudi Arabia,* 48.
5. "Interview with Commander Abu Abdel Aziz 'Barbaros.' "
6. Danner, "The Horrors of a Camp Called Omarska and the Serb Strategy."
7. Human Rights Watch, *War Crimes in Bosnia-Hercegovina,* 1.
8. "Interview with Commander Abu Abdel Aziz 'Barbaros.' "
9. As quoted in Kohlmann, "The Afghan-Bosnian Mujahideen Network in Europe."
10. "Bin Ladin Guard Interviewed on Saudi 'Coup' against Salafi Youth, Al-Qa'ida."
11. Pargeter, *The New Frontiers of Jihad,* 39.
12. Velikonja, *Religious Separation and Political Intolerance in Bosnia-Herzegovina,* 230.
13. As quoted in Kohlmann, *Al-Qaida's Jihad in Europe,* 92.
14. "Former Bin Ladin 'Bodyguard' Discusses 'Jihad' in Bosnia, Somalia, Later Stage."
15. "The Meeting of Emir Abdul Aziz, the Commander of the Arabs in Bosnia, with Sheikh Al-Albani."
16. "Help from the Holy Warriors."
17. "Interview with Commander Abu Abdel Aziz 'Barbaros.' "
18. As quoted in Pargeter, *The New Frontiers of Jihad,* 37.
19. Kepel, *Jihad;* Schindler, *Unholy Terror,* 167.
20. Hedges, "Muslims from Afar Joining 'Holy War' in Bosnia."
21. Kohlmann, "The Afghan-Bosnian Mujahideen Network in Europe."
22. Kohlmann, *Al-Qaida's Jihad in Europe,* 73.
23. "Interview with Commander Abu Abdel Aziz 'Barbaros.' "
24. Hegghammer, *Jihad in Saudi Arabia,* 51.
25. Kohlmann, *Al-Qaida's Jihad in Europe,* 25.
26. As quoted in Kohlmann, "The Afghan-Bosnian Mujahideen Network in Europe." See also Hegghammer, *Jihad in Saudi Arabia,* 51.
27. United States of America v. Enaam N. Arnaout, "Evidence Proffer," 17.
28. Hegghammer, *Violent Islamism in Saudi Arabia,* 35–36, 174–176; Dobbs, "Saudis Funded Weapons for Bosnia"; Pargeter, *The New Frontiers of Jihad,* 40; Abdullah, "Interview with Abdul-Aziz."
29. Hegghammer, *Jihad in Saudi Arabia,* 51.
30. As quoted in Hegghammer, *Jihad in Saudi Arabia,* 35.
31. "Bin Ladin Guard Interviewed on Saudi 'Coup' against Salafi Youth, Al-Qa'ida."
32. "Bosnian Muslims Turn to Kuwait for Money, Arms."
33. Kohlmann, *Al-Qaida's Jihad in Europe,* 40.
34. European Court of Human Rights, "Case of Al Husin v. Bosnia and Herzegovina," 3; Kohlmann, *Al-Qaida's Jihad in Europe,* 37; Kohlmann, "The Afghan-Bosnian Mujahideen Network in Europe"; United States of

America v. Enaam N. Arnaout, "Evidence Proffer," 30–31; "Bin Ladin Guard Interviewed on Saudi 'Coup' against Salafi Youth, Al-Qa'ida."

35. Tziampiris, "Assessing Islamic Terrorism in the Western Balkans."
36. United Nations International Tribunal, "Prosecutor v. Rasim Delic Public Judgment," 54. Hegghammer, *Violent Islamism in Saudi Arabia,* 203.
37. Mustapha, "The Mujahideen in Bosnia," 746; Rafael, "The Mujahidin Left Bosnia for Chechnya." Some go even higher. See, e.g., Tziampiris, "Assessing Islamic Terrorism in the Western Balkans," 213; Abdullah, "Interview with Abdul-Aziz."
38. Malet, "The European Experience with Foreign Fighters and Returnees," 12.
39. Rafael, "The Mujahidin Left Bosnia for Chechnya"; Pargeter, *The New Frontiers of Jihad,* 37–39.
40. Leiken, *Europe's Angry Muslims.*
41. Quoted in https://www.theguardian.com/media/2005/jul/22/theguardian. pressandpublishing1.
42. Bronitsky, "British Foreign Policy: The Rise of Islamism in Britain, 1992–1995," 12.
43. Sageman, *Leaderless Jihad,* 7.
44. Bronitsky, "British Foreign Policy: The Rise of Islamism in Britain, 1992–1995," 12.
45. Kohlmann, "The Afghan-Bosnian Mujahideen Network in Europe," 5.
46. United States of America v. Enaam N. Arnaout, "Evidence Proffer," 24.
47. http://www.historycommons.org/entity.jsp?entity=abu_zubair_al madani_ 1&printerfriendly=true. See also United States of America v. Enaam N. Arnaout, "Evidence Proffer," 25.
48. See the comments of a spokesman for Arab fighters in Bosnia at http:// archive.aawsat.com/details.asp?section=4&issueno=8585&article=106081# WW9tEvnyvcv.
49. As quoted in Kohlmann, "The Afghan-Bosnian Mujahideen Network in Europe."
50. "Former Bin Ladin 'Bodyguard' Discusses 'Jihad' in Bosnia, Somalia, Later Stage."
51. Abdullah, "Interview with Abdul-Aziz"; "The Meeting of Emir Abdul Aziz, the Commander of the Arabs in Bosnia, with Sheikh Al-Albani."
52. Kohlmann, *Al-Qaida's Jihad in Europe,* 18.
53. As quoted in United Nations International Tribunal, "Prosecutor v. Rasim Delic Public Judgment," 37–38.
54. As quoted in Tziampiris, "Assessing Islamic Terrorism in the Western Balkans," 213.
55. Director of Central Intelligence, "Combatant Forces in the Former Yugoslavia," iii. See also 25.
56. Kohlmann, *Al-Qaida's Jihad in Europe,* 126; the quote is on 128.

57. Pyes, Meyer, and Rempel, "Bosnia Seen as Hospitable Base and Sanctuary for Terrorists."

58. Kohlmann, *Al-Qaida's Jihad in Europe,* 91.

59. United Nations International Tribunal, "Prosecutor v. Rasim Delic Public Judgment," 50–51.

60. Ibid., 57.

61. Schindler, *Unholy Terror,* 164.

62. United Nations International Tribunal, "Prosecutor v. Rasim Delic Public Judgment," 50–51; Hegghammer, *Jihad in Saudi Arabia,* 50; Jadallah, "From Syria to Bosnia"; Schindler, *Unholy Terror,* 164; and Pyes, Meyer, and Rempel, "Bosnia Seen as Hospitable Base and Sanctuary for Terrorists."

63. Kohlmann, *Al-Qaida's Jihad in Europe,* 90.

64. Ibid., 130.

65. United Nations International Tribunal, "Prosecutor v. Rasim Delic Public Judgment," 4–5.

66. "Witness Testimony from ICTY–Delic Judgment: Ali Hamad," 4 and 8.

67. Gibas-Krzak, "Contemporary Terrorism in the Balkans," 209.

68. Pargeter, *The New Frontiers of Jihad,* 35.

69. "Witness Testimony from ICTY–Delic Judgment: Ali Hamad," 2.

70. "Interview with Commander Abu Abdel Aziz 'Barbaros.'"

71. Jadallah, "From Syria to Bosnia"; International Crisis Group, "Bin Laden and the Balkans," 11.

72. Hogg, "Arabs Join in Bosnia Battle."

73. Kohlmann, *Al-Qaida's Jihad in Europe,* 54.

74. Ibid.,125.

75. Ibid., 130.

76. As quoted in ibid., 131.

77. Schindler, *Unholy Terror,* 224.

78. Hegghammer, *Jihad in Saudi Arabia,* 35; Kohlmann, *Al-Qaida's Jihad in Europe,* 58–61.

79. "Witness Testimony from ICTY–Delic Judgment: Ali Hamad," 5.

80. European Court of Human Rights, "Case of Al Husin v. Bosnia and Herzegovina," 3.

81. Kohlmann, *Al-Qaida's Jihad in Europe,* 24.

82. "Interview with Commander Abu Abdel Aziz 'Barbaros.'"

83. "Witness Testimony from ICTY–Delic Judgment: Ali Hamad," 3.

84. Hogg, "Arabs Join in Bosnia Battle."

85. "Help from the Holy Warriors."

86. As quoted in Mitchell, "The Contradictory Effects of Ideology on *Jihadist* War-Fighting," 822–823.

87. "Witness Testimony from ICTY–Delic Judgment: Ali Hamad," 7.

88. Jadallah, "From Syria to Bosnia."

89. Khalifa, "Internal Memo for Arab-Afghans in Bosnia Reveals Significant Differences with Their Leaders."
90. Nasiri, *Inside the Jihad,* 37.
91. "Former Bin Ladin 'Bodyguard' Discusses 'Jihad' in Bosnia, Somalia, Later Stage."
92. Schindler, *Unholy Terror,* 128.
93. See United Nations International Tribunal, "Prosecutor v. Rasim Delic Public Judgment," 49.
94. Jadallah, "From Syria to Bosnia."
95. Schindler, *Unholy Terror,* 98.
96. Jadallah, "From Syria to Bosnia."
97. Kohlmann, *Al-Qaida's Jihad in Europe,* 81–83.
98. Ibid., 108.
99. Bowman, "Bosnia: U.S. Military Operations."
100. Abdel Baqi Khalifa, "Internal Memo for Arab-Afghans in Bosnia Reveals Significant Differences with Their Leaders," *Al Sharq Al Awsat,* November 20, 2001.
101. Rafael, "The Mujahidin Left Bosnia for Chechnya"; "Former Bin Ladin 'Bodyguard' Discusses 'Jihad' in Bosnia, Somalia, Later Stage."
102. As quoted in Schindler, *Unholy Terror,* 254.
103. Kohlmann, "The Afghan-Bosnian Mujahideen Network in Europe."
104. Schindler, *Unholy Terror,* 215.
105. European Court of Human Rights, "Case of Al Husin v. Bosnia and Herzegovina," 4; Hoare, *How Bosnia Armed,* 60; Oluic, "Radical Islam's Periphery," 6.
106. Schindler, *Unholy Terror,* 264–266.
107. Bardos, "Jihad in the Balkans," 75; Zosak, "Revoking Citizenship in the Name of Counterterrorism," 219.
108. Pyes, Meyer, and Rempel, "Bosnia Seen as Hospitable Base and Sanctuary for Terrorists."
109. Usama Bin Ladin, "The Bosnia Tragedy and the Custodian of the Two Holy Mosques" (Statement no. 18 from the Advice and Reform Committee, 1995).
110. "Interview with Commander Abdul-Aziz," n.d.
111. *The 9/11 Commission Report,* 155.
112. Flade, "The Islamic State Threat to Germany," 12.
113. Bardos, "Jihad in the Balkans," 74. *The 9/11 Commission Report,* 147.
114. Pyes, Meyer, and Rempel, "Bosnia Seen as Hospitable Base and Sanctuary for Terrorists."
115. Pyes, Meyer, and Rempel, "Bosnia Seen as Hospitable Base and Sanctuary for Terrorists."
116. Walton, "Bosnia Tackles 'Foreign Fighters.'"

Chapter 4

1. "Uncoventional Warfare," *GoArmy.com*, accessed October 18, 2017, https://www.goarmy.com/special-forces/primary-missions/unconventional-warfare.html.
2. A quoted in Lance, *Triple Cross,* xxx.
3. Weiser and Risen, "The Masking of a Militant."
4. As quoted in West Point Combating Terrorism Center, "Ali Mohamad."
5. Williams and McCormick, "Al Qaeda Terrorist Worked with FBI." For overview of Mohamad, see Lance, *Triple Cross*; West Point Combating Terrorism Center, "Ali Mohamad"; Weiser and Risen, "The Masking of a Militant"; Weiser, "Indicted Ex-Sergeant Says He Knows Who Bombed U.S. Embassies"; and Weiser, "Terror Case to End Secrets of Plea Deals by Informers."
6. Weiser and Risen, "The Masking of a Militant"; Statement of Patrick J. Fitzgerald, 4; West Point Combating Terrorism Center, "Ali Mohamad: A Biographical Sketch"; Williams and McCormick, "Bin Laden's Man in Silicon Valley."
7. Hays and Theimer, "In a Life of Double-Crosses, Egyptian Worked with Green Berets and Bin Laden"; Williams and McCormick, "Bin Laden's Man in Silicon Valley."
8. Williams and McCormick, "Bin Laden's Man in Silicon Valley."
9. "Turning Out Guerillas and Terrorists to Wage a Holy War"; Hamid and Farrall, *The Arabs at War in Afghanistan,* 135.
10. Berger, "Paving the Road to 9/11."
11. *The 9/11 Commission Report,* 68.
12. West Point Combating Terrorism Center, "Ali Mohamad: A Biographical Sketch."
13. Hamid and Farrall, *The Arabs at War in Afghanistan,* 136.
14. *The 9/11 Commission Report,* 57; West Point Combating Terrorism Center, "Ali Mohamad."
15. *The 9/11 Commission Report,* 58; Coll, *Ghost Wars,* 269.
16. *The 9/11 Commission Report,* 62–63.
17. Hamid and Farrall, *The Arabs at War in Afghanistan,* 230.
18. Nasiri, *Inside the Jihad,* 120.
19. *The 9/11 Commission Report,* 64; Hamid and Farrall, *The Arabs at War in Afghanistan,* 207.
20. "U.S. Pre-9/11 Memos."
21. Stenersen, "Blood Brothers of a Marriage of Convenience?" 3.
22. Stenersen, "Brothers in Jihad," 157–158.
23. "Former Bin Ladin 'Bodyguard' Recalls Al-Qa'ida Figures."
24. "Monograph on Terrorist Financing," 28.
25. Williams, "The 055 Brigade."

26. Williams, "On the Trail of the 'Lions of Islam,' " 7.

27. Stenersen, *Brothers in Jihad,* 297–313, with the quote on 310.

28. Coll, *Directorate S,* 20–22.

29. As quoted in Aaron, "In Their Own Words," 198.

30. "Former Bin Ladin 'Bodyguard' Discusses Al-Qa'ida Stance on Saudi, Iraqi Affairs."

31. "Turning Out Guerillas and Terrorists to Wage a Holy War."

32. "Jihad against Christians and Jews: World Islamic Front Statement."

33. Zawahiri, "Knights under the Prophet's Banner."

34. Abdul Sattar Khan, "Osama Urges Ummah to Continue Jihad," May 12, 2001.

35. "Interview with Jean-Pierre Filiu."

36. Hamid and Farrall, *The Arabs at War in Afghanistan,* 232–233.

37. Elias, "Video Offers Strong Bin Laden–USS Cole Link."

38. *The 9/11 Commission Report,* 66–67; Suri, *The Call for Global Islamic Resistance,* 896.

39. Felter and Brachman, "An Assessment of the 516 Combatant Status Review Tribunal (CSRT) Unclassified Summaries," 11.

40. "Bin Ladin Guard Interviewed on Saudi 'Coup' against Salafi Youth, Al-Qa'ida."

41. *The 9/11 Commission Report,* 148.

42. Onishi, "A Tale of the Mullah and Muhammad's Amazing Cloak."

43. Hamid and Farrall, *The Arabs at War in Afghanistan,* 270.

44. "Afghanistan."

45. Brynjar Lia, *Architect of Global Jihad,* 249–250.

46. Hamid and Farrall, *The Arabs at War in Afghanistan,* 6.

47. Holman, " 'Gonna Get Myself Connected.' "

48. *9/11 and Terrorist Travel,* 54.

49. Rohde and Chivers, "Qaeda's Grocery Lists and Manuals of Killing"; Felter and Brachman, "An Assessment of the 516 Combatant Status Review Tribunal (CSRT) Unclassified Summaries," 15.

50. United States of America v. Usama Bin Laden, "Testimony of Jamal Ahmed al-Fadl."

51. *9/11 and Terrorist Travel,* 56.

52. Evidence regarding the Iran-Al Qaeda relationship from the *9/11 Commission* can be found at http://www.meforum.org/670/irans-link-to-al-qaeda-the-9-11-commissions.

53. See *9/11 and Terrorist Travel.*

54. Aaron, "In Their Own Words," 288.

55. "Monograph on Terrorist Financing," 20. *The 9/11 Commission Report,* 55.

56. Statement of Patrick J. Fitzgerald, 3.

57. "Monograph on Terrorist Financing," 27–28.

58. Nasiri, *Inside the Jihad,* 169.

59. Stenersen, *Brothers in Jihad*, 95.
60. Nasiri, *Inside the Jihad*, 194 and 205.
61. "Bodyguard Interviewed on First Meeting with Bin-Ladin, Al-Qa'ida Beginnings."
62. United States of America v. Usama Bin Laden, "Testimony of Jamal Ahmed al-Fadl."
63. Rohde and Chivers, "Qaeda's Grocery Lists and Manuals of Killing."
64. Felter and Brachman. "An Assessment of the 516 Combatant Status Review Tribunal (CSRT) Unclassified Summaries," 16.
65. "Former Bin Ladin 'Bodyguard' Discusses Al-Qa'ida Training Methods, 'Libraries.'"
66. Faraj, *Dhikrayat Arabi Afghani: Abu Ja'far Al-Misri Al-Qandahari*, 30.
67. Nasiri, *Inside the Jihad*, 140.
68. "Turning Out Guerillas and Terrorists to Wage a Holy War."
69. "Bodyguard Interviewed on First Meeting with Bin-Ladin, Al-Qa'ida Beginnings."
70. Nasiri, *Inside the Jihad*, 2.
71. Ibid., 143.
72. Ibid., 209.
73. Rohde and Chivers, "Qaeda's Grocery Lists and Manuals of Killing."
74. Nasiri, *Inside the Jihad*, 219; "Turning Out Guerillas and Terrorists to Wage a Holy War."
75. Nasiri, *Inside the Jihad*, 167.
76. "Former Bin Ladin 'Bodyguard' Recalls Al-Qa'ida Figures," *Al-Quds Al-'Arabi*, March 31, 2005.
77. Bergen, "After the War in Iraq: What Will the Foreign Fighters Do?" 103.
78. United States of America v. Enaam N. Arnaout, "Evidence Proffer," 36.
79. Faraj, *Dhikrayat Arabi Afghani: Abu Ja'far Al-Misri Al-Qandahari*, 41.
80. Stenersen, *Brothers in Jihad*, 273.
81. Hamid and Farrall, *The Arabs at War in Afghanistan*, 117.
82. Nasiri, *Inside the Jihad*, 230.
83. Rohde and Chivers, "Qaeda's Grocery Lists and Manuals of Killing."
84. Ibid.
85. Nasiri, *Inside the Jihad*, 146–147.
86. "Bin Ladin Guard Interviewed on Saudi 'Coup' against Salafi Youth, Al-Qa'ida."
87. Nasiri, *Inside the Jihad*, 151; Tawil, *Brothers in Arms*, 38.
88. Rohde and Chivers, "Qaeda's Grocery Lists and Manuals of Killing."
89. "Former Bin Ladin 'Bodyguard' Discusses Al-Qa'ida Training Methods, 'Libraries.'"
90. Rohde and Chivers, "Qaeda's Grocery Lists and Manuals of Killing."
91. Nasiri, *Inside the Jihad*, 179.
92. Rohde and Chivers, "Qaeda's Grocery Lists and Manuals of Killing."

93. Nasiri, *Inside the Jihad,* 148.
94. Rohde and Chivers, "Qaeda's Grocery Lists and Manuals of Killing."
95. Hamid and Farrall, *The Arabs at War in Afghanistan,* 288.
96. Nasiri, *Inside the Jihad,* 234.
97. As quoted in Aaron, "In Their Own Words," 263.
98. Nasiri, *Inside the Jihad,* quotes on 178, 149, and 177.
99. Hamid and Farrall, *The Arabs at War in Afghanistan,* 230 and 259; Fishman, *The Master Plan,* 68; Stenersen, *Brothers in Jihad,* 262.
100. "Letter from Abu Yayha."
101. Ibrahim, "As Algerian Civil War Drags On, Atrocities Grow."
102. Hamid and Farrall, *The Arabs at War in Afghanistan,* 212.
103. Ibid., 5 and 104.
104. Ibid., 229; Fishman, *The Master Plan,* 13; Stenersen, "Blood Brothers of a Marriage of Convenience?" 11.
105. Nasiri, *Inside the Jihad,* 192.
106. Hamid and Farrall, *The Arabs at War in Afghanistan,* 221.
107. Khan, "Usama Bin Ladin' Al-Qaeda' Splits as Ideologue Parts Ways."
108. Wood, "The American Climbing the Ranks of ISIS"; Stenersen, *Brothers in Jihad,* 104–107.
109. *The 9/11 Commission Report,* 65.
110. As quoted in Stenersen, "Blood Brothers of a Marriage of Convenience?" 8.
111. Ibid., 5.
112. Al-Suri letter, as quoted in Fishman, *The Master Plan,* 13–14.
113. Bergen, *The Osama Bin Laden I Know,* 250.
114. Stenersen, *Brothers in Jihad,* 275–293.
115. "Samuel Berger, 9/11 Prepared Testimony."
116. National Commission on Terrorist Attacks upon the United States."
117. See "Monograph on Terrorist Financing," 30–40.
118. For a more complete review, see National Commission on Terrorist Attacks upon the United States ("The 9/11 Commission"). *9/11 and Terrorist Travel* and National Commission on Terrorist Attacks upon the United States, *The 9/11 Commission Report.*
119. As quoted in Stenersen, "Brothers in Jihad," 176.
120. Quoted in ibid., 200.
121. As quoted in ibid., 211. See also 252–253.
122. Lia, *Architect of Global Jihad,* 290.
123. Byman, *Al Qaeda, The Islamic State, and the Global Jihadist Movement,* n. 28.
124. "Interview with Jean-Pierre Filiu."
125. Stenersen, *Brothers in Jihad,* 303 and 327–335.
126. Wright, *The Looming Tower: Al-Qaeda and the Road to 9/11.*
127. See Berntsen and Pezzullo, *Jawbreaker;* and Coll, *Directorate S,* for an account of this campaign.
128. As quoted in Aaron, "In Their Own Words," 16.

129. Leigh Neville, *Special Forces in the War on Terror,* 50–51.

130. Hastert, "Operation Anaconda," 11.

131. Biddle, "Afghanistan and the Future of Warfare," vii.

132. Ibid., 28.

133. Hastert, "Operation Anaconda," 16.

134. See data compiled at http://hegghammer.com/text.cfm?path=2176.

135. Stenersen, "Al Qaeda's Foot Soldiers," 180.

136. Stenersen, "Al Qaeda's Foot Soldiers," 176–186; Coll, *Directorate S.*

137. Williams, "On the Trail of the 'Lions of Islam,'" 13; Coll, *Directorate S.* Fair, "Pakistan's Promises to Fight Terrorism Are a Bad Joke."

138. Stenersen, "Al Qaeda's Foot Soldiers," 185.

139. Stenersen, "Blood Brothers of a Marriage of Convenience?" 16–17.

140. Ibid., 11–19.

141. Hamid and Farrall, *The Arabs at War in Afghanistan,* 291.

142. Stenersen, "Blood Brothers of a Marriage of Convenience?" 2.

143. Stenersen, *Brothers in Jihad,* 341.

144. Williams, "Return of the Arabs."

145. "Petraeus: 'Double Digits' of al-Qaeda Fighters in Afghanistan," *Washington Independent,* June 17, 2010.

146. "Turning Out Guerillas and Terrorists to Wage a Holy War."

Chapter 5

1. Al-'Ubaydi, "Khattab," 1. The Sword of Islam label comes from WaIslamah. net, "The Life and Times of Khattab."

2. WaIslamah.net, "The Life and Times of Khattab."

3. Williams, "Allah's Foot Soldiers," 160.

4. WaIslamah.net, "The Life and Times of Khattab."

5. Williams, "Allah's Foot Soldiers," 165.

6. As quoted in Williams, "Allah's Foot Soldiers," 156.

7. Al-'Ubaydi, "Khattab," 10.

8. Moore and Tumelty, "Foreign Fighters and the Case of Chechnya," 424.

9. WaIslamah.net, "The Life and Times of Khattab."

10. Al-'Ubaydi, "Khattab," 14.

11. Suri, *The Call for Global Islamic Resistance,* 786.

12. WaIslamah.net, "The Life and Times of Khattab."

13. Al-'Ubaydi, "Khattab," 15.

14. Seely, *Russo-Chechen Conflict,* 60.

15. Tolstoy, *Hadji Murat,* 132.

16. Williams, *Inferno in Chechnya,* 20–30.

17. Moore, "Foreign Bodies," 407.

18. Moore and Tumelty, "Foreign Fighters and the Case of Chechnya," 416.

19. Al-Shishani, "The Rise and Fall of Arab Fighters in Chechnya," 7.

20. Moore and Tumelty, "Foreign Fighters and the Case of Chechnya," 415–416.
21. LaFraniere, "How Jihad Made Its Way to Chechnya."
22. Kroupenev, "Radical Islam in Chechnya."
23. Al-Shishani, "The Rise and Fall of Arab Fighters in Chechnya," 6.
24. Wilhelmsen, *When Separatists Become Islamists,* 12.
25. Williams, "Allah's Foot Soldiers," 157.
26. Kroupenev, "Radical Islam in Chechnya"; Wilhelmsen, *When Separatists Become Islamists,* 12; Al-Shishani, "The Rise and Fall of Arab Fighters in Chechnya," 7.
27. Amnesty International, "Russian Federation," 1.
28. Gall and De Wall, *Chechnya,* 242.
29. Figures listed on Wilhelmsen, *When Separatists Become Islamists,* 70.
30. WaIslamah.net, "The Life and Times of Khattab."
31. Williams, "Allah's Foot Soldiers," 161; McGregor, "Amir Abu Al-Walid"; United States of America v. Enaam N. Arnaout, "Evidence Proffer," 73–75.
32. Wilhelmsen, *Between a Rock and a Hard Place,* 40.
33. Souleimanov and Ditrych, "The Internationalisation of the Russian-Chechen Conflict," 1216.
34. Williams. *Inferno in Chechnya,* 100–104.
35. Kroupenev, "Radical Islam in Chechnya."
36. Williams, *Inferno in Chechnya,* 112–114.
37. Wilhelmsen, *When Separatists Become Islamists,* 13, 46
38. Ibid., 14.
39. LaFraniere, "How Jihad Made Its Way to Chechnya."
40. For this account, see Williams, "Allah's Foot Soldiers," 157.
41. Williams, "Allah's Foot Soldiers," 157.
42. Moore and Tumelty, "Foreign Fighters and the Case of Chechnya," 417.
43. Al 'Ubaydi, "Khattab," 29; McGregor, "Amir Abu Al-Walid."
44. Tumelty, "The Rise and Fall of Foreign Fighters in Chechnya."
45. WaIslamah.net, "The Life and Times of Khattab."
46. Vidino, "The Arab Foreign Fighters and the Sacralization of the Chechen Conflict," 7.
47. WaIslamah.net, "The Life and Times of Khattab."
48. Al-Shishani, "The Rise and Fall of Arab Fighters in Chechnya," 10–11.
49. United States of America v. Enaam N. Arnaout, "Evidence Proffer," 92.
50. Moore and Tumelty, "Foreign Fighters and the Case of Chechnya," 417.
51. Nesser, *Islamist Terrorism in Europe,* 37–44.
52. Tumelty, "The Rise and Fall of Foreign Fighters in Chechnya"; Moore, "Foreign Bodies," 400–404.
53. Al-Shishani, "The Rise and Fall of Arab Fighters in Chechnya," 11.
54. Moore and Tumelty, "Foreign Fighters and the Case of Chechnya," 418–421.

55. *The 9/11 Commission Report,* 149; Hegghammer, *Jihad in Saudi Arabia,* 56; WaIslamah.net, "The Life and Times of Khattab"; Williams, "Allah's Foot Soldiers," 161.

56. Williams, "Allah's Foot Soldiers," 162.

57. Williams, *Inferno in Chechnya,* 114.

58. Ibid., 112.

59. Wilhelmsen, *When Separatists Become Islamists,* 50–52.

60. Khuzam, "The Leader of the Arab Fighters in Chechnya."

61. Williams, "Allah's Foot Soldiers," 164.

62. Kroupenev, "Radical Islam in Chechnya."

63. Wilhelmsen, *When Separatists Become Islamists,* 31 and 49.

64. Ibid., 29.

65. Al-'Ubaydi, "Khattab," 21–22.

66. Moore, "Foreign Bodies," 400–405; Moore and Tumelty, "Foreign Fighters and the Case of Chechnya," 419.

67. Moore, "Foreign Bodies," 403; LaFraniere, "Moscow Eager to Tie Rebels in Chechnya to Bin Laden"; Al-Shishani, "Salafi-Jihadis and the North Caucasus," 17; Al-Shishani, "The Rise and Fall of Arab Fighters in Chechnya," 10; Williams, "Allah's Foot Soldiers," 164; Wilhelmsen, *When Separatists Become Islamists,* 33; WaIslamah.net, "The Life and Times of Khattab."

68. Al-'Ubaydi, "Khattab," 18–19; Al-Shishani, "The Rise and Fall of Arab Fighters in Chechnya," 4; Moore and Tumelty, "Foreign Fighters and the Case of Chechnya," 421.

69. Williams, "Allah's Foot Soldiers," 162.

70. Wilhelmsen, *When Separatists Become Islamists,* 16, 26–27, and 32.

71. Khuzam, "The Leader of the Arab Fighters in Chechnya."

72. As quoted in Vidino, "The Arab Foreign Fighters and the Sacralization of the Chechen Conflict," 2.

73. Balburov, "Shamil Basayev."

74. As quoted in Wilhelmsen, *When Separatists Become Islamists,* 56.

75. Kroupenev, "Radical Islam in Chechnya."

76. Moore and Tumelty, "Foreign Fighters and the Case of Chechnya," 419.

77. As quoted in Garner, "Chechnya and Kashmir," 425.

78. Wilhelmsen, *When Separatists Become Islamists,* 58.

79. See Geibel, "Khattab's Audacious Raid," 341–349 for an account.

80. Hamid and Farrall, *The Arabs at War in Afghanistan,* 248.

81. Al-'Ubaydi, "Khattab," 20; WaIslamah.net, "The Life and Times of Khattab."

82. Hegghammer, *Jihad in Saudi Arabia,* 37.

83. Al-'Ubaydi, "Khattab," 23.

84. Hamid and Farrall, *The Arabs at War in Afghanistan,* 169.

85. Moore, "Foreign Bodies," 399.

86. Moore and Tumelty, "Foreign Fighters and the Case of Chechnya," 422.

87. Williams, "Allah's Foot Soldiers," 169–170.

Chapter 6

1. LaFraniere, "How Jihad Made Its Way to Chechnya."
2. Wilhelmsen, *When Separatists Become Islamists,* 15.
3. Williams, "Allah's Foot Soldiers," 167.
4. LaFraniere, "How Jihad Made Its Way to Chechnya."
5. Vidino, "The Arab Foreign Fighters and the Sacralization of the Chechen Conflict," 5; "Russian Agency Carries Interview with Dagestan Insurgent Commander"; Moore and Tumelty, "Foreign Fighters and the Case of Chechnya," 420; Wilhelmsen, *When Separatists Become Islamists,* 34; and Williams, "Allah's Foot Soldiers," 165.
6. Zakriyev, "Chechen Warlord Denies Involvement in Terror Blasts."
7. As quoted in al-'Ubaydi, "Khattab," 27.
8. WaIslamah.net, "The Life and Times of Khattab."
9. "Scars Remain amid Chechen Revival."
10. Cohen, "Russia and Religious Terrorism."
11. Wilhelmsen, *When Separatists Become Islamists,* 24.
12. Ibid., 36.
13. Hegghammer, *Jihad in Saudi Arabia,* 79.
14. LaFraniere, "How Jihad Made Its Way to Chechnya."
15. McGregor, "Islam, Jamaats and Implications for the North Caucasus—Part 2."
16. Myers, *The New Tsar,* 243.
17. Bakke, "Help Wanted?" 179.
18. Seely, *Russo-Chechen Conflict,* 307–308.
19. Gall, "Muslim Fighters Embraces Warrior Mystique." Sindelar, "In Annals of Russian Crime, North Caucasians Remain Popular Scapegoat"; Zakriyev, "Chechen Warlord Denies Involvement in Terror Blasts."
20. William, *Inferno in Chechnya,* 145–150; Myers, *The New Tsar,* 158–161.
21. Myers, *The New Tsar,* 185.
22. Williams, "Allah's Foot Soldiers," 161.
23. Polling in Russia is often difficult, but the relatively independent Levada Center records a significant increase in trust in government as Putin led an aggressive response in Chechnya. See http://www.levada.ru/eng/approval-and-trust.
24. Zakriyev, "Chechen Warlord Denies Involvement in Terror Blasts"; McGregor, "Islam, Jamaats and Implications for the North Caucasus—Part 1."
25. Wilhelmsen, *When Separatists Become Islamists,* 62.
26. Al-Shishani, "Salafi-Jihadis and the North Caucasus," 7.
27. Moore and Tumelty, "Foreign Fighters and the Case of Chechnya," 425.
28. Kroupenev, "Radical Islam in Chechnya."
29. Vidino, "The Arab Foreign Fighters and the Sacralization of the Chechen Conflict," 7.

30. As quoted in Wilhelmsen, *When Separatists Become Islamists,* 31.
31. As quoted in ibid., 64.
32. Al-Shishani, "The Rise and Fall of Arab Fighters in Chechnya," 12.
33. Vidino, "The Arab Foreign Fighters and the Sacralization of the Chechen Conflict," 7.
34. McGregor, "The Amnesty Offensive."
35. McGregor, "New Fronts, New Focus."
36. As quoted in al-'Ubaydi, "Khattab," 6.
37. Moore and Tumelty, "Foreign Fighters and the Case of Chechnya," 422.
38. WaIslamah.net, "The Life and Times of Khattab."
39. Al-'Ubaydi, "Khattab," 32; Williams, "Allah's Foot Soldiers," 173.
40. Williams, *Inferno in Chechnya*, 195.
41. Moore, "Foreign Bodies," 403.
42. "Mastermind of Russian SchoolSiege Killed," *CNN.com* (July 10, 2006), http://www.cnn.com/2006/WORLD/europe/07/10/russia.basayev/index.html; Williams, *Inferno in Chechnya*, 201–202.
43. Williams, *Inferno in Chechnya*, 196–198; Myers, *The New Tsar,* 308.
44. Moore, "Foreign Bodies," 401.
45. Hegghammer, "Should I Stay or Should I Go?" 6.
46. Hegghammer, "The Rise of Muslim Foreign Fighters," 63.
47. Al-Shishani, "The Rise and Fall of Arab Fighters in Chechnya," 14.
48. Williams, *Inferno in Chechnya*, 203; Chivers, "Success of Chechen Amnesty Plan Is Contested."
49. Numbers on attacks in Chechnya are available via the Global Terrorism Database.
50. Coticchia, "The Military Impact of Foreign Fighters on the Battlefield," 132.
51. McGregor, "The Amnesty Offensive."
52. Garner, "Chechnya and Kashmir," 426.
53. Moore, "Foreign Bodies," 405.
54. Moore and Tumelty, "Foreign Fighters and the Case of Chechnya," 422.
55. Williams, "Allah's Foot Soldiers," 174.
56. Moore, "Foreign Bodies," 403.
57. Tumelty, "The Rise and Fall of Foreign Fighters in Chechnya."
58. Moore, "Foreign Bodies," 401.
59. Clifford, "The Cup and the Caliphate."
60. LaFraniere, "How Jihad Made Its Way to Chechnya"; McGregor, "Islam, Jamaats and Implications for the North Caucasus—Part 2."
61. Moore, "Foreign Bodies," 402.
62. Moore and Tumelty, "Foreign Fighters and the Case of Chechnya," 422.
63. Clifford, "The Cup and the Caliphate."
64. Moore, "Foreign Bodies," 408–409.
65. Williams, *Inferno in Chechnya*, 224–225.
66. Flood, "The Caucasus Emirate," 16–17.

67. Amnesty International, "Russian Federation," 302–306.
68. Clifford, "The Cup and the Caliphate."

Chapter 7

1. Fishman, *The Master Plan,* 5; Tønnessen, *Al-Qaida in Iraq,* 117; Abu Hanieh and Abu Rumman, "The 'Islamic State' Organization," 29.
2. Fishman, *The Master Plan,* 5.
3. Tønnessen, *Al-Qaida in Iraq,* 120.
4. Abu Hanieh and Abu Rumman, "The 'Islamic State' Organization," 31.
5. Husayn, "Al-Zarqawi."
6. Wright, *The Looming Tower,* 72; Slackman, "Bin Laden's Mother Tried to Stop Him"; Randal, *Osama,* 55.
7. See the testimony of Saif al-Adel in Husayn, "Al-Zarqawi."
8. Abu Hanieh and Abu Rumman, "The 'Islamic State' Organization," 33.
9. Fishman, *The Master Plan,* 14–15; Hamid and Farrall, *The Arabs at War in Afghanistan,* 257.
10. See the testimony of Saif al-Adel in Husayn, "Al-Zarqawi."
11. Al-Tawil, "Part 3: Al Zarqawi Is Given Al Qaida Control over Jihadist Routes to Iraq."
12. Winter and Al-Saud,"The Obscure Theologian Who Shaped ISIS."
13. Tønnessen, *Al-Qaida in Iraq,* 130–133.
14. Fishman, *The Master Plan,* 20.
15. See the testimony of Saif al-Adel in Husayn, "Al-Zarqawi."
16. Tønnessen, *Al-Qaida in Iraq,* 147.
17. Fishman, *The Master Plan,* 23–27; Tenet, *At the Center of the Storm,* 350.
18. Tønnessen, *Al-Qaida in Iraq,* 137.
19. "Letter to Abu Basir."
20. Tønnessen, *Al-Qaida in Iraq,* 206; Tønnessen, "Training on a Battlefield," 544; Camp, *Operation Phantom Fury,* 24.
21. As quoted in Aaron, "In Their Own Words," 233.
22. Tønnessen, "Training on a Battlefield," 544; Hoffman, "Insurgency and Counterinsurgency in Iraq," 105; Tønnessen, *Al-Qaida in Iraq,* 261.
23. Tønnessen, "Training on a Battlefield," 546.
24. Tønnessen, *Al-Qaida in Iraq,* 199–201, 214.
25. Husayn, "Al-Zarqawi."
26. As quoted in Aaron, "In Their Own Words," 234.
27. Tønnessen, "Training on a Battlefield," 543.
28. Fishman, *The Master Plan,* 52.
29. Tønnessen, *Al-Qaida in Iraq,* 220–223.
30. Tønnessen, "Training on a Battlefield," 549–555.
31. Malkasian, "Signaling Resolve, Democratization, and the First Battle of Fallujah," 428.

32. Malkasian, "Signaling Resolve, Democratization, and the First Battle of Fallujah," 431.

33. Camp, *Operation Phantom Fury*, 3, 17–18.

34. As quoted in Camp, *Operation Phantom Fury*, 3.

35. Camp, *Operation Phantom Fury*, 58.

36. Malkasian, "Signaling Resolve, Democratization, and the First Battle of Fallujah," 434.

37. Camp, *Operation Phantom Fury*, 58.

38. Malkasian, "Signaling Resolve, Democratization, and the First Battle of Fallujah," 424–437; Camp, *Operation Phantom Fury*, 13; Tønnessen, *Al-Qaida in Iraq*, 195–196, 241.

39. International Crisis Group, "In Their Own Words"; Malkasian, "Signaling Resolve, Democratization, and the First Battle of Fallujah," 438–441.

40. Tønnessen, *Al-Qaida in Iraq*, 231; Malkasian, "Signaling Resolve, Democratization, and the First Battle of Fallujah," 447.

41. See Bergen, *The Longest War*, 165.

42. Duyvesteyn and Peeters, "Fickle Foreign Fighters?" 18.

43. Tønnessen, *Al-Qaida in Iraq*, 237–239.

44. Malkasian, "Signaling Resolve, Democratization, and the First Battle of Fallujah," 447.

45. Tønnessen, *Al-Qaida in Iraq*, 245–247.

46. International Crisis Group, "In Their Own Words"; Stalinsky, Sosnow, and Khayat, "ISIS's Use of Twitter."

47. Tønnessen, *Al-Qaida in Iraq*, 234.

48. Husayn, "Al-Zarqawi."

49. Oukaci, "The 'Quagmire' of the Jihad."

50. See the testimony of Saif al-Adel in Husayn, "Al-Zarqawi."

51. Aaron, "In Their Own Words," 203.

52. Abu Hanieh and Abu Rumman, "The 'Islamic State' Organization," 50.

53. Cordesman, *Iraq's Insurgency and the Road to Civil Conflict*, 112–113.

54. "Foreign Terrorists in Fallujah."

55. Tønnessen, "Training on a Battlefield," 553.

56. "Interview with Jean-Pierre Filiu."

57. Tønnessen, *Al-Qaida in Iraq*, 244, 250–252.

58. Hegghammer, "Saudi Militants in Iraq," 10.

59. Whiteside, "A Pedigree of Terror," 4.

60. Holman, "French Foreign Fighters in Iraq"; Whiteside, "Lighting the Path"; Husayn, "Al-Zarqawi."

61. Ayman al-Zawahiri's letter to Abu Musab al-Zarqawi.

62. Zarqawi letter to Bin Laden.

63. Fishman, *Dysfunction and Decline*, 2.

64. Husayn, "Al-Zarqawi."

65. Fishman, *The Master Plan*, 60.

66. Aaron, "In Their Own Words," 103.

67. See the testimony of Maqdisi in Husayn, "Al-Zarqawi."

68. As quoted in Abu Hanieh and Abu Rumman, "The 'Islamic State' Organization," 45 and 48; Aaron, "In Their Own Words," 239.

69. Zarqawi letter. Available at ww.cpa-iraq.org/transcripts/2004021_zarqawi_full.html.

70. As quoted in Aaron, "In Their Own Words," 248.

71. Husayn, "Al-Zarqawi."

72. As quoted in Fishman, *The Master Plan*, 50.

73. Ibid., 51.

74. Felter and Fishman, "Al-Qa'ida's Foreign Fighters in Iraq," 20; Felter and Fishman, "Becoming a Foreign Fighter," 46–48; Hafez, *Suicide Bombers in Iraq*, 179; Obaid and Cordesman, "Saudi Militants in Iraq."

75. Brian Fishman and Joseph Felter, "Al-Qa'ida's Foreign Fighters in Iraq: A First Look at the Sinjar Records," Combating Terrorism Center at West Point, January 2, 2007.

76. Anonymous, "On the Ground from Syria to Iraq," in *Bombers, Bank Accounts, & Bleedout: Al-Qa'ida's Road in and out of Iraq*, 87.

77. Ibid., 88.

78. *Bombers, Bank Accounts, & Bleedout: Al-Qa'ida's Road in and out of Iraq*, 6.

79. Anonymous, "On the Ground from Syria to Iraq," 90.

80. Abu Hanieh and Abu Rumman, "The 'Islamic State' Organization," 100–101.

81. "Current and Projected National Security Threats to the United States," Hearing before the Select Committee on Intelligence of the U.S. Senate, January 11, 2007, 44.

82. Obaid and Cordesman, "Saudi Militants in Iraq."

83. Hegghammer, "Saudi Militants in Iraq," 12.

84. Zavis, "A Profile of Iraq's Foreign Insurgents"; Hegghammer, "Saudi Militants in Iraq," 12; Hafez, *Suicide Bombers in Iraq*, 175; Felter and Fishman, "Becoming a Foreign Fighter," 42; Abdul-Ahad, "Outside Iraq but Deep in the Fight." In the Sinjar Records only 157 of the 606 recorded fighters indicated a profession, but of those, 42.6% (67) were students, which includes high school, university, secondary school, and religious school. Felter and Fishman, "Al-Qa'ida's Foreign Fighters in Iraq," 17.

85. Watts, "Foreign Fighters: How Are They Being Recruited?"

86. Felter and Fishman, "Becoming a Foreign Fighter," 36 and 51.

87. Hafez (2007) documented 102 known suicide bombers from the publicized memorial biographies. Saudis were in the clear lead with forty-four, followed by eight Italians, seven Kuwaitis, seven Iraqis, six Syrians, three Libyans, three Jordanians, two Belgians, two Frenchmen, two Spaniards, two Egyptians, one Lebanese, one Tunisian, one Moroccan, one Briton, one Turk, and eleven unknown, for a total of 73.5% from Arab countries and 14.7% from Europe. Obaid and Cordesman used estimates provided by Saudi intelligence that claimed the breakdown for the estimated three thousand foreigners in Iraq was

Algeria 20%, Syria 18%, Yemen 17%, Sudan 15%, Egypt 13%, Saudi Arabia 12%, and other 5%. Alan B. Kreuger (2006) examined the 311 foreigners from twenty-seven countries captured by Coalition forces. The most came from Egypt 25%, followed by Syria 21%, Sudan 12%, Saudi Arabia 10%, and Jordan 5.5%. Finally, Felter and Fishman's analysis of the captured Sinjar documents of 595 fighter profiles identified Saudi Arabia 41% as providing almost half the recruits, with Libya at almost 20%.

88. Felter and Fishman, *Al-Qa'ida's Foreign Fighters*, 9.
89. Hegghammer, "Should I Stay or Should I Go," 5.
90. Abu Hanieh and Abu Rumman, "The 'Islamic State' Organization," 49.
91. Aaron, "In Their Own Words," 184.
92. As quoted in Felter and Fishman, "Becoming a Foreign Fighter," 38.
93. Felter and Fishman, "Becoming a Foreign Fighter," 59.
94. Ibid., 57.
95. "Addendum to the Report of the Islamic Maghreb."
96. Testimony of Treasury Acting Assistant Secretary Daniel L. Glaser, "Financing for the Iraqi Insurgency"; Burns and Semple, "US Finds Iraq Insurgency Has Funds to Sustain Itself"; Bahney et al., *An Economic Analysis of the Financial Records of al-Qa'ida in Iraq,* 36–37.
97. *Bombers, Bank Accounts, & Bleedout,* 11.
98. Shapiro, "Bureaucratic Terrorists," 74; "Analysis of the State of ISI," NMEC-2007-612449 (n.d., author unknown), published by the West Point Counterterrorism Center.
99. Bergen and Cruickshank, "Al Qa'ida in Iraq."
100. Fishman, *The Master Plan,* 25.
101. See, e.g., Harmony, "AQI Template for Leaving Iraq or Leaving the AQI Organization," NMEC-2007-657739.
102. Bowden, "The Ploy."
103. "U.S. raises Zarqawi reward to $25m."
104. Cuomo, McNiff, and ABC News Law and Justice Unit, "The Men in the Shadows"; Flynn, Juergens, and Cantrell, "Employing ISR," 57.
105. Cordesman, *Iraq's Insurgency and the Road to Civil Conflict,* 337–338.

Chapter 8

1. A Gallup poll in October 2006 found that 20 percent of Americans wanted to withdraw immediately and 34 percent within a year. Similarly, Pew Research Center polling in March 2006 found 50 percent of Americans thought the United States should "bring troops home as soon as possible." "Iraq," *Gallup*; "Public Attitudes toward the War in Iraq: 2003–2008," *Pew Research Center.*
2. Director of National Intelligence, "Declassified Key Judgments of the National Intelligence Estimate," *Trends in Global Terrorism: Implications for the United States,* April 2006.

3. Aaron, "In Their Own Words," 258.
4. Ayman al-Zawahiri, "Letter to Zarqawi."
5. Tønnessen, *Al-Qaida in Iraq,* 171.
6. Ibid., 186.
7. Roggio, "Who Is Abu Omar al Baghdadi?"
8. "Biography of Abu Omar al Baghdadi."
9. Wing, "Who Was Al Qaeda In Iraq's Abu Omar al-Baghdadi?"; Ingram and Whiteside, "Don't Kill the Caliph!"
10. Robertson, "Terrorist or Mythic Symbol."
11. Gordon, "Leader of Al Qaeda Group in Iraq Was Fictional, U.S. Military Says"; Roggio, "Islamic State of Iraq—An al Qaeda Front."
12. Whiteside, "Lighting the Path," 10.
13. See McCants, *The ISIS Apocalypse,* for a review.
14. Fishman, *The Master Plan,* 90.
15. Abu Hanieh and Abu Rumman, "The 'Islamic State' Organization," 64.
16. "Analysis of the State of ISI."
17. Ibid.
18. Fishman, *The Master Plan,* 109.
19. Fishman, *Dysfunction and Decline,* 1 and 18.
20. Pew Research Center, "Islamic Extremism."
21. As quoted in Fishman, *The Master Plan,* 77.
22. Pew Research Center, "The Great Divide."
23. Some estimates are even higher, up to 1,300 on the first day, according to Knichmeyer, "Blood on Our Hands."
24. Gettleman, "Bound, Blindfolded and Dead."
25. Kukis, "Ethnic Cleansing in a Baghdad Neighborhood?"
26. Fishman, *Dysfunction and Decline,* 2.
27. "Analysis of the State of ISI."
28. As quoted in Fishman, *Dysfunction and Decline,* 7.
29. "Response from Raja to Brother Abu al-'Abbas."
30. "Analysis of the State of ISI."
31. Ibid.
32. Fishman, *The Master Plan,* 130.
33. Ibid., 107.
34. "Analysis of the State of ISI."
35. Ibid.
36. Jung et al., "Managing a Transnational Insurgency," 18.
37. "Analysis of the State of ISI."
38. See Shapiro, "Bureaucratic Terrorists," 70–73.
39. Ibid., 72.
40. Ibid.
41. See Jung et al., "Managing a Transnational Insurgency," 16n18.
42. As quoted in Fishman, *Dysfunction and Decline,* 4.

43. Fishman, *The Master Plan,* 99.
44. Anonymous, "On the Ground from Syria to Iraq," 91.
45. International Crisis Group, "Exploiting Disorder," 16
46. "Analysis of the State of ISI."
47. Kaplan, "Man Versus Afghanistan."
48. "Analysis of the State of ISI."
49. Fishman, *The Master Plan,* 131.
50. Al-Hamdan, *Bay'ah to the Islamic State of Iraq,* 10.
51. "Analysis of the State of ISI."
52. Ibid.
53. "Hussein Cell/Network Status Update Report."
54. Fishman, *Dysfunction and Decline,* 15.
55. "Hussein Cell/Network Status Update Report."
56. Whiteside, "Lighting the Path," 8–12.
57. Abu Hanieh and Abu Rumman, "The 'Islamic State' Organization," 101.
58. Fishman, *The Master Plan,* 135.
59. "Analysis of the State of ISI." See also Hafez, "Jihad after Iraq," 86; and
    Bombers, Bank Accounts, & Bleedout, 6.
60. Couglin, "Foreign Fighters Pour in to Wage War on Coalition Forces."
61. Tønnessen, "Iraq as a Training Ground for Global Jihadis," 557.
62. Whiteside, *Lighting the Path,* 16.
63. Fishman, *The Master Plan,* 142; Whiteside, *The Smiling Scented Men,* 119
    and 145.
64. Fishman, *The Master Plan,* 147.
65. "Abdullah Anas: Zawahri Did Not Struggle in Afghanistan."
66. See Islamic Army of Iraq, "Reply of the Islamic Army in Iraq to the Speeches
    of Brother Abu Umar al-Baghdadi."
67. Fishman, *The Master Plan,* 48.
68. The visit was paid for by the Qaddafi Foundation and part of a Libyan
    government effort to win over terrorism experts and get them to support the
    regime's deradicalization program. It was clearly a propaganda effort, but the
    jihadist statements echoed those of jihads in other countries.
69. "Zawhari's Webchat."
70. Fishman, *The Master Plan,* 148–156.
71. Bergen, "After the War in Iraq," 112.
72. Bergen and Cruickshank, "The Iraq Effect."
73. "Analysis of the State of ISI."

Chapter 9

1. Abu Mansuur al-Amriki, "The Story of an American Jihaadi Part One," n.p.
2. Ibid.; Elliott, "The Jihadist Next Door."
3. Al-Amriki, "The Story of an American Jihaadi Part One," n.p.

4. Elliott, "The Jihadist Next Door."

5. Ibid.

6. Ibid.

7. Abu Mansuur al-Amriki, "The Story of an American Jihaadi Part One," n.p.

8. Bergen, *The United States of Jihad,* 173.

9. Elliott, "The Jihadist Next Door."

10. Abu Mansuur al-Amriki, "The Story of an American Jihaadi Part One," n.p.

11. Elliott, "The Jihadist Next Door."

12. Ibid.; Abu Mansuur al-Amriki, "The Story of an American Jihaadi Part One," n.p.

13. Abu Mansuur al-Amriki, "The Story of an American Jihaadi Part One," n.p.

14. Ibid.

15. Mueller, "The Evolution of Political Violence," 7.

16. Bridgman, "Bin Laden Praises Fighters in New Tape."

17. Elliott, "The Jihadist Next Door."

18. Abu Mansuur al-Amriki, "The Story of an American Jihaadi Part One," n.p.

19. International Crisis Group, "Somalia's Divided Islamists," 2, 3n8.

20. International Crisis Group, "Somalia: Al-Shabaab," 1.

21. Anzalone, "The Life and Death of Al-Shabab Leader Ahmed Godane."

22. Hansen, *Al-Shabaab in Somalia,* 20; International Crisis Group, "Somalia's Islamists," 3.

23. International Crisis Group, "Somalia's Islamists."

24. Marchal, "Islamic Political Dynamics in the Somali Civil War," 341.

25. International Crisis Group, "Somalia's Islamists," 6.

26. Marchal, "A Tentative Assessment of the Somali Harakat Al-Shabaab," 383; Hamid and Farrall, *The Arabs at War in Afghanistan,* 185.

27. Hansen, *Al-Shabaab in Somalia,* 21; International Crisis Group, "Somalia's Islamists," 9.

28. International Crisis Group, "Somalia's Islamists," 7–10.

29. Harmony, AFGP-2002-600104, 1, 189; Hamid and Farrall, *The Arabs at War in Afghanistan,* 189.

30. "Former Bin Ladin 'Bodyguard' Discusses 'Jihad' in Bosnia, Somalia, Later Stage."

31. International Crisis Group, "Counter-Terrorism in Somalia," 7.

32. United States Military Academy 2007, 20; AFGP-2002-600104, 5: United States Military Academy 2007, 22.

33. International Crisis Group, "Counter-Terrorism in Somalia," 6; Marchal, "A Tentative Assessment of the Somali Harakat Al-Shabaab."

34. Hansen, *Al-Shabaab in Somalia,* 21–22.

35. Hansen, *Al-Shabaab in Somalia,* 24.

36. Mueller, "The Evolution of Political Violence," 8.

37. Hansen, *Al-Shabaab in Somalia,* 26–27.

38. International Crisis Group, "Somalia's Islamists," December 12, 2005, 11.

39. Menkhaus, "The Somalia Crisis."

40. Marchal, "A Tentative Assessment of the Somali Harakat Al-Shabaab," 383.

41. Turbiville, Meservey, and Forest, "Countering the al-Shabaab Insurgency in Somalia," 8.

42. International Crisis Group, "Somalia's Islamists," 8.

43. Hansen, *Al-Shabaab in Somalia,* 47–49.

44. Gordon and Mazzetti, "U.S. Used Base in Ethiopia to Hunt Al Qaeda."

45. Turbiville, Meservey, and Forest, "Countering the al-Shabaab Insurgency in Somalia," 23.

46. Marchal, "A Tentative Assessment of the Somali Harakat Al-Shabaab," 392; International Crisis Group, "Somalia: Al-Shabaab," 17–18.

47. Turbiville, Meservey, and Forest, "Countering the al-Shabaab Insurgency in Somalia," 14.

48. Hansen, *Al-Shabaab in Somalia,* 46–51; 55.

49. Ibid., 9, 35, 45; Botha and Abdile, "Radicalisation and al-Shabaab Recruitment in Somalia."

50. Hansen, *Al-Shabaab in Somalia,* 63.

51. Shinn, "Al Shabaab's Foreign Threat to Somalia," 25–32.

52. Hansen, *Al-Shabaab in Somalia,* 43, 75.

53. Turbiville, Meservey, and Forest, "Countering the al-Shabaab Insurgency in Somalia," 26–27.

54. As quoted in "United States of America v. Yahya Farooq Mohammad," 7–8.

55. Marchal, "A Tentative Assessment of the Somali Harakat Al-Shabaab," 393.

56. Mueller, "The Evolution of Political Violence," 18; " 'Foreign Fighters Actively' Taking Part in Somalia Capital Clashes"; Nor and Houreld, "Somali Defector Reveals Foreigners' Role in War." Hansen, *Al-Shabaab in Somalia*, 50–54, 60–61; Marchal, "A Tentative Assessment of the Somali Harakat Al-Shabaab," 397; Turbiville, Meservey, and Forest, "Countering the al-Shabaab Insurgency in Somalia," 24.

57. Abu Mansuur al-Amriki, "The Story of an American Jihaadi Part One."

58. Ibid.

59. Hansen, *Al-Shabaab in Somalia,* 98.

60. Taarnby and Hallundbaek, "Al Shabaab"; Shinn, "Al Shabaab's Foreign Threat to Somalia."

61. Hansen, *Al-Shabaab in Somalia,* 58, 114; International Crisis Group, "Somalia: Al-Shabaab," 15.

62. Abu Mansuur al-Amriki, "The Story of an American Jihaadi Part One," n.p.

63. Ibid.

64. Ibid.

65. Ibid.

66. Ibid.

67. Ibid.

68. Hansen, *Al-Shabaab in Somalia,* 65.

69. Williams, "Fighting for Peace in Somalia," 240.

70. Anzalone, "The Life and Death of Al-Shabab Leader Ahmed Godane."

71. Ibid.

72. Hansen, *Al-Shabaab in Somalia,* 84–86, 91–92, 115.

73. Turbiville, Meservey, and Forest, "Countering the al-Shabaab Insurgency in Somalia," 12.

74. International Crisis Group, "Somalia: Al-Shabaab—It Will Be a Long War," June 26, 2014, 16.

75. Hiraal Institute, "The AS Finance System," 7.

76. Abu Mansuur al-Amriki, "The Story of an American Jihaadi Part One."

77. Ibid.

78. Hansen, *Al-Shabaab in Somalia,* 93.

79. International Crisis Group, "Somalia: Al-Shabaab—It Will Be a Long War," 4, 7–14.

80. Marchal, "A Tentative Assessment of the Somali Harakat Al-Shabaab," 388–389.

81. Turbiville, Meservey, and Forest, "Countering the al-Shabaab Insurgency in Somalia," 40.

82. Ibid., 35.

83. Hansen, *Al-Shabaab in Somalia,* 74, 84–85, 90.

84. International Crisis Group, "Counter-Terrorism in Somalia: Losing Hearts and Minds?" 4.

85. International Crisis Group, "Somalia's Divided Islamists," 9.

86. Turbiville, Meservey, and Forest, "Countering the al-Shabaab Insurgency in Somalia," 36.

87. Abu Mansuur al-Amriki, "The Story of an American Jihaadi Part One."

88. Schifrin and Fannin, "How Al-Shabab Is Recruiting Young Men from Kenya."

89. Abu Mansuur al-Amriki, "The Story of an American Jihaadi Part One."

90. Turbiville, Meservey, and Forest, "Countering the al-Shabaab Insurgency in Somalia," 37.

91. As quoted in International Crisis Group, "Somalia: Al-Shabaab: It Will Be a Long War."

92. Mueller, "The Evolution of Political Violence," 16.

93. Turbiville, Meservey, and Forest, "Countering the al-Shabaab Insurgency in Somalia," 33.

94. Hansen, *Al-Shabaab in Somalia,* 91–92, 102,115.

95. Shephard, "Inside the Secret Somalia Rehab Camp for Former Shabab Members."

96. Turbiville, Meservey, and Forest, "Countering the al-Shabaab Insurgency in Somalia," 39–41.

97. Anzalone, "The Life and Death of Al-Shabab Leader Ahmed Godane."

98. Roggio, "Shabaab Kills American Jihadist Omar Hammami and British Fighter."
99. Berger, "Omar and Me"; Anzalone, "The Life and Death of Al-Shabab Leader Ahmed Godane."
100. "Al-Amriki and al-Britani: Militants 'Killed' in Somalia."
101. Shephard, "Inside the Secret Somalia Rehab Camp for Former Shabab Members."
102. Statement of Philip Mudd before Senate Homeland Security Committee.
103. McCants, "How Zawahiri Lost al Qaeda."
104. International Crisis Group, "Somalia's Divided Islamists," 5.
105. As quoted in Mueller, "The Evolution of Political Violence," 10.
106. Hansen, *Al-Shabaab in Somalia,* 96.
107. Ibid., 126–131; Harding, "Somali Defector."
108. Gettleman, "Bomb Suspected in Deadly Explosion on Somali Jet."
109. Hansen, *Al-Shabaab in Somalia,* 104 and 150.
110. "New Ugandan Battle Group Arrives in Somalia."
111. "AMISOM Welcomes Burundi's Contribution to Restoring Peace in Somalia,"
112. Jeremy Binnie, "Ethiopia Withdrawing Troops from Somalia, but Not AMISOM."
113. Gordon and Mazzetti, "U.S. Used Base in Ethiopia to Hunt Al Qaeda."
114. Williams, "A Navy SEAL Was Killed in Somalia"; Whitlock, "US Has Deployed Military Advisors to Somalia."
115. Bruton and Williams, "Counterinsurgency in Somalia."
116. Williams, "A Navy SEAL Was Killed in Somalia."
117. *Department of Defense*, "Pentagon Confirms Death of Al-Shabab Co-founder"; McCrummen and DeYoung, "U.S. Airstrike Kills Somali Accused of Links to Al-Qaeda."
118. Mazzetti, Gettleman, and Schmitt, "In Somalia, U.S. Escalates a Shadow War."
119. Marchal, "A Tentative Assessment of the Somali Harakat Al-Shabaab," 398.
120. United Kingdom Home Office, *Country Policy and Information Note Somalia (South and Central): Fear of Al Shabaab*, 12–15.
121. International Crisis Group, "Somalia: Al-Shabaab—It Will Be a Long War," 2.
122. Turbiville, Meservey, and Forest, "Countering the al-Shabaab Insurgency in Somalia," 72.
123. Mazzetti, Gettleman, and Schmitt, "In Somalia, U.S. Escalates a Shadow War."
124. Marchal, "A Tentative Assessment of the Somali Harakat Al-Shabaab," 392.
125. International Crisis Group, "Somalia: Al-Shabaab—It Will Be a Long War," 12–13.
126. Turbiville, Meservey, and Forest, "Countering the al-Shabaab Insurgency in Somalia," 77.

127. Hiraal Institute, "The AS Finance System," 8.

128. Hansen, *Al-Shabaab in Somalia,* 113, 143.

Chapter 10

1. Lamothe, "Here's the Transcript of the Video Showing Steven Sotloff's Reported Execution."

2. Walsh, "Facing the Terrorists Accused of Killing a Friend"; Goldman and Schmitt, "2 of ISIS's Infamous British Fighters Are Captured by Syrian Kurds."

3. Mekhennet, "How a Journalist Uncovered the True Identity of Jihadi John."

4. Bradley, "My Son the ISIS Executioner."

5. Sengupta and Dearden, "ISIS Militants Hunted Down in Syria after Intelligence Extracted from Captured Members of 'The Beatles' Cell.'"

6. "Among the Believers Are Men: Abu Muharib al-Muhajir," *Dabiq* #13.

7. "The Emwazi emails." Mekhennet, "How a Journalist Uncovered the True Identity of Jihadi John."

8. "Mohammed Emzawi," "Counter Extremism Project."

9. Tinnes, "Although the (Dis-)Believers Dislike It."

10. "Department of Defense Press Briefing."

11. "Among the Believers Are Men: Abu Muharib al-Muhajir," *Dabiq* #13.

12. "Britons Accused of Being Islamic State 'Beatles' Call Beheadings 'Regrettable.'"

13. Walsh, "Facing the Terrorists Accused of Killing a Friend."

14. Sengupta and Dearden, "ISIS Militants Hunted Down in Syria after Intelligence Extracted from Captured Members of 'The Beatles' Cell.'"

15. According to David Malet, the Russian and Spanish civil wars drew 50,000 and 60,000 volunteers, respectively. If Shi'a foreigners fighting in Syria are included, the number in Syria probably exceeds 60,000. See Malet, "The European Experience with Foreign Fighters and Returnees," 9.

16. Poushter and Manevich, "Globally People Point to ISIS and Climate Change as Leading Security Threats."

17. International Crisis Group, "Exploiting Disorder," 17.

18. Abu Hanieh and Abu Rumman, "The 'Islamic State' Organization," 166.

19. Ramsay, "IS Files Reveal Assad's Deals with Militants."

20. Reuter, "Secret Files Reveal Structure of Islamic State."

21. Beirut NOW Lebanon, October 19, 2015.

22. International Crisis Group, "Exploiting Disorder," 17.

23. Abu Hanieh and Abu Rumman, "The 'Islamic State' Organization," 186.

24. Abu Bakr al-Baghdadi, "Bring Good Tidings to the Believers."

25. Abu Hanieh and Abu Rumman, "The 'Islamic State' Organization," 197–199, 204.

26. Abu Hanieh and Abu Rumman, "The 'Islamic State' Organization," 122–123.

27. Fisher, "In Rise of ISIS, No Single Missed Key but Many Strands of Blame."

28. As quoted in Abu Hanieh and Abu Rumman, "The 'Islamic State' Organization," 169.

29. Gartenstein-Ross, "How Many Fighters Does the Islamic State Really Have?"

30. Barrett, "Beyond the Caliphate," 7.

31. Interview conducted in May 2014.

32. As quoted in Azinović and Jusić, "The Lure of the Syrian War," 10.

33. *The Foreign Fighters Phenomenon in the European Union,* 53.

34. Hamed and Barrett, "Enhancing the Understanding of Foreign Terrorist Fighters Phenomenon in Syria," 3.

35. McDowall, "Saudi Opposition Clerics Make Sectarian Call to Jihad in Syria."

36. See Abu Bakr al-Baghdadi, "A Letter to the Holy Wars and the Muslim Community on the Month of Ramadan."

37. Hamed and Barrett, "Enhancing the Understanding of Foreign Terrorist Fighters Phenomenon in Syria," 17.

38. See Wood, *The Way of the Strangers,* for a description.

39. Dodwell, Milton, and Rassler, "The Caliphate's Global Workforce," 19.

40. Hamed and Barrett, "Enhancing the Understanding of Foreign Terrorist Fighters Phenomenon in Syria," 3.

41. Tinnes, "Although the (Dis-)Believers Dislike It."

42. Dawson and Amarasingam, "Talking to Foreign Fighters," 11.

43. Reinares, "Terrorist Mobilization, Undemocratic Salafism, and the Terrorist Threat to the EU."

44. Shtuni, "Ethnic Albanian Foreign Fighters in Iraq and Syria."

45. Gall, "How Kosovo Was Turned into Fertile Ground for ISIS."

46. Ibid.

47. Interview with Danish government official, May 2014.

48. Heil, "The Berlin Attack."

49. Abu Hanieh and Abu Rumman, "The 'Islamic State' Organization," 211.

50. As quoted in Abu Hanieh and Abu Rumman, "The 'Islamic State' Organization," 243.

51. *The Foreign Fighters Phenomenon in the European Union,* 53.

52. Coolsaet, "Facing the Fourth Foreign Fighters Wave," 3.

53. Azinović and Jusić, "The Lure of the Syrian War," 42.

54. International Crisis Group, "The North Caucasus Insurgency and Syria."

55. *The Foreign Fighters Phenomenon in the European Union,* 53; Barrett, "Beyond the Caliphate," 7.

56. Hamed and Barrett, "Enhancing the Understanding of Foreign Terrorist Fighters Phenomenon in Syria," 17 and 37.

57. Azinović and Jusić, "The Lure of the Syrian War," 7.

58. Heil, "The Berlin Attack."

59. Coolsaet, "Facing the Fourth Foreign Fighters Wave."

60. "Abdullah Anas, the Son-in-Law of the Spiritual Leader of the 'Afghan Arabs'."

61. See the tweets of Jenan Moussa based on documents she uncovered in Syria at https://twitter.com/jenanmoussa/status/976893098826588161

62. "Found at an Islamic State Training Camp."

63. Townsend, "Rape and Slavery Was Lure for UK ISIS Recruits."

64. Hamed and Barrett, "Enhancing the Understanding of Foreign Terrorist Fighters Phenomenon in Syria," 4.

65. Holman, "Belgian and French Foreign Fighters in Iraq 2003–2005," 605.

66. Abu Hanieh and Abu Rumman, "The 'Islamic State' Organization," 275.

67. Klausen, "Tweeting the Jihad," 1.

68. Carr, "With Videos of Killings, ISIS Sends Medieval Message by Modern Method."

69. Whiteside, Craig. 2016b. *Lighting the Path,* 19.

70. Abu Hanieh and Abu Rumman, "The 'Islamic State' Organization," 276.

71. Hamed and Barrett, "Enhancing the Understanding of Foreign Terrorist Fighters Phenomenon in Syria," 5.

72. Al-Tamimi, "The Archivist."

73. Stalinsky, Sosnow and Khayat, "ISIS's Use of Twitter, Other U.S. Social Media to Disseminate Images"; Cottee, "Inside Europol's Online War against ISIS."

74. Kibble, "Beheading, Raping, and Burning."

75. Quran 8:12. See Kibble, "Beheading, Raping, and Burning" for a discussion.

76. As quoted in Klausen, "Tweeting the Jihad," 4.

77. As quoted in Coolsaet, "Facing the Fourth Foreign Fighters Wave," 24 and 36.

78. Winter, "The Virtual 'Caliphate'," 29.

79. Coolsaet, "Facing the Fourth Foreign Fighters Wave," 17.

80. Berger, "Making CVE Work."

81. Pew Research Center, "Articles of Faith"; for a broader discussion, see McCants, *The Islamic State Apocalypse.*

82. Whiteside, Craig. 2016b. *Lighting the Path,* 26.

83. Winter, "An Integrated Approach to Islamic State Recruitment," 9.

84. Winter, "The Virtual 'Caliphate'," 7.

85. "Honor Is in Jihad."

86. Winter, "An Integrated Approach to Islamic State Recruitment," 10.

87. Klausen, "Tweeting the Jihad," 2.

88. Berger and Perez, *The Islamic State's Diminishing Returns on Twitter.*

89. Callimachi, "ISIS and the Lonely Young American."

90. Stevens and Neumann, "Countering Online Radicalisation," 12.

91. Homeland Security Committee, "Final Report of the Task Force on Combating Terrorist and Foreign Fighter Travel," 17–18.

92. Stein, "Islamic State Networks in Turkey."

93. Dawson and Amarasingam, "Talking to Foreign Fighters," 9.

94. Weggemans, Bakker, and Grol, "Who Are They and Why Do They Go?"

95. Winter, "The Virtual 'Caliphate'," 7.

96. Price and al-'Ubaydi, "The Islamic State's Internal Rifts and Social Media Ban."

97. Berger and Morgan, "The ISIS Twitter Census," 3.

98. Berger and Perez, "The Islamic State's Diminishing Returns on Twitter," 4.

99. Cottee, "Inside Europol's Online War against ISIS."

100. Stalinsky, Sosnow, and Khayat, "ISIS's Use of Twitter, Other U.S. Social Media to Disseminate Images."

101. See document provided by Charlie Winter at https://twitter.com/charliewinter/status/866325785728217088

102. Dodwell, Milton, and Rassler, "Then and Now," 7; Dodwell, Milton, and Rassler, "The Caliphate's Global Workforce," 9.

103. See Barrett, "Beyond the Caliphate."

104. Shih, "Uighurs Fighting in Syria Take Aim at China."

105. Watts, "Beyond Syria and Iraq, the Islamic State's HR Files Illuminate Dangerous Trends"; Gall, "How Kosovo Was Turned into Fertile Ground for ISIS"; Shtuni, "Ethnic Albanian Foreign Fighters in Iraq and Syria."

106. Dodwell, Milton, and Rassler, "Then and Now," 3–13; Dodwell, Milton, and Rassler, "The Caliphate's Global Workforce," iv.

107. Dodwell, Milton, and Rassler, "The Caliphate's Global Workforce," 15.

108. "Sterman and Rosenblatt, "All Jihad Is Local, Volume II," 5; Rosenblatt, "All Jihad Is Local," 5 and 20.

109. Shtuni, "Dynamics of Radicalization and Violent Extremism in Kosovo."

110. Rosenblatt, "All Jihad Is Local," 16.

111. Dodwell, Milton, and Rassler, "Then and Now," 11; Dodwell, Milton, and Rassler, "The Caliphate's Global Workforce," 27.

112. Cook and Vale, *From Daesh to 'Diaspora.'*

113. Manisera, " 'I Came for Jihad' "; Khan, "Hundreds of Foreign Women Who Joined ISIS Captured by Kurdish Forces in Syria."

114. Al-Tamimi, "The Archivist."

115. Milton and Dodwell, "Jihadi Brides?"

116. Barrett, "Beyond the Caliphate," 10–11; Milton and Dodwell, "Jihadi Brides?"

117. International Crisis Group, "The North Caucasus Insurgency and Syria."

118. Watts, "Beyond Syria and Iraq, the Islamic State's HR Files Illuminate Dangerous Trends."

119. Roth, "The Russian Village."

120. BBC, "Chechens Drawn South to Fight against Syria's Assad."

121. "BBC, "Chechnya Struggles to Stop Wave of Recruits Joining IS."

122. International Crisis Group, "The North Caucasus Insurgency and Syria."

123. Roth, "The Russian Village."

124. Quotes are from International Crisis Group, "The North Caucasus Insurgency and Syria."

125. Roth, "The Russian Village."

126. International Crisis Group, "The North Caucasus Insurgency and Syria."

127. Stein, "Islamic State Networks in Turkey."

128. Ibid.

129. Azinović and Jusić, "The Lure of the Syrian War," 36; Dodwell, Milton, and Rassler, "Then and Now," 14.

130. Winter, "An Integrated Approach to Islamic State Recruitment," 6 and 11.

131. Dodwell, Milton, and Rassler, "The Caliphate's Global Workforce," 26.

132. Stein, "Islamic State Networks in Turkey."

133. As quoted in Uslu, "Jihadist Highway to Jihadist Haven," 784.

134. Uslu, "Jihadist Highway to Jihadist Haven," 785–794.

135. Miller and Mekhennet, "Undercover Teams, Increased Surveillance and Hardened Borders."

136. Barrett, "Beyond the Caliphate," 16.

137. Arango, "Turkey Moves to Clamp Down on Border, Long a Revolving Door."

138. Stein, "Islamic State Networks in Turkey."

139. Barrett, "Beyond the Caliphate," 17.

140. International Crisis Group, "The North Caucasus Insurgency and Syria."

141. Osborne, "Isis Kills 'Raqqa Is Being Slaughtered Silently' Activist in Turkey."

142. Giglio and al-Awad, "The Escape."

143. Karadeniz and Dikmen, "Turkish Shelling Kills 55 Islamic State Militants in Syria."

144. Normark, Ranstorp, and Ahlin, "Financial Activities Linked to Persons from Sweden and Denmark," 10.

145. Barrett, "Beyond the Caliphate," 5.

146. Diehl, Lehberger, and Schlesier, "New Documents Help Identify Islamic State Returnees."

147. Dodwell, Milton, and Rassler, "The Caliphate's Global Workforce," 4.

148. Haq, "High-Profile Fighters Joined ISIS Army, Made Advances."

149. As quoted in Zelin, "The Others," 7.

150. "Found at an Islamic State Training Camp"; Flade, "The Islamic State Threat to Germany," 11; Coticchia, "The Military Impact of Foreign Fighters on the Battlefield: The Case of ISIL," 129.

151. Hamed and Barrett, "Enhancing the Understanding of Foreign Terrorist Fighters Phenomenon in Syria," 43.

152. "Found at an Islamic State Training Camp."

153. Shih, "Uighurs Fighting in Syria Take Aim at China."

154. Dawson and Amarasingam, "Talking to Foreign Fighters," 14. Lowercase use of ISIS in the original. For Islamic State rhetoric, see *Dabiq,* November 15, 2015.

155. Speckhard and Yayla, "Eyewitness Accounts from Recent Defectors from Islamic State," 107.

156. Abu Hanieh and Abu Rumman, "The 'Islamic State' Organization," 281.

157. Al-Tamimi, "The Archivist."
158. Homeland Security Committee, "Final Report of the Task Force on Combating Terrorist and Foreign Fighter Travel," 13.
159. Coticchia, "The Military Impact of Foreign Fighters on the Battlefield: The Case of ISIL," 131–134.
160. Abu Hanieh and Abu Rumman, "The 'Islamic State' Organization," 319.
161. International Crisis Group, "The North Caucasus Insurgency and Syria."
162. El-Ghobashy and Nabhan, "Foreign ISIS Fighters Increasingly Isolated in Mosul Battle"; Fine, "Operation Inherent Resolve: Report to the United States Congress, April 1, 2017–June 30, 2017."
163. Joscelyn, "The Terrorist Diaspora," 6–7; Winter, "War by Suicide," 5–11, 17–21.
164. Watts, "Beyond Syria and Iraq, the Islamic State's HR Files Illuminate Dangerous Trends."
165. Azinović and Jusić, "The Lure of the Syrian War," 46.
166. Hinnant and Schemm, "Death or Jail: The Cost of Leaving the Islamic State."
167. Azinović and Jusić, "The Lure of the Syrian War," 38.
168. Hassan, "The Secret World of ISIS Training Camps."
169. Reuters, "Secret Files Reveal Structure of Islamic State."
170. Speckhard and Yayla, "Eyewitness Accounts from Recent Defectors from Islamic State," 99.
171. Abdul-Ahad, "The Bureaucracy of Evil."
172. Reuters, "Secret Files Reveal Structure of Islamic State."
173. Dodwell, Milton, and Rassler, "The Caliphate's Global Workforce," 27.
174. Reuters, "Secret Files Reveal Structure of Islamic State."
175. Gartenstein-Ross and Barr, "Recent Attacks Illuminate the Islamic State's Europe Attack Network."
176. Whiteside, "A Pedigree of Terror."
177. Callimachi, "The Case of the Purloined Poultry."
178. Abdul-Ahad, "The Bureaucracy of Evil."
179. Callimachi, "The ISIS Files."
180. See Revkin, "The Legal Foundations of the Islamic State," 12. Quotes on 11 and 30.
181. Speckhard and Yayla, "Eyewitness Accounts from Recent Defectors from Islamic State," 103.
182. Callimachi, "The ISIS Files."
183. Revkin, "The Legal Foundations of the Islamic State," 23–29.
184. Callimachi, "The ISIS Files."
185. Revkin, "The Legal Foundations of the Islamic State," 17.
186. Callimachi, "The ISIS Files."
187. Chazan, "Brussels Museum Shooting Suspect 'Beheaded Baby.'"
188. Human Rights Watch, "Syria: ISIS Tortured Kobani Child Hostages."
189. Doornbos and Moussa, "Present at the Creation."

190. Speckhard and Yayla, "Eyewitness Accounts from Recent Defectors from Islamic State," 106.
191. Townsend, "Rape and Slavery Was Lure for UK ISIS Recruits."
192. Abu Hanieh and Abu Rumman, "The 'Islamic State' Organization," 278–279.
193. Heißner et al., "Caliphate in Decline"; Callimachi, "The ISIS Files."
194. "More Than 70 Nations Hold Talks on Terrorism Financing in Paris."
195. Abu Hanieh and Abu Rumman, "The 'Islamic State' Organization," 302.
196. Doornbos and Moussa, "Present at the Creation."
197. Reuter, "Secret Files Reveal Structure of Islamic State."
198. Revkin and Mhidi, "Why Syrians Are Abandoning the Group"; Bradley, "Rift Grows in Islamic State between Foreign, Local Fighters."
199. "How the People of Mosul Subverted Isis Apartheid."
200. Crowcraft and Limam, "ISIS: Foreign Fighters 'Live like Kings.'" See also Bradley, "Rift Grows in Islamic State between Foreign, Local Fighters."
201. Schmitt, "Thousands of ISIS Fighters Flee in Syria"; "After the Liberation of Mosul, an Orgy of Killing."
202. Eid, "French Jihadists Were ISIS Smart Bombs to Strike EU."
203. *The Foreign Fighters Phenomenon in the European Union,* 3; Barrett, "Beyond the Caliphate," 5.
204. Barrett, "Beyond the Caliphate."
205. Tufft, "ISIS 'Executes up to 200 Fighters' for Trying to Flee Jihad and Return Home"; Revkin and Mhidi, "Quitting ISIS"; Hinnant and Schemm, "Death or Jail: The Cost of Leaving the Islamic State."
206. Giglio and al-Awad, "The Escape."
207. Mironova, Sergatskova, and Alhamad, "The Lives of Foreign Fighters Who Left ISIS."
208. Speckhard and Yayla, "Eyewitness Accounts from Recent Defectors from Islamic State," 115–116.
209. Witte, "Westerners Fighting in Syria Disillusioned with Islamic State but Can't Go Home."
210. Mironova, Sergatskova, and Alhamad, "The Lives of Foreign Fighters Who Left ISIS"; Hamed and Barrett, "Enhancing the Understanding of Foreign Terrorist Fighters Phenomenon in Syria," 4.
211. For a review, see Zelin, "The Others."
212. Joscelyn, "The Terrorist Diaspora," 6; Evans et al., "Everything We Know about Manchester Suicide Bomber Salman Abedi"; Zelin, "The Others," 17; Callimachi and Schmitt, "Manchester Bomber Met with ISIS Unit in Libya, Officials Say."
213. Cragin, "Foreign Fighter 'Hot Potato.'"
214. General Intelligence and Security Service, "Life with ISIS."
215. Barrett, "Beyond the Caliphate," 14.
216. Van Vlierden, "Profile: Paris Attack Ringleader Abdelhamid Abaaoud."
217. Haq, "Islamic State's Fake Passports Disrupt the Alarm Bells of Foreign Intelligence."

218. Gartenstein-Ross and Barr, "Recent Attacks Illuminate the Islamic State's Europe Attack Network."

219. "How to Survive in the West."

220. Ibid.

221. Remnick, "Going the Distance."

222. "Remarks of Under Secretary for Terrorism and Financial Intelligence David Cohen before the Center for a New American Security on 'Confronting New Threats in Terrorist Financing.'"

223. Rosenblatt, "All Jihad Is Local," 20.

224. Data on airstrikes are available at the CENTCOM website for Operation Inherent Resolve. http://www.inherentresolve.mil/News/Strike-Releases/

225. "Ain Al Arab—Kubani." See also *Dabiq* number 5 for Kobani-focused propaganda.

226. Neumann, *Radicalized*, 104–105.

227. "Battle for Kobane."

228. Smith-Spark and Basil, "Kobani."

229. "ISIS Finally Admits Defeat in Kobani after Air Strikes Force Its Fighters to Retreat."

230. Smith-Spark and Basil, "Kobani"; Morris, "ISIS Still Strong Despite Major Defeat in Kobani."

231. Revkin and Mhidi, "Quitting ISIS."

232. Joscelyn, "The Terrorist Diaspora," 9.

233. Heißner, Neumann, Holland-McCowan, and Basra, "Caliphate in Decline: An Estimate of the Islamic State's Financial Fortunes."

234. El-Ghobashy and Salim, "Iraqi's Rapid Fire Trials Send Alleged ISIS Members—Including Foreigners—to the Gallows."

235. Coolsaet, "Facing the Fourth Foreign Fighters Wave," 39.

236. Hennessy-Fiske and Hennigan, "Civilian Casualties from Airstrikes Grow in Iraq and Syria"; Winter, "The ISIS Propaganda Decline."

237. Ryan and Raghavan, "U.S. Special Operations Troops Aiding Libyan Forces in Major Battle against Islamic State"; U.S. Department of Defense, August 17, 2016, "U.S. Airstrikes Hit ISIL Targets in Libya"; United States Africa Command, "AFRICOM Concludes Operation Odyssey Lightning"; Kirkpatrick, "Secret Alliance"; "Operation Freedom's Sentinel."

238. United Nations Security Council, "Resolution 2178."

239. Barrett, "Beyond the Caliphate," 18.

240. Cottee, "ISIS Will Fail, but What about the Idea of ISIS?"

Chapter 11

1. Sciolino, "Bombings in Madrid"; 11-M décimo aniversario."

2. Nesser, *Islamist Terrorism in Europe,* 66.

3. Reinares, *Al-Qaeda's Revenge* and Reinares, "The Evidence of Al-Qa'ida's Role in the 2004 Madrid Attack."

4. Ibid., 153.

5. As quoted in ibid., 96.

6. Ibid., 14–15.

7. Ibid., 102.

8. Quoted in ibid., 107.

9. Ibid., 17–19.

10. Ibid., 65–75.

11. Ibid., 111–112.

12. Ibid., 88.

13. Nesser, *Islamist Terrorism in Europe*, 1.

14. Interview with Danish terrorism expert, May 2014.

15. Kepel, *Jihad*, 260.

16. As quoted in Nesser, *Islamist Terrorism in Europe*, 72.

17. Travis, "Abu Qatada: From Refugee to Detainee."

18. See the testimony of Saif al-Adel in Husayn, "Al-Zarqawi."

19. Tremlett, "Islamist Cell Linked to UK Militants."

20. Aaron, "In Their Own Words," 105.

21. Shihab, "Heads of London-Based Extremist Islamic Organizations Interviewed."

22. Nesser, *Islamist Terrorism in Europe,* 39–47.

23. For an overview, see Hegghammer, *Jihadi Culture.*

24. Nasiri, *Inside the Jihad,* 279.

25. Nesser, *Islamist Terrorism in Europe,* 33 and 82.

26. Malet, "The European Experience with Foreign Fighters and Returnees," 10.

27. Nesser, *Islamist Terrorism in Europe*, 87, 96–97.

28. Ibid., 43.

29. Holman, "Belgian and French Foreign Fighters in Iraq 2003–2005," 603.

30. "7/7/ Bombings."

31. Hoffman, "The 7 July 2005 London Bombings."

32. Ibid.

33. Ibid., 34. As quoted in Van Ginkel and Minks, "Addressing the Challenge of Returnees," 58.

34. As quoted in Van Ginkel and Minks, "Addressing the Challenge of Returnees," 58.

35. Reinares and García-Calvo, "Moroccans and the Second Generation among Jihadists in Spain."

36. Interview conducted in Seville, Spain, June 2017.

37. Interview conducted in Seville, Spain, June 2017.

38. Interview with European counterterrorism official, August 2016.

39. De Bellaigue, "Are French Prisons 'Finishing Schools' for Terrorism?"

40. Mekhennet, "How a Journalist Uncovered the True Identity of Jihadi John."

41. Schmid and Tinnes, "Foreign (Terrorist) Fighters with IS."

42. Nesser, *Islamist Terrorism in Europe,* 60.

43. Ibid., 65.

44. Neumann, "Countering Violent Extremism and Radicalisation That Leads to Terrorism," 50.
45. De Bellaigue, "Are French Prisons 'Finishing Schools' for Terrorism?"; Renard and Coolsaet, "From the Kingdom to the Caliphate and Back," 32; Erickson, "Europe's Prisons Breed Terrorism."
46. Vidino, Marone, and Entenmann, "Fear Thy Neighbor," 12–17 and 23.
47. Heil, "The Berlin Attack."
48. Reinares, "Terrorist Mobilization, Undemocratic Salafism, and the Terrorist Threat to the EU."
49. Renard and Coolsaet, "From the Kingdom to the Caliphate and Back," 19.
50. Vidino, Marone, and Entenmann, "Fear Thy Neighbor," 81; Marone, "Italy's Jihadists in the Syrian Civil War."
51. Heinke and Raudszus, "Germany's Returning Foreign Fighters and What to Do about Them," 41–42.
52. Watts, "Beyond Syria and Iraq, the Islamic State's HR Files Illuminate Dangerous Trends"; Gall, "How Kosovo Was Turned into Fertile Ground for ISIS."
53. Crowell, "What Went Wrong with France's Deradicalization Program?"
54. Vidino, Marone, and Entenmann, "Fear Thy Neighbor," 16; *The Foreign Fighters Phenomenon in the European Union*, 4 and 32. Converts in Germany were about 15 percent of the group. Flade, "The Islamic State Threat to Germany," 12; Hamed and Barrett, "Enhancing the Understanding of Foreign Terrorist Fighters Phenomenon in Syria," 22–29; Neumann, *Radicalized*, 89–93.
55. Renard and Coolsaet, "From the Kingdom to the Caliphate and Back," 20.
56. Hecker, "137 Shades of Terrorism."
57. Reinares, "Terrorist Mobilization, Undemocratic Salafism, and the Terrorist Threat to the EU."
58. Moghadam, "The Jihadist Entrepreneur."
59. Vidino and Marone, "The Jihadist Threat in Italy."
60. Ibid.
61. Nasiri, *Inside the Jihad*, 9.
62. "Returnees," 3; See, e.g., Flade, "The Islamic State Threat to Germany," 11; Coolsaet, "Facing the Fourth Foreign Fighters Wave," 9; Barrett, "Beyond the Caliphate," 10; and Heinke and Raudszus, "Germany's Returning Foreign Fighters and What to Do about Them," 44. Renard and Coolsaet note that in some countries the returnee rate includes those who never made it to the war zone while in others it does not. "From the Kingdom to the Caliphate and Back," 19n5 and 23.
63. Hegghammer, "The Future of Jihadism in Europe," 160.
64. Hegghammer and Nesser, "Assessing the Islamic State's Commitment to Attacking the West."
65. Callimachi, "How ISIS Built the Machinery of Terror under Europe's Gaze."
66. Vidino, Marone, and Entenmann, "Fear Thy Neighbor," 34.

67. "How to Survive in the West," 5.
68. Al-Adnani, "Indeed Your Lord Is Ever Watchful."
69. Flade, "The Islamic State Threat to Germany," 11.
70. Cragin, "The November 2015 Paris Attacks," 212 and 221.
71. As quoted in Amarasingam, "An Interview with Rachid Kassim."
72. Malet, "The European Experience with Foreign Fighters and Returnees," 14.
73. Ibid., 4.
74. Nesser, *Islamist Terrorism in Europe,* 102–107.
75. Van Zuijdewijn, "The Foreign Fighter Phenomenon," 11.
76. Paulussen and Entenmann, "National Responses in Select Western European Countries to the Foreign Fighter Phenomenon," 394.
77. Renard and Coolsaet, "From the Kingdom to the Caliphate and Back," 23; Heinke and Raudszus, "Germany's Returning Foreign Fighters and What to Do about Them," 48.
78. Center for the Analysis of Terrorism, "Attentats, tentatives et projects d'attentats en relation avec le context syro-irakien dans les pays occidentaux," 8.
79. "Returnees," 3.
80. "Assessment of the Terror Threat to Denmark."
81. Schmitt, "ISIS Fighters Are Not Flooding Back Home to Wreak Havoc as Feared."
82. "Assessment of the Terror Threat to Denmark," 1.
83. Council of the European Union, "Outline of the Counter-Terrorism Strategy for Syria and Iraq."
84. Renard and Coolsaet, "From the Kingdom to the Caliphate and Back," 25.
85. Interview with European counterterrorism official, August 2016.
86. Interview with Danish terrorism expert, May 2014.
87. Normark, Ranstorp, and Ahlin, "Financial Activities Linked to Persons from Sweden and Denmark," 13.
88. Nesser, *Islamist Terrorism in Europe,* 121.
89. Azinović and Jusić, "The Lure of the Syrian War," 39.
90. Renard and Coolsaet, "From the Kingdom to the Caliphate and Back," 28.
91. "How to Survive in the West."
92. Al-Adnani, "Indeed Your Lord Is Ever Watchful."
93. Miller, "Senior Counterterrorism Official Expresses Concern about Access in U.S. to Lethal Weaponry."
94. Interview with European counterterrorism official, August 2016.
95. Interview with European counterterrorism official, June 2016.
96. "Returnees," 4.
97. Van Ginkel and Minks, "Addressing the Challenge of Returnees," 58.
98. McCann, "'The Only Way' of Dealing with British Islamic State Fighters Is to Kill Them in Almost Every Case."
99. Hookkharn, "SAS in Iraq Get Kill List of British Jihadis."

100. Meichtry and Barnes, "Europe Balks at Taking Back ISIS Fighters."
101. Heinke and Raudszus, "Germany's Returning Foreign Fighters and What to Do about Them," 49.
102. Interview with European counterterrorism official, August 2016.
103. Meichtry and Barnes, "Europe Balks at Taking Back ISIS Fighters."
104. Interview with lawyers in France, 2014.
105. Vidino and Marone, "The Jihadist Threat in Italy: A Primer."
106. Van Zuijdewijn, "The Foreign Fighter Phenomenon"; Hecker, "137 Shades of Terrorism," 34.
107. Hecker, "137 Shades of Terrorism," 31–33.
108. Moutot, "Jailbird Jihadists."
109. "Returnees," 5.
110. Van Ginkel and Minks, "Addressing the Challenge of Returnees," 61.
111. Interview with Danish government official, May 2014.
112. Neumann, "Countering Violent Extremism and Radicalisation That Leads to Terrorism," 76–77.
113. Cruickshank, "A View from the CT Foxhole," 8.
114. Interview with European counterterrorism official, August 2016.
115. Cook and Vale, *From Daesh to "Diaspora."*
116. Normark, Ranstorp, and Ahlin, "Financial Activities Linked to Persons from Sweden and Denmark," 8; Renard and Coolsaet, "From the Kingdom to the Caliphate and Back," 19; Simcox, "The Terrorist Diaspora," 2.
117. Simcox, "The Terrorist Diaspora," 2.
118. Cruickshank, "A View from the CT Foxhole," 7.

Chapter 12

1. Warrick, "Aulaqi Incited Young Muslims to Attacks against West."
2. As quoted in Bergen, *The United States of Jihad,* 144.
3. Shane, "The Enduring Influence of Anwar al-Awlaki," 15; Awlaki, "The Hereafter."
4. As quoted in "Zachary Chesser."
5. See Ito, "ACLU Lens: American Citizen Anwar Al-Aulaqi Killed without Judicial Process." Numerous other groups have issued similar statements.
6. "Killing Al-Awlaki Raises Obama's Approval on Terrorism Eight Points."
7. Wallace and Townshend, "The Case for Removing Extremist Videos from the Internet"; Nelson, "Comey: FBI Began Investigating Orlando Shooter in May 2013"; "Anwar Awlaki Email Exchange with Fort Hood Shooter Nidal Hassan."
8. For background on Hussain and the Legion, see Goldman and Schmitt, "One by One, ISIS Social Media Experts Are Killed as Result of F.B.I. Program"; Hamid, "The British Hacker Who Became the Islamic State's Chief Terror Cybercoach"; Wilber, "Here's How the FBI Tracked Down a

Tech-Savvy Terrorist Recruiter for the Islamic State"; Hughes and Meleagrou-Hitchens, "The Threat to the United States from the Islamic State's Virtual Entrepreneurs"; and Larner, "Junaid Hussain."

9. Hughes and Meleagrou-Hitchens, "The Threat to the United States from the Islamic State's Virtual Entrepreneurs."

10. Meleagrou-Hitchens, Hughes, and Clifford, "The Travelers," 82.

11. Hughes and Meleagrou-Hitchens, "The Threat to the United States from the Islamic State's Virtual Entrepreneurs."

12. Hamid, "The British Hacker Who Became the Islamic State's Chief Terror Cybercoach."

13. Hamid, "The British Hacker Who Became the Islamic State's Chief Terror Cybercoach"; Goldman and Schmitt, "One by One, ISIS Social Media Experts Are Killed as Result of F.B.I. Program"; Hughes and Meleagrou-Hitchens, "The Threat to the United States from the Islamic State's Virtual Entrepreneurs."

14. Hughes, "The Only Islamic State-Funded Plot in the U.S."

15. Mueller, "The Cybercoaching of Terrorists," 33.

16. Jenkins, "When Jihadis Come Marching Home"; Berger, *Jihad Joe,* 8.

17. Meleagrou-Hitchens, Hughes, and Clifford, "The Travelers," 16 and 75.

18. Bergen, *The United States of Jihad,* 16.

19. Mona El-Naggar and Quynhahn Do, "Video Released of U.S. Bomber in Syria," *New York Times,* July 31, 2014.

20. Vidino and Hughes, "ISIS in America: From Retweets to Raqqa," 22.

21. National Consortium for the Study of Terrorism and Responses to Terrorism (START), "Understanding the Threat," 2; Meleagrou-Hitchens, Hughes, and Clifford, "The Travelers," 16.

22. Bergen, "Jihad 2.0," 2; Vidino and Hughes, "ISIS in America: From Retweets to Raqqa," 5.

23. National Consortium for the Study of Terrorism and Responses to Terrorism (START), "Overview"; Meleagrou-Hitchens, Hughes, and Clifford, "The Travelers," 39; Bergen, "Jihad 2.0," 4.

24. National Consortium for the Study of Terrorism and Responses to Terrorism (START), "Overview."

25. Bergen, *The United States of Jihad,* 15 and 46–50.

26. Vidino, Marone, and Entenmann, "Fear Thy Neighbor," 55; Vidino and Hughes, "ISIS in America: From Retweets to Raqqa," 6.

27. "How to Survive in the West."

28. Silber and Bhatt, "Radicalization in the West."

29. Hughes, Meleagrou-Hitchens, and Clifford, "A New American Leader Rises in ISIS."

30. National Consortium for the Study of Terrorism and Responses to Terrorism (START), "Profiles of Individual Radicalization in the United States."

31. Mueller, "The Cybercoaching of Terrorists: Cause for Alarm?," 29–30.

32. Hughes, Meleagrou-Hitchens, and Clifford, "A New American Leader Rises in ISIS."
33. *The 9/11 Commission Report,* 233.
34. National Consortium for the Study of Terrorism and Responses to Terrorism (START), "Understanding the Threat," 2.
35. National Consortium for the Study of Terrorism and Responses to Terrorism (START), "Overview: Profiles of Individual Radicalization in the United States."
36. Jenkins, "When Jihadis Come Marching Home."
37. Meleagrou-Hitchens, Hughes, and Clifford, "The Travelers," 71–85.
38. Taylor, "Omar Mateen May Not Have Understood the Difference between ISIS, Al-Qaeda and Hezbollah."
39. Hughes, "The Only Islamic State-Funded Plot in the U.S."
40. "Director Rasmussen Opening Remarks."
41. Lister, "ISIS Rides Waves of Attacks Even as Its Territory Shrinks."
42. Precise numbers are difficult, as it is often unclear how lonely Lone Wolves are. The San Bernardino killers were married, and Nidal Hassan maintained email contact with Anwar al-Awlaki. Callimachi, "Not 'Lone Wolves' after All."
43. Gladwell, "Thresholds of Violence."
44. McCarthy, "Worry about Terrorist Attacks in U.S. High but Not Top Concern."
45. *The 9/11 Commission Report,* 71–100.
46. "Counterterrorism Spending," The Stimson Center.
47. Brill, "Is America Any Safer?"; "Countering Terrorism in the United States"; Miller, "When Preventing Another 9/11 Is Your Day Job."
48. Doyle, "Terrorist Material Support."
49. Meleagrou-Hitchens, Hughes, and Clifford, "The Travelers," 52–53.
50. See the criminal complaint against Nicholas Teausant, 6.
51. As quoted in Homeland Security Committee, "Final Report of the Task Force on Combating Terrorist and Foreign Fighter Travel," 18.
52. Clarke, "The Terrorist Diaspora," 6.
53. See the criminal complaint against Aaron Daniels, 9.
54. National Consortium for the Study of Terrorism and Responses to Terrorism (START), "Understanding the Threat," 2.
55. See the criminal complaint of Akram Museleh, 8.
56. Vidino and Hughes, "ISIS in America," 1.
57. United States of America v. Mohamed Abdihamid Farah et al., "Criminal Complaint."
58. Lichtblau, "F.B.I. Steps Up Use of Stings in ISIS Cases"; and Osnos, "Do F.B.I. Stings Help the Fight against ISIS?"
59. Bergen, *The United States of Jihad,* 33.
60. Aaron, "In Their Own Words," 219.

61. Gartenstein-Ross, "What Does the Recent Spate of Lone Wolf Terrorist Attacks Mean?"

62. Pew Research Center, "How the U.S. General Public Views Muslims and Islam."

63. National Consortium for the Study of Terrorism and Responses to Terrorism (START), "Profiles of Individual Radicalization in the United States."

64. Malik, "I Reported Omar Mateen to the FBI."

65. U.S. Government Accountability Office, "Counterterrorism"; The White House, "Fact Sheet: U.S. Security Sector Assistance Policy."

66. "Stories and Scenes from Mosul (1)."

67. Byman, "The Intelligence War on Terrorism."

68. Zelin and Prohov, "How Western Non-EU States Are Responding to Foreign Fighters," 428.

69. Schmitt, "ISIS Fighters Are Not Flooding Back Home to Wreak Havoc as Feared."

70. Bergen, "Jihad 2.0," 8.

71. National Consortium for the Study of Terrorism and Responses to Terrorism (START), "Overview: Profiles of Individual Radicalization in the United States."

72. Meleagrou-Hitchens, Hughes, and Clifford, "The Travelers," 76–77.

Chapter 13

1. Schmid, "Public Opinion Survey Data to Measure Sympathy and Support for Islamist Terrorism."

2. Interview with European counterterrorism official, June 2016.

3. Temple-Raston, "Enemy Within?"

4. Homeland Security Committee, "Final Report of the Task Force on Combating Terrorist and Foreign Fighter Travel," 28–29.

5. "Zachary Chesser."

6. Kirkpatrick, "New Freedoms in Tunisia Drive Support for ISIS."

7. Interview with French government official, May 2014.

8. Geller, "Why ISIS Is Winning the Online Propaganda War."

9. Berger, "Making CVE Work."

10. See Mansour, "Mum, I'm Fighting for Allah Now."

11. Al-Barei, "Disillusioned by al-Qaeda: Saudi Fighter in Syria Airs Confessions."

12. "UK Carries Out Cyber-attack on Islamic State."

13. "Egypt Adds New Measures against Terror Recruitment."

14. Cruickshank, "A View from the CT Foxhole," 8.

15. Watts, "Beyond Iraq and Afghanistan." Italics in the original.

16. Vidino and Hughes, "ISIS in America: From Retweets to Raqqa," 9; "Zachary Chesser," 23.

17. Al-Shishani, "The Challenge of Keeping Denmark's Muslims out of Syria."

18. Azinović and Jusić, "The Lure of the Syrian War," 37.

19. National Commission on Terrorist Attacks upon the United States, 69.

20. "Letter about Matter of the Islamic Maghreb."

21. Canadian Security and Intelligence Service, "Mobilization to Violence (Terrorism) Research."

22. See National Commission on Terrorist Attacks upon the United States, 9/11 and Terrorist Travel, 150–161.

23. "Director Rasmussen Opening Remarks."

24. Watts, "Hammami Thinks the Grass Might be Greener in Syria."

25. See Byman, "Why Drones Work" for quotes and for a broader description of how drones work for counterterrorism.

26. Arntsen, "Yemen's Al-Qaida."

27. See Karlin, Building Militaries in Fragile States for more on problems with training foreign partners.

28. Sambanis, "What Is a Civil War?"

29. El-Ghobashy and Kesling, "Iraqi Troops Fly Shiite Flags, Exacerbating Tensions."

30. George, "Officials Have Cast."

31. Quinlivan, "Coup Proofing.

32. Bodetti, "Fatal Attraction"; Boghani, "How People Are Using Technology against ISIS."

33. "Director Rasmussen Opening Remarks."

34. Rudner, "Hunters and Gatherers," 219.

35. Hamed and Barrett, "Enhancing the Understanding of Foreign Terrorist Fighters Phenomenon in Syria," 42.

36. Al-Shafey, "ISIS Tightens Up Its Entry Requirements."

37. See the data at the Brown University "Costs of War" at http://watson.brown. edu/costsofwar/.

38. Hegghammer and Nesser, "Assessing the Islamic State's Commitment to Attacking the West."

39. Malet and Hayes, "Foreign Fighter Returnees."

40. Stewart, "Jihadist Watch to Cost $8m a Suspect."

41. Interview with European intelligence officials, May 2014.

42. Neumann, "Countering Violent Extremism and Radicalisation That Leads to Terrorism," 49,

43. Bergen, The United States of Jihad, 42.

44. Filiu, "Ansar al-Fatah and 'Iraqi' Networks in France," 358. One review from 2010 found that less than 5 percent of those sent to prison are likely to become involved again in terrorism, but with large numbers going to jail that number is significant. For the figure, see Horgan and Braddock, "Rehabilitating the Terrorists?"

45. Interview with Shiraz Maher and Peter Neumann, June 17, 2014.

46. Malet, "Foreign Fighter Mobilization and Persistance in a Global Context."
47. Vermeulen, "Suspect Communities: Targeting Violent Extremism at the Local Level."
48. Interview with Floris Vermeulen, July 2014.
49. Taylor, "Saudi Arabia Aays 12 Percent of Its 'Rehabilitated' Terrorists Have Returned to Terror." See also Ansary, "Combating Extremism," 112–113.
50. Horgan and Braddock, "Rehabilitating the Terrorists?," 273.
51. Keaten, "French Police Arrest 6 Suspected Syria Jihadists."
52. "Toulouse: les deux apprentis jihadistes retracent leur périple en garde à vue."
53. Interview with Floris Vermuelen, July 2014; interview with Danish official, May 2014.
54. Shih, "Uighurs Fighting in Syria Take Aim at China."
55. Kramer, "Raised by ISIS, Returned to Chechnya."

REFERENCES

Aaron, David. 2008. *In Their Own Words: Voices of Jihad.* Santa Monica, CA: RAND.

Abdul-Ahad, Ghaith. June 8, 2005. "Outside Iraq but Deep in the Fight." *Washington Post.*

Abdul-Ahad, Ghaith. January 29, 2018. "The Bureaucracy of Evil: How Islamic State Ran a City." *The Guardian.*

Abdullah, Maher. October 26, 1992. "Interview with Abdul-Aziz." *Al-Wasat.*

Aboul-Enein, Youssef. 2008. *The Late Sheikh Abdullah Azzam's Books.* West Point, NY: Combating Terrorism Center, United States Military Academy.

Abu Hanieh, Hassan, and Mohammad Abu Rumman. 2015. *The "Islamic State" Organization: The Sunni Crisis and the Struggle of Global Jihadism.* Amman, Jordan: Friedrich-Ebert-Stiftung Jordan & Iraq.

"Addendum to the Report of the Islamic Maghreb." n.d. Washington, DC: Office of the Director of National Intelligence. https://www.dni.gov/files/documents/ubl2017/english/Addendum%20to%20the%20report%20of%20the%20Islamic%20Maghreb.pdf.

African Union Mission in Somalia. n.d. *Uganda—UPDF.* N.p.: Mogadishu, Somalia. http://amisom-au.org/uganda-updf/.

Ahmad, Aisha. 2015. "The Security Bazaar: Business Interests and Islamist Power in Civil War Somalia." *International Security* 39, no. 3: 89–117.

Al-Adnani, Abu Muhammad [Ash-Shami]. September 2014. "Indeed Your Lord Is Ever Watchful." *Al Hayat Media.*

Al-Amriiki, Abu Mansuur. n.d. *The Story of an American Jihaadi: Part One.* https://azelin.files.wordpress.com/2012/05/omar-hammami-abc5ab-mane1b9a3c5abr-al-amrc4abkc4ab-22the-story-of-an-american-jihc481dc4ab-part-122.pdf.

Al Arabiya. September 27, 2005. "Abdullah Anas: Zawahri Did Not Struggle in Afghanistan."

Al Arabiya. November 28, 2017. "Detained Abu Hamza Al-Belgiki Narrates Details of His Time with ISIS." http://english.alarabiya.net/en/features/2017/11/28/Detained-Abu-Hamza-al-Belgiki-narrates-details-of-his-time-with-ISIS.html.

Al-Awlaki, Anwar. n.d. "The Hereafter." Internet archive. Accessed February 12, 2018. https://archive.org/details/nooor90.

Al-Baghdadi, Abu Bakr. n.d. "A Letter to the Holy Wars and the Muslim Community on the Month of Ramadan." *Al-Furqan Media Foundation*.

Al-Baghdadi, Abu Bakr. April 2013. "Bring Good Tidings to the Believers." *Al-Furqan Media Foundation*.

Al-Baghdadi, Abu Bakr. 2014. "A Message to the Mujahidin and the Islamic Ummah in the Month of Ramadan." *Al-Furqan Media Foundation*.

Al-Barei, Sultan. March 20, 2014. "Disillusioned by al-Qaeda: Saudi Fighter in Syria Airs Confessions." *Al-Shorfa*.

Al-Hamdan, Ahmed. 2016. "Bay'ah to the Islamic State of Iraq: An Untold Story of Al-Qaida's Mistake." Translated by *Al Muwahideen Media*. *Al Muwahideen Media* (blog).

Al-Hammadi, Khalid. 2005a. "Part 1—Al Qaeda from Within, as Narrated by Abu Jandal (Nasir Al-Bahri), Bin Laden's Bodyguard." *Al Quds al-Arabi*, March 18, 2005.

Al-Hammadi, Khalid. 2005b. "Part 2—Al Qaeda from Within, as Narrated by Abu Jandal (Nasir Al-Bahri), Bin Laden's Bodyguard." *Al Quds al-Arabi*, March 19–20, 2005.

Al-Hammadi, Khalid. 2005c. "Part 4—Al Qaeda from Within, as Narrated by Abu Jandal (Nasir Al-Bahri), Bin Laden's Bodyguard." *Al Quds al-Arabi*, March 22, 2005.

Al-Hammadi, Khalid. 2005d. "Part 5—Al Qaeda from Within, as Narrated by Abu Jandal (Nasir Al-Bahri), Bin Laden's Bodyguard." *Al Quds al-Arabi*, March 23, 2005.

Al-Hammadi, Khalid. 2005e. "Part 8—Al Qaeda from Within, as Narrated by Abu Jandal (Nasir Al-Bahri), Bin Laden's Bodyguard." *Al Quds al-Arabi*, March 26–27, 2005.

Al-Hammadi, Khalid. 2005f. "Part X—Al Qaeda from Within, as Narrated by Abu Jandal (Nasir Al-Bahri), Bin Laden's Bodyguard." *Al Quds al-Arabi*, March 28, 2005.

Al-Hammadi, Khalid. 2005g. "Part 10—Al Qaeda from Within, as Narrated by Abu Jandal (Nasir Al-Bahri), Bin Laden's Bodyguard." *Al Quds al-Arabi*, March 29, 2005.

Al Husin v. Bosnia and Herzegovina (No. 3727/08). February 7, 2012. Council of Europe: European Court of Human Rights. http://www.refworld.org/cases,ECHR,4f310b822.html.

Ali Mohamed: A Biographical Sketch. 2011. West Point, NY: Combating Terrorism Center. https://ctc.usma.edu/app/uploads/2011/06/Ali-Mohammed.pdf.

Al Jazeera. February 20, 2003. "Abdullah Azzam Documentary." http://www. aljazeera.net/programs/infocus/2005/1/10/%D8%B9%D8%A8%D8%AF-%D8%A7%D9%84%D9%84%D9%87-%D8%B9%D8%B2%D8%A7%D9%85-%D8%AD1.

Al Jazeera. February 27, 2003. "Abdullah Azzam Documentary (Part Two)." *http://www.aljazeera.net/programs/infocus/2005/1/10/ %D8%B9%D8%A8%D8%AF-%D8%A7%D9%84%D9%84%D9%87-%D8%B9%D8%B2%D8%A7%D9%85-%D8%AD2.*

Al Jazeera. February 3, 2010. "Bosnian Police Raid Muslim Houses." http://www. aljazeera.com/news/europe/2010/02/201022184657620696.html.

Al-Shafey, Mohammed. November 9, 2014. "ISIS Tightens Up Its Entry Requirements." *Asharq Al-Awsat.* https://eng-archive.aawsat.com/m-alshafey/ features/isis-tightens-up-its-entry-requirements.

Al Sharq al-Awsat. February 8, 2014. "Abdullah Anas, the Son-in-Law of the Spiritual Leader of the 'Afghan Arabs.'"

Al-Shishani, Murad Batal. 2010. "Salafi-Jihadis and the North Caucasus: Is There a New Phase of the War in the Making?" *Terrorism Monitor* 8, no. 27: 6–9.

Al-Shishani, Murad Batal. 2012. "The Rise and Fall of Arab Fighters in Chechnya." In *Volatile Borderland: Russia and the North Caucasus,* ed. Glen E. Howard, 286–316. Washington, DC: Jamestown Foundation.

Al-Shishani, Murad Batal. November 20, 2013. "Chechens Drawn South to Fight against Syria's Assad." *BBC News.* http://www.bbc.com/news/ world-middle-east-24999697.

Al-Shishani, Murad Batal. May 19, 2014. "The Challenge of Keeping Denmark's Muslims out of Syria." *BBC News. http://www.bbc.com/news/world-europe-27423789.*

Al-Suri, Abu Mus'ab. 2006. *The Call for a Global Islamic Resistance.* Arlington, VA: CENTRA Technology.

Al-Tamimi, Aymenn Jawad. August 24, 2016. "The Archivist: Stories of the Mujahideen." *Jihadology.*

Al-Ubaydi, Muhammad. 2015. *Khattab (1969–2002): Jihadi Bios Project.* West Point, NY: Combating Terrorism Center, United States Military Academy.

Amarasingam, Amarnath. November 18, 2016. "An Interview with Rachid Kassim, Jihadist Orchestrating Attacks in France." *Jihadology.* http://jihadology.net/2016/ 11/18/guest-post-an-interview-with-rachid-kassim-jihadist-orchestrating-attacks-in-france/.

AMISOM. January 23, 2014. "Ethiopian Troops Formally Join AMISOM Peacekeepers in Somalia." http://amisom-au.org/2014/01/ethiopian-troops-formally-join-amisom-peacekeepers-in-somalia/.

AMISOM. 2017a. "AMISOM Lauds Contribution by Burundi towards Restoration of Peace in Somalia." January 29, 2017. http://amisom-au.org/2017/01/amisom-lauds-contribution-by-burundi-towards-restoration-of-peace-in-somalia/.

AMISOM. 2017b. "New Ugandan Battle Group Arrives in Somalia." April 7, 2017. http://amisom-au.org/2017/04/new-ugandan-battle-group-arrives-in-somalia/.

Analysis of the State of ISI. n.d. NMEC-2007-612449. West Point, NY: Combating Terrorism Center. https://ctc.usma.edu/harmony-program/analysis-of-the-state-of-isi-original-language-2/.

Anas, Abdallah. 2002. *Weladt "Al Afghan Al Arab": Sirt Abdallah Anas bayn Massoud wa Abdallah Azzam* [The Birth of the Afghan Arabs: The Life of Abdallah Anas between Masoud and Abdallah Azzam]. London: Dar Al Saqi.

Anonymous. 2009. "On the Ground from Syria to Iraq." In *Bombers, Bank Accounts, & Bleedout: Al-Qa'ida's Road in Iraq and Out of Iraq,* ed. Brian Fishman, 81–97. West Point, NY: Combating Terrorism Center.

Ansary, Abdullah F. Summer 2008. "Combating Extremism: A Brief Overview of Saudi Arabia's Approach." *Middle East Policy* 15, no. 2: 112–113.

"Anwar Awlaki Email Exchange with Fort Hood Shooter Nidal Hassan." July 19, 2012. *Intelwire.* http://news.intelwire.com/2012/07/the-following-e-mails-between-maj.html.

Anzalone, Christopher. 2014 "The Life and Death of Al-Shabab Leader Ahmed Godane." *CTC Sentinel* 7, no. 9: 19–23. https://ctc.usma.edu/posts/the-life-and-death-of-al-shabab-leader-ahmed-godane.

AQI Template for Leaving Iraq or the AQI Organization 2 n.d. NMEC-2007-657739. West Point, NY: Combating Terrorism Center. https://ctc.usma.edu/harmony-program/aqi-template-for-leaving-iraq-or-the-aqi-organization-2-original-language-2/.

Arango, Tim. December 22, 2015. "Turkey Moves to Clamp Down on Border, Long a Revolving Door." *New York Times.*

Arntsen, Erlend Ofte. April 16, 2017. "Yemen's Al-Qaida: Entered Agreement with Tribal Leaders Not to Attack the West." *AG.* https://www.vg.no/nyheter/utenriks/i/knEWk/yemen-s-al-qaida-entered-agreement-with-tribal-leaders-not-to-attack-the-west

Assessment of the Terror Threat to Denmark. January 12, 2018. Søborg, Denmark: Center for Terror Analysis, Politiets Efterretningstjeneste, Danish Security and Intelligence Service. https://www.pet.dk/~/media/VTD%202018/VTD2018ENGpdf.ashx.

Associated Press. August 16, 2007. "U.S. Pre-9/11 Memos: Pakistan Backs the Taliban." http://www.nbcnews.com/id/20300129/ns/world_news-south_and_central_asia/t/us-pre--memos-pakistan-backs-taliban/#.WuRyUm6UuUk.

Ayn Al-Haqiqah [pseud]. March 5, 2003. "The Al-Qa'ida Organization Writes a Letter to the Iraqi People." *Alfjr.com* (chatroom).

Azinović, Vlado, and Muhamed Jusić. 2015. *The Lure of the Syrian War: The Foreign Fighters' Bosnian contingent.* Sarajevo, Bosnia and Herzegovina: Atlantic Initiative. http://atlanticinitiative.org/images/THE_LURE_OF_THE_SYRIAN_WAR_THE_FOREIGN_FIGHTERS_BOSNIAN_CONTINGENT/The_Lure_of_the_Syrian_War_-_The_Foreign_Fighters_Bosnian_Contingent.pdf.

Azzam, Abdullah. n.d.a "Defense of the Muslim Lands, The First Obligation after Iman." Internet archive. Accessed February 1, 2018. http://archive.org/stream/Defense_of_the_Muslim_Lands/Defense_of_the_Muslim_Lands_djvu.txt.

Azzam, Abdullah. n.d.b. "Join the Caravan." Internet archive. Accessed February 1, 2018. https://archive.org/stream/JoinTheCaravan/JoinTheCaravan_djvu.txt.

Azzam, Abdullah. n.d.c. "Martyrs: The Building Blocks of Nations." http://www.religioscope.com/info/doc/jihad/azzam_martyrs.htm.

Azzam, Abdullah. n.d.d. "The Signs of Allah the Most Merciful in the Jihad of Afghanistan." Internet archive. Accessed February 2, 2018. https://archive.org/details/MiraclesOfJihadInAfghanistan-AbdullahAzzam.

Bahney, Benjamin, Howard J. Shatz, Carroll Ganier, Renny McPherson, Barbara Sude, Sara Beth Elson, and Ghassan Schbley. 2010. *An Economic Analysis of the Financial Records of Al-Qa'ida in Iraq.* Santa Monica, CA: RAND Corporation.

Bakke, Kristin N. Spring 2014. "Help Wanted? The Mixed Record of Foreign Fighters in Domestic Insurgencies." *International Security* 38, no. 4: 150–187.

Balburov, Dmitry. April 14, 1999. "Shamil Basayev: 'Let Russia Lock Horns with Uncle Sam.'" *Moscow News.*

Bardos, Gordon N. 2014. "Jihad in the Balkans: The Next Generation." *World Affairs* 177, no. 3: 73–79.

Barrett, Richard. 2017. *Beyond the Caliphate: Foreign Fighters and the Threat of Returnees.* New York: Soufan Center.

Bayoumi, Yara. September 22, 2014. "ISIS Urges More Attacks on Western Disbelievers." *The Independent.*

BBC News. September 12, 2013. "Al-Amriki and Al-Britani: Militants 'Killed' in Somalia." http://www.bbc.com/news/world-africa-24060558.

BBC News. June 25, 2015. "Battle for Kobane: Key Events." *http://www.bbc.com/news/world-middle-east-29688108.*

BBC News. April 12, 2018. "UK Carries Out Cyber-attack on Islamic State." http://www.bbc.com/news/technology-43738953.

Bergema, Reinier, and Peter Wijninga. February 15, 2018. "Coming Home: Explaining the Variance in Jihadi Foreign Fighter Returnees across Western Europe." *Jihadology.net.*

Bergen, Peter. 2001 *Holy War, Inc.: Inside the Secret World of Osama Bin Laden.* New York: Simon & Schuster.

Bergen, Peter. 2006. *The Osama bin Laden I Know: An Oral History of al Qaeda's Leader.* New York: Simon & Schuster.

Bergen, Peter. 2009. "After the War in Iraq: What Will the Foreign Fighters Do?" In *Bombers, Bank Accounts, & Bleedout: Al-Qa'ida's Road in Iraq and Out of Iraq,* ed. Brian Fishman, 98–122. West Point, NY: Combating Terrorism Center.

Bergen, Peter. 2011. *The Longest War: The Enduring Conflict Between America and Al-Qaeda.* New York: Simon & Schuster.

Bergen, Peter. 2016. *United States of Jihad: Investigating America's Homegrown Terrorists.* New York: Crown Publishers.

Bergen, Peter, and Paul Cruickshank. March 1, 2007. "The Iraq Effect." *Mother Jones.*

Berger, Carol. January 28, 1993. "Bosnian Muslims Turn to Kuwait for money, Arms." *Christian Science Monitor.* https://www.csmonitor.com/1993/0128/28062.html.

Berger, J. M. September 29, 2006. "The Man Who Paved the Road to 9/11." *INTELWIRE.* http://news.intelwire.com/2006/09/man-who-paved-road-to-911.html.

Berger, J. M. 2011. *Jihad Joe: Americans Who Go to War in the Name of Islam.* Washington, DC: Potomac Books.

Berger, J. M. September 17, 2013. "Omar and Me." *Foreign Policy.* http://foreignpolicy.com/2013/09/17/omar-and-me/.

Berger, J. M. May 2016. "Making CVE Work: A Focused Approach Based on Process Disruption." The Hague, The Netherlands, International Centre for Counter-Terrorism. https://www.icct.nl/wp-content/uploads/2016/05/J.-M.-Berger-Making-CVE-Work-A-Focused-Approach-Based-on-Process-Disruption-.pdf.

Berger, J. M., and Heather Perez. 2016. *The Islamic State's Diminishing Returns on Twitter: How Suspensions are Limiting the Social networks of English-Speaking ISIS Supporters.* Washington, DC: George Washington University Program on Extremism.

Berger, J. M., and Jonathon Morgan. 2015. *The ISIS Twitter Census: Defining and Describing the Population of ISIS Supporters on Twitter.* Washington, DC: Brookings Institution.

Berntsen, Gary, and Ralph Pezzullo. 2005. *Jawbreaker: The Attack on Bin Laden and Al Qaeda: A Personal Account by the CIA's Key Field Commander.* New York: Crown Publishing.

Beuze, Canelle. March 2017. *Terrorist Attacks, Failed Attacks and Plots in the West linked to the Syrian-Iraqi Context (2013–2016).* Paris, France: Center for the Analysis of Terrorism, 8. http://cat-int.org/wp-content/uploads/2017/04/Terrorist-attacks-Report-2013-2016.pdf.

Biddle, Stephen. 2002. *Afghanistan and the Future of Warfare: Implications for Army and Defense Policy.* Carlisle, PA: Strategic Studies Institute, U.S. Army War College.

Biddle, Stephen, Julia Macdonald, and Ryan Baker. 2017. "Small Footprint, Small Payoff: The Military Effectiveness of Security Force Assistance." *Journal of Strategic Studies* 41, nos. 1–2: 89–142.

Bin Laden, Osama. 1995. "The Bosnia Tragedy and the Treason of the Custodian of the Two Holy Mosques." Statement no. 18, Advice and Reform Committee. https://books.google.com/books?id=bNLODP6w6GkC&pg=PA36&lpg=PA36&dq=The+Bosnia+Tragedy+and+the+Treason+of+the+Custodian+of+the+Two+Holy+Mosques.+Statement+no.+18,+Advice+and+Reform+Committee&source=bl&ots=DNbX-WgAA9&sig=4UyFUbfYH89SCLuNQun

xmJYYwSs&hl=en&sa=X&ved=0ahUKEwjV6bqLzaDbAhXos1kKHVR-
CRkQ6AEIKTAA#v=onepage&q=The%20Bosnia%20Tragedy%20and%20
the%20Treason%20of%20the%20Custodian%20of%20the%20Two%20Holy%20
Mosques.%20Statement%20no.%2018%2C%20Advice%20and%20Reform%20
Committee&f=false.

Bin Laden, Osama, Ayman Zawahiri, Abu- Yasir Rifa'i Ahmad Taha, Mir
Hamza, and Fazlur Rahman. February 23, 1998. "Jihad against Jews and
Crusaders: World Islamic Front Statement." Washington, DC: Federation of
American Scientists. https://fas.org/irp/world/para/docs/980223-fatwa.htm.

Binnie, Jeremy. October 28, 2016. "Ethiopia Withdrawing Troops from Somalia,
but Not AMISOM." *Jane's 360. www.janes.com.*

Blanchard, Christopher M., and Alfred B. Prados. 2007. *Saudi Arabic: Terrorist
Financing Issues.* CRS Report No. RL32499. Washington, DC: Congressional
Research Service. https://fas.org/sgp/crs/terror/RL32499.pdf.

Bodetti, Austin. January 3, 2017. "Fatal Attraction: ISIS Just Can't
Resist Social Media." *Daily Beast.* https://www.thedailybeast.com/
fatal-attraction-isis-just-cant-resist-social-media.

Boghani, Priyanka. July 14, 2014. "How People Are Using Technology Against
ISIS." *FRONTLINE PBS. https://www.pbs.org/wgbh/frontline/article/how-people-are-
using-technology-against-isis/.*

Boghani, Priyanka. March 21, 2017. "Iraq's Shia Militias: The Double-Edged Sword
Against ISIS." *FRONTLINE PBS.* http://www.pbs.org/wgbh/frontline/article/
iraqs-shia-militias-the-double-edged-sword-against-isis/.

Bonner, Michael. 2006. *Jihad in Islamic History: Doctrines and Practice.* Princeton,
NJ: Princeton University Press.

Botha, Anneli, and Mahdi Abdile. September 2014. *Radicalisation and Al-Shabaab
Recruitment in Somalia.* Pretoria, South Africa: Institute for Security Studies.
https://issafrica.s3.amazonaws.com/site/uploads/Paper266.pdf.

Bowden, Mark. May 2007. "The Ploy." *The Atlantic.*

Bowman, Steven R. 2003. *Bosnia: U.S. Military Operation.* Washington,
DC: Congressional Research Service. http://www.au.af.mil/au/awc/awcgate/crs/
ib93056.pdf.

Bradley, Jane. May 23, 2016. "My Son the ISIS Executioner." *BuzzFeed News.*
https://www.buzzfeed.com/janebradley/my-son-the-isis-executioner?utm_term=.
ouOndn7PD#.iwA3R3O5l.

Bradley, Matt. March 25, 2016. "Rift Grows in Islamic State Between Foreign, Local
Fighters." *Wall Street Journal.*

Braithwaite, Alex, and Tiffany S. Chu. May 22, 2017. "Civil Conflicts Abroad,
Foreign Fighters, and Terrorism at Home." *Journal of Conflict Resolution:*1–25.

Bridgman, Andrew. July 1, 2006. "Bin Laden Praises Fighters in New Tape." *CBS
News.* https://www.cbsnews.com/news/bin-laden-praises-fighters-in-new-tape/.

Brill, Steve. September 2016. "Is America Any Safer?" *The Atlantic.* https://www.
theatlantic.com/magazine/archive/2016/09/are-we-any-safer/492761/.

Bronitsky, Jonathan. 2010. *British Foreign Policy and Bosnia: The Rise of Islamism in Britain, 1992–1995.* London: International Center for the Study of Radicalisation and Political Violence. http://icsr.info/wp-content/uploads/2012/10/1289583399ICSRPaper_BritishForeignPolicyPaperandBosnia_JBronitsky.pdf.

Bronitsky, Jonathan. September 3, 2014. "Crescent over the Thames." *War on the Rocks.* https://warontherocks.com/2014/09/crescent-over-the-thames/.

Brown, Vahid. 2009. "Foreign Fighters in Historical Perspective: The Case of Afghanistan." In *Bombers, Bank Accounts, & Bleedout: Al-Qa'ida's Road in Iraq and Out of Iraq,* ed. Brian Fishman, 16–31. West Point, NY: Combating Terrorism Center.

Bruton, Bronwyn E., and Paul D. Williams. September 18, 2014. "Counterinsurgency in Somalia: Lessons Learned from the African Union Mission in Somalia, 2007–2013." Tampa, FL: Joint Special Operations University http://www.dtic.mil/dtic/tr/fulltext/u2/a616394.pdf.

Brynjar, Lia. 2008. *Architect of Global Jihad: The Life of Al-Qaida Strategist Abu Mus'ab Al-Suri.* New York: Columbia University Press.

Bryson, Rachel. 2017. *For Caliph and Country: Exploring How British Jihadis Join a Global Movement.* London: Tony Blair Institute for Global Change.

Burke, Jason. October 21, 2017. "Rise and Fall of ISIS: Its Dream of a Caliphate Is Over, So What Now?" *The Guardian.*

Burns, John F., and Kirk Semple. November 26, 2006. "U.S. Finds Iraq Insurgency Has Funds to Sustain Itself." *New York Times.*

Byman, Daniel. 2014. "The Intelligence War on Terrorism." *Intelligence and National Security* 29, no. 6: 837–863.

Byman, Daniel. 2013. "Why Drones Work: The Case for Washington's Weapon of Choice." *Foreign Affairs* 92, no. 4: 32–43.

CAGE. 2015. *The Emwazi Emails: CAGE Releases Its Correspondences with Emwazi in Full.* London. https://cage.ngo/uncategorized/emwazi-emails-cage-releases-its-correspondences-emwazi-full/.

Callimachi, Rukmini. June 27, 2015. "ISIS and the Lonely Young American." *New York Times.*

Callimachi, Rukmini. March 29, 2016. "How ISIS Built the Machinery of Terror under Europe's Gaze." *New York Times.*

Callimachi, Rukmini. April 4, 2018. "The ISIS Files." *New York Times.*

Callimachi, Rukmini. July 1, 2018. "The Case of the Purloined Poultry: How ISIS Prosecuted Petty Crime." *New York Times.* https://www.nytimes.com/2018/07/01/world/middleeast/islamic-state-iraq.html.

Callimachi, Rukmini, and Eric Schmitt. June 3, 2017. "Manchester Bomber Met with ISIS Unit in Libya, Officials Say." *New York Times.*

Camp, Dick. 2009. *Operation Phantom Fury: The Assault and Capture of Fallujah, Iraq.* St. Paul, MN: Zenith Press.

Canadian Security Intelligence Service. 2018. "Mobilization to Violence (Terrorism) Research: Key Findings." https://csis.gc.ca/pblctns/thrpblctns/2018-02-05-en.php

Carr, David. September 7, 2014. "With Videos of Killings, ISIS Sends Medieval Message by Modern Method." *New York Times*.

CATO Institute. 2017. "Countering Terrorism in the United States." CATO Handbook for Policymakers. https://www.cato.org/cato-handbook-policymakers/cato-handbook-policy-makers-8th-edition-2017/countering-terrorism-united.

Cendrowicz, Leo, Adam Lusher, and Alistair Dawber. November 16, 2015. "Paris Terror: Intelligence Agencies Missed Series of Key Clues before Attacks." *The Independent*.

Center for the Analysis of Terrorism. March 2017. "Attentats, tentatives et projects d'attentats en relation avec le context syro-irakien dans les pays occidentaux (2013–2016)." http://cat-int.org/wp-content/uploads/2017/03/Etude_Attentats_2013_2016-VF.pdf.

Central Intelligence Agency, Directorate of Intelligence. 1983. *Afghanistan: Goals and Prospects for the Insurgents*. Washington, DC. https://www.cia.gov/library/readingroom/docs/CIA-RDP84S00556R000200080004-3.pdf.

Central Intelligence Agency, Director of Central Intelligence. 1993. *Combatant Forces in the Former Yugoslavia: Volume II–Supporting Analysis*. Washington, DC. https://www.cia.gov/library/readingroom/docs/DOC_0005621706.pdf.

Chazan, David. September 7, 2014. "Brussels Museum Shooting Suspect 'Beheaded Baby.' " *The Telegraph*.

Chivers, C. J., and David Rohde. March 18, 2002. "Turning Out Guerrillas and Terrorists to Wage a Holy War." *New York Times*.

Chivers, C. J. January 16, 2007. "Success of Chechen Amnesty Plan Is Contested." *New York Times*.

Chu, Tiffany S., and Alex Braithwaite. July–September 2017. "The Impact of Foreign Fighters on Civil Conflict Outcomes." *Research and Politics*: 1–7.

Chulov, Martin. March 25, 2016. "How ISIS Laid Out Its Plans to Export Chaos in Europe." *The Guardian*.

Clarke, Colin. July 13, 2017. "The Terrorist Diaspora: After the Fall of the Caliphate." Testimony before the House Homeland Security Committee Task Force on Denying Terrorists Entry into the United States.

Clifford, Bennett. June 22, 2018. "The Cup and the Caliphate: Russia's Counterterrorism Operations before Major Sporting Events and the Global Jihadist Movement." https://www.lawfareblog.com/cup-and-caliphate-russias-counterterrorism-operations-major-sporting-events-and-global-jihadist.

Clinton, William. January 29, 2002. "Clinton Transcript." Berkeley: University of California Press. http://www.berkeley.edu/news/features/2002/clinton/clinton-transcript.html.

CNN.com. July 1, 2004. "U.S. Raises Zarqawi Reward to $25m." http://www.cnn.com/2004/WORLD/meast/07/01/iraq.zarqawi.reward/index.html.

CNN.com. July 10, 2006. "Mastermind of Russian School Siege Killed." http://www.cnn.com/2006/WORLD/europe/07/10/russia.basayev/index.html.

Cohen, Ariel. January 6, 2003. "Russia and Religious Terrorism: Shifting Dangers." *Eurasianet*. https://eurasianet.org/s/russia-and-religious-terrorism-shifting-dangers.

Coll, Steve. 2004. *Ghost Wars: The Secret History of the CIA, Afghanistan, and Bin Laden, from the Soviet Invasion to September 10, 2001*. New York: Penguin Press.

Coll, Steve. 2018. *Directorate S: The C.I.A. and America's Secret Wars in Afghanistan and Pakistan*. New York: Penguin Press.

Coolsaet, Rik. 2016. *Facing the Fourth Foreign Fighters Wave: What Drives Europeans to Syria, and the Islamic State? Insights from the Belgian Case*. Brussels: Egmont, The Royal Institute for International Relations.

Cook, Joanna, and Gina Vale. 2018. *From Daesh to "Diaspora": Tracing the Women and Minors of the Islamic State*. London: ICSR. https://icsr.info/wp-content/uploads/2018/07/Women-in-ISIS-report_20180719_web.pdf.

Cooper, Helene. July 27, 2007. "Saudis' Role in Iraq Frustrates U.S. Officials." *New York Times*. http://www.nytimes.com/2007/07/27/world/middleeast/27saudi.html?mcubz=1.

Cordesman, Anthony H., and Emma R. Davies. 2008. *Iraq's Insurgency and the Road to Civil Conflict*. Westport, CT: Praeger Security International.

Coticchia, Fabrizio. 2016. "The Military Impact of Foreign Fighters on the Battlefield: The Case of the ISIL." In *Foreign Fighters under International Law and Beyond*, ed. Andrea de Guttry, Francesca Capone, and Christophe Paulussen, 121–141. The Hague: T.M.C. Asser Press.

Cottee, Simon. April 13, 2016. "Europe's Joint-Smoking, Gay-Club Hopping Terrorists." *Foreign Policy*.

Cottee, Simon. March 23, 2017. "ISIS Will Fail, but What About the Idea of ISIS?" *The Atlantic*. https://www.theatlantic.com/international/archive/2017/03/idea-of-isis-will-outlive-caliphate/520224/.

Cottee, Simon. April 10, 2018. "Inside Europol's Online War against ISIS." *Vice*. *https://www.vice.com/en_uk/article/59jw8z/inside-europols-online-war-against-isi*.

Counter Extremism Project. *Mohammed Emwazi*. n.d. https://www.counterextremism.com/extremists/mohammed-emwazi.

Cragin, R. Kim. 2017a. "The Challenge of Foreign Fighter Returnees." *Journal of Contemporary Criminal Justice* 33, no. 3: 292–312.

Cragin, R. Kim. 2017b. "The November 2015 Paris Attacks: The Impact of Foreign Fighter Returnees." *Orbis* 61, no. 2: 212–226.

Crowcroft, Orlando, and Arij Limam. March 12, 2015. "ISIS: Foreign Fighters 'Live Like Kings' in Syrian Raqqa Stronghold of Islamic State." *International Business Times*.

Crowell, Maddy. September 28, 2017. "What Went Wrong with France's Deradicalization Program?" *The Atlantic*.

Cruickshank, Paul. 2016. "A View from the CT Foxhole: Hazim Fouad and Behnam Said, Analysts at the Bremen and Hamburg Verfassungsschutz." *CTC Sentinel* 9, no. 7: 7–10.

Cruickshank, Paul, and Peter Bergen. October 31, 2007. "Al Qaeda in Iraq: Self-Fulfilling Prophecy." *Mother Jones.*

Cullison, Alan, and Andrew Higgins. August 2, 2002. "A Once-Stormy Terror Alliance Was Solidified by Cruise Missiles." *Wall Street Journal.*

Cuomo, Chris, Eamon McNiff, and ABC News Law and Justice Unit. June 9, 2006. "The Men in the Shadows—Hunting Al-Zarqawi." *ABC News.* http://abcnews.go.com/GMA/Terrorism/story?id=2056386&page=1.

Current and Projected National Security Threats to the United States: Hearing before the Select Committee on Intelligence of the United States, 110th Cong. 2007. 1. https://fas.org/irp/congress/2007_hr/threat.pdf.

Dabiq, Issue 12. Available at https://azelin.files.wordpress.com/2015/11/the-islamic-state-e2809cdc481biq-magazine-12e280b3.pdf.

Danner, Mark. December 4, 1997. "America and the Bosnia Genocide." *New York Review of Books.* http://www.nybooks.com/articles/1997/12/04/america-and-the-bosnia-genocide/.

Dawoud, Khaled, Julian Borger, and Nicholas Watt. November 20, 2001. "Doomed Arab Unites Prepare for Final Battle against the Odds." *The Guardian.* https://www.theguardian.com/world/2001/nov/20/afghanistan.terrorism4.

Dawson, Lorne L., and Amarnath Amarasingam. 2017. "Talking to Foreign Fighters: Insights into the Motivations for Hijrah to Syria and Iraq." *Studies in Conflict & Terrorism* 40, no. 3: 191–220.

De Bellaigue, Christopher. March 17, 2016. "Are French Prisons 'Finishing Schools' for Terrorism?" *The Guardian.* https://www.theguardian.com/world/2016/mar/17/are-french-prisons-finishing-schools-for-terrorism.

Department of Defense. September 5, 2014. "Pentagon Confirms Death of Al-Shabab Co-founder." Washington, DC. https://www.defense.gov/News/Article/Article/603193/.

Department of Defense. November 18, 2015. "Department of Defense Press Briefing by Col. Warren via DVISD from Baghdad, Iraq." Washington, DC. https://www.defense.gov/News/Transcripts/Transcript-View/Article/630393/department-of-defense-press-briefing-by-col-warren-via-dvids-from-baghdad-iraq/.

Department of Defense. June 1, 2016. "Statement by Pentagon Press Secretary Peter Cook on U.S. Airstrike in Somalia." Washington, DC. https://www.defense.gov/News/News-Releases/News-Release-View/Article/788062/statement-by-pentagon-press-secretary-peter-cook-on-us-airstrike-in-somalia/.

Department of Treasury. March 4, 2014. "Remarks of Under Secretary for Terrorism and Financial Intelligence David Cohen before the Center for a New American Security on 'Confronting New Threats in Terrorist Financing.'" Washington, DC. https://www.treasury.gov/press-center/press-releases/Pages/jl2308.aspx.

Diehl, Jorg, Roman Lehberger, and Vanessa Schlesier. July 18, 2016. "Terrorist Bookkeepers: New Documents Help Identify Islamic State Returnees." *SpiegelOnline.* http://www.spiegel.de/international/world/new-islamic-state-data-trove-a-help-for-german-prosecutors-a-1103194.html.

Dobbs, Michael. February 2, 1996. "Saudis Funded Weapons for Bosnia, Official Says." *Washington Post*. https://www.washingtonpost.com/archive/politics/1996/02/02/saudis-funded-weapons-for-bosnia-official-says/1a163310-2064-49f6-bd11-84bc67092ce2/?utm_term=.c7c74fb531b2.

Dodwell, Brian, Daniel Milton, and Don Rassler. 2016a. *The Caliphate's Global Workforce: An Inside Look at the Islamic State's Foreign Fighter Paper Trail*. West Point, NY: Combating Terrorism Center.

Dodwell, Brian, Daniel Milton, and Don Rassler. 2016b. *Then and Now: Comparing the Flow of Foreign Fighters to AQI and the Islamic State*. West Point, NY: Combating Terrorism Center

Doornbos, Harald, and Jenan Moussa. August 16, 2016. "Present at the Creation: The Never-Told-Before Story of the Meeting That Led to the Creation of ISIS, as Explained by an Islamic State Insider." *Foreign Policy*.

Doyle, Charles. 2016. "Terrorist Material Support: An Overview of 18 U.S.C. §2339A and §2339B." Washington, DC: Congressional Research Service.

Duyvesteyn, Isabelle, and Bram Peeters. 2015. *Fickle Foreign Fighters? A Cross-Case Analysis of Seven Muslim Foreign Fighter Mobilizations (1980–2015)*. The Hague: International Center for Counter-Terrorism.

"Egypt Adds New Measures against Terror Recruitment." June 12, 2014. The *Independent*. http://www.egyptindependent.com//news/egypt-adds-new-measures-against-terror-recruitment.

Eid, Ali. October 15, 2017. "French Jihadists Were ISIS Smart Bombs to Strike EU: Leaks." https://en.zamanalwsl.net/news/articles/130.

Elias, Dina. June 19, 2001. "Video Offers Strong Bin Laden–USS Cole Link." *ABC News*. http://abcnews.go.com/International/story?id=80896&page=1

El-Ghobashy, Tamer, and Ali A. Nabhan. March 16, 2017. "Foreign ISIS Fighters Increasingly Isolated in Mosul Battle." *Wall Street Journal*. https://www.wsj.com/articles/foreign-isis-fighters-increasingly-isolated-in-mosul-battle-1489676887.

El-Ghobashy, Tamer, and Ben Kesling. October 21, 2016. "Iraqi Troops Fly Shiite Flags, Exacerbating Tensions." *Wall Street Journal*. https://www.wsj.com/articles/iraqi-troops-stoke-sectarian-tensions-in-mosul-fight-1477042201.

El-Ghobashy, Tamer, and Mustafa Salim. December 28, 2017. "Iraq's Rapid-Fire Trials Send Alleged ISIS Members—Including Foreigners—to the Gallows." *Washington Post*.

El-Naggar, Mona, and Quynhanh Do. July 31, 2014. "Video Released of U.S. Bomber in Syria." *New York Times*. https://www.nytimes.com/video/world/middleeast/100000003029549/video-of-us-bomber-moner-mohammad-abusalha-in-syria.html.

El Pais. "11-M décimo aniversario." https://elpais.com/especiales/2014/aniversario-11-m/graficos/.

El-Said, Hamed, and Richard Barrett. 2017. *Enhancing the Understanding of the Foreign Terrorist Fighters Phenomenon in Syria*. New York: United Nations Office of

Counter-Terrorism. http://www.un.org/en/counterterrorism/assets/img/Report_
Final_20170727.pdf.

Elliott, Andrea. January 27, 2010. "The Jihadist Next Door." *New York Times.*

Erickson, Amanda. July 26, 2018. "Europe's Prisons Breed Terrorism. Can
Anything Be Done?" *Washington Post. https://www.washingtonpost.com/news/
worldviews/wp/2018/07/26/europes-prisons-breed-terrorism-can-anything-be-done/?utm_
term=.0959f0b984f5*

European Union. March 15, 2017. *Directive (EU) 2017/541 of the European Parliament
and of the Council of 15 March 2017 on Combating Terrorism and Replacing Council
Framework Decision 2002/475/JHA and Amending Council Decision 2005/671/
JHA.* http://eur-lex.europa.eu/legal-content/EN/TXT/?uri=uriserv:OJ.L_
.2017.088.01.0006.01.ENG.

Exum, Andrew. Summer 2008. "Return of the Jihadi." *DemocracyJournal.org.*

Faiola, Anthony, and Souad Mekhennet. December 20, 2015. "The Islamic
State Creates a New Type of Jihadist: Part Terrorist, Part Gangster."
Washington Post.

Faiola, Anthony, and Souad Mekhennet. April 22, 2016. "Tracing the Path of Four
Terrorists Sent to Europe by the Islamic State." *Washington Post.*

Fair, Christine. 2017. "Pakistan's Promises to Fight Terrorism Are a Bad Joke."
https://www.youtube.com/watch?v=nYyXx9c3J94.

Faraj, Ayman Sabri. 2002. *Dhikrayat Arabi Afghani: Abu Ja'far Al-Misri Al-
Qandahari {Memoirs of an Arab Afghan: Abu Ja'afar Al-Masri Al-Qandahari}.*
Cairo: Dar Al Shorouk.

Farrall, Leah. December 2017. "Revisiting al-Qaida's Foundation and Early History."
Perspectives on Terrorism. http://www.terrorismanalysts.com/pt/index.php/pot/
article/view/654.

Federation of American Scientists. October 28, 1994. "Arab Veterans of Afghanistan
War Lead New Islamic Holy War." Washington, DC. https://fas.org/irp/news/
1994/afghan_war_vetrans.html.

Felter, Joseph, and Brian Fishman. 2009. "Becoming a Foreign Fighter: A
Second Look at the Sinjar Records." In *Bombers, Bank Accounts, & Bleedout: Al-
Qa'ida's Road in Iraq and Out of Iraq,* ed. Brian Fishman, 32–65. West Point,
NY: Combating Terrorism Center.

Felter, Joseph, and Jarret Brachman. 2007. *An Assessment of 516 Combatant Status
Review Tribunal (CSRT) Unclassified Summaries.* West Point, NY: Combating
Terrorism Center.

Fernandez, Alberto. 2012. "The State Department's Center for Strategic
Counterterrorism Communications: Mission, Operations, and Impact," Pub.
L. No. 112–164, § Subcommittee on Terrorism, Nonproliferation, and Trade of
the Committee on Foreign Affairs, 5, http://www.gpo.gov/fdsys/.

*Financing of Insurgency Operation in Iraq: Hearing before the House Financial Services
Subcommittee on Oversight and Investigations and the House Armed Services Subcommittee*

on *Terrorism*, 109th Cong. 1. July 28, 2005. Testimony of Daniel L. Glaser, Acting Assistant Secretary, Office of Terrorist Financing and Financial Crimes, U.S. Department of Treasury. https://financialservices.house.gov/media/pdf/072805dg.pdf.

Fine, Glenn A. April 2017. "Operation Inherent Resolve: Report to the United States Congress, April 1, 2017–June 30, 2017." Lead Inspector General for Overseas Contingency Operations, Washington, DC: Department of Defense. https://media.defense.gov/2017/Dec/20/2001859239/-1/-1/1/FY2017_LIG_OCO_OIR_Q3_REPORT_REV1.PDF.

Fisher, Ian. November 18, 2015. "In Rise of ISIS, No Single Missed Key but Many Strands of Blame." *New York Times*.

Fishman, Brian. 2009a. *Dysfunction and Decline: Lessons Learned from Inside Al-Qa'ida in Iraq*. West Point, NY: Combating Terrorism Center, Unites States Military Academy.

Fishman, Brian. 2009b. *Bombers, Bank Accounts, & Bleedout: Al-Qa'ida's Road in Iraq and Out of Iraq*. West Point, NY: Combating Terrorism Center.

Fishman, Brian. 2016. *The Master Plan: ISIS, al-Qaeda, and the Jihadi Strategy for Final Victory*. New Haven, CT: Yale University Press.

Flade, Florian. 2016. "The Islamic State Threat to Germany: Evidence from the Investigations." *CTC Sentinel* 9, no. 7: 11–14.

Flood, Derek Henry. 2014. "The Caucasus Emirate: From Anti-Colonialist Roots to Salafi-Jihad." *CTC Sentinel* 7, no. 3: 13–17.

Flynn, Michael T., Rich Juergens, and Thomas L. Cantrell. 2008. "Employing ISR: SOF Best Practices." *Joint Forces Quarterly* 50, no. 3: 56–61.

Galdini, Franco. December 19, 2013. "From Syria to Bosnia: Memoirs of a Mujahid in Limbo." *The Nation*. https://www.thenation.com/article/syria-bosnia-memoirs-mujahid-limbo/.

Gall, Carlotta. October 17, 1999. "Muslim Fighter Embraces Warrior Mystique." *New York Times*. http://www.nytimes.com/1999/10/17/world/muslim-fighter-embraces-warrior-mystique.html.

Gall, Carlotta. May 21, 2016. "How Kosovo Was Turned into Fertile Ground for ISIS." *New York Times*.

Gall, Carlotta, and Thomas De Waal. 1997. *Chechnya: A Small Victorious War*. London: Pan.

Gallup. "Iraq." n.d. Accessed February 20, 2018. http://news.gallup.com/poll/1633/iraq.aspx.

Gargan, Edward A. April 8, 1993. "Radical Arabs Use Pakistan as Base for Holy War." *New York Times*. http://www.nytimes.com/1993/04/08/world/radical-arabs-use-pakistan-as-base-for-holy-war.html.

Garner, George. 2013. "Chechnya and Kashmir: The Jihadist Evolution of Nationalism to Jihad and Beyond." *Terrorism and Political Violence* 25, no. 3: 419–434.

Gartenstein-Ross, Daveed. February 9, 2015. "How Many Fighters Does the Islamic State Really Have?" *Warontherocks.com*. https://warontherocks.com/2015/02/how-many-fighters-does-the-islamic-state-really-have/.

Gartenstein-Ross, Daveed, and Nathaniel Barr. 2016. *Recent Attacks Illuminate the Islamic State's Europe Attack Network.* Washington, DC: Jamestown Foundation.

Geibel, Adam. 2000. "Khattab's Audacious Raid (22 December 1997): Prelude to the Second Chechen War." *Central Asian Survey* 19, nos. 3/4: 339–347.

Geller, Eric. March 29, 2016. "Why ISIS Is Winning the Online Propaganda War." *Daily Dot.*

General Intelligence and Security Service. 2016. "Life with ISIS: The Myth Unravelled." https://english.nctv.nl/binaries/Life%20with%20ISIS%20-%20the%20Myth%20Unravelled_tcm32-90366.pdf

General Secretariat of the Council. 2015. *Outline of the Counter-Terrorism Strategy for Syria and Iraq, with Particular Focus on Foreign Fighters.* Brussels: Council of the European Union. http://data.consilium.europa.eu/doc/document/ST-5369-2015-INIT/en/pdf.

George, Sussannah. January 21, 2016. "Officials Have Cast the Iraqi Military's Victory over Islamic State Extremists in Ramadi as Proof That Coalition Training Efforts Have Paid Off and the Country's Troops Have Improved Since Their Catastrophic Collapse in 2014." *Associated Press.* https://www.usnews.com/news/world/articles/2016-01-26/iraqs-military-is-still-struggling-despite-us-training.

2016. "Foreign Fighters and the War on Terror: An Interview with Ambassador Thomas Krajeski." *Georgetown Journal of International Affairs* 17, no. 2: 5–9.

Gerstein, Josh, and Jennifer Scholtes. September 27, 2016. "Comey Warns of Post-ISIL Terrorist 'Diaspora.'" *Politico.*

Gettleman, Jeffrey. March 26, 2006. "Bound, Blindfolded and Dead: The Face of Revenge in Baghdad." *New York Times.*

Gettleman, Jeffrey. February 3, 2016. "Bomb Suspected in Deadly Explosion on Somali Jet." *New York Times.*

Gibas-Krzak, Danuta. 2013. "Contemporary Terrorism in the Balkans: A Real Threat to Security in Europe." *Journal of Slavic Military Studies* 26, no. 2: 203–218.

Giglio, Mike, and Munzer al-Awad. December 19, 2015. "The Escape: How ISIS Members Fled The Caliphate, Perhaps To Fight Another Day." *Buzzfeed.* https://www.buzzfeed.com/mikegiglio/how-isis-members-fled-the-caliphate-perhaps-to-fight?utm_term=.ayQ4d7mZ7#.lrzBmrvwr

Giglio, Mike, and Munzer Al-Awad. December 19, 2017. "How ISIS Members Fled the Caliphate, Perhaps to Fight Another Day." *BuzzFeed News.* https://www.buzzfeed.com/mikegiglio/how-isis-members-fled-the-caliphate-perhaps-to-fight?utm_term=.wgKpV509N#.rd4E7P9ng.

Gladwell, Malcolm. October 19, 2015. "Thresholds of Violence." *New Yorker.* https://www.newyorker.com/magazine/2015/10/19/thresholds-of-violence.

"A Global Battleground: The Fight against Islamist Extremism at Home and Abroad." Hearing before the Committee on Homeland Security, 114th Cong. 1. 2015. https://www.gpo.gov/fdsys/pkg/CHRG-114hhrg94886/pdf/CHRG-114hhrg94886.pdf.

Gold, Dore. 2012. *Hatred's Kingdom: How Saudi Arabia Supports the New Global Terrorism.* Washington, DC: Regnery Publishing.

Goldberg, Noah, and Victoria Bekiempis. "Bronx Man Who Got 'Terrorist Propaganda' from Chelsea Bomber Laughs during Court Appearance." *New York Daily News.*

Goldman, Adam, and Greg Miller. November 10, 2014. "American Suicide Bomber's Travels in U.S., Middle East Went Unmonitored." *Washington Post.* https://www.washingtonpost.com/world/national-security/american-suicide-bombers-travels-in-us-middle-east-went-unmonitored/2014/10/11/38a3228e-4fe8-11e4-aa5e-7153e466a02d_story.html?utm_term=.6c141d958a53.

Goldman, Adam, and Eric Schmitt. November 24, 2016. "One by One, ISIS Social Media Experts Are Killed as Result of F.B.I. Program." *New York Times.*

Goldman, Adam and Eric Schmitt. February 8, 2018. "2 of ISIS's Infamous British Fighters Are Captured by Syrian Kurds." *New York Times.*

Gordon, Michael R. July 18, 2007. "Leader of Al Qaeda Group in Iraq Was Fictional, U.S. Military Says." *New York Times.*

Gordon, Michael R., and Mark Mazzetti. February 23, 2007. "U.S. Used Base in Ethiopia to Hunt Al Qaeda." *New York Times.*

Greene, Leonard. January 24, 2016. "Video Shows ISIS Thugs Planning Paris Terror Attacks." *New York Daily News.* http://www.nydailynews.com/news/world/video-shows-isis-thugs-planning-paris-terror-attacks-article-1.2508087.

The Guardian. July 22, 2005. "Background: The Guardian and Dilpazier Aslam." https://www.theguardian.com/media/2005/jul/22/theguardian.pressandpublishing1.

The Guardian. January 31, 2015. "ISIS Finally Admits Defeat in Kobani after Air Strikes Force Its Fighters to Retreat." https://www.theguardian.com/world/2015/jan/31/isis-kobani-islamic-state-syria.

The Guardian. November 21, 2017. "After the Liberation of Mosul, an Orgy of Killing." https://www.theguardian.com/world/2017/nov/21/after-the-liberation-of-mosul-an-orgy-of-killing.

The Guardian. January 30, 2018. "How the People of Mosul Subverted ISIS Apartheid." https://www.theguardian.com/cities/2018/jan/30/mosul-isis-apartheid.

Hafez, Mohammed M. 2007. *Suicide Bombers in Iraq: The Strategy and Ideology of Martyrdom.* Washington, DC: United States Institute of Peace Press.

Hafez, Mohammed M. 2008. "Jihad after Iraq: Lessons from the Arab Afghans Phenomenon." *Studies in Conflict & Terrorism* 32, no. 2: 73–94.

Hamid, Mustafa, and Leah Farrall. 2015 *The Arabs at War in Afghanistan.* London: Hurst.

Hamid, Nafees. April 2018 "The British Hacker Who Became the Islamic State's Chief Terror Cybercoach: A Profile of Junaid Hussain." *CTC Sentinel.* pp. 30–37.

Hansen, Stig Jarle. 2013 *Al-Shabaab in Somalia: The History and Ideology of a Militant Islamist Group, 2005–2012.* New York: Oxford University Press.

Haq, Ethar Abdul. March 24, 2016. "Islamic State's Fake Passports Disrupt the Alarm Bells of Foreign Intelligence: New Documents." https://en.zamanalwsl.net/news/articles/130.

Haq, Ethar Abdul. April 26, 2016. "High-Profile Fighters Joined ISIS Army, Made Advances: Leaked Data Shows." https://en.zamanalwsl.net/news/articles/130.

Harding, Andrew. May 20, 2015 "Somali Defector: Why I Left Al-Shabab." *BBC News*.

Hassan, Hassan. January 24, 2015 "The Secret World of ISIS Training Camps— Ruled by Sacred Texts and the Sword." *The Guardian*.

Hassan, Hassan. October 25, 2017. "ISIL and the Numbers Game: What Exactly Is the Size of Its Army?" *The National*.

Hastert, Paul L. 2005. "Operation Anaconda: Perception Meets Reality in the Hills of Afghanistan." *Studies in Conflict & Terrorism* 28, no. 1: 11–20.

Hays, Tom, and Sharon Theimer. December 26, 2001. "In Life of Double-Crosses, Egyptian Worked with Green Berets and Bin Laden." *Black Hills Pioneer*. http://www.bhpioneer.com/in-life-of-double-crosses-egyptian-worked-with-green-berets/article_264a0132-b8e9-59b0-b2b2-174098a908fc.html.

Heavey, Susan, and Ian Simpson. March 31, 2017. "The FBI Arrested a Teen at a South Carolina Airport for Trying to Join ISIS." *Reuters*. http://www.businessinsider.com/charleston-international-airport-isis-2017-3.

Hecker, Marc. April 2018. "137 Shades of Terrorism: French Jihadists before the Courts." Security Studies Center (IFRI)

Hedges, Chris. December 5, 1992. "Muslims from Afar Joining 'Holy War' in Bosnia." *New York Times*. http://www.nytimes.com/1992/12/05/world/muslims-from-afar-joining-holy-war-in-bosnia.html.

Hegghammer, Thomas. 2007a. *Saudi Militants in Iraq: Backgrounds and Recruitment Patterns*. Kjeller, Norway: Norwegian Defence Research Establishment, Forsvarets Forskningsinstitutt (FFI). http://www.ffi.no/no/Rapporter/06-03875.pdf.

Hegghammer, Thomas. 2007b. "Violent Islamism in Saudi Arabia, 1979– 2006: The Power and Perils of Pan-Islamic Nationalism." PhD diss. (unpublished), Institut d'Etudes Politiques de Paris. http://hegghammer.com/_files/Hegghammer_-_Thesis_-_Violent_Islamism_in_Saudi_Arabia_-_FULL_VERSION.pdf.

Hegghammer, Thomas. 2008. "Azzam." In Gilles Kepel and Jean-Pierre Milelli, eds., *Al Qaeda in Its Own Words*. Cambridge, MA: Harvard University Press.

Hegghammer, Thomas. 2010a. *Jihad in Saudi Arabia: Violence and Pan-Islamism since 1979*. Cambridge, UK: Cambridge University Press.

Hegghammer, Thomas. 2010b. "The Rise of Muslim Foreign Fighters: Islam and the Globalization of Jihad." *International Security* 35, no. 3: 53–94.

Hegghammer, Thomas. 2013a. "Abdallah Azzam and Palestine." *Welt des Islams* 53, nos. 3/4: 353–387.

Hegghammer, Thomas. 2013b. "Should I Stay or Should I Go? Explaining Variation in Western Jihadists' Choice between Domestic and Foreign Fighting." *American Political Science Review* 107, no. 1: 1–15.

Hegghammer, Thomas. 2016. "The Future of Jihadism in Europe: A Pessimistic View." *Perspectives on Terrorism* 10, no. 6: 156–170.

Hegghammer, Thomas. Ed. 2017. *Jihadi Culture.* Cambridge, UK: Cambridge University Press

Hegghammer, Thomas, and Petter Nesser. 2015. "Assessing the Islamic State's Commitment to Attacking the West." *Perspectives on Terrorism* 9, no. 4: 14–30.

Hegghammer, Thomas, and Aaron Y. Zelin. July 3, 2013. "How Syria's Civil War Became a Holy Crusade." *Foreign Affairs.* https://www.foreignaffairs.com/articles/middle-east/2013-07-03/how-syrias-civil-war-became-holy-crusade.

Heißner, Stefan, Peter R. Neumann, John Holland-McCowan, and Rajan Basra. 2017. "Caliphate in Decline: An Estimate of the Islamic State's Financial Fortunes." London: International Centre for the Study of Radicalisation and Political Violence. http://icsr.info/wp-content/uploads/2017/02/ICSR-Report-Caliphate-in-Decline-An-Estimate-of-Islamic-States-Financial-Fortunes.pdf.

Heil, Georg. 2017. "The Berlin Attack and the 'Abu Walaa' Islamic State Recruitment Network." *CTC Sentinel* 10, no. 2: 1–11.

Heinke, Daniel H. 2016. *German Jihadists in Syria and Iraq: An Update."* London: International Centre for the Study of Radicalisation and Political Violence. http://icsr.info/2016/02/icsr-insight-german-jihadists-syria-iraq-update/.

Heinke, Daniel H., and Jan Raudszus. 2018. "Germany's Returning Foreign Fighters and What to Do about Them." In "Returnees: Who Are They, Why Are They (Not) Coming Back and How Should We Deal with Them?" *Egmont Paper* 101, Thomas Renard and Rik Coolsaet, eds., 41–54. http://www.egmontinstitute.be/content/uploads/2018/02/egmont.papers.101_online_v1-3.pdf?type=pdf.

Hennessy-Fiske, Molly, and W. J. Hennigan. April 21, 2017. "Civilian Casualties from Airstrikes Grow in Iraq and Syria. But few are Ever Investigated." *Los Angeles Times.*

Hinnant, Lori, and Paul Schemm. February 3, 2015. "The Cost of Leaving Islamic State: Death or Jail." *Japan Today.* https://japantoday.com/category/world/the-cost-of-leaving-islamic-state-death-or-jail.

Hiraal Institute. July 2018. "The AS Finance System.s" https://hiraalinstitute.org/the-as-finance-system/

History Commons. n.d. "Profile: Abu Zubair Al Madani." http://www.historycommons.org/entity.jsp?entity=abu_zubair_al_madani_1&printerfriendly=true.

Hoare, Marko Attila. 2004. *How Bosnia Armed.* London: Saqi.

Hoffman, Bruce. 2006. "Insurgency and Counterinsurgency in Iraq." *Studies in Conflict & Terrorism* 29, no. 2: 103–121.

Hoffman, Bruce. 2014. "The 7 July 2005 London Bombings." In *The Evolution of the Global Terrorist Threat: From 9/11 to Osama bin Laden's Death*, ed. Bruce Hoffman and Fernando Reinares, 192–223. New York: Columbia University Press.

Hogg, Andrew. August 30, 1992. "Arabs Join in Bosnian War." *Sunday Times* (London).

Holley, Peter. November 16, 2015. "Paris Suspect Bragged of Eluding Bloated Crusader Intelligence." *Washington Post.* https://www.washingtonpost.com/news/worldviews/wp/2015/11/16/paris-terror-suspect-bragged-of-eluding-bloated-crusader-intelligence/?utm_term=.c11dd7689585.

Holman, Timothy. 2015. "Belgian and French Foreign Fighters in Iraq 2003–2005: A Comparative Case Study." *Studies in Conflict & Terrorism* 38, no. 8: 603–621.

Holman, Timothy. January 16, 2015. "The Clear Banner: French Foreign Fighters in Iraq 2003–2008." *Jihadology.* http://jihadology.net/2015/01/16/the-clear-banner-french-foreign-fighters-in-iraq-2003-2008-2/.

Holman, Timothy. 2016. " 'Gonna Get Myself Connected': The Role of Facilitation in Foreign Fighter Mobilizations." *Perspectives on Terrorism* 10, no. 2: 2–23.

Homeland Security Committee. 2015. *Final Report of the Task Force on Combating Terrorist and Foreign Fighter Travel.* https://homeland.house.gov/wp-content/uploads/2015/09/TaskForceFinalReport.pdf.

Homeland Security Committee. 2012. A Report by: Majority and Minority Staff Senate Committee on Homeland Security and Governmental Affairs. *Zachary Chesser: A Case Study in Online Islamist Radicalization and Its Meaning for the Threat of Homegrown Terrorism.* https://www.hsgac.senate.gov/imo/media/doc/CHESSER%20FINAL%20REPORT(1)?.pdf.

Hookham, Mark. November 6, 2016. "SAS in Iraq Gets Kill List of British Jihadis." *The Times.*

Horgan, John, and Kurt Braddock. 2010. "Rehabilitating the Terrorists? Challenges in Assessing the Effectiveness of De-radicalization Programs." *Terrorism and Political Violence* 23: 267–291.

Horwitz, Sari, and Adam Goldman. May 2, 2014. "FBI Director: Number of Americans Traveling to Fight in Syria Increasing." *Washington Post.* https://www.washingtonpost.com/world/national-security/fbi-director-number-of-americans-traveling-to-fight-in-syria-increasing/2014/05/02/6fa3d84e-d222-11e3-937f-d3026234b51c_story.html?utm_term=.26a0f71fd9af.

Hughes, Seamus. March 7, 2018. "The Only Islamic State–Funded Plot in the U.S.: The Curious Case of Mohamed Elshinawy." *Lawfareblog.* https://www.lawfareblog.com/only-islamic-state-funded-plot-us-curious-case-mohamed-elshinawy.

Hughes, Seamus, and Alexander Meleagrou-Hitchens. March 2017. "The Virtual Entrepreneurs of the Islamic State." *CTC Sentinel* 10, no. 3: 1–8.

Hughes, Seamus, Alexander Meleagrou-Hitchens, and Bennett Clifford. June 13, 2018. "A New American Leader Rises in ISIS." *The Atlantic.*

Human Rights Watch. 1992. *War Crimes in Bosnia-Hercegovina.* https://www.hrw.org/reports/pdfs/y/yugoslav/yugo.928/yugo928full.pdf.

Human Rights Watch. November 4, 2014. "Syria: ISIS Tortured Kobani Child Hostages." https://www.hrw.org/news/2014/11/04/syria-isis-tortured-kobani-child-hostages.

Husayn, Fu'ad. June 10, 2006. "Al-Zarqawi: The Second Generation of Al-Qa'ida."

Hussein Cell/Network Status Update Report. 2007. Reference Number: NMEC-2007-658086. West Point, NY: Combating Terrorism Center. https://ctc.usma.edu/harmony-program/hussein-cellnetwork-status-update-report-original-language-2/.

Hyman, Anthony. 1994. "Arab Involvement in the Afghan War." *Beirut Review* 7 (spring): 73–89.

Ibrahim, Youssef. December 28, 1997. "As Algerian Civil War Drags On, Atrocities Grow." *New York Times.* https://www.nytimes.com/1997/12/28/world/as-algerian-civil-war-drags-on-atrocities-grow.html.

Iley, Chrissy. May 16, 2011. "Vidal Sassoon Interview." *The Telegraph.* http://fashion.telegraph.co.uk/news-features/TMG8480525/Vidal-Sassoon-interview.html

The Independent. July 6, 2015. "7/7 Bombings: Profiles of the Four Bombers Who Killed 52 People in the London Attacks." https://www.independent.co.uk/news/uk/home-news/77-bombings-london-anniversary-live-profiles-of-the-four-bombers-who-killed-52-people-in-london-10369984.html.

"Inside the world of Saudi Islamic State members." May 5, 2016. The *New Arab.*

Ingram, Haroro J., and Craig Whiteside. June 2, 2016. "Don't Kill the Caliph! The Islamic State and the Pitfalls of Leadership Decapitation." *War on the Rocks.* https://warontherocks.com/2016/06/dont-kill-the-caliph-the-islamic-state-and-the-pitfalls-of-leadership-decapitation/.

Internal document: Harmony, AFGP-2002-600104, 1. 2007. Translated/compiled in United States Military Academy, 189. https://ctc.usma.edu/harmony-program/the-ogaden-file-operation-holding-al-msk-original-language-2/

International Crisis Group. 2001. *Bin Laden and the Balkans: The Politics of Anti-Terrorism.* Washington, DC. https://d2071andvip0wj.cloudfront.net/119-bin-laden-and-the-balkans-the-politics-of-anti-terrorism.pdf.

International Crisis Group. 2005. *Counter-Terrorism in Somalia: Losing Hearts and Minds?* Washington, DC, https://d2071andvip0wj.cloudfront.net/95-counter-terrorism-in-somalia-losing-hearts-and-minds.pdf.

International Crisis Group. 2006. *In Their Own Words: Reading the Iraqi Insurgency.* Washington, DC, https://d2071andvip0wj.cloudfront.net/50-in-their-own-words-reading-the-iraqi-insurgency.pdf.

International Crisis Group. 2010. *Somalia's Divided Islamists.* https://d2071andvip0wj.cloudfront.net/b74-somalia-s-divided-islamists.pdf.

International Crisis Group. 2014. *Somalia: Al-Shabaab—It Will Be a Long War.* https://d2071andvip0wj.cloudfront.net/somalia-al-shabaab-it-will-be-a-long-war.pdf.

International Crisis Group. 2016. *Exploiting Disorder: Al-Qaeda and the Islamic State.* Washington, DC. https://www.crisisgroup.org/global/exploiting-disorder-al-qaeda-and-islamic-state.

International Crisis Group. 2016. *The North Caucasus Insurgency and Syria: An Exported Jihad?* Washington, DC. https://www.crisisgroup.org/europe-central-asia/caucasus/north-caucasus/north-caucasus-insurgency-and-syria-exported-jihad.

"Interview with Commander Abdul-Aziz." n.d. In *I Am Muslim.* http://www.alalbany.me/play.php?catsmktba=15923.

"Interview with Jean-Pierre Filiu." February 11, 2007. *La Nouvelle Republique.*

Islamic Army of Iraq. April 5, 2007. "Reply of the Islamic Army in Iraq to the Speeches of Brother Abu Umar Al-Baghdadi." *Al-Boraq Media Center.* Document archive provided by Brian Fishman.

Islamic News Agency. October 24, 2014. "Ain Al Arab—Kubani."

Islamic New Agency. October 29, 2016. "Stories and Scenes from Mosul (1): Fighters of Different Nationalities Like You Are in the World Cup."

Ito, Suzanne. September 30, 2011. "ACLU Lens: American Citizen Anwar Al-Aulaqi Killed without Judicial Process." *American Civil Liberties Union.* http://www.aclu.org/blog/national-security/aclu-lens-american-citizen-anwar-al-aulaqi-killed-without-judicial-process..

James, Patrick, Michael Jensen, and Herbert Tinsley. 2015. *Understanding the Threat: What Data Tells Us about U.S. Foreign Fighters.* College Park, MD: National Consortium for the Study of Terrorism and Responses to Terrorism. http://www.start.umd.edu/pubs/START_PIRUS_WhatDataTellUsAbo utForeignFighters_AnalyticalBrief_Sept2015.pdf.

Jehl, Douglas. March 7, 1993. "The Twin Towers; Rahman Errors Admitted." *New York Times.* http://www.nytimes.com/1993/03/07/nyregion/the-twin-towers-rahman-errors-admitted.html.

Jenkins, Brian. 2014. "When Jihadis Come Marching Home: The Terrorist Threat Posed by Westerners Returning from Iraq and Syria." Santa Monica, CA: RAND Corporation.

Jensen, Michael, Patrick James, and Herbert Tinsley. 2016. *Overview: Profiles of Individual Radicalization in the United States–Foreign Fighters (PIRUS-FF).* College Park, MD: National Consortium for the Study of Terrorism and Responses to Terrorism. https://www.start.umd.edu/sites/default/files/publications/local_attachments/START_PIRUS-FF_InfographicSeries_April2016_0.pdf.

Jihad 2.0: Social Media in the Next Evolution of Terrorist Recruitment: Testimony before the Committee on Homeland Security and Governmental Affairs, 114th Cong. 1. 2015. Statement of Peter Bergen, Director, International Security Program, New America and Professor of Practice at Arizona State University.

Jihadology. June 4, 2015. "Al-Hayat Media Center Presents a New Video Message from the Islamic State: 'Honor is in Jihad: A Message to the People of the Balkans.'" http://jihadology.net/2015/06/04/

al-%E1%B8%A5ayat-media-center-presents-a-new-video-message-from-the-islamic-state-honor-is-in-jihad-a-message-to-the-people-of-the-balkans/.

Jung, Danielle F., Pat Ryan, Jacob N. Shapiro, and Jon Wallace. 2014. *Managing a Transnational Insurgency: The Islamic State of Iraq's "Paper Trail," 2005–2010*. West Point, NY: Combating Terrorism Center. https://ctc.usma.edu/app/uploads/2014/12/Managing-a-Transnational-Insurgency-ISI-FINAL1.pdf.

Kaplan, Robert D. April 2010. "Man Versus Afghanistan." *The Atlantic*.

Karadeniz, Tulay, and Yesim Dikmen. May 8, 2016. "Turkish Shelling Kills 55 Islamic State Militants in Syria: Military Sources." *Reuters*. https://www.reuters.com/article/us-mideast-crisis-syria-turkey/turkish-shelling-kills-55-islamic-state-militants-in-syria-military-sources-idUSKCN0XZ05R.

Karlin, Mara E. 2017. *Building Militaries in Fragile States: Challenges for the United States*. Philadelphia: University of Pennsylvania Press.

Keaten, Jamey. May 13, 2014. "French Police Arrest 6 Suspected Syria Jihadists." *Associated Press*. http://bigstory.ap.org/article/french-police-arrest-6-suspected-syria-jihadists.

Mogadishu: African Union Mission in Somalia. n.d. *Kenya—KDF*. http://amisom-au.org/kenya-kdf/.

Kepel, Gilles. 2003. *Jihad: The Trail of Political Islam*. Cambridge, MA: Harvard University Press.

Khalifa, Abdel Baqi. November 20, 2001. "Internal Memo for Arab-Afghans in Bosnia Reveals Significant Differences with Their Leaders." *Asharq Al-Awsat*. http://archive.aawsat.com/details.asp?section=1&issueno=8393&article=67213&feature=#.Wnxr7K6nHcs.

Khalifa, Abdel Baqi. May 31, 2002. "The Spokesman for Arab Fighters in Bosnia: Bin Laden Opposed Sending Arab Volunteers to Bosnia." *Asharq Al-Awsat* [Arabic]. http://archive.aawsat.com/details.asp?section=4&issueno=8585&article=106081#.Wnxpha6nHcv.

Khan, Abdul Sattar. May 12, 2001. "Osama Urges Ummah to Continue Jihad." *The News*.

Khan, Ismail. July 31, 2000. "Usama Bin Ladin's Al-Qaeda Splits as Ideologue Parts Ways." *The News* (Islamabad).

Khan, Shehab. February 10, 2018. "Hundreds of Foreign Women Who Joined ISIS Captured by Kurdish Forces in Syria." *The Independent*. https://www.independent.co.uk/news/world/middle-east/isis-foreign-women-islamic-state-detained-human-rights-watch-a8204686.html.

Khuzam, Akram. May 1997. "The Leader of the Arab Fighters in Chechnya." *Al Jazeera*. https://www.youtube.com/watch?v=97fOtZ0zM0c

Kibble, David G. 2016. "Beheading, Raping, and Burning: How the Islamic State Justifies Its Actions." *Military Review* 96, no. 2: 28–35.

"Killing Al-Awlaki Raises Obama's Approval on Terrorism Eight Points." October 7, 2011. The Economist/YouGov poll. http://today.yougov.com/news/2011/10/07/killing-al-awlaki-raises-obamas-approval-terrorism/.

Kinzer, Stephen. January 21, 1996. "Ferry Hijacking Raises Turkey-Russia Tension." *New York Times*. http://www.nytimes.com/1996/01/21/world/ferry-hijacking-raises-turkey-russia-tension.html.

Kirkpatrick, David. February 3, 2018. "Secret Alliance: Israel Carries Out Airstrikes in Egypt, with Cairo's Okay." *New York Times*. https://www.nytimes.com/2018/02/03/world/middleeast/israel-airstrikes-sinai-egypt.html.

Klausen, Jytte. 2015. "Tweeting the Jihad: Social Media Networks of Western Foreign Fighters in Syria and Iraq." *Studies in Conflict & Terrorism* 38, no. 1: 1–22.

Knickmeyer, Ellen. October 25, 2010. "Blood on Our Hands." *Foreign Policy*.

Kohlmann, Evan F. 2004. *Al-Qaida's Jihad in Europe: The Afghan Bosnian Network*. Oxford, UK: Berg.

Kohlmann, Evan F. 2006. *The Afghan-Bosnian Mujahedeen Network in Europe*. Swedish National Defence College. http://www.aina.org/reports/tabmnie.pdf.

Kolind, Torsten. 2008. *Post-War Identification: Everyday Muslim Counter-Discourse in Bosnia Herzegovina*. Aarhus, Denmark: Aarhus University Press.

Kramer, Andrew E. February 24, 2018. "Raised by ISIS, Returned to Chechnya: 'These Children Saw Terrible Things.'" *New York Times*.

Kristo, Ivana Kiendl. 2016. *Framework Decision 2002/475/JHA on Combating Terrorism*. Brussels: European Parliamentary Research Service. http://www.europarl.europa.eu/RegData/etudes/BRIE/2016/581393/EPRS_BRI2016581393_EN.pdf.

Kroupenev, Artem. 2009. *Radical Islam in Chechnya*. Herzliya, Israel, International Institute for Counter-Terrorism. https://www.ict.org.il/Article.aspx?ID=1057#gsc.tab=0.

Krueger, Alan B. 2006. "The National Origins of Foreign Fighters in Iraq." Unpublished, Princeton University.

Kukis, Mark. October 25, 2006. "Ethnic Cleansing in a Baghdad Neighborhood?" *Time*.

Lafitte, Pracille. November 9, 2018. "How the Planners of the 2015 Paris Attacks Were Systematically Eliminated." *France 24*. https://www.france24.com/en/20181108-france-intelligence-2015-paris-attacks-masterminds-eliminated-suc-book-islamic-state

LaFraniere, Sharon. September 26, 2001. "Moscow Eager to Tie Rebels in Chechnya to Bin Laden." *Washington Post*. https://www.washingtonpost.com/archive/politics/2001/09/26/moscow-eager-to-tie-rebels-in-chechnya-to-bin-laden/741c6b8a-3e18-4aa6-a0ac-6b338c33b807/?utm_term=.d1c0347ad091.

LaFraniere, Sharon. April 26, 2003. "How Jihad Made Its Way to Chechnya." *Washington Post*. https://www.washingtonpost.com/archive/politics/2003/04/26/how-jihad-made-its-way-to-chechnya/5b941796-ed50-4f65-9a2b-18a90155e571/?utm_term=.bd1933273f75.

Lamothe, Dan. September 2, 2014. "Here's the Transcript of the Video Showing Steven Sotloff's Reported Execution." *Washington Post*. https://www.washingtonpost.com/news/checkpoint/wp/2014/09/02/

heres-the-transcript-of-the-video-showing-steven-sotloffs-reported-execution/
?utm_term=.98fdd9700909.

Larner, Tony. December 10, 2017. "Junaid Hussain: How Birmingham ISIS Terrorist Was Linked to THIRTY Plots across the World." *Birmingham Live.* https://www.birminghammail.co.uk/news/midlands-news/junaid-hussain-how-birmingham-isis-14016336.

Lawler, David, Isabelle Fraser, Raziye Akkoc, and David Millward. November 20, 2015. "Paris Attacks: Police Warn of EU Border Failures—As It Happened on Thursday Nov 19." *The Telegraph.* https://www.telegraph.co.uk/news/worldnews/europe/france/12007011/Paris-attacks-as-it-happened-on-Thursday-Nov-19.html.

Leiken, Robert S. 2012. *Europe's Angry Muslims: The Revolt of the Second Generation.* New York: Oxford University Press.

"Letter about Matter of the Islamic Maghreb." n.d. Documents gathered by Brian Fishman. Available at https://static1.squarespace.com/static/57a2ce8503596ee87a205a0d/t/57b7999d5016e192aad6e5c5/1471650206041/Letter+about+matter+of+the+Islamic+Maghreb.pdf.

"Letter to Abu Basir." n.d. Available at https://www.dni.gov/files/documents/ubl2017/english/Letter%20to%20Abu%20Basir.pdf.

"Letter from Abu Yayha." n.d. Available at https://www.dni.gov/files/documents/ubl2017/english/Letter%20from%20Abu%20Yahya.pdf.

Levada Center. 2014. *Approval and Trust.* Moscow, Russia. https://www.levada.ru/en/2014/09/29/approval-and-trust/.

Levitt, Matthew. 2008. "Al-Qaʿida's Finances: Evidence of Organizational Decline?" *CTC Sentinel* 1, no. 5: 7–9.

Levitt, Matthew, and Michael Jacobson. 2008. *The Money Trail: Finding, Following, and Freezing Terrorist Finances.* Washington, DC: Washington Institute for Near East Policy. https://www.washingtoninstitute.org/uploads/Documents/pubs/PolicyFocus89.pdf.

Lia, Brynjar. Winter 2016. "Jihadism in the Arab World after 2011: Explaining Its Expansion." *Middle East Policy Journal* 33, no. 4. https://onlinelibrary.wiley.com/doi/pdf/10.1111/mepo.12234.

Lichtblau, Eric. June 7, 2016. "F.B.I. Steps Up Use of Stings in ISIS Cases." *New York Times.* https://www.nytimes.com/2016/06/08/us/fbi-isis-terrorism-stings.html.

Life with ISIS: The Myth Unraveled. 2016. General Intelligence and Security Service, Ministry of the Interior and Kingdom Relation. The Hague, The Netherlands. https://english.nctv.nl/binaries/Life%20with%20ISIS%20-%20the%20Myth%20Unravelled_tcm32-90366.pdf.

Lister, Tim. June 14, 2016. "ISIS Rides Waves of Attacks Even as Its Territory Shrinks." *CNN.com.* https://www.cnn.com/2016/06/14/middleeast/isis-territory-attacks-lister/.

Lokshina, Tanya. 2016. *Like Walking a Minefield: Vicious Crackdown on Critics in Russia's Chechen Republic.* Human Rights Watch.

https://www.hrw.org/report/2016/08/30/walking-minefield/
vicious-crackdown-critics-russias-chechen-republic#page.

Malet, David. 2013. *Foreign Fighters: Transnational Identity in Civil Conflicts.* Oxford, UK: Oxford University Press.

Malet, David. 2015. "Foreign Fighter Mobilization and Persistence in a Global Context." *Terrorism and Political Violence* 27, no. 3: 454–473.

Malet, David. 2018. "The European Experience with Foreign Fighters and Returnees." In *Returnees: Who Are They, Why Are They (Not) Coming Back and How Should We Deal with Them?*" 2018. *Egmont Paper* 101, Thomas Renard and Rik Coolsaet, eds., pp. 6–18.

Malet, David, and Rachel Hayes. 2018. "Foreign Fighter Returnees: An Indefinite Threat?" *Terrorism and Political Violence* 1: 1–19.

Malik, Mohammad A. June 20, 2016. "I Reported Omar Mateen to the FBI." *Washington Post.* https://www.washingtonpost.com/posteverything/wp/2016/06/20/i-reported-omar-mateen-to-the-fbi-trump-is-wrong-that-muslims-dont-do-our-part/?utm_term=.3c4c75f07f3d.

Malkasian, Carter. 2006. "Signaling Resolve, Democratization, and the First Battle of Fallujah." *Journal of Strategic Studies* 29, no. 3: 423–452.

Manisera, Sara. September 29, 2017. " 'I Came for the Jihad': Women Tell of Life in the Islamic State." *Syria Deeply.* https://www.newsdeeply.com/syria/articles/2017/09/29/i-came-for-the-jihad-women-tell-of-life-in-the-islamic-state.

Mansour, Ahmad. February 6, 2014. "Mum, I'm Fighting for Allah Now." *Fikra Forum.* http://fikraforum.org/?p=4599.

Marchal, Roland. 2009. "A Tentative Assessment of the Somali Harakat Al-Shabaab." *Journal of Eastern African Studies* 3, no. 3: 381–404.

Marchal, Roland. 2013. "Islamic Political Dynamics in the Somali Civil War." In *Islam in Africa South of the Sahara: Essays in Gender Relations and Political Reform,* ed. Paade Badru, Brigid M. Sackey, and Roland Marchal, 331–354. Lanham, MD: Scarecrow Press.

Marone, Francesco. 2016. *Italy's Jihadists in the Syrian Civil War.* The Hague: International Center for Counter-Terrorism.

"Massacres of Hazaras in Afghanistan." February 2001. Human Rights Watch. https://www.hrw.org/report/2001/02/01/massacres-hazaras-afghanistan.

Mazzetti, Mark, Jeffrey Gettleman, and Eric Schmitt. October 16, 2016. "In Somalia, U.S. Escalates a Shadow War." *New York Times.*

McCann, Kate. October 22, 2017. " 'The Only Way' of Dealing with British Islamic State Fighters Is to Kill Them in Almost Every Case, Minister Says." *The Telegraph.*

McCants, William. Ed. 2006. *Militant Ideology Atlas.* West Point NYL Combating Terrorism Center. https://ctc.usma.edu/app/uploads/2012/04/Atlas-ResearchCompendium1.pdf.

McCants, William. November 19, 2013. "How Zawahiri Lost Al Qaeda." *Foreign Affairs.*

McCants, William. 2015. *The ISIS Apocalypse: The History, Strategy, and Doomsday Vision of the Islamic State.* New York: St. Martin's Press.

McCarthy, Justin. March 23, 2016. "Worry about Terrorist Attacks in U.S. High but Not Top Concern." *Gallup.* http://news.gallup.com/poll/190253/worry-terror-attacks-high-not-top-concern.aspx?g_source=position1&g_medium=related&g_campaign=tiles.

McCrummen, Stephanie, and Karen DeYoung. May 2, 2008. "U.S. Airstrike Kills Somali Accused of Links to Al-Qaeda." *Washington Post.*

McDowall, Angus. October 5, 2015. "Saudi Opposition Clerics Make Sectarian Call to Jihad in Syria." *Reuters.* https://www.reuters.com/article/us-mideast-crisis-saudi-clerics/saudi-opposition-clerics-make-sectarian-call-to-jihad-in-syria-idUSKCN0RZ1IW20151005.

McGregor, Andrew. 2003. *Amir Abu Al-Walid and the Islamic Component of the Chechen War.* Central Asia-Caucasus Institute Analyst. https://www.cacianalyst.org/publications/analytical-articles/item/7260-analytical-articles-caci-analyst-2003-2-26-art-7260.html.

McGregor, Andrew. 2006a. "Islam, Jamaats and Implications for the North Caucasus—Part 1." *Terrorism Monitor* 4, no. 11. https://jamestown.org/program/islam-jamaats-and-implications-for-the-north-caucasus-part-1/.

McGregor, Andrew. 2006b. "Islam, Jamaats and Implications for the North Caucasus—Part 2." *Terrorism Monitor* 4, no. 12. https://jamestown.org/program/islam-jamaats-and-implications-for-the-north-caucasus-part-2/.

McGregor, Andrew. 2006c. " 'Jihad and the Rifle Alone': 'Abdullah 'Azzam and the Islamist Revolution." *Journal of Conflict Studies* 23, no. 2: 92–113.

McGregor, Andrew. 2006d. "The Amnesty Offensive: Breaking Down Basaev's Network." *North Caucasus Weekly* 7, no. 30. https://jamestown.org/program/the-amnesty-offensive-breaking-down-basaevs-network/.

McGregor, Andrew. 2006e. "New Fronts, New Focus: Dokku Umarov's War on Russia." *North Caucasus Weekly* 7, no. 26. https://jamestown.org/program/new-fronts-new-focus-dokku-umarovs-war-on-russia/.

"The Meeting of Emir Abdul Aziz, the Commander of the Arabs in Bosnia, with Sheikh Al-Albani." n.d. http://www.alalbany.me/play.php?catsmktba=15923.

Meichtry, Stacy, and Julian E. Barnes. February 13, 2018. "Europe Balks at Taking Back ISIS Fighters." *Wall Street Journal.*

Mekhennet, Souad. August 16, 2017. "How a Journalist Uncovered the True Identity of Jihadi John." *Longreads.* https://longreads.com/2017/08/16/how-a-journalist-uncovered-the-true-identity-of-jihadi-john/.

Meleagrou-Hitchens, Alexander, and Seamus Hughes. 2017. "The Threat to the United States from the Islamic State's Virtual Entrepreneurs." *CTC Sentinel* 10, no. 3: 1–8.

Meleagrou-Hitchens, Alexander, Seamus Hughes, and Bennett Clifford. 2018. "The Travelers: American Jihadists in Syria and Iraq." Washington, DC: George

Washington University Program on Extremism. https://extremism.gwu.edu/sites/
extremism.gwu.edu/files/TravelersAmericanJihadistsinSyriaandIraq.pdf

Menkhaus, Ken. 2007. "The Crisis in Somalia: Tragedy in Five Acts." *African Affairs*
106, no. 424: 357–390.

Menkhaus, Ken. 2009. "Somalia: 'They Created a Desert and Called it Peace
(Building).'" *Review of African Political Economy* 36, no. 120: 223–233.

Meservey, Joshua, and Kelsey Lilley. October 26, 2016. "Is the Coalition Fighting
Al-Shabaab Falling Apart?" *War on the Rocks*. https://warontherocks.com/2016/10/
is-the-coalition-fighting-al-shabaab-falling-apart/.

Middle East Forum. 2004. *Iran's Link to Al-Qaeda: The 9-11 Commission's
Evidence*. Philadelphia, Pennsylvania. http://www.meforum.org/670/
irans-link-to-al-qaeda-the-9-11-commissions.

Miller, Greg. December 22, 2017. "Senior Counterterrorism Official Expresses
Concern about Access in U.S. to Lethal Weaponry." *Washington Post*. https://www.
washingtonpost.com/world/national-security/senior-counterterrorism-official-
expresses-concern-about-access-in-us-to-lethal-weaponry/2017/12/21/dad95cce-
e664-11e7-833f-155031558ff4_story.html?utm_term=.e023b117b11d.

Miller, Greg, and Souad Mekhennet. March 6, 2016. "Undercover Teams, Increased
Surveillance and Hardened Borders: Turkey Cracks Down on Foreign Fighters."
Washington Post.

Miller, Greg, and Souad Mekhennet. April 10, 2016. "One Woman Helped
the Mastermind of the Paris Attacks. The Other Turned Him In." *The
Washington Post*.

Miller, John. September 9, 2016. "When Preventing Another 9/11 Is Your Day Job."
Esquire. https://www.esquire.com/news-politics/a48456/current-terrorism-threats/

Milton, Daniel, and Brian Dodwell. May 2018. "Jihadi Brides? Examining a Female
Guesthouse Registry from the Islamic State's Caliphate." *CTC Sentinel* 11,
no. 5: 16–23.

Mironova, Vera, Ekaterina Sergatskova, and Karam Alhamad. October 27, 2017.
"The Lives of Foreign Fighters Who Left ISIS." *Foreign Affairs*.

Mitchell, Jeni. 2008. "The Contradictory Effects of Ideology on Jihadist
War-Fighting: The Bosnia Precedent." *Studies in Conflict & Terrorism* 31,
no. 9: 808–828.

MI5 Security Service. "Foreign Fighters." London. https://www.mi5.gov.uk/
foreign-fighters

Moghadam, Assaf. September 15, 2016. "The Jihadist Entrepreneur: What the
Anjem Choudary Case Can Teach Us." *War on the Rocks*. https://warontherocks.
com/2016/09/the-jihadist-entrepreneur-what-the-anjem-choudary-case-can-teach-
us/.

*Money Laundering and Terror Financing Issues in the Middle East: Hearing before
the Committee on Banking, Housing, and Urban Affairs*, 109th Cong. 1. 2005.
Wtatement of Stuart Levey, Under Secretary, Office of Terrorism and Financial

Intelligence, U.S. Department of Treasury. https://www.treasury.gov/press-center/press-releases/Pages/js2629.aspx.

Moore, Cerwyn. 2015. "Foreign Bodies: Transnational Activism, the Insurgency in the North Caucasus and 'Beyond.'" *Terrorism & Political Violence* 27, no. 3: 395–415.

Moore, Cerwyn, and Paul Tumelty. 2008. "Foreign Fighters and the Case of Chechnya: A Critical Assessment." *Studies in Conflict & Terrorism* 31, no. 5: 412–433.

"More Than 70 Nations Hold Talks on Terrorism Financing in Paris." April 25, 2018. *Associated Press*. https://www.washingtonpost.com/world/europe/more-than-70-nations-hold-talks-on-terror-financing-in-paris/2018/04/25/0b5a86f4-485b-11e8-8082-105a446d19b8_story.html?noredirect=on&utm_term=.c15888bb0b96.

Morris, Harvey. January 27, 2015. "ISIS Still Strong Despite Major Defeat in Kobani." *Time*.

Moutot, Michel. March 19, 2018. "Jailbird Jihadists, a Security Threat for Europe." *AFP*.

Mueller, Jason C. May 2016. "The Evolution of Political Violence: The Case of Somalia's al-Shabaab." *Terrorism and Political Violence*: 1556–1836.

Mueller, John. October 2017. "The Cybercoaching of Terrorists: Cause for Alarm?" *CTC Sentinel* 10, no. 9: 29–35.

Mueller, John. Ed. March 2014. *Terrorism since 9/11: The American Cases*. http://politicalscience.osu.edu/faculty/jmueller//since.html.

Mukhaybar, Nayil, Sa'id Al-Quwaysi, and Muhammad Al-Zahir. December 1, 1995. "Arab Afghans Said to Launch Worldwide Terrorist War." *Paris Al-Watan Al-Arabi*, 22–24, FBIS-TOT-96-010-L.

Muhammad, Basil. 1991. *Safahat Min Sijill An-Ansar Al-Aarb Fi Afghanistan {Pages from the Record of the Arab Supporters in Afghanistan: Part One}*. Jeddah, Saudi Arabia: Dar Al-A'lem Press.

A Mujahid Guide: How to Survive in the West. 2015. Washington, DC: Investigative Project on Terrorism. https://www.investigativeproject.org/documents/misc/863.pdf. (Originally published by the Islamic State.)

Mustapha, Jennifer. 2013. "The Mujahideen in Bosnia: The Foreign Fighter as Cosmopolitan Citizen and/or Terrorist." *Citizenship Studies* 17, nos. 6/7: 742–755.

Myers, Steven Lee. 2015. *The New Tsar: The Rise and Reign of Vladimir Putin*. New York: Vintage Books.

Naji, Abu Bakr. 2006 *The Managements of Savagery: The Most Critical Stage Through Which the Umma will Pass*. Translated by William McCants. Cambridge, MA: John M. Olin Institute for Strategic Studies, Harvard University.

Nasiri, Omar. 2006. *Inside the Jihad: My Life with Al Qaeda: A Spy's Story*. New York: Basic Books.

National Commission on Terrorist Attacks upon the United States ("The 9/11 Commission"). 2004a. *9/11 and Terrorist Travel. Staff Report of the National*

Commission on Terrorist Attacks upon the United States. Ed. Thomas R. Eldridge, Susan Ginsburg, Walter T. Hempel II, Janice L. Kephart, and Kelly Moore. http://govinfo.library.unt.edu/911/staff_statements/911_TerrTrav_Monograph.pdf.

National Commission on Terrorist Attacks upon the United States ("The 9/11 Commission"). 2004b. *Monograph on Terrorist Financing. Staff Report to the Commission.* Ed. John Roth, Douglas Greenburg, and Serena Wille. http://govinfo.library.unt.edu/911/staff_statements/911_TerrFin_Monograph.pdf.

National Commission on Terrorist Attacks upon the United States ("The 9/11 Commission"). 2004c. *The 9/11 Commission Report: Final Report of the National Commission on Terrorist Attacks upon the United States.* Washington, DC, Government Printing Office. https://www.gpo.gov/fdsys/pkg/GPO-911REPORT/pdf/PO-911REPORT.pdf.

National Intelligence Council, Director of National Intelligence. 2006. *Declassified Key Judgments of the National Intelligence Estimate "Trends in Global Terrorism: Implications for the United States."* https://www.hsdl.org/?view&did=466878.

Nelson, Louis. June 13, 2016. "Comey: FBI Began Investigating Orlando Shooter in May 2013." https://www.politico.com/story/2016/06/omar-mateen-fbi-investigated-224266.

Nesser, Petter. 2015. *Islamist Terrorism in Europe: A History.* New York: Oxford University Press.

Neumann, Peter R. 2015. *Victims, Perpetrators, Assets: The Narratives of Islamic State Defectors.* London: International Center for the Study of Radicalisation and Political Violence. http://icsr.info/wp-content/uploads/2015/09/ICSR-Report-Victims-Perpertrators-Assets-The-Narratives-of-Islamic-State-Defectors.pdf.

Neumann, Peter R. 2016. *Radicalized: New Jihadists and the Threat to the West.* New York: I. B. Tauris.

Neumann, Peter R. 2017. *Countering Violent Extremism and Radicalization That Lead to Terrorism: Ideas, Recommendations, and Good Practices from the OSCE Region.* Organization for Security and Co-operation in Europe. http://www.osce.org/chairmanship/346841?download=true.

Neville, Leigh. 2015. *Special Forces in the War on Terror.* New York: Osprey Publishing.

New York Times. March 9, 1996. "Pro-Chechen Hijacker of Turkish Jet Surrenders in Germany." http://www.nytimes.com/1996/03/09/world/pro-chechen-hijacker-of-turkish-jet-surrenders-in-germany.html.

New York Times. March 31, 2018. "Britons Accused of Being Islamic State 'Beatles' Call Beheadings 'Regrettable.' "

Newsweek. October 4, 1992. "Help from the Holy Warriors." http://www.newsweek.com/help-holy-warriors-199918.

Newton-Small, Jay. September 27, 2013. "An Alleged Terrorist's Family Waits in Hope and Fear." *Time.* http://nation.time.com/2013/09/27/a-terrorists-family-waits-in-hope-and-fear/.

Schifrin, Nick, and Zach Fanin. 2016. "How Al-Shabab Is Recruiting Young Men from Kenya." *PBS News Hour* Video, 07:54. April 10, 2016. https://www.pbs.org/newshour/show/how-al-shabaab-is-recruiting-young-men-from-kenya.

The 9/11 Plot: Statement before the National Commission on Terrorist Attacks upon the United States. 2004. Twelfth public hearing of the National Commission on Terrorist Attacks upon the United States. Statement of Patrick J. Fitzgerald, United States Attorney for the Northern District of Illinois.

Nor, Mohamed Sheikh, and Katharine Houreld. March 2, 2011. "Somali Defector Reveals Foreigners' Role in War." *Associated Press.*

Normark, Magnus, Magnus Ranstorp, and Filip Ahlin. 2017. *Financial Activities Linked to Persons from Sweden and Denmark who Joined Terrorist Groups in Syria and Iraq during the Perion 2013–2016.* Stockholm, Center for Asymmetric Threat Studies, Swedish Defence University.

Obaid, Nawaf, and Anthony Cordesman. 2005. *Saudi Militants in Iraq: Assessment and Kingdom's Response.* Washington, DC: Center for Strategic and International Studies.

Oluic, Steven. 2006. "Radical Islam's Periphery: Bosnia & Herzegovina's Extremist Threat." *Pennsylvania Geographer* 44, no. 2: 3–18.

Oluic, Steven. 2008. "Radical Islam on Europe's Frontier—Bosnia & Herzegovina." *National Security and the Future* 9, nos. 1–2: 35–52.

Onishi, Norimitsu. December 19, 2001. "A Tale of the Mullah and Muhammad's Amazing Cloak." *New York Times.*

"Operation Freedom's Sentinel." October 2017–December 2017. Office of the Inspector General Report to the United States Congress. https://oig.state.gov/system/files/fy2018_lig_oco_ofs_q1_dec2017.pdf.

Osborne, Samuel. December 27, 2015. "Isis Kills 'Raqqa Is Being Slaughtered Silently' Activist in Turkey." *The Independent.* https://www.independent.co.uk/news/world/middle-east/isis-kills-raqqa-is-being-slaughtered-silently-activist-in-turkey-a6787751.html.

Osnos, Evan. June 10, 2016. "Do F.B.I. Stings Help the Fight against ISIS?" *New Yorker.* https://www.newyorker.com/news/news-desk/do-f-b-i-stings-help-the-fight-against-isis.

Oukaci, Faycal. January 18, 2007. "The 'Quagmire' of the Jihad: 'The Road to Baghdad.'" *L'Expression.*

Pantucci, Raffaello. 2016. "The Islamic State Threat to Britain: Evidence from Recent Terror Trials." *CTC Sentinel* 9, no. 3: 19–23.

Pargeter, Alison. 2008. *The New Frontiers of Jihad: Radical Islam in Europe.* Philadelphia: University of Pennsylvania Press.

Paulussen, Christophe, and Eva Entenmann. 2016. "National Responses in Select Western European Countries to the Foreign Fighter Phenomenon." In *Foreign Fighters under International Law and Beyond*, ed. Andrea de Guttry, Francesca Capone, and Christophe Paulussen, 391–422. The Hague: T.M.C. Asser Press.

Le Parisien. January 29, 2014. "Toulouse: les deux apprentis jihadistes retracent leur périple en garde à vue." http://www.leparisien.fr/faits-divers/video-toulouse-les-deux-ados-candidats-au-jihad-en-garde-a-vue-29-01-2014-3539361.php.

Pelligrini-Bettoli. May 26, 2017. "Intrepid Sisters Reveal How ISIS Depends on Role of Women." *Syria Deeply.* https://www.newsdeeply.com/syria/articles/2017/05/26/intrepid-sisters-reveal-how-isis-depends-on-role-of-women.

Petraeus, David. June 17, 2010. " 'Double Digits' of Al-Qaeda Fighters in Afghanistan." *Washington Independent.*

Pew Research Center. 2005. *Islamic Extremism: Common Concern for Muslim and Western Publics.* Washington, DC. http://www.pewglobal.org/2005/07/14/islamic-extremism-common-concern-for-muslim-and-western-publics/.

Pew Research Institute. 2006. *The Great Divide: How Westerners and Muslims View Each Other.* Washington, DC. http://www.pewglobal.org/2006/06/22/the-great-divide-how-westerners-and-muslims-view-each-other/.

Pew Research Center. 2008. *Public Attitudes Toward the War in Iraq: 2003–2008.* Washington, DC. http://www.pewresearch.org/2008/03/19/public-attitudes-toward-the-war-in-iraq-20032008/.

Pew Research Center. 2012. "Articles of Faith." In *The World's Muslims: Unity and Diversity,* 57–66. Washington, DC.

Pew Research Center. June 26, 2017. *How the U.S. General Public Views Muslims and Islam.* Washington, DC. http://www.pewforum.org/2017/07/26/how-the-u-s-general-public-views-muslims-and-islam/.

Poushter, Jacob, and Dorothy Manevich. 2017. *Globally, People Point to ISIS and Climate Change as Leading Security Threats.* Washington, DC: Pew Research Center. http://www.pewglobal.org/2017/08/01/globally-people-point-to-isis-and-climate-change-as-leading-security-threats/.

Priante, Andrea. May 11, 2016. "From Belluno to ISIL Army." *Corriere della Sera.*

Price, Bryan, and Muhammad Al-Ubaydi. 2017. *The Islamic State's Internal Rifts and Social Media Ban.* West Point, NY: Combating Terrorism Center.

Prochazkova, Petra. September 9, 1999. "Rebel Leader Basayev on Dagestan Conflict." *Lidove Noviny.*

Prosecutor v. Rasim Delic No. IT0483T. September 15, 2008. United Nations International Tribunal for the Prosecution of Persons Responsible for Serious Violations of International Humanitarian Law Committed in the Territory of the Former Yugoslavia since 1991. http://www.icty.org/x/cases/delic/tjug/en/080915.pdf

Pyes, Craig, Josh Meyer, and William C. Rempel. October 7, 2001. "Bosnia Seen as Hospitable Base and Sanctuary for Terrorists." *Los Angeles Times.*

Quinlivan, James. 1999. "Coup Proofing: Its Practice and Consequences in the Middle East." *International Security* 24, no. 2: 131–165.

Rafael, Jamil. March 31, 1996. "The Mujahidin Left Bosnia for Chechnya and the Iranians Were Expelled from Tuzla." *Al-Hayah.*

Rainsford, Sarah. January 4, 2016. "Chechnya Struggles to Stop Wave of Recruits Joining IS." *BBC News.* http://www.bbc.com/news/world-europe-35197985.

Ramsay, Stuart. May 2, 2016. "IS Files Reveal Assad's Deals with Militants." *Sky News.* https://news.sky.com/story/is-files-reveal-assads-deals-with-militants-10267238.

Randal, Jonathan. 2011. *Osama: The Making of a Terrorist.* New York: I. B. Tauris.

Rashid, Ahmed. 2010. *Taliban.* New Haven, CT: Yale University Press.

Rasmussen, Nicholas. May 3, 2017. "Director Rasmussen Opening Remarks." CNAS Keynote Policy Address.

Ratelle, Jean-François. 2016. "North Caucasian Foreign Fighters in Syria and Iraq: Assessing the Threat of Returnees to the Russian Federation." *Caucasus Survey* 4, no. 3: 218–238.

Rayner, Gordon. November 19, 2015. "Who Is Abdelhamid Abaaoud?" *Telegraph.* https://www.telegraph.co.uk/news/worldnews/islamic-state/11998252/Paris-attacks-who-is-suspected-ringleader-Abdelhamid-Abaaoud.html.

Reinares, Fernando. 2012. "The Evidence of Al-Qaʾida's Role in the 2004 Madrid Attack." *CTC Sentinel* 5, no. 3: 1–6.

Reinares, Fernando. 2017a. *Al-Qaeda's Revenge: The 2004 Madrid Train Bombings.* New York: Columbia University Press.

Reinares, Fernando. 2017b. *Jihadist Mobilisation, Undemocratic Salafism and Terrorist Threat in the EU.* Madrid: Elcano Royal Institute. http://www.realinstitutoelcano.org/wps/wcm/connect/af85ab1e-72bc-4b26-ba25-54dae9d60eb4/Commentary-Reinares-Jihadist-mobilisation-undemocratic-Salafism-terrorist-threat-EU.pdf?MOD=AJPERES&CACHEID=af85ab1e-72bc-4b26-ba25-54dae9d60eb4.

Reinares, Fernando. 2017c. "Jihadist Mobilization, Undemocratic Salafism, and Terrorist Threat in the European Union." *The Georgetown Security Studies Review,* Special Issue: What the New Administration Needs to Know About Terrorism and Counterterrorism, 70–76.

Reinares, Fernando, and Carola García-Calvo. June 27, 2018. "Moroccans and the Second Generation among Jihadists in Spain." Elcano Royal Institute. http://www.realinstitutoelcano.org/wps/portal/rielcano_en/contenido?WCM_GLOBAL_CONTEXT=/elcano/elcano_in/zonas_in/ari82-2018-reinares-garciacalvo-moroccans-second-generation-among-jihadists-spain.

Remnick, David. January 27, 2014. "Going the Distance." *New Yorker.* https://www.newyorker.com/magazine/2014/01/27/going-the-distance-david-remnick.

Renard, Thomas, and Rik Coolsaet. 2018. "From the Kingdom to the Caliphate and Back: Returnees in Belgium." In "Returnees: Who Are They, Why Are They (Not) Coming Back and How Should We Deal with Them?" *Egmont Paper* 101, ed. Thomas Renard and Rik Coolsaet, 19–40.

"Response from Raja to Brother Abu al-'Abbas." n.d. Documents gathered by Brian Fishman. Available at https://static1.squarespace.com/static/57a2ce8503596ee87a205a0d/t/57b798305016e192aad6dc49/1471649841029/Dear+Brother+Abu+al-%E2%80%98Abbas.pdf.

Reuter, Christoph. April 18, 2015. "The Terror Strategist: Secret Files Reveal the Structure of Islamic State." *SpiegelOnline*. http://www.spiegel.de/international/world/islamic-state-files-show-structure-of-islamist-terror-group-a-1029274.html.

Revkin, Mara. 2016. *The Legal Foundations of the Islamic State*. Washington, DC: Brookings Institution Press.

Revkin, Mara, and Ahmad Mhidi. May 1, 2016. "Quitting ISIS: Why Syrians Are Abandoning the Group." *Foreign Affairs*.

Riedel, Bruce. 2012. *Deadly Embrace: Pakistan, America, and the Future of the Global Jihad*. Washington, DC: Brookings Institution Press.

Riedel, Bruce, and Bilal Y. Saab. 2008. "Al Qaeda's Third Front: Saudi Arabia." *Washington Quarterly* 31, no. 2: 33–46.

Robertson, Campbell. May 30, 2009. "Terrorist or Mythic Symbol: A Tale of Iraqi Politics." *New York Times*.

Robin Simcox. July 13, 2017. "The Terrorist Diaspora: After the Fall of the Caliphate." Testimony before the House Homeland Security Committee Task Force on Denying Terrorists Entry into the United States.

Roggio, Bill. July 2007. "Islamic State of Iraq—an Al Qaeda Front." *FDD's Long War Journal*. https://www.longwarjournal.org/archives/2007/07/islamic_state_of_ira.php.

Roggio, Bill. September 2008. "Who Is Abu Omar Al Baghdadi?" *FDD's long War Journal*. https://www.longwarjournal.org/archives/2008/09/who_is_abu_omar_al_b.php.

Roggio, Bill. September 2013. "Shabaab Kills American Jihadist Omar Hammami and British Fighter." *FDD's Long War Journal*. https://www.longwarjournal.org/archives/2013/09/shabaab_kills_americ.php.

Rohde, David. October 30, 2007. "Foreign Fighters of Harsher Bent Bolster Taliban." *New York Times*.

Rohde, David, and C. J. Chivers. March 17, 2002. "A Nation Challenged: Qaeda's Grocery Lists and Manuals of Killing." *New York Times*.

Rosenblatt, Nate. July 2016. "All Jihad Is Local: What ISIS' Files Tell Us about Its Fighters." *New America*.

Roth, Andrew. October 27, 2015. "The Russian Village That Sent 20 Men to Wage Jihad in Syria." *Washington Post*.

Rubin, Alissa J. 2018. January 11, 2018. "She Left France to Fight in Syria. Now She Wants to Return. But Can She?" *New York Times*. https://www.nytimes.com/2018/01/11/world/europe/emilie-konig-france-islamic-state.html.

"Russian Agency Carries Interview with Dagestan Insurgent Commander." August 11, 1999. Interfax News Agency, supplied by BBC Worldwide Monitoring.

"Russian Federation: Brief Summary of Concerns about Human Rights Violations in the Chechen Republic." 1996. Amnesty International. http://www.refworld.org/docid/3ae6a9c52c.html.

"Russian Federation." 2016. *Amnesty International Report 2015/2016: The State of the World's Human Rights.* N.p.: Amnesty International, 302–306. https://www. amnesty.org/en/latest/research/2016/02/annual-report-201516/.

Ryan, Missy, and Sudarsan Raghavan. August 9, 2016. "U.S. Special Operations troops aiding Libyan forces in major battle against Islamic State." *Washington Post.* https://www.washingtonpost.com/news/checkpoint/wp/2016/08/09/u-s-special-operations-forces-are-providing-direct-on-the-ground-support-for-the-first-time-in-libya/?utm_term=.5a6ca3f6c440.

Sageman, Marc. 2008. *Leaderless Jihad: Terror Networks in the Twenty-First Century.* Philadelphia: University of Pennsylvania Press.

Sambanis, Nicholas. 2004. "What Is a Civil War?" *Journal of Conflict Resolution* 48, no. 6: 814–858.

"Samuel Berger 9/11 Prepared Testimony." March 24, 2004. http://www.nbcnews. com/id/4593926/ns/us_news-security/t/samuel-berger-prepared-testimony/ #.WuRrIm6UuUk.

"Scars Remain amid Chechen Revival." March 3, 2007. *BBC News.* http://news.bbc. co.uk/2/hi/programmes/from_our_own_correspondent/6414603.stm.

Schechner, Sam, and Benoit Faucon. September 11, 2016. "New Tricks Make ISIS, Once Easily Tracked, a Sophisticated Opponent." *Wall Street Journal.*

Scheuer, Michael. 2011. *Osama bin Laden.* New York: Oxford University Press.

Schindler, John R. 2007. *Unholy Terror: Bosnia, Al-Qa'ida, and the Rise of Global Jihad.* St. Paul: Zenith Press.

Schmid, Alex P. February 2017. "Public Opinion Survey Data to Measure Sympathy and Support for Islamist Terrorism." International Centre for Counter-Terrorism—the Hague. https://icct.nl/wp-content/uploads/2017/02/ ICCT-Schmid-Muslim-Opinion-Polls-Jan2017-1.pdf.

Schmid, Alex P., and Judith Tinnes. 2015. *Foreign Terrorist Fighters with IS: A European Perspective.* The Hague: International Center for Counter-Terrorism. https://icct.nl/wp-content/uploads/2015/12/ICCT-Schmid-Foreign-Terrorist-Fighters-with-IS-A-European-Perspective-December2015.pdf.

Schmitt, Eric. October 22, 2017. "ISIS Fighters Are Not Flooding Back Home to Wreak Havoc as Feared." *New York Times.*

Schmitt, Eric. February 4, 2018. "Thousands of ISIS Fighters Flee in Syria, Many to Fight Another Day." *New York Times.*

Sciolino, Elaine. March 12, 2004. "Bombings in Madrid: The Attack; 10 Bombs Shatter Trains in Madrid, Killing 192." *New York Times.* https://www.nytimes. com/2004/03/12/world/bombings-in-madrid-the-attack-10-bombs-shatter-trains-in-madrid-killing-192.html.

Seely, Robert. 2001. *Russo-Chechen Conflict, 1800–2000: A Deadly Embrace.* Portland, OR: Frank Cass.

Sengupta, Kim, and Lizzie Dearden. February 9, 2018. "ISIS Militants Hunted Down in Syria after Intelligence Extracted from Captured Members of 'The Beatles' Cell." *Independent.* http://www.independent.co.uk/news/uk/home-news/

isis-british-the-beatles-militants-captured-syria-intelligence-operations-us-britain-kotey-elsheikh-a8203421.html.

Shafaq News. December 3, 2016. "Found at an Islamic State Training Camp: Bunk Beds, Weapons Manuals, Steroids."

Shane, Scott. 2016. "The Enduring Influence of Anwar Al-Awlaki in the Age of the Islamic State." *CTC Sentinel* 9, no. 7: 15–19.

Shapiro, Jacob. 2009. "Bureaucratic Terrorists: Al-Qa'ida in Iraq's Management and Finances." In *Bombers, Bank Accounts, & Bleedout: Al-Qa'ida's Road in Iraq and Out of Iraq,* ed. Brian Fishman, 66–80. West Point, NY: Combating Terrorism Center.

Shephard, Michelle. June 25, 2016. "Inside the Secret Somalia Rehab Camp for Former Shabab Members." *TheStar.com.* https://www.thestar.com/news/atkinsonseries/generation911/2016/06/25/inside-the-secret-somalia-rehab-camp-for-former-shabab-members.html.

Shih, Gerry. December 23, 2017. "Uighurs Fighting in Syria Take Aim at China." *Associated Press.*

Shihab, Zaki. November 9, 2000. "Heads of London-Based Extremist Islamic Organizations Interviewed." *Abha Al-Watan,* 11.

Shinn, David. 2011. "Al Shabaab's Foreign Threat to Somalia." *Orbis* 55, no. 2: 203–215.

Shtuni, Adrian. April 30, 2015. "Ethnic Albanian Foreign Fighters in Iraq and Syria." *CTC Sentinel* 8, no. 4: 11–19.

Shtuni, Adrian. December 2016. "Dynamics of Radicalization and Violent Extremism in Kosovo." Washington, DC: United States Institute of Peace.

Silber, Mitchell, and Arvin Bhatt. 2007. "Radicalization in the West: The Homegrown Threat." New York: New York City Police Department. https://sethgodin.typepad.com/seths_blog/files/NYPD_Report-Radicalization_in_the_West.pdf.

Sinclair, Daisy. March 9, 2015. "In Annals of Russian Crime, North Caucasians Remain Popular Scapegoat." *Radio Free Europe, Radio Liberty.* http://www.rferl.org/content/russia-north-caucasus-popular-scapegoat/26890029.html.

Slackman, Michael. November 13, 2001. "Bin Laden's Mother Tried to Stop Him, Syrian Kin Say." *Chicago Tribune.* http://www.chicagotribune.com/chi-0111130207nov13-story.html.

Smith-Spark, Laura, and Yousuf Basil. January 31, 2015. "Kobani." *CNN.*

Solahudin. 2013. *The Roots of Terrorism in Indonesia: From Darul Islam to Jema'ah Islamiyah.* Trans. Dave McRae. Ithaca, NY: Cornell University Press.

Souleimanov, Emil, and Ondrej Ditrych. 2008. "The Internationalisation of the Russian-Chechen Conflict: Myths and Reality." *Europe-Asia Studies* 60, no. 7: 1199–1222.

Speckhard, Anne, and Ahmet S. Yayla. December 2015. "Eyewitness Accounts from Recent Defectors from Islamic State: Why They Joined, What They Saw, Why They Quit." *Perspectives on Terrorism* 9, no. 6: 95–117.

Stalinsky, Steven, R. Sosnow, and M. Khayat. 2016. *ISIS's Use of Twitter, Other U.S. Social Media to Disseminate Images, Videos of Islamic Religious Punishments— Beheading, Crucifixion, Stoning, Burning, Drowning, Throwing from Buildings— Free Speech?* Washington, DC: Middle East Media Research Institute, Cyber Jihad Lab.

Stein, Aaron. 2016. *Islamic State Networks in Turkey: Recruitment for the Caliphate.* Washington, DC: Atlantic Council.

Stenersen, Anne. February 15–18, 2009. "Blood Brothers or a Marriage of Convenience? The Ideological Relationship between al-Qaida and the Taliban." Paper presented at the International Studies Association, New York, New York.

Stenersen, Anne. 2011a. "Al Qaeda's Foot Soldiers: A Study of the Biographies of Foreign Fighters Killed in Afghanistan and Pakistan between 2002 and 2006." *Studies in Conflict & Terrorism* 34, no. 3: 171–198.

Stenersen, Anne. 2011b. "Brothers in Jihad: Explaining the Relationship Between al-Qaida and the Taliban, 1996–2001." PhD diss., University of Oslo.

Stenersen, Anne. 2017. *Al-Qaida in Afghanistan.* Cambridge, UK: Cambridge University Press.

Sterman, David, and Nate Rosenblatt. April 2018. "All Jihad Is Local, Volume II: ISIS in North Africa and the Arabian Peninsula." *New America.*

Stevens, Tim, and Peter R. Neumann. 2009. *Countering Online Radicalisation: A Strategy for Action.* London: The International Center for the Study of Radicalisation and Political Violence.

Stewart, Cameron. August 8, 2014. "Jihadist Watch to Cost $8m a Suspect." *The Australian.* http://www.theaustralian.com.au/national-affairs/defence/jihadist-watch-to-cost-8m-a-suspect/story-e6frg8yo-1227017233690#.

Stimson Center. May 2018. "Counterterrorism Spending: Protecting American While Promoting Efficiencies and Accountability." https://www.stimson.org/sites/default/files/file-attachments/CT_Spending_Report_0.pdf.

Susman, Tina. November 19, 2015. "Islamic State Presence in U.S. Is 'the New Normal,' FBI Director Says." *Los Angeles Times.* http://www.latimes.com/nation/la-na-isis-us-20151120-story.html.

Taarnby, Michael, and Lars Hallundbaek. 2010. *Al-Shabaab: The Internationalization of Militant Islamism in Somalia and the Implications for Radicalisation Processes in Europe.* Copenhagen: Ministry of Justice of Denmark. http://justitsministeriet.dk/sites/default/files/media/Arbejdsomraader/Forskning/Forskningspuljen/2011/2010/alshabaab.pdf.

Tawfiq Tabib. August 1994. "Understanding Jihad: Interview with Sheikh Al-Mujahideen Abu Abdel Aziz 'Barbaros.'" *Al-Sirat Al-Mustaqeem:* 33.

Tawil, Camille. October 28, 2010. "Part 3: Al-Zarqawi Is Given Al-Qaida Control over Jihadist Routes to Iraq." *Al-Hayat.*

Tawil, Camille. 2011. *Brothers in Arms: The Story of al-Qa'ida and the Arab Jihadists.* London: Saqi.

Taylor, Adam. November 28, 2014. "Saudi Arabia Says 12 Percent of Its
'Rehabilitated' Terrorists Have Returned to Terror." *Washington Post.* http://www.
washingtonpost.com/blogs/worldviews/wp/2014/11/28/saudi-arabia-says-12-
percent-of-its-rehabilitated-terrorists-have-returned-to-terror/.

Taylor, Adam. June 13, 2016. "Omar Mateen May Not Have Understood the
Difference between ISIS, Al-Qaeda and Hezbollah." *Washington Post.*

Temple-Raston, Dina. September 7, 2007. "Enemy Within? Not Quite." *Washington
Post.* http://www.washingtonpost.com/wp-dyn/content/article/2007/09/07/
AR2007090702049.html.

Tenet, George. 2007. *At the Center of the Storm: The CIA during America's Time of
Crisis.* New York: Harper Perennial.

Thomas, Joscelyn. July 13, 2017. "The Terrorist Diaspora: After the Fall of the
Caliphate." Testimony before the House Homeland Security Committee Task
Force on Denying Terrorists Entry into the United States.

Tinnes, Judith. 2015. "Although the (Dis-)Believers Dislike It: A Backgrounder
on IS Hostage Videos—August—December 2014." *Perspectives on Terrorism* 9,
no. 1: 76–94.

Tolstoy, Leo. 1965. *Hadji Murat: A Tale of the Caucasus.* New York: McGraw-Hill.

Tønnessen, Truls Hallberg. 2008. "Training on a Battlefield: Iraq as a Training
Ground for Global Jihadis." *Terrorism & Political Violence* 20, no. 4: 543–562.

Tønnessen, Truls Hallberg. 2015a. "Al-Qaida in Iraq: The Rise, the Fall and the
Comeback." PhD diss., University of Oslo.

Tønnessen, Truls Hallberg. 2015b. "Heirs of Zarqawi or Saddam? The Relationship
between Al-Qaida in Iraq and the Islamic State." *Perspectives on Terrorism* 9,
no. 4: 48 60.

Townsend, Mark. October 7, 2017. "Rape and Slavery Was Lure for UK ISIS
Recruits with History of Sexual Violence." *The Guardian.*

Travis, Alan. February 18, 2009. "Abu Qatada: From Refugee to Detainee." *The
Guardian.* https://www.theguardian.com/world/2009/feb/19/abu-qatada-profile.

Tremlett, Giles. November 19, 2001. "Islamist Cell Linked to UK Militants." *The
Guardian.* https://www.theguardian.com/uk/2001/nov/20/september11.world1.

Tufft, Ben. December 29, 2014. "ISIS 'Executes Up to 200 Fighters' for Trying to
Flee Jihad and Return Home." The *Independent.*

Tumelty, Paul. 2006. "The Rise and Fall of Foreign Fighters in Chechnya." *Terrorism
Monitor* 4, no. 2. https://jamestown.org/program/the-rise-and-fall-of-foreign-
fighters-in-chechnya/.

Turbiville, Graham, Josh Meservey, and James Forest. 2014. *Countering the Al-
Shabaab Insurgency in Somalia: Lessons for U.S. Special Operations Forces.* Tampa,
FL: Joint Special Operations University.

Tziampiris, Aristotle. 2009. "Assessing Islamic Terrorism in the Western
Balkans: The State of the Debate." *Journal of Balkan and Near Eastern Studies* 11,
no. 2: 209–219.

United Kingdom Home Office. July 2017. *Country Policy and Information Note: Somalia South and Central: Fear of Al Shabaab.* London. https://www.justice.gov/eoir/page/file/982591/download, 12–15.

United Nations Security Council, 72nd Meeting. September 24, 2014. *Resolution 2178 {Foreign Terrorist Fighters}.* S/RES/2178. https://www.un.org/en/sc/ctc/docs/2015/SCR%202178_2014_EN.pdf.

United Nations Security Council, Counter-Terrorism Committee Executive Directorate. March 2018. *The Challenge of Returning and Relocating Foreign Terrorist Fighters: Research Perspectives.* https://www.un.org/sc/ctc/wp-content/uploads/2018/04/CTED-Trends-Report-March-2018.pdf.

United States Africa Command. December 20, 2016. "AFRICOM Concludes Operation Odyssey Lightning." http://www.africom.mil/media-room/pressrelease/28564/africom-concludes-operation-odyssey-lightning.

United States Army. n.d. "Unconventional Warfare: Training Covertly for Success." Accessed February 2, 2018. https://www.goarmy.com/special-forces/primary-missions/unconventional-warfare.html.

United States of America v. Aaron T. Daniels, "Criminal Complaint" and "Arrest Warrant." No. 2:16MJ534. November 7, 2016. United States District Court, Southern District of Ohio. https://www.investigativeproject.org/documents/case_docs/3131.pdf.

United States of America v. Akram I. Musleh, "Criminal Complaint" No. 1:16MJ00444. June 21, 2016. United States District Court, Southern District of Indiana. https://cchs.gwu.edu/sites/cchs.gwu.edu/files/downloads/Musleh%20Complaint.pdf.

United States of America v. Enaam M. Arnaout No. 02CR892. January 6, 2003. United States District Court, Northern District of Illinois, Eastern Division. http://news.findlaw.com/hdocs/docs/bif/usarnaout10603prof.pdf.

United States of America v. Mohamad Jamal Khweis No. 1:16MJ213JFA. May 11, 2016. United States District Court, Eastern District of Virginia. https://www.justice.gov/opa/file/865806/download.

United States of America v. Mohamed Abdihamid Farah et al. April 18, 2016. United States District Court, District of Minnesota. https://www.slideshare.net/BigJoe5/farah-et-al-criminal-complaint-dmn-april-18-2015.

United States of America v. Nicholas Michael Teausant, "Criminal Complaint" No. 2:14MJ0064. March 17, 2014. United States District Court, Eastern District of California. https://extremism.gwu.edu/sites/extremism.gwu.edu/files/Teausant%20Criminal%20Complaint.pdf.

United States of America v. Usama Bin Laden. February 6, 2001. "Testimony of Jamal Ahmed al-Fadl." https://cryptome.org/usa-v-ubl-02.htm.

United States of America v. Yahya Farooq Mohammad et al. No. 3:15CR00358. September 30, 2015. United States District Court, Northern District of Ohio, Western Division. https://www.justice.gov/opa/file/790971/download.

United States Department of State. 2004. *Zarqawi Letter.* https://2001-2009.state.gov/p/nea/rls/31694.htm.

United States Department of State. 2015. *Russia 2015 Human Rights Report.* https://www.state.gov/documents/organization/253105.pdf.

U.S. Department of Defense. August 17, 2016. "U.S. Airstrikes Hit ISIL Targets in Libya." https://www.defense.gov/News/Article/Article/917245/us-airstrikes-hit-isil-targets-in-libya/.

U.S. Government Accountability Office. April 18, 2016. "Counterterrorism." Washington, DC. https://www.gao.gov/products/GAO-16-368.

Uslu, Emrullah. 2016. "Jihadist Highway to Jihadist Haven: Turkey's Jihadi Policies and Western Security." *Studies in Conflict & Terrorism* 39, no. 9: 781–802.

Van Buren, Peter. June 2, 2015. "Dude, Where's My Humvee: Iraq Losing Equipment to the Islamic State at a Staggering Rate." *Reuters.* http://blogs.reuters.com/great-debate/2015/06/02/dude-wheres-my-humvee-iraqi-equipment-losses-to-islamic-state-are-out-of-control/.

Van Ginkel, Bibi, and Eva Entenmann. Eds. 2016. *The Foreign Fighters Phenomenon in the European Union: Profiles, Threats & Policies.* The Hague: International Center for Counter-Terrorism. https://icct.nl/wp-content/uploads/2016/03/ICCT-Report_Foreign-Fighters-Phenomenon-in-the-EU_1-April-2016_including-AnnexesLinks.pdf.

Van Ginkel, Bibi, and Simon Minks. 2018. "Addressing the Challenge of Returnees: Threat Perceptions, Policies and Practices in the Netherlands." In *Egmont Paper* 101, ed. Thomas Renard and Rik Coolsaet, 55–70.

Van Vlierden, Guy. November/December 2015. "Profile: Paris Attack Ringleader Abdelhamid Abaaoud." *CTC Sentinel* 8, no. 11: 30–33. https://ctc.usma.edu/app/uploads/2015/12/CTCSentinel-Vol8Iss112.pdf.

Van Zuijdewijn, Jeanine de Roy. May 2017. "The Foreign Fighter Phenomenon: Case Study of the Netherlands." In *Not Only Syria? The Phenomenon of Foreign Fighters in Comparative Perspective*, edited by Kacper Rekawek. NATO IOS Press.

Van Zuijdewijn, Jeanine de Roy, and Edwin Bakker. June 2014. "Returning Western Foreign Fighters: The Case of Afghanistan, Bosnia, and Somalia." The Hague: International Centre for Counter-Terrorism.

Velikonja, Mitja. 2003. *Religious Separation and Political Intolerance in Bosnia-Herzegovina.* College Station: Texas A&M University Press.

Vermeulen, Floris. 2014. "Suspect Communities: Targeting Violent Extremism at the Local Level." *Terrorism and Political Violence* 26, no. 2: 286–306. http://www.tandfonline.com/doi/abs/10.1080/09546553.2012.705254#preview.

Vidino, Lorenzo. Spring 2006. "The Arab Foreign Fighters and the Sacralization of the Chechen Conflict" *Al Nakhlah*: 1–9.

Vidino, Lorenzo, and Francesco Marone. November 2017. "The Jihadist Threat in Italy: A Primer." Institute Per Gli Studi Di Politica Internazionale. http://www.ispionline.it/it/pubblicazione/jihadist-threat-italy-primer-1854.

Vidino, Lorenzo, and Seamus Hughes. 2015. *ISIS in America: From Retweets to Raqqa.* Washington, DC: George Washington University Program on Extremism.

Vidino, Lorenzo, Francesco Marone, and Eva Entenmann. 2017. *Fear Thy Neighbor: Radicalization and Jihadist Attacks in the West*. Milan: Ledizioni.

Violent Islamist Extremism: Al-Shabaab Recruitment in America: Hearing before the Committee of Homeland Security and Governmental Affairs. 2009. 111th Cong. 1 (statement of Philip Mudd, Associate Executive Assistant Director, National Security Branch, Federal Bureau of Investigation). https://www.hsgac.senate.gov/imo/media/doc/031109Mudd.pdf?attempt=2.

Wagemakers, Joas. 2017. "Revisiting Wiktorowicz: Categorising and Defining the Branches of Salafism." In *Salafism after the Arab Awakening: Contending with People's Power*, ed. Francesco Cavatorta and Fabio Merone, 7–24. Oxford, UK: Oxford University Press.

WaIslamah.net. n.d. "The Life and Times of Khattab." Was previously at https://www.youtube.com/watchv=hBt7J81FEJs but taken down in 2017. Arabic with English subtitles.

Wallace, Mark, and Frances Townsend. November 30, 2017. "The Case for Removing Extremist Videos from the Internet." *New York Times*.

Walsh, Nick Paton. April 11, 2018. "Facing the Terrorists Accused of Killing a Friend." *CNN*.

Walton, Nicholas. April 12, 2007. "Bosnia Tackles 'Foreign Fighters.'" *BBC News*. http://news.bbc.co.uk/2/hi/europe/6547287.stm.

Warrick, Joby. September 30, 2011. "Aulaqi Incited Young Muslims to Attacks against West." *Washington Post*. https://www.washingtonpost.com/world/national-security/aulaqi-incited-young-muslims-to-attacks-against-west/2011/09/30/gIQACMaKAL_story.html?utm_term=.2c8d997e564a.

Washington Times. December 13, 2004. "Foreign Terrorists in Fallujah." https://www.washingtontimes.com/news/2004/dec/13/20041213-103108-2737r/.

Watts, Clint. n.d. "Beyond Iraq and Afghanistan: What Foreign Fighter Data Reveals about the Future of Terrorism." *Small Wars Journal*. http://smallwarsjournal.com/jrnl/art/beyond-iraq-and-afghanistan.

Watts, Clint. June 1, 2016. "Beyond Syria and Iraq, the Islamic State's HR Files Illuminate Dangerous Trends." *War on the Rocks*. https://warontherocks.com/2016/06/beyond-syria-and-iraq-the-islamic-states-hr-files-illuminate-dangerous-trends/.

Watts, Clinton. June 22, 2008. "Foreign Fighters: How Are They Being Recruited? Two Imperfect Recruitment Models." *Small Wars Journal*.

Watts, Clinton. January 15, 2013. "Hammami Thinks the Grass Might be Greener in Syria." *Selected Wisdom*.

Weaver, Mary Anne. July/August 2006. "The Short, Violent Life of Abu Musab al-Zarqawi." *The Atlantic*.

Weggemans, Daan, Edwin Bakker, and Peter Grol. 2014. "Who Are They and Why Do They Go? The Radicalisation and Preparatory Processes of Dutch Jihadist Foreign Fighters." *Perspective on Terrorism* 8, no. 4: 100–110.

Weiser, Benjamin, and James Risen. December 1, 1998. "The Masking of a Militant." *New York Times*.

Weiser, Benjamin. June 5, 1999. "Indicted Ex-Sergeant Says He Knows Who Bombed U.S. Embassies." *New York Times.*

Weiser, Benjamin. May 12, 2001. "Terror Case to End Secrets of Please Deals by Informers." *New York Times.*

"What Happened at the Bataclan?" December 9, 2015. *BBC News.* http://www.bbc.com/news/world-europe-34827497.

The White House. April 5, 2013. "Fact Sheet: U.S. Security Sector Assistance Policy." Washington, DC. https://fas.org/irp/offdocs/ppd/ssa.pdf.

The White House. September 10, 2014. "Statement by the President on ISIL." Washington, DC. https://obamawhitehouse.archives.gov/the-press-office/2014/09/10/statement-president-isil-1.

Whiteside, Craig. 2014. "The Smiling Scented Men: The Political Worldview of the Islamic State of Iraq, 2003–2013." PhD diss., Washington State University.

Whiteside, Craig. 2016a. "Biography of Abu Omar Al Baghdadi." *Craig Whiteside, Naval War College Monterey* (blog), May 25, 2016. https://whitesidenwc.wordpress.com/2016/05/25/biography-of-abu-omar-al-baghdadi/.

Whiteside, Craig. 2016b. *Lighting the Path: The Evolution of the Islamic State Media Enterprise (2003–2016).* The Hague: International Center for Counter-Terrorism.

Whiteside, Craig. 2017. "A Pedigree of Terror: The Myth of the Ba'athist Influence in the Islamic State Movement." *Perspectives on Terrorism* 11, no. 3: 2–18.

Whitlock, Craig. January 10, 2014. "US Has Deployed Military Advisors to Somalia, Officials Say." *Washington Post.*

Wilber, Del Quentin. April 3, 2017. "Here's How the FBI Tracked Down a Tech-Savvy Terrorist Recruiter for the Islamic State." *Los Angeles Times.* http://www.latimes.com/politics/la-fg-islamic-state-recruiter-20170406-story.html.

Wilhelmsen, Julie. 2004. *When Separatists Become Islamists: The Case of Chechnya.* Kjeller, Norwegian Defence Research Establishment, Forsvarets Forskningsinstitutt (FFI). https://www.ffi.no/no/Rapporter/04-00445.pdf.

Wilhelmsen, Julie. 2005. "Between a Rock and a Hard Place: The Islamisation of the Chechen Separatist Movement." *Europe-Asia Studies* 57, no. 1: 35–59.

Williams, Brian Glyn. 2007. "Allah's Foot Soldiers: An Assessment of the Role of Foreign Fighters and Al-Qa'ida in the Chechen Insurgency." In *Ethno-Nationalism, Islam and the State in the Caucasus: Post-Soviet Disorder*, ed. Moshe Gammer, 156–178. London: Routledge.

Williams, Brian Glyn. 2008a. "Return of the Arabs: Al-Qa'ida's Current Military Role in the Afghan Insurgency." *CTC Sentinel* 1 no. 3: 22–25.

Williams, Brian Glyn. 2008b. "The Al-Qaida We Don't Know: The 055 Brigade." *World Politics Review*, October 26, 2008. https://www.worldpoliticsreview.com/articles/2821/the-055-brigade.

Williams, Brian Glyn. 2011. "On the Trail of the 'Lions of Islam': Foreign Fighters in Afghanistan and Pakistan, 1980–2010." *Orbis* 55: 216–239.

Williams, Brian Glyn. 2015. *Inferno in Chechnya: The Russian-Chechen Wars, the Al Qaeda Myth, and the Boston Marathon Bombings.* Lebanon, NH: ForeEdge.

Williams, Brian Glyn. 2017. *Counter Jihad: America's Military Experience in Afghanistan, Iraq, and Syria.* Philadelphia: University of Pennsylvania Press.

Williams, Lance, and Erin McCormick. September 21, 2001. "Bin Laden's Man in Silicon Valley." *San Francisco Chronicle.* https://www.sfgate.com/bayarea/article/Bin-Laden-s-man-in-Silicon-Valley-Mohamed-the-2875779.php.

Williams, Lance, and Erin McCormick. November 4, 2001. "Al Qaeda Terrorist Worked with FBI/Ex-Silicon Valley Resident Plotted Embassy Attacks." *SFGate.* http://www.sfgate.com/news/article/Al-Qaeda-terrorist-worked-with-FBI-Ex-Silicon-2861719.php.

Williams, Paul D. 2013. "Fighting for Peace in Somalia: AMISOM's Seven Strategic Challenges." *Journal of International Peacekeeping* 17: 222–247.

Williams, Paul D. May 8, 2017. "A Navy SEAL Was Killed in Somalia. Here's What You Need to Know about U.S. Operations There." *Washington Post.*

Wing, Joel. June 13, 2016. "Who Was Al Qaeda in Iraq's Abu Omar Al-Baghdadi? Interview with Naval War College's Prof Craig Whiteside." *Musings on Iraq* (blog). http://musingsoniraq.blogspot.com/2016/06/who-was-al-qaeda-in-iraqs-abu-omar-al.html.

Winter, Charlie. 2015. *The Virtual "Caliphate": Understanding Islamic State's Propaganda Strategy.* London: Quilliam.

Winter, Charlie. 2016. *An Integrated Approach to Islamic State Recruitment.* Canberra: Australian Strategic Policy Institute.

Winter, Charlie. 2017a. *War by Suicide: A Statistical Analysis of the Islamic State's Martyrdom Industry.* The Hague: International Center for Counter-Terrorism.

Winter, Charlie. 2017b. *The ISIS Propaganda Decline.* London: The International Centre for the Study of Radicalisation and Political Violence. http://icsr.info/2017/03/icsr-insight-isis-propaganda-decline/.

Winter, Charlie @charliewinter. 2017c. "Statement from Delegated Committee *Bans* #IS Soldiers from Using Social Media Platforms on Account of Security Concerns. Looks Real to Me." Twitter, May 21, 2017, 9:12 a.m. https://twitter.com/charliewinter/status/866325785728217088.

Winter, Charlie, and Abdullah K. Al-Saud. December 4, 2016. "The Obscure Theologian Who Shaped ISIS." *The Atlantic.*

Witness Testimony from ICTY-Delic Judgment: Ali Hamad. 2005. Bosnia Foreign Fighters Research. International Criminal Tribunal for the former Yugoslavia. http://www.icty.org/x/cases/delic/trans/en/070907IT.htm

Witte, Griff. September 12, 2014. "Westerners Fighting in Syria Disillusioned with Islamic State but Can't Go Home." *Washington Post.* https://www.washingtonpost.com/world/europe/westerners-fighting-in-syria-disillusioned-with-islamic-state-but-cant-go-home/2014/09/11/cdadc12c-2c27-47c4-8258-b053e45c0852_story.html?utm_term=.c0bb960d3a84.

Woehrel, Steven. 2005. *Islamic Terrorism and the Balkans.* CRS Report No. RL33012. Washington, DC: Congressional Research Service. https://fas.org/sgp/crs/terror/RL33012.pdf.

Wood, Graeme. March 2017. "The American Climbing the Ranks of ISIS." *The Atlantic.* https://www.theatlantic.com/magazine/archive/2017/03/the-american-leader-in-the-islamic-state/510872/?utm_source=twb.

Wood, Graeme. 2017. *The Way of the Strangers: Encounters with the Islamic State.* New York: Random House.

Wright, Lawrence. 2006. *The Looming Tower: Al-Qaeda and the Road to 9/11.* New York: Alfred A. Knopf.

Wright, Robin. December 12, 2016. "After the Islamic State." *New Yorker.* https://www.newyorker.com/magazine/2016/12/12/after-the-islamic-state.

Wright, Robin. July 27, 2017. "Are We Nearing the Endgame with ISIS?" *New Yorker.* https://www.newyorker.com/news/news-desk/are-we-nearing-the-endgame-with-isis.

Yaakov, Yifa. June 4, 2014. "France Was Warned in Advance about Brussels Killer." *Times of Israel.* http://www.timesofisrael.com/france-was-warned-in-advance-about-brussels-killer/.

Zakriyev, Alvi. September 13, 1999. "Chechen Warlord Denies Involvement in Terror Blasts." *Agence France Press.*

Zavis, Alexandra. March 17, 2008. "A Profile of Iraq's Foreign Insurgents." *Los Angeles Times.*

Zawahiri, Ayman. n.d. "Knights under the Prophet's Banner." WordPress. Accessed February 1, 2018. https://azelin.files.wordpress.com/2010/11/6759609-knights-under-the-prophet-banner.pdf.

"Zawahiri's Letter to Zarqawi." 2005. West Point, NY: Combating Terrorism Center, United States Military Academy. https://ctc.usma.edu/harmony-program/zawahiris-letter-to-zarqawi-original-language-2/.

"Zawahiri's Webchat." 2008. Full text at http://www.washingtonpost.com/wp-dyn/content/graphic/2008/04/03/GR2008040300575.html.

Zein Eddine, Jalal. October 15, 2015. "How Russia Has Served ISIS." *NOW.* https://now.mmedia.me/lb/en/commentary/566045-how-russia-has-served-isis.

Zelin, Aaron Y. 2018. "The Others: Foreign Fighters in Libya." Washington Instittue for Near East Policy.

Zelin, Aaron Y., and Jonathan Prohov. 2016. "How Western Non-EU States Are Responding to Foreign Fighters: A Glance at the USA, Canada, Australia, and New Zealand's Laws and Policies." In *Foreign Fighters under International Law and Beyond*, ed. Andrea de Guttry, Francesca Capone, and Christophe Paulussen, 423–444. The Hague: T.M.C. Asser Press.

Zosak, Stephanie. 2010. "Revoking Citizenship in the Name of Counterterrorism: The Citizenship Review Commission Violates Human Rights in Bosnia and Herzegovina." *Northwestern Journal of International Human Rights* 8, no. 2: 216–232.

INDEX

imprisonment of, 264
propaganda developed and
    distributed by, 18–19, 151
Al Qaeda in the Arabian Peninsula
    leadership of, 229
Al Qaeda recruitment by, 230
Al Shebaab and, 151, 230
US citizenship of, 229–30
US killing of, 18–19, 229, 230
Ayro, Aden Hashi Farah, 147–48,
    149, 162
Azerbaijan, 181*t*
Azizi, Amer, 18–19, 205–7, 258–59
Azzam, Abdallah
    "Arab Afghan" network of foreign
        fighters developed by, 18, 20–21,
        22, 24, 25, 26–27, 28–29, 31, 32,
        33, 40, 51
    Bin Laden and, 20–21, 22
    on the Caliphate, 24–25
    education of, 21–22
    on Egypt's ruling regime, 25
    "Encyclopedia of Afghan Jihad"
        and, 57
    fundraising strategies of, 28
    jihadist ideology of, 22–23,
        24–25, 31, 61
    jihadists inspired by, 154, 169–70,
        205, 249, 255
    killing of, 32
    kuffar doctrine rejected by,
        25, 26–27
    Massud and, 60
    on Muslims' duty to remove foreign
        occupiers from Muslim lands, 9,
        22–23, 24, 106
    Pakistan and, 31
    Palestinian fight against Israel
        and, 21, 24
    propaganda developed and
        distributed by, 20–21, 28–29,
        40–41, 175, 234
    Al Qaeda and, 32

recruitment of foreign fighters and, 69
religious leaders courted by, 27
Sada training camp and, 66
on Saudi Arabia's ruling regime, 25
sermons recorded and
    distributed by, 27
Services Bureau and, 22, 28–29
terrorism opposed by, 32
in the United States, 28
Western reporters welcomed by, 174

Badr operation (Bosnia war), 50
Badr Organization (Iraq), 130–31
al-Baghdadi, Abu Bakr, 126, 169, 170,
    172, 190
al-Baghdadi, Abu Umar, 127, 137, 139
Bakri Mohammed, Omar, 45–46,
    209–10, 212
"Barbaros" (Abd al-Rahman al-Dawsary)
    Afghanistan-Soviet war experiences
        (1980s) of, 18, 40, 249,
        255, 258–59
    Bosnia war (1991-95) and, 3–4, 18,
        40–41, 42–45, 46, 47, 48, 49, 51,
        85–86, 249, 251
    El Mudzahid unit led by, 48
    fundraising for jihad in Bosnia by,
        43–45, 48
    on human rights abuses against
        Muslims in Bosnia, 42
    religious leaders courted by, 43
    Saudi Arabia and, 3–4, 54, 250
    on Shia Muslims, 42–43
    in the United States, 44–45
Barre, Siad, 146
Basaev, Shamil
    in Abkhazia, 86, 94
    Beslan siege (2004) and, 97
    Budyonnovsk attack (1995) and, 86–87
    call for independence of the Caucus
        from Russia by, 97
    Chechnya war and, 86–87, 94
    Dagestan and, 87, 94, 95

military campaign against Islamic
State and, 220
Prophet Muhammad cartoon
controversy (2005) in, 214
Dernah (Libya), 121, 182–83, 256
Derunta training camp
(Afghanistan), 66
Djibouti, 160
Djibouti Agreement (2009), 155
Druze population (Syria), 167, 169–70
Dubrovka Theater siege (Moscow,
2002), 97
Dudaev, Dzhokhar, 84–85, 89–90

Edmonds, Hasan, 244–45
Egypt
"apostate government" cited as
motivation for jihadists in, 9,
69–70, 71–72
Arab Spring (2011) in,
167–68, 215–16
foreign fighters in Afghanistan from,
35–36, 37–38, 63, 70, 74
foreign fighters in Bosnia war from,
45, 49, 53
foreign fighters in Chechnya from, 91
foreign fighters in Iraq from, 120
Iran and, 65
Islamic Jihad organization, 26–27,
35–36, 55–56, 64, 68, 126
Islamic State in, 170, 202, 249
Islamist forces in, 20, 21–23, 26–27,
35, 47, 126, 250
Islamist government (2011-13)
in, 173–74
Pakistan and, 35
September 11 terrorist attacks
and, 75
Sudan and, 59
United States and, 61
El Mudzahid unit (Bosnia war),
48, 49, 53
Elsheikh, El Shafee, 164–65, 166

Elshinawy, Mohamed, 240
Emzawi, Mohammed ("John the
Beatle"), 164–65, 166,
249, 258–59
"Encyclopedia of Afghan Jihad," 57
English Defense League, 231–32
Erdogan, Recep Tayyip, 186
Eritrea, 149, 150, 158
Ethiopia
African Union Somalia force soldiers
from, 161
Al-Itihaad al-Islamiya and, 146–47
Somalia invaded (2006-9) by, 149,
150, 155
Somali population in, 149,
150–51, 160
US counterterrorism funding
to, 246
European Muslim communities. See also
individual countries
Algerian civil war and, 207–8, 209
cross-border connections among
jihadists and, 207
de-radicalization programs and,
226–27, 254, 256
discrimination against, 215, 218
foreign fighters' role in creating
jihadist cells in, 204
Iraq War (2003-12) and, 207–8, 211,
212–13, 214
Islamic State fighters from, 216
negative public opinion and hostility
regarding, 15–16, 17, 214
prison populations and, 215, 226
Al Qaeda's attempts to develop
jihadist cells among, 211–12
radical preachers and, 45–46, 88,
173, 206, 209–11, 212–13, 218,
221, 224, 228, 251
return of foreign fighters to, 219
second-generation communities in,
214, 218–19
Somali populations and, 151

Christian populations targeted by,
192–93, 198
converts to Islam recruited to,
217–18, 237
criminal background among recruits
to, 174, 236, 252
demographic profile of foreign
fighters in, 181–82, 217–18
ex-Baath Party officers in, 191
foreign donors supporting, 194
foreign fighters' decisions to leave,
195–96, 197, 265
foreign fighters recruited by, 1, 2–3,
5, 10, 11–12, 18–19, 166, 171,
172, 173–84, 185, 187, 196–97,
200, 201, 216, 219–20, 231, 232–
33, 237–38, 243–45
foreign fighters' relations with local
populations and, 190, 194–95
foreign fighters' roles in military
operations of, 188–90, 198
foreign fighters trained by, 6, 14, 188
foreign fighters' understanding of
Islam and, 172
in Iraq, 6, 16, 166, 170, 172, 188,
189, 191, 192, 194–95, 198–99,
200, 201, 202
Jabhat al-Nusra and, 169–70,
188, 253–54
kidnappings by, 194
"The Legion" recruiting unit in, 18–
19, 231, 232–33, 238
in Libya, 170, 196–97, 198–99,
202, 249
"lone wolf attacks" and, 222, 240–41
Mosul (Iraq) and, 170, 172, 189, 191–
92, 200, 202, 246, 260–61
Obama on, 199
oil revenues and, 194, 201–2
online presence of, 2–3, 11, 18–
19, 175, 177–79, 185, 231–32,
237–38, 255
Paris attacks (2015) and, 1–2

propaganda developed and
distributed by, 1–3, 11, 175–78,
179, 182–83, 202, 203, 221, 231,
254, 255
Al Qaeda in Iraq and the origins
of, 4–5, 127, 140–41, 167,
169, 171–72
Raqqa controlled (2013-17) by, 169,
170, 189, 190, 202
Salafist mosques and recruitment for,
172–73, 178
Shi'a populations targeted by,
169–70, 171–72, 177, 193, 194,
198, 200
suicide bombing and, 11–12,
188, 189
in Syria, 1, 6, 9, 16, 18, 166, 167,
169–70, 171, 172, 174, 175, 179,
188–89, 190–91, 193–95, 198–
99, 200–1, 202
taxes collected by, 10, 194
travel logistics for foreign fighters in,
184–85, 186, 187, 222–23, 243
Turkey and, 5–6, 186–87,
199–201, 203
US law enforcement responses to
potential recruits to, 243, 244
US-led military campaign against,
3–4, 6, 10, 16, 166, 178, 186,
200, 201–2, 220, 233, 246, 259
weapons acquisition by, 224
Western hostages in Syria executed
by, 193, 194
women recruited by, 2–3, 183,
217–18, 227
Yazidi population targeted by, 170,
174–75, 192–93
Israel. *See also* Palestine
Islamic State and, 202
Al Qaeda and, 59, 107
suicide bombings in, 121
United States and, 69–70
War of Independence (1948) in, 4

Mosul (Iraq)
    Christian population in, 192–93
    Islamic State's bureaucratic successes
        in, 191–92, 261
    Islamic State's control (2014-17) over,
        170, 172, 189, 191–92, 200, 202,
        246, 260–61
Mubarak, Hosni, 36–37, 59,
    71–72, 126
Mueller, John, 238
al-Muhajir, Abu Hamza. *See* al-Masri,
    Abu Ayyub
al-Muhajir, Sheikh Abu Abdallah,
    107, 173
Al Muhajiroun, 210, 224, 252–53
Muhammad (The Prophet), 23, 63, 177
Muslim Brotherhood, 7, 126,
    145, 173–74

Nabhan training camp (Somalia), 156
Nagorno-Karabakh, 81
Nairobi (Kenya) attacks (1998), 54, 55,
    56, 57, 62
Najaf attacks (Iraq, 2004), 117
Nasiri, Omar, 66–71, 218–19
Nemmouche, Mehdi, 193, 219–20
Nesser, Petter, 207, 263
The Netherlands
    foreign fighters' return to, 226
    international military campaign
        against Islamic State and, 220
    Islamic State fighters from, 217,
        219, 221–22
    Al Qaeda in Iraq fighters from, 120
    sentencing for terrorism crimes
        in, 226
Neumann, Peter, 177
Nice terrorist attacks (2016), 216
Niger, 246
Nigeria, 170, 198–99
Nolen, Alton, 240
Norway, 182*t*, 215–16
Nosair, El Sayyid, 56

Obama, Barack, 6, 152, 199, 229,
    230, 259
Odierno, Ray, 138
Oklahoma City bombings (1995), 37–38
Omar, Mullah, 60, 63, 73, 74–75
Operation Gallant Phoenix, 247
O'Reilly, Bill, 111
Organization of Monotheism and Jihad
    (Zarqawi), 106–7, 108, 109, 114.
    See also Al Qaeda in Iraq
Orwell, George, 4, 138–39
Othman, Omar Mahmoud (Abu
    Qatada), 45–46, 206,
    209–10, 251

Pakistan
    Afghanistan and, 13, 20–21, 22, 26,
        29–31, 34, 35, 46, 47, 58, 59–61,
        64, 70, 75–76
    Azzam and, 31
    Bosnia war and, 43–44
    Chechnya and, 96
    Egypt and, 35
    foreign fighters in, 77–78, 81
    Islamic State attacks in, 198
    Kashmir and, 35–36, 59–60
    Al Qaeda and, 35, 58, 59–60, 70,
        73–74, 75–76, 77–78, 138, 205,
        212–13, 215–16, 246
    Saudi Arabia and, 30
    Shia Muslims in, 77–78
    Soviet Union and, 30–31
    suicide bombings in, 77–78
    The Taliban and, 60, 72, 77
    United States's relationship with, 35,
        77–78, 246
    US drone strikes, 230, 259
    vacillating approach toward foreign
        fighters by government in, 13–14,
        20–21, 59–60, 64, 77–78, 81
Palestine, 24, 69–70, 96, 107, 121, 206–
    7. *See also* Israel
Palmyra (Syria), 168

Russia (*Cont.*)
Chechnya border controls and, 11, 63, 89, 90, 101
counterterrorism policy of allowing jihadists to leave, 183–84
First Chechen War (1994-96) and, 84, 86–88, 89–90
foreign fighters' return to, 265
Islamic State attack on commercial airliner (2015) from, 197
Islamic State attacks (2018) in, 104
Islamic State fighters from, 183–84, 189, 195–96
Second Chechen War (1999-2009) and, 95–97, 98–101, 102–3
suicide bombings in, 97, 102
Syrian civil war and, 184
Rutte, Mark, 224–25
Ryazan bombing attempt (Russia, 1999), 98

Sadat, Anwar, 21–22, 55–56
Sada training camp (Pakistan), 29, 66, 105–6
al-Sadr, Moktada, 130–31
Sadulayev, Abdul-Khalim, 101
Said, Qari, 208
Salafism
Afghanistan-Soviet war (1980s) and, 23–24, 25, 30
Bosnia war and, 42–43
in Chechnya, 83–84, 90–91
in Dagestan, 84, 90–91, 95
fundamentalist interpretation of Islam in, 23–24
Islamic State recruitment networks within, 178
jihadist fighting of "nonbelievers" and, 7, 23, 25
quietism within, 24
in Saudi Arabia, 15, 23–24
Shia Muslims targeted by, 7, 23–24, 26–27, 63–64, 69–70, 72, 107

in Somalia, 145–46
Sufism attacked in, 23–24
The Taliban and, 72, 107
Saleh, Ali Abdallah, 184–85
San Bernardino attacks (2015), 240
Sanchez, Ricardo, 111–12
Sassoon, Vidal, 4
Saudi Arabia
Afghanistan civil war fighters from, 63, 70–71
Afghanistan-Soviet war (1980s) and, 22, 30, 31, 33–34
"apostate government" as motivation for foreign fighters in, 9, 106
"Barbaros" and, 3–4, 54, 250
Bin Laden and, 58–59, 71–72, 93, 250
Bosnia war (1991-95) and, 43–44, 49, 50
Chechnya conflict and, 93, 96
crackdown on jihadist financing (2000s) in, 102, 122
de-radicalization programs in, 264–65
donations to Islamic State from, 194
foreign fighters in Afghanistan from, 35–36
foreign fighters in Chechnya from, 91, 96
foreign fighters in Iraq from, 110, 114, 118, 119, 120, 121, 289–90n87
foreign fighters return from Bosnia to, 54
Iran and, 30, 37–38, 65
Islamic State attacks in, 198
Islamic State fighters from, 179–82, 181*t*, 189, 195–96, 200
Al-Itihaad al-Islamiya and, 147
Khattab on, 80–81, 93, 250
Khobar Towers attacks (1996) in, 37–38, 54
Kosovo and, 172–73
Mecca siege (1979) in, 20
Pakistan and, 30

Al Shebaab (*Cont.*)

Tanweer, Shehzad, 212–13
Tanzania embassy bombing (1998), 54, 55, 56, 57, 62
Tolstoy, Leo, 82
Trinidad and Tobago, 179–81, 181*t*, 182*t*
Trump, Donald, 6, 161–62, 233, 259
Tunisia
    Arab Spring uprising (2011) in, 167–68, 215–16
    Islamic State fighters from, 181*t*, 182–83, 184, 195–97
    Islamist government in, 173–74
    Salafism in, 184–85
Turkey
    Assad regime in Syria and, 185–86, 187
    Bosnia war and, 43–44
    Central Asian jihadists in, 184
    counterterrorism policies in, 185
    crackdown against Islamic State fighters in, 196, 257
    foreign fighters in Chechnya from, 101
    foreign fighters travel to Syria via, 11, 16, 184, 185, 186, 187, 221, 223, 243, 255–56, 257
    Islamic State and, 5–6, 186–87, 199–201, 203
    Istanbul bombings (2003) in, 110
    Jabhat al-Nusra and, 185–86
    jihadist cells in, 107–8
    Kurdish population in, 185–86, 199–200
    military campaign against Islamic State and, 186, 187
    United States and, 185, 186
    vacillating approach toward foreign fighters by government in, 13–14, 223

Uganda, 160, 161–62
Umarov, Doku, 101, 102–3
United Arab Emirates, 73–74, 184–85, 194
United Kingdom

counterterrorism operations in Syria by, 166
de-radicalization programs in, 227, 254, 256
foreign fighters in Bosnia war from, 45–46
foreign fighters in Iraq from, 120
foreign fighters in Somalia from, 8, 151
foreign fighters in Syria from, 5–6, 175, 231–33
Hizb ut-Tahrir in, 45–46
international military campaign against Islamic State and, 220
Iraq War (2003-12) and, 212–13
Islamic State fighters from, 179–81, 217, 224–25, 227–28, 231–33
London terrorist attacks (2005) in, 3, 12, 54, 212–14
Manchester terrorist attack (2017) and, 196–97, 216
Pakistani population in, 212, 213, 235–36
Al Qaeda and, 212–14
radical Muslim preachers in, 45–46, 88, 206, 209–11, 212–13, 218, 221, 224, 251
Somali population in, 147
United Nations Operation in Somalia (UNISOM), 146–47, 157–58, 161, 162
United Nations Security Council Resolution 2178, 202–3, 222–23, 256–57
United Nations Security Council Resolution 2396, 203
United States
    Afghanistan-Soviet war (1980s) and, 22, 28, 30–31
    Afghanistan War (2001-) and, 13–14, 75–76, 78, 108, 246
    airstrikes against Al Qaeda (1998) by, 74–75

anti-Muslim sentiments in, 15–16, 17, 245

Bosnia war and, 39–40, 43, 44–45, 52

Chechnya and, 61, 99, 101

counterterrorism policy changes following September 11 attacks and, 13, 15, 17, 18–19, 54, 73–74, 161, 242–43, 251, 256, 266–67

de-radicalization programs in, 238, 244

Egypt and, 61

Ethiopian invasion of Somalia (2006) and, 149

foreign fighters in Afghan-Soviet war from, 234

foreign fighters in Al Qaeda from, 234

foreign fighters in Al Shebaab from, 234, 235t, 251

foreign fighters in Somalia from, 150, 151, 163, 232–33, 235–36

foreign fighters in Syria from, 163

global intelligence operations of, 17, 247

Gulf War (1991) and, 43

India and, 61

Iraq War (2003-12) and, 14, 68, 108–9, 111–14, 115–17, 123–24, 125, 129, 134–37, 138, 140, 144, 167, 207–8, 211, 212, 214

Islamic State recruits from, 178, 234–35, 235t, 236–38, 243–45, 251

Islamic State targeted by, 3–4, 6, 10, 16, 166, 178, 186, 200, 201–2, 220, 233, 246, 259

Israel and, 69–70

Jabhat al-Nusra fighters from, 234, 235t, 239–40

Pakistan and, 35, 77–78, 246

Al Qaeda recruits from, 231, 235t

Saudi Arabia and, 44, 59, 61, 119

Al Shebaab targeted by, 148, 149, 161–62, 242–43, 246, 259

Somalia peacekeeping efforts (1990s) and, 55–56, 61–62, 146–47

Sudan and, 59

Turkey and, 185, 186

Yemen and, 14, 150–51, 229, 230–31

USS Cole bombing (2000), 54, 61–62, 230

Van Gogh, Theo, 214

Vilks, Lars, 214

Volgograd bombings (2013), 102

Wahhabism, 23–24, 72–73, 145–46. *See also* Salafism

Watts, Clinton, 119, 190, 256, 259

Westheimer, Ruth, 4

Williams, Brian Glyn, 78

Winter, Charlie, 176–77, 178

World Islamic Front, 61

World Trade Center bombing (1993), 36–38, 47, 56

World Trade Center terrorist attacks (2001). *See* September 11 terrorist attacks

Yandarbiyev, Zelimkhan, 89–90, 100–1

Yarysh Mardy attack (Chechnya, 1996), 87

Yazidis (ethnic group in Iraq), 128–29, 170, 174–75, 192–93

Yeltsin, Boris, 86–87, 90, 95–96

Yemen

civil war (1990s) in, 14, 35–36

civil war (2010s) in, 163, 184–85

de-radicalization programs in, 264–65

foreign fighters in, 14, 35–36

foreign fighters in Afghanistan from, 35–36, 63

foreign fighters in Chechnya from, 91

foreign fighters in Iraq from, 120

foreign fighters in Somalia from, 150–51

foreign fighters in Syria from, 5–6

Iran and, 184–85

Islamic State attacks in, 198

Islamic State fighters from, 2, 189